HARVARD COMPOSERS

Walter Piston and His Students, from Elliott Carter to Frederic Rzewski

by
HOWARD POLLACK

The Scarecrow Press, Inc.
Metuchen, N.J., & London
1992

British Library Cataloguing-in-Publication data available

Library of Congress Cataloging-in-Publication Data

Pollack, Howard.
 Harvard composers : essays on Walter Piston and his
students : from Elliott Carter to Frederic Rzewski / by
Howard Pollack.
  p.   cm.
 Includes index.
 ISBN 0-8108-2493-0 (alk. paper)
 1. Composers—United States. 2. Harvard University.
Dept. of Music. 3. Piston, Walter, 1894–1976. 4. Car-
ter, Elliott, 1908– . 5. Rzewski, Frederic. I. Title.
ML390.P745   1992
780'.92'27444—dc20   91-46438

To my parents

CONTENTS

Acknowledgments   vii
Introduction   xi

1. Two American Classicists: Walter Piston and James Gould Cozzens   1
2. Songs Without Words: The Orchestral Miniatures of Leroy Anderson   20
3. Regional Voices: John Vincent and Gail Kubik   41
4. Classicism Pursued: Everett Helm and Ellis Kohs   62
5. New Forms, New Meanings: The Music of Arthur Berger   78
6. Expanding the Modernist Tradition: Elliott Carter and Leonard Bernstein   104
7. Adventures in Wonderland: Irving Fine and His Music   131
8. A Midcentury Masterwork: Harold Shapero's *Symphony for Classical Orchestra*   166
9. A Heritage Upheld: Daniel Pinkham   189
10. Favored Sons: Robert Middleton and Allen Sapp   208
11. In Bartók's Wake: John Bavicchi, Nicholas Van Slyck, and Noël Lee   231
12. The Center Holding: Gordon Binkerd   254
13. A Life in Music: The Symphonies of Samuel Adler   273
14. "Carter and the Postwar Composers" Revisited: Billy Jim Layton, Yehudi Wyner, and Martin Boykan   295
15. Music with New Perspectives: Robert Moevs, Karl Kohn, Claudio Spies, Peter Westergaard, and John MacIvor Perkins   323

16. Four Women: Eugenia Frothingham, Victoria
    Glaser, Betsy Warren, and Rosamond Brenner   357
17. A New Age and a New Left: David Behrman
    and Frederic Rzewski   370
18. The Elusive Balance: John Harbison   397
    Conclusion: Walter Piston and His Students
    in Widening Contexts   417
    Index   449
    About the Author   490

ACKNOWLEDGMENTS

FOR PERMISSION TO REPRODUCE excerpts from copyrighted materials, grateful acknowledgment is made to the following publishers, composers, and other copyright holders:

American Composers Alliance for *A Short Concert* (String Quartet No. 2) © 1964 Ellis B. Kohs and for the *Inventions*. All rights reserved by the composer. Reprinted by permission of American Composers Alliance, New York.

Arthur Berger for Bagatelle No. 1. © 1975 Arthur Berger. Reprinted by permission of the composer.

Boosey & Hawkes, Inc. for *Trouble in Tahiti*. Copyright 1953 by Leonard Bernstein; copyright renewed. Used by permission of Jalni Publications, Inc., publisher, and Boosey & Hawkes, Inc., sales agent.

Martin Boykan for *String Quartet No 1*. Copyright by Martin Boykan. Used by permission of the composer.

Columbia Pictures Publications for Leroy Anderson, *Sleigh Ride*. © 1948 by Mills Music, Inc., © 1950 by Mills Music, Inc. International copyright secured. Made in USA. All rights reserved. Used by permission.

Carl Fischer, Inc. for Arthur Berger, *Five Pieces for Piano*. Copyright © 1965 by Carl Fischer, Inc., New York. Copyright renewed. Used by permission.

Eugenia Frothingham for *Simplicity*. Copyright by Eugenia Frothingham. Used by permission of the composer.

E. C. Schirmer Music Company Inc. for *Cantilena and Capriccio.* © 1957 by Daniel Pinkham. © assigned 1972 to Ione Press Inc. Sole selling agents: E. C. Schirmer Music Co. Inc., Boston, Mass. Reprinted by permission.

Trudi Van Slyck for *Finger Paints* and *Piano Partners.* Copyright 1980 and 1982. Used by permission.

Peter Westergaard for *Mr. and Mrs. Discobbolus.* Copyright 1968. Used by permission of the composer.

INTRODUCTION

THIS BOOK IS ABOUT WALTER PISTON and thirty-three composers who studied with him at Harvard. It is about these men and women as individuals—about their music, their writings, their ideals, and their lives.

Naturally, one asks: how and to what extent does this group constitute a whole, a unity? To someone like this author, who believes that Piston's influence has been grossly overlooked, this is a question of considerable concern. It is a question, however, that figures only in the background of this survey, and one that is not addressed forthrightly until the study's conclusion.

Of course, there exists the unity of time and place: most of these students were American, most grew up during the 1920s and '30s, and most served in the Second World War in some capacity. This background naturally had far-reaching consequences, consequences which similarly affected many other composers of their generation and nationality.

More specifically, these particular composers reflected tastes and sensibilities that, for all their myriad differences, were nurtured and refined at Harvard and in Boston. And this often meant a susceptibility to influences that transcended that of any one particular person. Indeed, for some, what was learned from Piston was secondary to what was owed to performances by Koussevitzky and the Boston Symphony, Fiedler and the Pops, and Davison and the Harvard Glee Club; extended visits by Stravinsky, Copland, Boulanger, and Hindemith; the early music scholarship of Apel, Davison, and Merritt; the aesthetics of D. W. Prall, and the literary criticism of F. O. Matthiessen; the productions of Harvard's Classic Club and Hasty Pudding; the religious liberalism of Boston's Unitarian churches and Reformed synagogues, and

the rowdy fun of its bars and burlesque joints; the eventual
emergence of Tanglewood and Sarah Caldwell; and, in a more
negative sense, a certain distance from the great centers of
ballet, opera, theater, jazz, and avant-garde art.

Taking off from H. Wiley Hitchcock, it might be appropriate to speak of these composers, or the majority of them, as
yet another "New England School," this one a "third" one,
with Piston filling a role comparable to that filled by another
Down-Easterner, John Knowles Paine, in the "second" one.
To trace all these regional threads, while observing, too, how
those composers who left Boston differed from those who
continued to contribute to its musical and academic life,
requires its own book, but one for which this study should
provide some foundation.

Piston, in any event, stood very much at the center of this
vortex. He was the best Boston-based composer of the
century, and the first to win real international renown; his
chamber and orchestral music was played around the world,
and his textbooks were translated into numerous languages.
Moreover, his critical articles, especially his piece on Roy
Harris, were widely admired. Many of his students dedicated
compositions to him; few wrote some music, whether a
melody or a whole symphony, that did not owe some debt to
his music or teaching. (This study naturally emphasizes such
debts, possibly at the expense of other connections just as, if
not more, important.)

Two limitations of Piston's influence, however, might be
noted at once. The first is that nearly all of his students looked
to some other composer, be it Hindemith, Stravinsky, Copland, Bartók, or Schoenberg, for a surer guide. As it happened, this earned Piston's tacit, or perhaps slyly ironic approval—it accorded with his own cosmopolitan outlook, and
allowed him a comfortably reticent role. He appeared happy
that his students should perceive him more the congenial,
polished uncle (with Copland often seconding as the compassionate older brother) than the forbidding, titanic father.

The other limitation was that Piston's influence waned over
time. His decline trailed Hindemith's by a few years, but it
proved to be even more obliterating. It is consequently only
by way of a sort of epilogue that we include in this survey four

of the composers (Perkins, Behrman, Rzewski, and Harbison) who studied with him in the late 1950s, after this "decline" had set in. Certainly, from the very beginning, with Carter and Anderson, Piston's students accomplished some variation on the modernist tradition that he himself exemplified. But now the break was more dramatic, in part because the new heroes were younger and so different. Perkins responded directly to Boulez. Behrman ultimately joined the very un-Bostonian avant-garde that formed around Cage; Rzewski, along with his friend Cornelius Cardew, at first looked to Stockhausen, and then agreed to reject him in the interest of the international student-worker movement; and Harbison, responding to the achievement of Britten, strove for his kind of success. If there was anything that these younger composers could agree on, it was probably that, on the whole, Piston's music was not central to their concerns (though, as we shall see, their Harvard years left their mark, nonetheless). After 1960, it was rare for even Piston's most devoted former students to pursue the study of some early work (no matter how fondly remembered), let alone investigate some new work from the 1960s or '70s.

The history of Piston's influence on his students, along with the limitations of this influence, is, in short, complex and subtle, and can be considered only after some exploration of these students in their own light.

Who were these students? They were born between 1902 and 1941. Most came from the Northeast, especially the Boston area. Most were men, though there were some women, too, mostly Radcliffe undergraduates. A large percentage of these students were Jewish, thereby repudiating the anti-Semitism that had tainted the music department in previous years. The very few blacks included Coleridge Braithwaite, who attended Harvard in the late 1930s, and was, in fact, the only black in his entire graduating class. (Braithwaite often sat in class behind Leonard Bernstein, who would write a senior thesis on "The Absorption of Race Elements into American Music.") And finally, some students came from abroad, most notably, Yorgos Sicilianos from Greece. The fact that musicians came from around the world to study with Piston itself signified Piston's importance, and signaled a turning point in America's musical maturation.

Piston's teaching was limited to Harvard to a surprising degree. He rarely accepted private students, and did so only early in his career. He never served as visiting professor, never gave seminars, never taught at Tanglewood. His students came to him as Harvard students. Some came as undergraduates, and some as graduate students, often after study at another area school, like the New England Conservatory, Boston University, or Yale. The graduates in nearly all cases came specifically to study with Piston; by the late 1930s, the undergraduates were also attracted by Piston's presence, but they tended to enroll more simply because Harvard was Harvard. In any event, admission was selective, and Piston had a large say in the matter, as in the matter of scholarships and assistantships. It might be fair to say that if a "Piston school" existed, it was as much a matter of Piston's selecting his students as their choosing him.

Of the relatively small number accepted during Piston's thirty-four years at Harvard (1926–1960), scores of eminent composers and musicologists emerged. The total number is held in secret in the Harvard archives. But Piston's classes were never very big, often averaging about ten in number. Over the years, the following students earned some reputation for their music, even if this consisted merely of occasional performances and a listing in some reference book:

John Vincent (1902–1977)
Henry Leland Clarke
    (1907)
Elliott Carter (1908)
Leroy Anderson (1908–
    1975)
Henry Lasker (1909–
    1976)
Josef Alexander (1910–
    1992)
Arthur Berger (1912)
Everett Helm (1913)
Norman Cazden (1914)
Gail Kubik (1914–1984)

Irving Fine (1914–1962)
Gordon Binkerd (1916)
Ellis Kohs (1916)
Coleridge Braithwaite (1917)
Leonard Bernstein (1918–
    1990)
Charles Shackford (1918)
Victoria Glaser (1918)
Joseph Goodman (1918)
Roslyn Brogue (1919–
    1981)
Robert Middleton (1920)
Robert Moevs (1920)
Paul Des Marais (1920)

Harold Shapero (1920)
Betsy Warren (1921)
Douglas Allanbrook (1921)
Allen Sapp (1922)
John Bavicchi (1922)
Yorgos Sicilianos (1922)
Nicholas Van Slyck (1922–
  1983)
Russell Woollen (1923)
Daniel Pinkham (1923)
Noël Lee (1924)
Billy Jim Layton (1924)
Klaus George Roy (1924)
Claudio Spies (1925)
Karl Kohn (1926)

Samuel Adler (1928)
Yehudi Wyner (1929)
Archibald Davison (1930)
Rosamond Brenner (1931)
Martin Boykan (1931)
Peter Westergaard (1931)
John MacIvor Perkins
  (1935)
Anthony Zano (1937)
David Behrman (1937)
Frederic Rzewski (1938)
John Harbison (1938)
Mark DeVoto (1940)
Joel Lazar (1941)

Of these forty-nine composers, at least twenty-three had notable careers, most spectacularly, Carter and Bernstein, Piston's only students to gain an international reputation greater than his own. Another student, Leroy Anderson, rivaled all of Piston's students, and Piston himself, in terms of sheer popularity, without attracting serious critical attention. Four composers—Berger, Fine, Shapero, and Pinkham—earned solid national reputations. Also highly regarded, though in a more ephemeral, local, or limited way, were Kubik, Binkerd, Moevs, Layton, Wyner, Adler, Kohn and Behrman; specialists of one sort or another would be familiar with their work. In the 1980s, two more, Rzewski and Harbison, went beyond specialists to win an attention comparable to Berger and Pinkham in the 1950s. (John Adams, another Harvard composer to gain prominence in the 1980s, takes us into post-Piston Harvard.) The names Vincent, Helm, Kohs, Spies, and Westergaard were fairly familiar, but more for their writings than for their music. Lee, far more famous as a pianist than as a composer, and better known as a composer in France than in the United States, was altogether unique.

This book considers these twenty-three composers in some detail. Another nine composers—Middleton, Sapp, Bavicchi, Van Slyck, Glaser, Warren, Brenner, Boykan, and Perkins—are also included, as is Eugenia Frothingham (b. 1908), who never attended Harvard or Radcliffe, but who studied

privately with Piston and Merritt. These lesser-known composers are discussed, albeit briefly in some cases, because
they represent an intriguing style or viewpoint. Furthermore,
they help round out the whole of our study; consider, for
instance, the influence of Sapp's analyses of Schoenberg's
12-tone music on Irving Fine, Gordon Binkerd, Peter
Westergaard, and others. I would have liked to have discussed
Braithwaite and Sicilianos as well, but their music is unavail-
able. As for Henry Leland Clarke, an interesting figure in his
own right, he is omitted because his slight contact with Piston
occurred at a very late stage of his formal education.

Whether or not a composer receives a whole chapter, the
study of each individual composer is independent enough so
that a reader can easily use the book as a reference source. On
the other hand, the connections among these composers are
so extensive that the study of any one figure can profit from
some consideration of the others. These connections, observed throughout the whole, are brought together in the
book's conclusion.

It was decided, too, to say something about Piston himself,
and this took the form of a comparison with a contemporary
novelist, James Gould Cozzens. For more on Piston, the
reader might consult my study of the composer (*Walter
Piston,* UMI, 1981), as well as David Thompson's *History of
Harmonic Theory in the United States* (Kent State University,
1980). This last work makes large claims for Piston's
Harmony, not only because the 1941 text offered the first
cogent explanation of secondary dominant chords, or because
it attempted the first systematic discussion of harmonic
rhythm, or because it proposed the interchangeability of the
major and minor modes, but, above all, because "it marked a
reversal of philosophy: the concept of an acoustical basis had
given way to the procedure of deriving theory solely from the
observation of musical practice," thereby ushering in the
modern period of harmonic theory, including the later work
of Hindemith, Sessions, Wallace Berry, William Christ, Paul
Harder, Richard Franko Goldman, and many others. Need-
less to say, Piston's own students were often the first to profit.

Because I wrote this book in the late 1980s, I did not have
the opportunity to study much music written after 1985. I
consequently used that year as a kind of cut-off point.

Unfortunately, this left the younger composers, such as Rzewski and Harbison, dangling, so to speak, in mid-career. One could imagine new and surprising developments from them, as well as from many of their more established seniors.

This project enjoyed the help of many of the subjects themselves. Nearly all agreed to be interviewed, or else answered letters, sometimes engaging in extensive correspondence with the author. Furthermore, a number of composers—Kohs, Binkerd, Sapp, Middleton, Pinkham, Bavicchi, Adler, Frothingham, Glaser, Brenner, Layton, Moevs, Spies, Kohn, and Behrman—generously supplied me with a wealth of scores and tapes. This helped to fill in numerous gaps, though I have emphasized, as far as seemed appropriate, works that are commonly available either in score or on record.

Eleanor Anderson, Verna Fine, and Trudi Van Slyck also agreed to interviews, and allowed me to examine unpublished scores and other materials not yet deposited in any library. Verna Fine, moreover, permitted me use of the Fine Collection at the Library of Congress.

Of many reference and scholarly books, I am most indebted to David Ewen's *Dictionary of American Composers* (G. P. Putnam's, 1982); for those composers discussed in both sources, one well might want to consult Ewen for facts and details not mentioned here. As for helpful writings on individual composers, they are cited in the course of the text.

Verna Fine, Eleanor and Kurt Anderson, Trudi Van Slyck, and many of the subjects themselves helpfully corrected portions of the text. Ed Murray supervised my analysis of Boykan's *First Quartet*. Naturally, I take full responsibility for any erroneous or misleading content.

Alex Jeschke, longtime friend of many composers, and Darryl Wexler helped edit and proofread my manuscript.

Victor Smith prepared the musical examples, assisted by a grant from the University of Houston. Aaminah Durrani's help in compiling the index turned this often routine task into an adventure.

Parker Pringle, Roland Vazquez, Maggie Jackson, Carol Roth, and Linda and Michael Storey helped make research trips to Boston and Washington possible. Linda Patterson, Sara Brakefield, and Sam Hyde, librarians at the University of

Houston, assisted me in numerous ways, as did my colleagues, Robert Lynn and John Snyder. Throughout, my parents, Walter and Adele Pollack, and David Bischoping gave support and encouragement.

Special acknowledgment is due Professors Sam Adler and William Austin for their generosity and guidance. Both provided me with material from their private libraries, and, further, made available to me the rich holdings of Eastman's Sibley Library and Cornell's Music Library. Austin's comments on individual chapters were also helpful; indeed, in some ways, this book is intended as a detailed gloss to p. 441 of his own *Music in the 20th Century* (Norton, 1966).

HOWARD POLLACK
University of Houston
Houston, TX

1. TWO AMERICAN CLASSICISTS: WALTER PISTON AND JAMES GOULD COZZENS

WALTER PISTON'S SONATA FOR FLUTE AND PIANO (1930) was his first really successful work: It quickly established itself as a repertory staple. Although the work was only the composer's third to be published, it fully reflected the confident maturity of its not-so-young author, now thirty-five and on the faculty of his alma mater, Harvard University. Even Piston's very first published work, the 1925 *Three Pieces for Flute, Clarinet and Bassoon* (a work still well-known among wind players) was the kind of skillful and individual work that made people take notice. This debut, however, was more obviously derivative of Stravinsky, perhaps because Piston wrote it under Nadia Boulanger;[1] in fact, Paul Dukas, with whom Piston also was studying, called the work, "Stravinskique," half-disapprovingly, as the composer remembered.[2] (For Dukas, Piston wrote the more somber and grand *Piano Sonata* of 1926.) The three works from the later 1920s that followed (only one of which, the *Suite for Orchestra,* was published) similarly took part in contemporary trends of one sort or another. The *Flute Sonata,* on the other hand, marked the kind of synthesis that would characterize the mature Piston.

On one level, the synthesis represented by the *Flute Sonata* drew upon techniques, ideas and moods found in some of the composer's earlier music. One discovered in its three-movement form something of the cool, witty, polished tone of the *Three Pieces;* the somber, romantic, brooding quality of the *Piano Sonata;* and the warm, genial, jazzy playfulness of

1

the *Suite for Orchestra*. Piston often attempted such a variety of moods within the confines of a highly unified and individual style.

The synthesis, however, also involved a deep response to past styles and traditions. The opening phrase (Ex. 1) itself indicated this. The flute melody—arched, poised, neatly spun-out—reminded one of Bach to the extent that if labels were needed, neobaroque was more accurate than neoclassic, as Piston himself once suggested.[3] (The neobaroque flavor of the work's second movement was even more pronounced, with the melodic lines lasting much longer than this one.) Its careful articulation of small phrases was perhaps more like Mozart, so that the label neoclassical was not inaccurate after

Example 1. Walter Piston, *Sonata for Flute and Piano*, I (Associated Music, 1933).

all. Piston's nineteenth-century heroes—Chopin and Brahms—were in ready evidence, too: Chopin in the whirling, chromatic piano figuration; Brahms in the cross-rhythms between piano and flute. Add to this the melodic flexibility of Debussy, the polytonality of Stravinsky, the chromatic manipulations of Schoenberg and Webern, and the rhythmic energy of Hindemith, and one deduced the broad framework of the composer's stylistic orientation.

One needed to study the work's entire movement to see how such models determined formal procedures. One noted, for example, a thorough-going motivic unity characteristic of Bach—but applied, in the modernist way, to all three movements. And yet one found, concurrently, a formal lucidity and elegance that betokened, above all, Mozart. Each part of the traditional sonata form fell into place with the utmost clarity, with almost a super-clarity. Indeed, the first theme group consisted of only one large antecedent-consequent structure (mm. 1–28) and another, smaller such structure (mm. 29–36). The way Piston treated melodies in, say, recapitulations, however, looked to the more spontaneous procedures of, once again, Chopin and Brahms.

What, then, constituted the work's individuality? One had to begin, first, with the synthesis itself. One would be hard-pressed to find another American who took such a wide range of European traditions, and who assimilated them with such ease and flair. When Virgil Thomson derided "such an indigestible mixture, such a cocktail of culture as the international neo-classic style," it was pretty clear that he was satirizing, above all, his old friend and rival, Piston.[4] No one else but perhaps an American with a profound sympathy and knowledge of European music, and without any particular allegiance to one or another nationality, could perhaps have pulled it off in the first place.

But it went further than that. Far from "indigestible," the music bore no stamp of eclecticism. The opening flute melody, for example, exhibited that lilting, gently sad quality that was Piston's own. From a fairly neutral beginning— reminiscent of the kind of modally ambiguous melodies that Brahms loved—followed, characteristically, the almost spontaneously melancholy E^b; the expressive, surprising jump of a seventh; the climax on the high F; and the poignant semitone cadence, which returned, once again, to neutral fourths and fifths.

The harmonic sense, further, showed an individual and highly refined sense of chromatic materials. One recognized some kind of tonality; the phrase seemed to have a tonal center of D, and the strong arrival of A at measure eight appeared to be a kind of dominant. The movement, as well as the entire work, not surprisingly ended in D. One intimated other roots as well, and a harmonic rhythm that increased in speed until the cadence at measure eight. The prevailing sonority, however, was the highly ambiguous chord, D-G#-C#, and its various permutations and transpositions (the composer apparently had Schoenberg's 12-tone method somewhat in mind while composing the piano part [5]). Further, the flute part asserted its own harmonic and tonal identity, except at measures 7–9, when the composer suggested the progression, C# Major—A (Minor). This particular progression sounded right, its VII-v implications functioning as V/V-V might in common practice harmony. But even here, the piano's right hand contributed contradictory tritones and major sevenths. The harmonic language, in short, constituted a rational and logical one, though one that was not conventionally tonal, polytonal, or atonal.

The music's individuality often suggested, subtly, the composer's American provenance. The flute melody, for instance, bore some resemblance to folk tunes from Piston's native Maine, tunes his grandfather, seaman Anthony (Antonio) Piston (Pistone), may have played on the flute.[6] Piston made explicit, programmatic use of this folk idiom in two later works: the *Three New England Sketches* and the *Pine Tree Fantasy,* both for orchestra. He also considered writing an opera with a Maine coastal setting. The connection here was ultrarefined, perhaps only subliminal. As for the music's quirky, astringent harmonic quality, it bespoke some connection to jazz.

There were other, more overt references to popular, vernacular styles in the Flute Sonata. The first movement's second theme, for instance, had the ironic wit of the popular music of the 1920s (Ex. 2). Similarly, the last movement used march, tango, and polka rhythms in a way later popularized by

Example 2. Walter Piston, *Sonata for Flute and Piano,* first 9 measures of movement I (p. 3), last 2 lines of p. 5. Copyright by Associated Music Publishers, Inc. All rights reserved by permission.

the composer in his biggest success, the ballet *The Incredible Flutist.* The whole work had a brisk, detached, laconic quality that seemed like the kind one might expect from a New Englander.

In 1930, the year Piston wrote his *Flute Sonata,* James Gould Cozzens wrote his fifth novel, *S. S. San Pedro.* Shorter than its now-forgotten predecessors, the *San Pedro,* actually a novella, was Cozzens's first book to display that tautness of construction and confinement of time and space characteristic of his mature work. All action took place on board ship within three days, the time limit, too, of such later and far more expansive books as *Guard of Honor* and *By Love Possessed.* The form was neat; its four chapters described, in succession, the flawed ship laying dockside in Hoboken, on course to Argentina, in the throes of a gale, and, finally, sinking.

Except for the absence of those rhetorical flourishes and classical allusions that embellish his later fiction, the content and style of *San Pedro* was recognizably that of the mature Cozzens. For example, here follows a paragraph from the second chapter:

> Left alone, Anthony Bradell finished his shaving. A fresh uniform lay on his bunk and he considered it without pleasure while he put away his shaving things, restoring his cabin to its brutally bare and immaculate good order. It was an idea of the company that some officers not on duty should go down after dinner when the passengers were dancing in the widened waist of the promenade-deck and make themselves agreeable. On most of the company's vessels leadership in this fell conveniently to the chief officer, who stood no watch. Mr. Driscoll of the *San Pedro* was not a success socially. Captain Clendening had selected Anthony instead. He did not, he told his senior officer when he gave the order, know what the hell the sea had come to, but the *San Pedro* might as well make as good a showing as possible. Anthony could leave at ten o'clock, and he needn't come onto the morning watch until four bells on such nights. Mr. Fenton, who acted as his junior watch-officer, was perfectly competent. Anthony agreed about the fourth officer's competence. He did not consider sleep precisely a vice, but any concern about it failed to fit in with the efficient asceticism he had brought himself to practice. He would continue to be called as usual.[7]

This excerpt vividly illustrates Cozzens's preoccupation with the drama inherent in the daily activity of men; the way one furnishes a room or interacts socially or regards sleep intrigued the novelist, especially when it provided the background to a crisis, in this case, the sinking of a ship.

The excerpt also reveals the cool severity of Cozzens's prose; indeed, the "*S. S. San Pedro* is the first novel in which he consistently maintained the objective tone and detached point of view that defines his major fiction," according to his biographer.[8] This was accomplished through matter-of-fact statement ("Mr. Driscoll of the *San Pedro* was not a success socially"), technical precision ("widened waist of the promenade-deck"), and changing perspectives (between Bradell and Clendening). Cozzens's objectivity was reinforced and enlivened by a strong and pervasive irony, in this example targeting the company ("make themselves agreeable"), Clendening ("He did not . . . know what the hell the sea had come to"), and Bradell ("He did not consider sleep precisely a vice"). Cozzens liked to distinguish between clarity and simplicity, always aiming for the former,[9] and irony was the principal means with which he gave his clear prose depth and intelligence.

S. S. San Pedro was also fairly characteristic in its cast of characters, a cast that includes a broad range of ages, classes, races, and religions, all interconnected by an intricate web of needs and responsibilities. Here the community was at sea, but beginning with Cozzens's 1933 novel *The Last Adam,* the community was typically a small town in the eastern United States. *San Pedro's* protagonist, Anthony Bradell, was, like most of Cozzens's central characters, an intelligent, reserved figure in confrontation with the haphazardness of fate and the irrationality of human emotion. Cozzens's synopsis for *By Love Possessed* could stand as the thematic centerpiece of the *San Pedro,* indeed, for all his mature fiction: "He ends face to face with the fact of this life—the underlying, everlasting opposition of thinking and feeling, with life's simple disaster of passion and reason, self-division's cause."[10]

This theme, though nothing new, as the above allusion to Fulke Greville intimated, was newly treated, partly because Cozzens recognized his time's uncertainties, including its shifting moral and spiritual climate. Further, he described in realistic detail the contemporary world—its manners, dress, music, technology, and so forth. (The *San Pedro's* repulsive and ghostly Doctor Percival represented an untypical excursion into a German-like expressionistic mode, one that was given total rein in the 1934 *Castaway,* and subsequently incorporated into a classically restrained style.) There was often some existentialist malaise about Cozzens, including *San Pedro;* Marilee's poignant question, "How can I help where I lose my heart?", echoed Hemingway's Brett Ashley. His early novels were full of this sort of despair, and even in later books, many characters succumbed to a variety of emotions, some very destructive. But there were always a few characters who faced life's irrational waywardness with admirable, even heroic, dignity.

Piston and Cozzens shared a corresponding place in American arts and letters. They generally were regarded as major artists of their generation, but because of their elegance and conservatism, not typical of this generation.[11] Their principal virtue, most agreed, lay in their consistently impeccable craftsmanship, their greatest weakness in what was alleged to be a certain emotional reticence, even tepidness. No colorful controversy marked their careers,[12] but neither met with unchallenged acceptance. Cozzens recognized in his work,

> a kind of writing that must have some emotion-arousing quality that makes those who like it unable to see its faults; and those who don't like it, unable to see its merits. The result is no critical middle ground. The likers, in effect, love it and give it the highest praise; the dislikers are not just bored or indifferent. In effect, they hate it; actively and loudly they assert it's as bad as possible.[13]

Listeners responded to Piston similarly. This "emotion-arousing quality" perhaps involved the notable lack of sentimentality and bombast in their work. It was argued, too, that their kind of artistic finish was itself, paradoxically, a liability. Compare, for instance, the following observations of Theodore Chanler and Bernard DeVoto on Piston and Cozzens, respectively.

> . . . (Piston's *String Quartet No. 1*) had that aloofness of music which does exactly what it sets out to do, without tentativeness or strain of any kind. It had, properly speaking, no potentialities, since everything was cast in its definitive form. People were inclined to find it uninteresting on that account. They didn't feel needed.[14]
> . . . (Cozzens's novels) contain no fog of confused thinking on which, as on a screen, criticism can project its diagrams of meanings which the novelist did not know were there. There is no mass of unshaped emotion, the novelist's emotions or the characters', from which criticism can dredge up significance that becomes portentous as the critic calls our attention, and the novelist's, to it. Worse still, they are written with such justness that criticism cannot get a toehold to tell him and us how they should have been written.[15]

A similar lexicon was used for Piston and Cozzens, depending on one's perspective: to the takers, they were classical, lucid, elegant, wry; to others, they were cerebral, dry, dreary, cold.

This criticism to some extent was subject to changing standards and tastes. Their works from the 1930s, for instance, won a rather limited following, although the more fashionably modernistic works, like the *Flute Sonata* and the *S. S. San Pedro*, were well-touted in progressive circles, and the more accessible works, like Piston's *The Incredible Flutist* and Cozzens's *The Last Adam*, won a measure of popular acclaim, both at home and abroad. The years 1946 to 1960 were conducive to more widespread appreciation. During this time, Piston won two Pulitzer Prizes, the first in 1947 for his *Third Symphony*, the second in 1960 for his *Seventh Symphony*. Cozzens similarly earned a Pulitzer Prize in 1948 for *Guard of Honor*, and the prestigious William Dean Howells Award in 1960 for *By Love Possessed*, making too, in 1957, the cover of *Time*. The 1960s and '70s witnessed a sharp reaction, almost revulsion, toward their work, and they died (Piston in 1976; Cozzens in 1978) respected, but thoroughly unfashionable. Their first biographies were published in the early 1980s, a time that, in general, gave evidence of revival and reassessment.

These similarities suggested some sort of bond between Piston and Cozzens. If one existed, it was unintentional. There was no concrete link between the two other than the fact that Piston owned a copy of *By Love Possessed*.[16] There was, it is true, opportunity for at least casual acquaintance. Both were students at Harvard in 1922–24, and both were in Paris in 1926. Cozzens's college friends included Lucius Beebe and Dudley Fitts, who, in turn, were friendly with Jack Wheelwright, Gordon Bassett, and Conrad Aiken, all friends of Piston, especially Aiken. Another connection was Cozzens's wife, Bernice Baumgarten, who was Aiken's literary agent. This social network notwithstanding, Piston and Cozzens probably only knew of one another, as they were both fairly reclusive.

Nor is there any evidence that they were interested in each other's work. As mentioned, Piston owned a copy of *By Love Possessed*, a not quite so insignificant fact considering that the American literature in his private library was limited to works by Emerson, Hawthorne, Thoreau, Longfellow, Melville, Henry James, Hemingway, Faulkner, Steinbeck, and Edwin O'Connor. But its importance paled beside, say, his extensive collection of novels by Alberto Moravia.

As for Cozzens, he had virtually no interest in concert music. During his youth, he forced himself to listen to recordings and to attend concerts and operas,[17] but he soon gave it up, writing to his mother in 1931, "I rest easier now that I've formally acknowledged the fact that I have no ear for music and don't know one piece from another until I've heard it twenty times."[18] He enthusiastically collected records of popular music from the 1920s, however,[19] and could assert with confidence, "Nobody ever wrote musical comedy pieces like Gershwin and probably nobody ever will." All he knew of modern concert music was that it "seems to have (I judge from more competent and interested opinion than my own) the music boobs merely stunned."[20]

But Piston and Cozzens shared a number of common or comparable interests that can be grouped into four categories: 18th century classicism, French art, New England traditions, and 1920s modernism.

The European classics, especially those of the 18th century, were preeminent in shaping the ideals and aspirations of both men. Throughout his career, Cozzens stated a preference for Shakespeare, Swift, Steele, Gibbon, Austen, and Hazlitt.[21] Piston similarly had the highest regard for Bach, Mozart, and Beethoven, and singled out Bach when once asked about his artistic development.[22] Consequently, both men most admired 19th-century artists who in their estimation came closest to this classic ideal, for example, George Eliot and Brahms, Flaubert and Fauré.

Early in their careers, they even tried their hands at antiquated idioms: Cozzens in his second book, *Michael Scarlett* (1925), a historical novel set in Elizabethan England, and written in the style of the 16th-century, and Piston in the 1927 *Minuetto in Stile Vecchio* for string quartet. Very soon, however, classical models came to serve more as a background reference against which their imagination freely took wing. In Cozzens's 1934 *Castaway,* the author used Defoe's *Robinson Crusoe* as its point of departure, but the book was a psychological thriller about a man hunted by an idiot in a deserted department store, a thriller that had critics talking about the ego, the id, and the corruption of Western civilization. Similarly, Piston's *Prelude and Fugue* for orchestra, written in the same year as *Castaway*, obviously was indebted to Bach, but its grim edge and acerbic wit was adventurous and daring, too daring for Bruno Walter, who refused to conduct its scheduled premiere.[23] To take another example, one might consider the boisterously ironic treatment of Renaissance themes in Piston's 1938 *Carnival Song* and Cozzens's 1940 *Ask Me Tomorrow*. Their later works took less recourse to this sort of parody, but remained clearly resonant of classic literature by way of their elegantly controlled style and crisp, cool tone.

Both inherited from the classical tradition a concern about form. Piston sought to find "the perfect balance between expression and form";[24] Cozzens worked "to fit the wording, the syntax and the structure to the material."[25] Both valued the balance, coherence, and succinctness of 18-century masterworks to an extraordinary degree. Underlying this enthusiasm was an unflinching commitment to reason and order, even in the face of 20th-century madness. Discussing his interest in law, an interest that found prominent expression in his later novels, Cozzens once noted:

> I never realized it before, but in the main, it (the law) is, of course, the 18th century speaking and you can hardly help hearing it with pleasure for its perfect sophistication, the way it takes human nature as it is, without evasion or apology, and then sees what can be done by firmness and reason to give it a modicum of dignity and order. There is, I suppose something about it close to what I would have to admit was my own feeling about life—it is absurd to pretend that there is any plan or meaning in it, but never mind, we will make a plan and the meaning will be that we are men and not dogs.[26]

For Piston, a similar disposition encouraged a lifelong and, through his textbooks, world-famous study of common practice harmony, counterpoint, and orchestration, as well as a thorough consideration of the modern writings of Schoenberg and others (though he was ever careful not to impute historical or acoustical absolutes to any theory, old or new).[27]

And he rejected chance music as an abrogation of the composer's responsibility.[28]

Both Piston and Cozzens, however, agreed that artistic genius, in Cozzens's words, "so far transcends your reasonable expectation that you see that it couldn't have been done merely by intelligence, or training, or hard trying, and must simply have been born in a sort of triumphant flash outside the ordinary process of thought."[29] Piston, for his part, spoke of "the elusive side of music."[30] Both men discouraged probing critics and interviewers by saying that they really did not know what they were doing. This was as much the classical legacy as was the steady exercise of reason and clarity.

Another important influence, especially during their formative years, was French art of the late 1800s and early 1900s. Cozzens's first novel, *Confusion* (1924), whose protagonist, Cerise D'Atrée, is herself half French, was inspired by Flaubert's *Madame Bovary* and Jules Payot's *The Education of the Will*. Of *Madame Bovary*, Cozzens wrote in his diary:

> It is of course the most exquisitely written thing I have ever read, the beautiful construction stands thru the translation, the clarity of thought and sincerity of feeling, all with that incomparable style, you sense it at once as an aristocrat of books, very close to *the* aristocrat. I know I shall be able to write better for knowing *Madame Bovary*, I could hardly help thinking better.[31]

Flaubert also proved a model for Cozzens's exacting, fastidious working methods (which were very much like Piston's).[32] In 1925, Cozzens translated Gide's *The Immoralist* to keep up his French, and wrote to his mother:

> Just what I want is harder to say, but a less ornate style for one thing. I have never, as I noted long ago, seen it in English, but it's André Gide's better stuff in French—perfectly stark, smooth and lucid, a result not so much of simplicity as of an agonisingly careful choice of words.[33]

During these same years, Piston was closely involved with modern French music. From 1917 to 1921, he played violin in the MacDowell Club and the Boston Musical Association, both under the direction of George Longy, principal oboe with the Boston Symphony Orchestra, and indefatigable advocate of things French. The Boston Symphony itself, under the leadership of Rabaud and Monteux, was at this time well-disposed toward the French repertory, while at Harvard, all but one of the music faculty had French academic backgrounds, including E. B. Hill, who wrote a detailed book on *Modern French Music*. Piston's postgraduate studies in Paris with Dukas and Boulanger only widened his already extensive and intimate familiarity with French music. Not surprisingly, his earliest music showed traces of Fauré, Dukas, Ravel, and others. One work, the *Suite for Oboe and Piano,* was even a sort of homage to some French masters, subtly evoking as it does pieces by Satie, Ravel, Debussy, and Roussel.

Relative to the broad, cosmopolitan range of their interests, how important was French art to their artistic development? This is a difficult question made more so by their reluctance to publicly evaluate other artists' work, claiming that such opinions were limited by their own work.[34] Such opinions, nonetheless, were occasionally offered, most often privately. Cozzens once remarked, for instance, "All German novels are 100 pages too long," and Piston similarly felt that much modern German music was overblown.[35] Of contemporary Englishmen, they most admired Maugham and Holst, who were themselves, significantly, deeply influenced by the French.[36] Both could be highly critical of even their most celebrated American contemporaries, and many of these criticisms were even to similar effect: Roy Harris and John Steinbeck were marred by their sentimentality; Virgil Thomson and Sinclair Lewis lacked depth; Roger Sessions and William Faulkner were convoluted; the later works of Aaron Copland and Ernest Hemingway merely echoed their admittedly brilliant early ones.[37] Given these perspectives, French art seemed particularly decisive to their artistic development.

Their relation to 18th-century classicism and French art sometimes obscured their shared regional heritage. Both came from old New England families of modest circumstance; they even had seafaring uncles. They were brought up Episcopalian, and although neither attended church in adulthood, the Episcopal Church remained the basic framework for their mature religious views, Piston veering more, perhaps, towards Unitarianism-Universalism. As for politics, they shared that ingrained New England aversion to an aggressive, centralized government; they found the policies of Roosevelt and Kennedy irksome, and supported Eisenhower for both terms.[38] Their temperaments were also characteristically regional: aloof and self-reliant, they led quiet, secluded lives. They disliked formality, celebrity, and state occasions (both turned down invitations to the Kennedy White House), and viewed artists, critics, and the intelligentsia with no little skepticism. They had, too, an almost Puritan coolness toward theater and opera.

This background did not surface prominently in their work overall. Occasionally, there was a telling regional feature— the town-hall meeting in Cozzens's *The Last Adam,* or the evocation of country fiddling in Piston's *Fourth Symphony.* And some late works engaged in frank reminiscence of childhood in New England: Cozzens's *Children and Others* and *Morning Noon and Night;* Piston's *Three New England Sketches* and *Pine Tree Fantasy.* But by and large, picturesque quaintness and ethnic color served their work only marginally. Only a few Cozzens novels, in fact, took New England as their locale, the others being set in New York City, the Delaware Valley, Florida, Cuba, England, and continental Europe. Piston was equally international, using Spanish, French, Italian, and other idioms as it suited him; wrote Copland, somewhat exaggeratedly, "There is nothing especially 'American' about his work."[39]

Nonetheless, their New England background left its mark on their work, not only in its laconic wit, but in the very substance of its material. In Cozzens's novels, whatever the setting, the characters were often New Englanders by birth or education. Moreover, the principal themes—the conflict between passion and reason, free will and fate—were historically endemic to the region. Similarly, many of Piston's themes were related to traditional New England chanteys, hymns, reels, and marches, and his textures were as crisp as autumn in Maine.

Both men recognized these connections, and, given the nationalist views fashionable in their time, spoke of them with understandable defiance. Cozzens wrote:

> It (New England) is my country; the people are my
> people and so, of course, they seem to me the only
> people in the world who are altogether right, the way
> people ought to be. If I have an eye for their faults, it is
> because I have them myself and know where to look for
> faults. . . . My pride in my people is a matter rooted
> deeper than vanity or any concern about getting them
> whitewashed for inspection by New Yorkers or Middle
> Westerners.[40]

And Piston once asked:

> Is the Dust Bowl more American than, say, a corner in
> the Boston Athenaeum? Would not a Vermont village
> furnish as American a background for a composition as
> the Great Plains? The self-conscious striving for nation-
> alism gets in the way of the establishment of a strong
> school of composition and even of significant individual
> expression.[41]

Finally, Piston and Cozzens shared a number of traits
common among '20s-styled modernists, the so-called "lost
generation": a disillusionment with the 19th-century concept
of progress; a contempt for Victorian prudishness and
sentimentality; a respect for the vigorous, stoical individual;
an enthusiasm for jazz and the motion pictures; an attraction
to Latin America and Spain; and a romantic fascination with
alcohol. Copland selected Piston, along with Harris, Thomson, Sessions, and himself, as significant, representative
composers of their generation, both for a series of one-man
concerts in 1935, and later, for a book on 20th-century music
(for which he also included Marc Blitzstein and Carlos
Chávez).[42] Cozzens's first work, *Confusion,* was frequently
compared to Fitzgerald's *This Side of Paradise;* his ensuing
novels well might have evoked other such comparisons: *Cock
Pit* with Hemingway's *The Sun Also Rises, San Pedro* with
Thornton Wilder's *The Bridge of San Luis Rey, The Last Adam*
with Lewis's *Arrowsmith,* and *Men and Brethren* with O'Hara's
Butterfield 8.

In later years, Piston and Cozzens, it is true, reflected new
trends, namely, the social consciousness of the 1930s and
'40s, and the confessional individuality of the 1950s and '60s.

Indeed, they proved trenchant observers of the changing American temper from the 1920s through the 1960s, and, in Piston's case, to the mid-1970s. They were realists, and their principal inspiration was the world in which they lived. But they unquestionably brought to everything they wrote a cool and ironic sensibility shaped by the 1920s.

In conclusion, Piston and Cozzens seemed to share dialectical tensions of a similar nature. Both, for instance, encompassed the witty, charming elegance and rationality of the eighteenth century along with the uncertainty, the irreverence, and the stoic heroism of the 1920s. Similarly, their work looked at once to the elaborate sophistication of modern European, and especially French art, and to the modesty and reticence of their Puritan, or at least, New England backgrounds. These dialectics helped to explain why their careers unfolded so similarly, and why they won such a comparable niche in America's artistic history. For while such dialectic tensions were common enough in the twentieth century, these particular ones were fairly unusual. In the case of Cozzens, the immediate historical ramifications of such an achievement apparently were minimal, whatever the ultimate value placed on his novels; Piston's achievement, on the contrary, was to wield a profound influence on many outstanding American composers, no matter how different, ultimately, these composers proved to be.

Notes

1. Peter Westergaard, "Conversation with Walter Piston," *Perspectives on American Composers,* edited by Boretz and Cone (New York: W. W. Norton, 1971), p. 159. *Three Pieces* was not dedicated to Boulanger, but to his wife, the painter Kathryn Nason. It was not until 1967 that Piston, in honor of her eightieth birthday, dedicated a piece to Boulanger, namely, the *Souvenirs* for flute, viola, and harp (AMP, 1991). To Boulanger he also dedicated his 1933 textbook, *Principles of Harmonic Analysis.*
2. Piston, taped interview with Robert Lurtsema, "Morning Pro Musica," WGBH Boston, January 19, 1974, privately held.
3. Piston, taped interview.

4. Thomson, *The State of Music* (New York: William Morrow, 1939), pp. 98–102.
5. Piston Collection, Boston Public Library.
6. Howard Pollack, *Walter Piston* (Ann Arbor: UMI, 1981), p. 15.
7. Cozzens, *S. S. San Pedro* (New York: Harcourt Brace, 1930), p. 36.
8. Matthew J. Bruccoli, *James Gould Cozzens. A Life Apart* (New York: Harcourt Brace Jovanovich, 1983), p. 103.
9. Bruccoli, pp. 302–303.
10. Bruccoli, p. 203.
11. For a Piston bibliography, see Pollack, pp. 225–237; for a Cozzens bibliography, see Bruccoli, p. 314.
12. The controversy surrounding the publication of *By Love Possessed,* marked by charges of racism and anti-Semitism, was exceptional. It seems, in retrospect, that much of the furor was off target, as it confused the author with one of his characters, a fairly embittered one, too. Ironically, one of Cozzens's central concerns was the independence of virtue from race, religion, class, and family. Aside from this particular episode, Cozzens's career unfolded in relative obscurity, as suggested by the title of Bruccoli's biography, *A Life Apart.*
13. Bruccoli, p. xv.
14. Chanler, "New York, 1934," *Modern Music* 11 (1934), p. 142. This description of Piston's *Quartet* was contrasted with the enthusiasm that greeted Roy Harris's *Sextet* performed at the same concert.
15. DeVoto, "The Easy Chair," *Harper's* 198 (February, 1949), p. 72.
16. Piston Collection.
17. Cozzens was encouraged to take up music by a friend, George Bartlett, who, incidentally, held up Roger Sessions as the model of the well-rounded artist. In a letter dated July 31, 1920 (Cozzens Collection, Princeton University Library), Bartlett described a rapturous evening listening to Sessions play *Pelléas* and *Tristan* at the piano. Sessions played the "Liebestod," Bartlett wrote Cozzens, "without excitement, with the transcendental calm of the complete union of love—beyond the realm of passions." Bartlett continued: "For years he was in some ways the guide to my life. He introduced me to Meredith, Ibsen, Santayana, and to the whole world of orchestral music. I forgot to add Freud to the list and many other things far more important than these." In response, Cozzens wondered whether Sessions lacked "soul."
18. Cozzens, letter to Bertha Cozzens, May 7, 1931, Cozzens Collection. There was a relevant autobiographical bit in *Ask Me*

Tomorrow (New York: Harcourt Brace, 1940), p. 24: "Music was not one of Francis's natural interests or pleasures, for he was practically tone-deaf; but the love of it is a mark of superior culture, and so he had heard a great deal of music while he was at college and supported with disciplined patience many concerts and evenings of opera rather than have his friends suppose he was in any respect their esthetic inferior." Many of Cozzens's own music-loving college friends were gay, which helps explain the frequent association of classical music and homosexuality found in his fiction.

19. Bruccoli, p. 128. In a letter dated June 18, 1957 (Cozzens Collection), Cozzens wrote to John McCallum at Harcourt, in a thank-you note for the gift of a Tom Lehrer record, "For years I've contented myself with a 78 rpm job because my flawless musical taste (except for being tone-deaf) mostly confined me to my really unexampled collection of the records of my youth. (If you want to hear a mint-condition Marian Harris' Left All Alone Again Blues; or Ted Lewis' original Unreconstructed Margie, or Down the Old Church Aisle; or Paul Whiteman's 1921 Ka-lu-a; or Frank Crumit singing as who else could or would, Sweet Lady, or The Love Nest, you only have to stop by.)"

20. Cozzens, letter to Bertha Cozzens, December 8, 1932, Cozzens Collection.

21. Bruccoli, p. 156.

22. Pollack, p. 29.

23. Pollack, p. 40.

24. William Austin, *Music in the 20th Century* (New York: W. W. Norton, 1966), p. 440.

25. Bruccoli, p. 211.

26. Bruccoli, p. 148.

27. Pollack, pp. 163–176.

28. Piston, taped interview with Margaret Fairbanks, Rodgers and Hammerstein Archive, New York Public Library, c. 1967.

29. Bruccoli, p. 129.

30. Austin, p. 440.

31. Bruccoli, p. 36.

32. Bruccoli, pp. 176–177; Pollack, p. 177.

33. Bruccoli, p. 76.

34. Bruccoli, p. 302; Pollack, p. 175.

35. Bruccoli, p. 86; interview with Richard French, January 4, 1978.

36. Bruccoli, p. 277, and Cozzens, letter to Bertha Cozzens, December 17, 1940, Cozzens Collection; Pollack, p. 175.

37. Bruccoli, p. 137, and Cozzens, letter to Bertha Cozzens, July 14, 1939, Cozzens Collection; Pollack, pp. 173–175, French interview, and interview with David Diamond, August 2, 1979.

38. In 1956, Piston joined CASE (Committee of the Arts and Sciences for Eisenhower), Piston Collection, Library of Congress. Cozzens, however, refused to do so, writing, "Privately, I'm of your committee's opinion; but since I've long made it my rule to mind my own business, which is nothing but writing, I don't feel able to add my name to your list." Letter to J. Donald Adams, October 9, 1956, Cozzens Collection.

39. Copland, *The New Music 1900–1960,* revised and enlarged (New York: W. W. Norton, 1968), p. 131.

40. Bruccoli, p. 116.

41. Pollack, p. 66.

42. Copland, pp. 118–144.

2. SONGS WITHOUT WORDS: THE ORCHESTRAL MINIATURES OF LEROY ANDERSON

LEROY ANDERSON'S ORCHESTRAL MINIATURES, including *The Syncopated Clock, Sleigh Ride,* and *Blue Tango,* were among the best-known American concert music written after Gershwin's *Rhapsody in Blue* and Copland's *Appalachian Spring.* For most people who knew his music, however (and every American knew his music), he was an obscure figure. Leading chroniclers of American music, including Chase, Mellers, Hitchcock, and Hamm, omitted him from their surveys. (Historians of the American musical, more understandably, perhaps, similarly tended to omit mention of *Goldilocks,* his one venture on Broadway.) Local Connecticut newspapers, however, regularly published features on the composer, and with the additional help of unpublished material belonging to Mrs. Eleanor Anderson, the following sketch could be drawn.[1]

Leroy Anderson, born on June 29, 1908 in Cambridge, Massachusetts, was, like Gershwin and Copland, the son of immigrants. His parents had come to the United States from Sweden as young children; his father, Brewer Anton, was from Christianstad, and his mother, Anna Margareta Johnson, from Stockholm. His parents spoke Swedish at home, and thus Leroy picked up the language. In later years, the composer remembered with great relish the smorgasbord of a traditional Swedish Christmas: hogshead cheese, pickled herring, pickled beets, sausages, and rice pudding.

Both parents were musical. His mother was a church

organist and a pianist, and his father played the mandolin in his spare time from his job as a postal employee. Anderson learned to play organ and piano sitting in his mother's lap. The whole family sang popular American songs at home and in the car.

Anderson once noted that the "long haul" of his formal education transpired on one street in Cambridge: Broadway. It was on Broadway that he attended primary school, Harvard Grammar School, Cambridge High and Latin School, and, finally, Harvard. Had he walked a little further down Broadway, from Paine Hall to the Law School, he quipped, he might have become a lawyer. In high school, well on his way to his adult height of six feet, Anderson took up the double bass, his principal instrument, which he studied with the Boston Symphony's Gaston Dufresne. He also studied organ with Henry Gideon in Boston. His father further encouraged him to learn trombone, so that he could march with the Harvard University Band at football games. During his student years, Anderson's pleasant baritone voice was also in some demand, and throughout his life, he was happy to sing some popular song by Gershwin, Porter, or Rodgers at friendly gatherings.

Anderson began composing music in high school. He wrote three class songs for Cambridge High, the last of which he orchestrated himself. By his junior year, he was writing instrumental compositions. These included some pieces for string quartet, one of which, a 1923 *Menuet,* he showed to George Chadwick, who edited it slightly.

Anderson entered Harvard as a music major in the fall of 1925. He studied theory and vocal composition with Spalding, counterpoint with Ballantine, fugue with Heilman, and orchestration and composition with Piston. He also studied composition briefly with visiting professor Georges Enescu. His courses outside of music included history, English, astronomy, and foreign languages. During these years, he wrote songs to German 19th-century verse for Spalding, and a *Rondo* for piano for Piston. His major academic effort was a paper entitled, "Music, Romanticism, and Rousseau." Anderson fastidiously preserved his college class notes, examinations, compositions, and orchestrations, materials which soon

are to be publicly available as part of Yale University's
Anderson Collection.

In a 1953 interview for the *Boston Sunday Post*, Anderson
credited Enescu with teaching him "craftsmanship," and
Piston for teaching him "how to be objective."[2] He expanded
at some length on this last point:

> The general tendency of a composer is to fall in love
> with what he does. Piston always advised us to listen to
> our compositions as though someone else had written
> them. My biggest disappointment came the day he
> handed me back one of my pieces with the comment
> that it sounded like improvisation. I was crushed. . . .But
> he was right. Every church organist improvises and that
> was my trouble. I had been playing the organ at the East
> Congregational Church in Milton for $10 a Sunday and
> sure enough, I had fallen into the habit of improvising to
> fill the gaps that always occurred. Piston's advice was
> good and I've never forgotten it.

Piston's comments marked in red pencil throughout the
manuscript of Anderson's *Rondo* suggest yet other aspects of
his teaching: "Why not keep to same style? Too many literal
repetitions of opening phrase in principal theme? Too many
root positions? Same modulation as in principal theme. Is
triple time really advisable? Avoid anticipation of A^b I before
entry of the theme." Piston concluded, "Too many repetitions. First episodes not sufficiently contrasted rhythmically
with principal theme. Subdominant would have been better
key for second episode. Would gain much by greater variety."
Characteristically, Piston balanced questions and statements,
as well as concerns for both unity and variety.

Anderson received his BA, magna cum laude and Phi Beta
Kappa, in 1929, and his MA in 1930. He subsequently
applied for a Paine Traveling Fellowship, which "in those days
was the next step in a career in music." He hoped in particular
to study with Nadia Boulanger. After being turned down in
1930, he took E.B. Hill's advice and gave up directing the
Harvard Band, an activity which, according to Hill, "did not
indicate a proper attitude." But after a second refusal in 1931,
he resumed leadership of the Band and started work on a PhD

in Harvard's German Department, majoring in Scandinavian languages.

Eventually, Anderson mastered German, Swedish, Norwegian, Danish, 'and Icelandic. He also studied French, Italian, and Portuguese. At the same time, he earned his living by tutoring music at Radcliffe (1930–1932); serving as organist and choir director at the East Congregational Church in Milton (1929–1935); directing the Harvard Band (1929–1930, 1932–1936); playing piano, double bass, and tuba in dance bands and radio orchestras, a few conducted by himself, and nearly all under Ruby Newman's management (1931–1935); playing solo engagements as an accordionist; and working as a free-lance arranger and orchestrator! In 1934, he gave up his graduate studies before completing the PhD and soon was working almost exclusively as a professional arranger.

Anderson's earliest arrangements had been occasional pieces for the Harvard Band. He also orchestrated musical revues staged by the Vincent Club and the Hasty Pudding Club. By the mid-1930s, he was writing dozens of dance-band arrangements of songs by Foster, Romberg, Kern, Gershwin, Porter, Rodgers, and others for Ruby Newman. His big turning point came in 1936 when George Judd, manager of the Boston Symphony, asked Anderson to arrange some Harvard songs for the Boston Pops' Harvard Night. Anderson recalled the circumstances well:

> He (Judd) knew that I'd written some stuff and had arranged medleys for the Harvard band and he wanted me to arrange a symphonic medley of Harvard songs, and conduct that segment myself. So I wrote this piece, which I called *Harvard Fantasy,* rehearsed it with the Pops orchestra, and then at the appropriate point during the concert Fiedler called me out and I conducted this and a few other college songs. It was quite a thrill.[3]

It was also the start of a remarkable association between Anderson and Arthur Fiedler, director of the Boston Pops Orchestra from 1930–1979.

Anderson had long known Fiedler as the versatile musician who played six different instruments for the Boston Symphony, in addition to being "the handsomest man in the Orchestra."[4] Fiedler vaguely knew Anderson as the leader of a dance band at the Ritz Carlton with whom he once had posed for a photograph at the hotel president's request. Impressed with the orchestration of the young man's *Harvard Fantasy*, Fiedler asked Anderson for more scores. Two years later, Anderson submitted an original composition for the string orchestra, pizzicato, called *Jazz Pizzicato*, a work intended as "a little encore number, à la Fiedler." Anderson conducted the premiere himself on May 23, 1938. The piece was an immediate hit with Pops audiences, and Fiedler conducted it frequently for the rest of the season. Fiedler subsequently suggested a companion piece, so that he could record both on one side of a 78 rpm disc, for which Anderson composed *Jazz Legato*, also for strings. Fiedler and the Pops recorded both pieces on June 29, 1939, at a session at which Piston's *Suite from The Incredible Flutist* was also recorded.

It is not difficult to understand the success of *Jazz Pizzicato* and *Jazz Legato:* urbane, witty, and, as their titles promise, jazzy, they have not lost their charm. But more importantly, they answered to the specific needs of the Boston Pops and, soon enough, its many imitators. The Boston Pops was founded to provide light summertime fare that would have broad popular appeal, and that at the same time would please sophisticated tastes and be worthy of the great Boston Symphony Orchestra. This proved to be no easy feat, and over the years, the Pops alternately were accused of being too serious, as during Casella's tenure in the 1920s, or too frivolous, as in Fiedler's later years. Its golden age may well have been the 1930s, when the level of American popular music was exceptionally high, and when American serious music often enjoyed a popular strain. During that decade, Piston wrote his ballet, *The Incredible Flutist*, for the Boston Pops; even Elliott Carter hoped to have the Pops play his music (though even then, that was rather out of the question).

The major problem confronting the Boston Pops was finding an appropriate repertoire. Neither of the two major resources—19th-century overtures and modern arrangements of popular songs—were entirely satisfactory. The former could be dull and old-fashioned; the latter could be banal and meretricious. Most modern orchestral composers wrote in styles that would leave young couples too nonplused to drink their lemonades. Anderson's *Jazz Pizzicato* and a whole series of orchestral miniatures to follow, however, hit the spot perfectly.

Light, diverting instrumental miniatures were, of course, not unknown. The French Baroque harpsichord literature was particularly rich in them, as was the piano literature from the 19th and 20th centuries in general, as Anderson well knew. Then, too, there were the little gems of Kreisler, the dance music of the Strauss family, and a lively tradition of American novelty compositions for small bands or jazz combos, the most famous examples including Arthur Pryor's *The Whistler and His Dog* and Zez Confrey's *Kitten on the Keys*. Anderson's innovation, however, was twofold. First, his compositions were intended for a topnotch orchestra, as so few instrumental miniatures had been. Second, he combined classic, popular, and contemporary features with great flair and humor, bringing him at least in range of contemporary modernists like Berger, Shapero, and Bernstein. (Anderson's possible influence on these younger Harvard composers, in fact, should not be disregarded offhand.) Anderson stood, further, in special relation to Piston, perhaps somewhat as Johann Strauss, Jr., did to Brahms.

When the War came in 1942, Anderson enlisted as a private in the Army and was sent to Iceland to serve as translator and interpreter for U.S. counterintelligence. In 1943, after Officer's School at Fort Monmouth, he was assigned to Military Intelligence Service in Washington, D.C., where he was Chief of the Scandinavian Desk. Released in 1946 with the rank of Captain, he was asked to remain in the Army as a military attaché in Oslo or Stockholm, but he chose to return to his musical career.

Even before the War ended, Fiedler had asked Anderson to write something for a Boston Pops' Army Night on May 28, 1945. Finding a few free hours from the Pentagon, Anderson wrote the sprightly *Promenade*. While scoring the work, the title of another work came to mind, *The Syncopated Clock*. "It occurred to me," remembered Anderson, "that hundreds of composers had written music imitating or suggesting clocks, but that all these clocks were ordinary ones that beat in a regular rhythm. No one had described a 'syncopated' clock and this idea seemed to present the opportunity to write something different."[5] He found time to compose this piece as well, and obtaining a three-day pass, he conducted the premiere of both *Promenade* and *The Syncopated Clock* in uniform.

Returning to civilian life, Anderson became one of the Boston Pops' principal arrangers. He arranged medleys from *South Pacific, Annie Get Your Gun,* and other Broadway shows, and orchestrated piano pieces by Chopin, Fauré, and others. His growing success as a composer meant that by the 1950s he could give up arranging as a livelihood, but he continued to arrange nonetheless, albeit at a less harried pace. Much of 1955, in fact, was given over to arranging three *Suites of Carols* for brass choir, string orchestra, and woodwind ensemble, respectively. His very last work was a 1974 arrangement of music from Gershwin's *Girl Crazy* for Fiedler and the Pops.

Immediately after the War, Anderson and his family[6] settled in New York City, but in the late '40s, they moved to Woodbury, Connecticut, a picturesque and historic town in the western part of the state. Anderson purchased nine acres of hilltop property, and built a house whose modern architecture provoked some local consternation. He lived there quietly for the rest of his life, leaving only for the occasional conducting engagement, trip abroad, commute to New York, and the like. Most of his friends were Woodbury business executives. His few musician friends included Johnny Green, composer of "Body and Soul" and other hits. Anderson had known Green at Harvard, but saw him only rarely after Green moved to Hollywood to work for MGM. (Anderson, for his part, had no interest in writing for the motion pictures, and periodically turned down such offers, as from the producers of *Mr. Roberts.*) Throughout, he remained very close to Fiedler, sympathizing with the conductor's troubles with certain players, his unwillingness to renounce his Judaism in deference to the Catholic Church at the time of his marriage, and his desire to expand the scope of the Boston Pops.[7] And he valued Fiedler's constructive criticism:

> You would take a number to Fiedler and after giving it careful consideration he'd hand it back and say, "No

good. Try again." But he would tell you why. He'd show you that it was aimless, that it missed the point, and you would learn.[8]

Following the success of his early works, Anderson continued to write original novelty pieces for the Boston Pops, twenty-four in all from 1946 to 1954. *Chicken Reel* came first in 1946, though it was not published until 1963. In 1947 the composer wrote his first big hit, a brilliant and witty perpetual motion for strings entitled *Fiddle-Faddle* (the enormous popularity of *The Syncopated Clock* still lay ahead). The work was recorded by the Boston Pops on RCA Records, and even earlier by England's Kingsway Orchestra on London Records, giving many the notion that the little-known Anderson was an English composer. In this same year Anderson wrote the suave, Latin American-inspired *Serenata,* a piece that became a favorite not only with Fiedler, but with a number of jazz musicians.[9]

In 1948 Anderson wrote *Saraband,* a work that epitomized the composer's inimitable blend of classic poise and contemporary wit (Ex. 3). 1948 was also the year of *Sleigh Ride,* which over time became his most frequently recorded work, and the *Governor Bradford March,* one of his few unpublished works. *A Trumpeter's Lullaby* followed in 1949. It was written at the request of the Boston Symphony's first trumpet, Roger Voisin, who requested an encore piece that would show off the trumpet's tenderer side.

In 1950 Anderson wrote *The Waltzing Cat* and *The Typewriter.* Anderson's use of an actual typewriter as a percussion instrument in the latter looked back to Satie, as well as to his friend Johnny Green, but it was Anderson's novel and ingenious touch to use a desk bell to simulate the ring of the carriage return.

1951 was a particularly fruitful year with seven new works: *Blue Tango, China Doll, Belle of the Ball, The Phantom Regiment, The Penny-Whistle Song, Horse and Buggy,* and *Plink, Plank, Plunk!*

Up until this point, Anderson's fame was limited largely to the Boston area. But in 1950 he began to record his orchestral miniatures, and things changed quickly. For one, the producers at WCBS-TV, New York, happened to hear his recording

Example 3. Leroy Anderson, *Saraband* (Mills Music, 1950).

of *The Syncopated Clock,* and decided to use it as the theme music for a new television program of old movies being launched, *The Late Show.* Anderson's unusual clock piece became an overnight sensation, and its continued success was evident by the fact that CBS used it for the next twenty-five years.

Even more astounding was the success of Anderson's recording of *Blue Tango.* Released in the fall of 1951, it sold over a million and a quarter copies by the fall of 1952. In addition, it was the first instrumental work ever to reach the top of the Hit Parade, where it stayed for fifteen weeks in early 1952. Anderson recalled, "The whole thing was completely unbelievable to me, because the kind of music I write was not popular music, it was concert music."[10] He subsequently made a guest appearance on the *Ed Sullivan Show.* It soon became apparent that Anderson's miniatures could meet the needs not only of Pops concerts, but of radio, television, and Muzak. This, in turn, encouraged more orchestras to play him, and in 1953 a study conducted by the American Symphony Orchestra League showed him to be the American composer most frequently performed by American orchestras, ahead of Copland, Gershwin, and Barber.

Anderson's immense popularity encouraged his publisher, Mills, to put out some of his miniatures as songs, which was no hardship, considering that their tunefulness and songlike forms made many of them easy to adapt as such. For this venture, they drafted Mitchell Parish, well-known for putting words to instrumental music, having done so for Hoagy Carmichael's *Stardust* and Duke Ellington's *Sophisticated Lady*. Parish and Anderson collaborated on seven lyrics: *Sleigh Ride* (1950), *The Syncopated Clock* (1950), *Serenata* (1950), *The Waltzing Cat* (1951), *Blue Tango* (1952), *Belle of the Ball* (1953), and *Forgotten Dreams* (1962). Anderson particularly liked the lyrics for *The Waltzing Cat,* while his favorite performance was Sarah Vaughan's rendition of *Serenata.* None of these songs, however, rivaled the popularity of their purely instrumental versions, with the possible exception of *Sleigh Ride,* which was useful for Christmas albums (though both song and instrumental version were intended as winter landscapes, not as Christmas pieces per se).

In 1951 Anderson was recalled to active duty to aid intelligence in the Korean War. After serving at Fort Riley, Fort Bragg, and finally the Office of the Assistant Chief of Staff, Intelligence, in Washington, he was released in December of 1952.

In 1953 he wrote three more miniatures (*Song of the Bells, Summer Skies,* and *The Girl in Satin*), but spent most of the year on a three-movement *Concerto in C for Piano and Orchestra.* Premiered by Eugene List and the Chicago Summer Symphony, the work was withdrawn soon after its premiere. Anderson's instincts were probably right. He intended it as a needed addition to a repertory that included Gershwin's *Rhapsody in Blue* and *Concerto in F.* But the end result sounded uncomfortably like the movie scores for contemporary Hollywood melodramas, as had Richard Addinsell's *Warsaw Concerto.* The composer tackled the demands of a larger form with routine literalness, including a fairly strained fugal episode in the first movement's development. In general, little of the distinctive wit and sharpness of the

miniatures shone through, even in the folksy finale. As might
be expected, however, the melodies were quite tuneful, for
example, the second theme from the first movement (Ex. 4).
A planned revival of the work might prove its usefulness after
all.

Anderson never again attempted a large, instrumental

Example 4. Leroy Anderson, *Concerto for Piano and Orchestra* (Woodbury
Music, 1978).

work. In 1954 he returned to miniatures, writing *Forgotten Dreams, The First Day of Spring, The Sandpaper Ballet* (which called for coarse, medium, and fine sandpaper), and *Bugler's Holiday* (a fantasy about three buglers on their day off playing bugle calls "they wouldn't get away with on the post"[11]).

The years 1954 to 1962 were spent working on, and recovering from, a musical comedy venture, *Goldilocks*. His collaborators were Walter Kerr, drama critic; Kerr's wife Jean, author of the best-selling novel, *Please Don't Eat the Daisies;* and Joan Ford. The Kerrs recently had completed their first musical, *The Vamp* (1956), a spoof on the silent movies. *Goldilocks* similarly was set in the early days of filmmaking (1913, New York). The story's heroine, Maggie Harris, is a Broadway star who is leaving the stage to marry upper-class George Randolph Brown, but who must first fulfill a forgotten contractual agreement to star in a movie directed by the struggling, hard-boiled, tyrannical Max Grady (perhaps inspired by D.W. Griffith).[12] After two acts of bickering, Maggie and Max decide to marry and make more movies, leaving George to be consoled by Lois, a chorus girl. It was a congenial vehicle for Anderson, who loved Charlie Chaplin and P.G. Wodehouse, and who even knew some Marx Brothers routines by heart. Producer David Merrick, unwilling to back a composer who never had been known to write a song, let alone a Broadway musical, left the show over the Kerrs' insistence on Anderson. This and other "behind-the-scene accounts of the musical *Goldilocks*" were discussed in an article by George Wright Briggs, Jr.[13]

Anderson wrote the score quickly, finding it easier than writing instrumental music.[14] One song, "I Never Know When," was composed overnight.[15] The score lacked some of the dazzle and originality of some of the decade's more enduring musical comedies, but it was distinguished by its tunefulness and its high level of craftsmanship. Best, perhaps, were the sweet, romantic ballads given to George: "Save a Kiss" (Ex. 5) and "Shall I Take My Heart and Go." The more comic numbers, while handled adequately, were not Anderson's real milieu, as they were, say, Bernstein's or Styne's. Anderson orchestrated a few of the show's numbers himself, and supervised Philip Lang on the others.[16] These orchestrations proved altogether superior for a Broadway musical.

Goldilocks opened in Philadelphia's Erlanger Theatre on September 2, 1958.[17] The lavish production cost close to $400,000. Kerr directed, Peter Larkin did the sets, Castillo designed the costumes, Agnes de Mille choreographed, and Lehman Engel conducted the orchestra. The cast included Barry Sullivan (Max), Elaine Stritch (Maggie), Russell Nype (George), and Pat Stanley (Lois), with Nathaniel Frey and Margaret Hamilton in minor roles. (Max originally was to be played by Ben Gazzara.) During the work's Boston run at the Schubert Theatre, Sullivan left the show and was replaced by Don Ameche. *Goldilocks* opened in New York's Lunt-Fontanne Theatre on October 11, 1958, and closed on February 23, 1959, after 161 performances, losing more than $300,000. Critics found the emotional life of the story wanting, especially as the spurned George has the work's two romantic ballads, an assessment with which Kerr himself concurred.[18]

Although *Goldilocks* as a show quickly was forgotten, the cast album was available continually until 1986. Further, Anderson arranged six of its numbers for symphony orchestra and recorded them in 1962. He also arranged three of the songs for concert purposes. Some of these proved as viable as the orchestral miniatures; in 1982, they were recorded by Muzak, and subsequently piped into department stores and elevators.

Not thoroughly daunted, Anderson accepted an offer from David Selznick to write another musical, this one with poet Ogden Nash, after Margaret Mitchell's *Gone with the Wind.* The project had to be shelved because of legal complications, but not before Anderson and Nash completed a few songs, which can be found among the composer's papers.

In 1962 Anderson resumed the writing of orchestral miniatures, producing *Arietta, Balladette, The Golden Years, Clarinet Candy, Home Stretch* (which sought to capture the excitement of a horse race's final moments), and *The Captains and the Kings* after Kipling (in which the kings, depicted in the middle section, were thought of as "ordinary people like the rest of us; it's just that they have an exalted position"[19]). Whether because of lingering bitterness over *Goldilocks* (Anderson thought the work a "flop"[20]), or flagging inspiration, or less sympathetic times, these works had much less success than the earlier ones. He published no new works after this. In 1969 he revised the *Harvard Fantasy,* calling it *A Harvard Festival,* and in 1970 he wrote four short works (*Lullaby of the Drums, Birthday Party, Waltz Around the Scale,* and a later-withdrawn *March of the Two Left Feet*) for local Connecticut orchestras. He died of lung cancer on May 18, 1975.

The continued success of Anderson's best orchestral miniatures could be explained in part by the composer's careful, meticulous workmanship. Anderson composed painstakingly, often spending whole months on a single three- or four-minute piece.[21] Just the introductory four measures to the *Penny-Whistle Song,* he tells us, took four days to write. Occasionally the search for a general concept or title, with which his compositional process usually began, itself took weeks of pacing about the house, a habit, he was interested to learn, he shared with Irving Berlin. This concept or title was

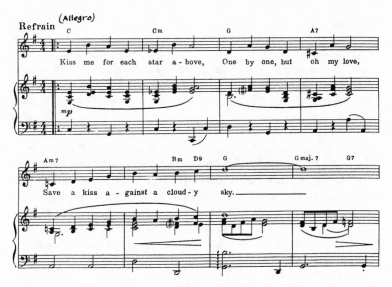

Example 5. Leroy Anderson, "Save a Kiss," *Goldilocks* (Ankerford Music, 1958).

usually associated with some rhythm, an association epitomized by his own description of *Belle of the Ball:* "Whenever
you hear a waltz going like that, you can see some beautiful
girl in a long, flowing gown just waltzing around the place."[22]
After finding the basic concept and rhythm, Anderson
created a harmonic context, sometimes tried out at the piano,
and then a principal melody, never worked out at the piano
for fear of falling into conventional habits. He then wrote out
a three-stave condensed score, and finally orchestrated it in
full score.

Within the wide world of moving objects, the ideas that
inspired Anderson were quite varied: cats and horses,
typewriters and clocks, belles and soldiers, buglers and
penny-whistlers, pizzicato and perpetual motion. The dance
was naturally of special importance to Anderson, and many of
his titles alluded to dances of one sort or another, including
*Promenade, Chicken Reel, Saraband, Governor Bradford March,
The Waltzing Cat, Blue Tango,* and *Sandpaper Ballet,* which
was a kind of soft-shoe number. Other numbers were
essentially dances without being called so: *Jazz Pizzicato/Jazz
Legato* (fox-trot), *Fiddle-Faddle* (reel), *Serenata* (beguine), *Belle
of the Ball* (waltz), *The Girl in Satin* (tango), *Bugler's Holiday*
(polka), and *The Captains and the Kings* (march and polonaise). Even such musical landscapes as *Summer Skies* and *The
First Day of Spring* seemed related to the dance, more
specifically, to the "Adagios" of classical ballet. Performed
one after the other, Anderson's miniatures, in fact, seemed to
resemble nothing so much as the court entertainments from
the Tchaikovsky ballets.

Having found some suitable idea, there was some tendency
to use it a second time, for example, a trotting horse in *Sleigh
Ride* and *Horse and Buggy,* the tango in *Blue Tango* and *The
Girl in Satin,* and violin pizzicato in *Jazz Pizzicato* and *Plink,
Plank, Plunk!* The second of these couplings was usually not
as inspired as the original, but nonetheless gave a new,
distinctive dimension to the shared idea.

One noted, too, in the course of Anderson's career a
stylistic development that can be said to comprise three
periods. The first of these (1937 to 1950) was characterized
by the sly irreverence and improbability of *Jazz Pizzicato, The
Syncopated Clock, Trumpeter's Lullaby,* and *The Waltzing Cat.*

The second period (1951–1954) was more romantic and nostalgic with its *Belle of the Ball, Horse and Buggy, Summer Skies,* and *Forgotten Dreams.* The third period (consisting primarily of only one year, 1962) had a cool, restrained, somewhat abstract quality, as in *Arietta* and *Balladette.* Audiences liked the earliest pieces best.

Throughout Anderson's career, but especially in his second period, there was often a quaint, homey, American quality that perhaps could be compared with a popular illustrator like Norman Rockwell, but at the same time an ironic urbanity that seemed closer to a sophisticated cartoonist like James Thurber. As for Anderson's polish and elegance, it had at least some relation to his collegiate enthusiasm for the French clavecin school and Rousseau.

How Anderson's style and technique served his ideas is best seen by a close look at one of his works, such as *Sleigh Ride.*

Like many Anderson miniatures, *Sleigh Ride* was in ternary ABA form. Both the A and B sections were related to popular song forms: A was in aabbaa form (close enough to the conventional aaba form, to be sure, though the composer's elaboration is worth noting), and B was in abab form. And like popular songs, these smaller phrases were typically eight measures in length. (Only rarely did Anderson's subjects inspire unusual phrase lengths. In *The Typewriter,* for instance, an expected 4-measure phrase was extended to six measures to depict the typist's breathless pace; while in *A Trumpeter's Lullaby,* phrase lengths were varied to suggest a singer's rubato.)

Sleigh Ride's schematic form notwithstanding, the composer unified its varied parts with flair and skill. The opening rhythmic motive in the bass (Ex. 6a), for instance, not only prepared the main theme (Ex. 6b), but reappeared throughout the work, most ingeniously at m. 31 (Ex. 6c). Similarly, the opening accompanimental figure itself not only prefigured the pick-up to the main theme, but later was transformed into a secondary contrasting theme (Ex. 7).

Such formal niceties in themselves were clearly not as winning as was Anderson's ability to interrelate the musical elements to impart a vivid sense of some idea, in this case a sleigh ride. For example, the surprising move to E minor (ii of

Example 6a. Leroy Anderson, *Sleigh Ride* (Mills Music, 1948).

III) at m. 29 (see Ex. 6c), meant to evoke some new thrill, was matched by added rhythmic activity—the "giddy-yap" triplets—and the introduction of the temple block. Another surprise, the arrival in G major at m. 63 (see Ex. 7), was similarly matched by a dramatic crescendo, the introduction of the whip, and a more expansive harmonic rhythm. The last big surprise, the return of the main theme in swing style (m.

Example 6b.

Example 6c.

101), intensified the merriment and momentum (furthermore, it at once reflected a modern, American sensibility, and
offered, in classic tradition, an ornamented da capo). In this
piece, as in some others, Anderson does what Piston warned
him against in the early *Rondo:* he anticipates the main theme
with an arrival in the tonic (m. 9; m. 99). This too served
programmatic intentions, for it mitigated against suggesting
any firm arrival before the work's final measure.

There were many other descriptive touches. The opening
harmony, a second-inversion major triad with a suspended
fourth, perfectly matched the sound of sleigh bells. Similarly,

Example 7. Leroy Anderson, *Sleigh Ride* (Mills Music, 1948).

the penultimate chord, C^b-E^b-F, itself derived from the opening harmony except that the fifth has become an augmented fourth, brilliantly suggested the tightening of the horse's reins. Also descriptive were Anderson's use of sleigh bells, wood block, and whip, not to mention the trumpet whinny at the work's close. *Sleigh Ride,* however, used no instrument that would not be found in the standard modern orchestra. The popular association of Anderson with sound effects can find support in only two works: *The Typewriter* and *Sandpaper Ballet.* It could be his music was so descriptive, it frequently gave the illusion of sound effects.

Shortly before his death, at a 1973 Yale University lecture, Anderson spoke at some length about two musicological "myths" that were popular during his college days in the 1920s. The first was that enduring composers were not admired in their own lifetime. This myth, he claimed, was fabricated by Wagnerites in order to conceal the offensiveness of Wagner's character. The historical facts, as reported by Ernest Newman, told another story; and to give another example, Anderson cited, in German, Schubert's eulogy of Beethoven. He suspected that in the course of the 20th century this myth had been discredited by the success of Stravinsky and Prokofiev.

The other myth, still widespread, in his opinion, was that only serious music survived. He recalled reading a passage in Ebenezer Prout's music text that named three late 19th-century German composers that the author surely thought would endure: Richard Wagner, Johannes Brahms, and Joachim Raff. Anderson remembered thinking that had Prout cited Johann Strauss, Jr., instead of Raff, his statement would have been considerably more accurate. But Strauss wrote waltzes, whereas Raff wrote symphonies, and the academic assumption was that symphonies, not waltzes, survived. Anderson suspected that this myth was losing currency also.

Anderson made no allusion to himself in this discussion, but by inference it was clearly a defense of his own life's work. The confidence and ease with which he spoke suggested that he had no regrets. He seemed quite reconciled to let future audiences decide his fate. And, indeed, in 1988 he was inducted posthumously into the Songwriter's Hall of Fame, a singular, but somehow appropriate honor for this unusual composer of orchestral songs without words.

Notes

1. Some of these local newspaper features were reprinted in *Leroy Anderson (Almost Complete)* (Melville, NY: Belwin Mills, 1978). Other published material includes "Leroy Anderson," *Current Biography* (September, 1952), and "Leroy Anderson, Wrote Pop Music," *New York Times* (May 19, 1975). Unpublished sources used for this chapter include taped conversations of Anderson from 1962 (WTIC-AM), 1970 (WTIC-TV), 1972 (U.S. Air Force Band concert), 1972 (Evening at the Boston Pops), and 1973 (Yale University Radio); and an interview with Mrs. Eleanor Anderson and Kurt Anderson, November 22, 1983.
2. Eleanor Roberts, *Boston Sunday Post,* March 22, 1953.
3. Robin Moore, *Fiedler* (Boston: Little, Brown and Company, 1968), p. 157.
4. Anderson, Evening at the Boston Pops.
5. Anderson, "The Syncopated Clock Still Ticks," *Music Journal* 26 (September, 1968), p. 31.
6. Anderson married Eleanor Jane Firke on October 31, 1942. They had four children: Jane (b. 1944), Eric (b. 1947), Rolf (b. 1952), and Kurt (b. 1954).
7. Moore, pp. 93, 152, 157–159, 187.
8. Roberts.
9. *Serenata* was recorded by Teddy Wilson, Joe Pass, and Sarah Vaughan.
10. Anderson, WTIC-TV.
11. Anderson, Evening at the Boston Pops.
12. Walter and Jean Kerr, *Goldilocks* (NY: Samuel French, 1958).
13. Briggs, Jr., "Leroy Anderson on Broadway: Behind-the-Scene Accounts of the Musical *Goldilocks,*" *American Music* Vol. 3, No. 3 (1985), pp. 329–336.
14. "New Broadway Composer Likes to Be Different," *St. Louis Globe Democrat,* November 23, 1958.
15. Briggs, p. 333.
16. Anderson orchestrated the Overture, the Entr'acte, "The Pussy Foot," and "Heart of Stone" (Briggs).
17. The source material concerning *Goldilocks,* including reviews, financial statements, and press clippings, is found in the

Goldilocks files of the Theater Department, New York Public Library at Lincoln Center.

18. Kerr reflected, "What we should have done was forget all about working for more comedy whatsoever, and straighten out the emotional line instead. I mean, make something real seem to happen between the principals, emotionally," *On Broadway,* William and Jane Scott, eds. (NY: Da Capo Press, 1978), p. 323.

19. Anderson, U.S. Air Force Band concert.

20. Briggs, p. 330.

21. There were exceptions: *The Syncopated Clock,* for instance, took two days to write.

22. Anderson, U.S. Air Force Band concert.

3. REGIONAL VOICES: JOHN VINCENT AND GAIL KUBIK

ROM THE STANDPOINT of Piston's students as a group, John
Nathaniel Vincent, Jr., cut an unusual figure. Whereas
most of these students came from the East or Midwest,
Vincent hailed from Birmingham, Alabama. Born on May 17,
1902, he was also the oldest of Piston's students, and
considerably older than his Harvard classmates in the mid-
'30s. His age and background helped form a relatively
conservative disposition which was further conditioned by an
impassioned, lifelong study of the diatonic modes, also
unusual in a time that inspired all sorts of chromatic
adventures.

Vincent's interest in modes stemmed from a boyhood love
for the folk and church music of Southern blacks and
backwoods whites. In fact, he did pioneering ethnographic
work in this field, recording and transcribing Southern folk
music, work later donated to the Library of Congress. Vincent
also studied the flute, which he pursued with Georges
Laurent at the New England Conservatory (1922–1926). He
stayed on at the Conservatory an extra year (1926–1927) to
attend classes given by Converse and Chadwick, whose
course on modal theory intrigued him. Vincent subsequently
taught at Nashville's George Peabody College, where he
earned a master's degree in 1933. Sometime along the way he
befriended fellow Southerner John Powell, who encouraged
him to develop his own modal theories.[1]

At Harvard from 1933 to 1935, he studied with Leichtentritt, but principally with Piston, "whose penetrating criticisms did much to insure the validity of my ideas during the
development stage."[2] Probably on Piston's advice, he studied

with Boulanger from 1935 to 1937 in Paris at the Ecole Normale, where he wrote his first significant work, the *String Quartet No. 1 in G* (1936). Vincent's formal education finally ended with some work with Roy Harris at Cornell, where he received a PhD in 1942 for the ballet *3 Jacks* and the a cappella chorus, *Three Grecian Songs*. He served a number of educational institutions before replacing Schoenberg at UCLA, where he taught form 1946 to 1969. He composed until his death in Santa Monica on January 21, 1977. Outstanding were two orchestral works from the '50s, *Symphony in D* and the *Symphonic Poem after Descartes*, both championed by Eugene Ormandy and the Philadelphia Orchestra. He was best known, however, for the treatise *The Diatonic Modes in Modern Music* (1951).

The Diatonic Modes in Modern Music had value far exceeding its obvious importance to any serious study of Vincent's music. Indeed, it was quickly acknowledged as a major contribution in its field. The book proposed a dialectic in Western music between diatony and chromaticism that regularly expressed itself in cycles. This dichotomy entailed complex ambiguities the author chose to skirt, for diatony was made to include the "diatonic modes" of Graeco-Christian tradition (Vincent argued strenuously for the inclusion of the controversial locrian mode), the "tonality" of Monteverdi, and the "harmonic modality" of Fauré; chromaticism, meanwhile, included the "chromatic genera" of ancient Greece, as well as Gesualdo and Wagner.

The book's dialectical premise, however, was not its main focus. The author aimed more specifically to trace the survival of the seven modes throughout Western music history despite the ascendency of the major mode set into motion by the medieval practice of "musica ficta." Vincent observed this survival in European sacred music, folk music, and more tenuously in some art music, including that of the eccentric Charles Henri de Blainville (1711–1769), who wrote much publicized pieces in the phrygian mode, and Jean Francois Lesueur (1760–1837), whose students included Berlioz, Gounod, and Ernest Boulanger, Nadia's father. But it was only with Musorgsky and Fauré, argued Vincent, that the modes made a real return to Western art music: the works of Blainville and Lesueur, like many modal passages in music from Monteverdi to Franck, subordinated modal melodies to tonal harmonic practice, or else used them for effect, usually ecclesiastic (Berlioz) or folkloric (Glinka). Musorgsky and Fauré, on the other hand, created a new usage which "emancipated modality from the role of a mere coloristic device of romanticism and transformed it into a neoclassic technique."[3]

This new usage involved the "principle of interchangeability," in which any of the seven modes could be used interchangeably, much as the major and minor modes were used interchangeably since the early 19th century. Vincent called this usage "harmonic modality," and found it especially applicable to the music of Brahms, Grieg, Dvořák, Saint-Saëns, Glazunov, Debussy, Pizzetti, Ravel, Respighi, Malipiero, and, incidentally, himself. He passingly found connections with jazz, the blues, and George Gershwin as well. The Wagner-Bruckner-Strauss-Schoenberg line, in contrast, was seen more or less as a chromatic degeneracy of the tonal system, comparable to the "extravagancies of Gesualdo."[4] The author showed less certainty about modes outside the seven church ones, those, for instance, with an augmented second, and, consequently, about Stravinsky, Bartók, and even Borodin. He was likewise uncertain about the "empirical" modal-chromaticism of Hindemith, and one might add by inference, Piston. These and other ambiguities may have been clarified in Vincent's 1974 revision of *The Diatonic Modes,* still not yet generally available.

Many ambiguities colored not only Vincent's historiography, but his actual analytical method. Inspired by Piston's *Principles of Harmonic Analysis,* the analyses were largely harmonic, this itself a sticking point, as modal theory lends itself more naturally to a linear than to a vertical approach. Extending Piston's concept of interchangeability of the major and minor modes, Vincent listed all possible triads derived from the seven modes in relation to a given tonic note, and illustrated their use in numerous examples. Some of the listed chords could not be positively identified: for instance, a major triad on the tonic, according to Vincent, could be an Ionian I, a Lydian I, or a Mixolydian I. Such overlapping notwithstanding, Vincent's method allowed him to extend labels and propose meanings to unusual chordal relations, even including a major triad on the flatted dominant (Locrian V). On the other hand, there was no place in this method for such familiar harmonies as the augmented triad or the augmented sixth chord.

The absence of familiar harmonies and the overlapping identities of others posed but some of the problems of Vincent's methodology. There was also, for instance, the question of relating "modal interchangeability" to traditional concepts of modulation and harmonic rhythm. Acknowledging the contributions of Piutti, Riemann, and Piston, Vincent hoped that his method could supersede their concepts of half-modulations, substitute tones, and secondary chords, respectively. But sidestepping the whole question of modulation, calling a Neapolitan chord a Phrygian II, and treating a V of V as a Lydian II, suggested a certain untenable extremism and reductionism, especially when applied as freely to Mozart as to Stravinsky. And unlike Piston's *Principles,* no whole work, or even movement, was offered to place such details in some larger context. In all fairness, Vincent provided dual modal/tonal analyses without necessarily claiming preference for one over the other. Moreover, the attempt to integrate new kinds of harmonic relations was a much needed one, and many analysts have profited from it, and will doubtless continue to do so.

Vincent's treatise on the *Diatonic Modes* further shed light on his own music, especially the 1936 *String Quartet* and the 1942 *Three Grecian Songs.* In fact, his book often cited the second and fourth movements of the *Quartet,* not for any self-promoting reasons (Vincent easily could have quoted many other examples from his work), but for much needed evidence to support the existence of a locrian mode and its corollary, the tonic diminished triad. These citations made clear, consequently, the fact that both movements were in G locrian; the second movement, "Andante cantabile con moto," even had the proper key signature of four flats (whereas the more chromatic finale had a noncommittally blank key signature).

Virgil Thomson noted, too, that the *Quartet's* third movement was in E phrygian (here the lack of a key signature was modally appropriate) and that the first movement was in G aeolian.[5] This first movement, however, seemed more ambig-

uous than that to this listener. Unlike the "Andante cantabile," which periodically came to rest on its strange tonic
triad, G-B♭-D♭ (Ex. 8; see also mm. 26, 38, 62, 85, 97,
111–113), this first movement contained no clear internal
cadences, and furthermore, closed with an evocative tritone,
C-F#. There was some evidence to suggest that the movement was actually in D phrygian. First, the main theme
emphasized the pitch D, and came to a cadence of sorts on a
D minor triad on the last quarter note of m. 4. Assuming, too,
that this was a "traditional sonata-form," as Thomson notes, a
tonal center of D fit better, for the second theme was in A
mixolydian in the exposition and D mixolydian in the
recapitulation. This would allow an interpretation of the final
tritone as a kind of rest in D mixolydian, as well as a
preparation for the G tonic of the second and fourth
movements. Of course, considering the G center for movements two and four, classical precedence would support
Thomson's claim of a G tonic for the first movement after all;
and in any case, listeners are sooner likely to hear the piece in

Example 8. John Vincent, *String Quartet,* II (Mills Music, 1948).

G aeolian than in D phrygian. Vincent's key signature of two
flats supported either view.

Whether or not the larger modal contexts in the *String
Quartet* and the *Three Grecian Songs* were clear, their smaller
details were without doubt ambiguous. Vincent minimized
leading tone functions and cadential patterns, which resulted
in long, diatonic passages full of shadowy meanings, or
chromatic passages vaguer still. Some fairly direct modulations occurred, for example, in the movement to A
mixolydian in the first movement, as mentioned, and the
movement to A aeolian for the scherzo's trio section, to take
another example. Similarly, the last movement ingeniously
exploited modal inversion by having a fugal episode in the
locrian mode (mm. 37ff.) reappear inverted in the lydian
mode (mm. 125ff.). For some good examples of modal
interchangeability, see the movement from A^b ionian to A^b
mixolydian and back again in the last of the *Three Grecian
Songs;* and the scrambled use of D mixolydian, ionian,
aeolian, and phrygian in the last nine measures of the
Quartet's first movement (if, indeed, the movement is in D).

These modal features helped give Vincent's music a
Southern flavor, recognized as such by Thomson. Just as
important in defining its regional character were the pentatonic melodic inflections, the refined textures, the long,
leisurely lines, and the waltz, gallop, and faintly jazzy
rhythms. The resultant sweetness and nostalgia deserved
comparison with a contemporary writer like Eudora Welty.
Vincent learned a great deal from the famous Americanisms
of his teachers, and one found something of Chadwick's
quaintness, Piston's sophistication, and Harris's earnestness
in his work. There were also resemblances to Thomson and
Barber. But Vincent never seems to have entertained a
folkloric tone; indeed, there was little nationalistic about his
work, unless one considers nationalistic his arrangement of an
odd little string quartet supposedly written by Benjamin
Franklin, a work whose homely cheer and 18th-century
coolness he could have warmed to understandably enough.
The composer's aspirations, as his postwar orchestral works
made clear, were more in line with Dukas or Roussel than
typically was encountered in an American composer of his
generation.

These postwar orchestral works showed, too, the impact of Vincent's adopted Los Angeles, for one found in them some Hollywood glamour, particularly in their glitzy orchestrations and snazzy rhythms. The first of these, the *Symphony in D. A Festival Piece in One Movement* (1954, revised 1957), was probably Vincent's most successful accomplishment. The composer's modal penchants were still evident, but here tempered by traditional tonal resources, including modulation and dominant functions. A large sonata movement, the *Symphony* consisted of a slow introduction in D major with some minor inflections, somewhat reminiscent of Harris (mm. 1–114); a fast main theme in D aeolian, demonstrating how this mode can be used for festive effect (mm. 115–206); a lyrical second theme in G dorian (mm. 207–246); a fugal development, mostly in E and A major (mm. 247–318); a false recapituation in B aeolian (mm. 319–334); a return of the main theme in D aeolian (mm. 335–361) and the second theme in B dorian (mm. 362–408); and a coda that returns to D major (mm. 409–507). The whole belonged most in the tradition of Piston, especially the soaring second theme (Ex. 9). Also noteworthy was a passage in the coda (mm. 418–433) in which the return of the second theme in B dorian was supported by ostinati using the pitches C and G, and a bass part outlining the E^b lydian scale, a refreshing polymodal touch that is probably heard as some kind of C lydian.

Vincent's *Symphonic Poem after Descartes* (1958), dedicated to Ormandy, was another one-movement orchestral work, this one more ambitious and intriguing, but less endearing. Inspired by conversations with historian Will Durant, Vincent musically set out to depict aspects of Descartes and his philosophy, theology, and mathematics; he arranged these aspects into eight contiguous sections divided into two parts. The composer's detailed program was spelled out in a four-page preface to Mills' 1960 edition of the work. Suffice to say here, Vincent employs four principal musico-poetic ideas: a rhythm inspired by Descartes's famous deduction, "Cogito, Ergo Sum" (see the timpani part, m. 1, for "cogito," and m. 10, for "ergo sum"); the overtone series, with its minor seventh and augmented fourth, meant to symbolize the factual premise of "Cogito, Ergo Sum," and from which Vincent constructs most of the work's thematic material (the

Example 9. John Vincent, *Symphony in D* (Mills Music, 1957).

overtone series is put forth in harmonics in the cello, m. 12);
a melody called the "philosopher's theme," which uses the
notes from the overtone series (first hinted at in the oboe, m.
15); and a Latin hymn, "Aeterne Rerum Conditor," intended
to represent Descartes's Catholicism, and to provide musical
contrast (lower strings, m. 24). Vincent's program was
audible, but its literalness and grandiosity tended to get in the
way: the music was just not that deep, and the effect, perhaps,
was to trivialize its subject. Fortunately, the work's lucid form
could stand on its own without any literary interpretation.
Particularly impressive was the work's orchestration, outstanding not only in its expertise, but in its lushness. Of
historical interest was the way in which the work anticipated
fashionable motion picture scores of later years, such as those
by John Williams; indeed, Vincent's position at UCLA must

have left a mark on the film industry (considering that many movie composers, like John Williams, studied there).

Less endearing still was Vincent's last major orchestral work, *Symphony No. 2* for piano and string orchestra, actually a little-changed arrangement of a three-movement chamber piece from 1960, *Consort* for piano quartet. The title's Elizabethan connotation was matched by the music's modal flavor, but stylistically, the work, with its unison string melodies accompanied by piano arpeggios, displayed much greater affinity with late Romantic music. As always, Vincent demonstrated splendid formal control, but the long lines seemed weary, and the background harmonies mere wash.

After 1960 Vincent composed a few more works, including *The Phoenix, Fabulous Bird,* a symphonic poem for the city of Phoenix (premiered in 1966); a *Second String Quartet* (1967); and a large setting of the Stabat Mater, in the composer's own English translation, for soprano solo, chorus, and organ, entitled *Mary at Calvary* (1972). To some extent, these later works, especially *Mary at Calvary,* a big, heartfelt work in eleven movements, returned somewhat to the modal ambiguities and oddities of Vincent's work from the 1930s. None of these later works were particularly successful and the earlier orchestral works seemed more likely candidates for revival.

Gail Thompson Kubik (1914–1984) was a composer at once more individual and more fashionable than Vincent, but his music similarly had a strong regional flavor, with roots, however, in Middle America, not the deep South. Kubik was born in Coffeyville, Oklahoma, and grew up in Kansas. During the Depression, he toured the Dust Bowl with his family, playing violin in an ensemble, the Kubik Ensemble, that also included his mother, a concert singer who had studied with Ernestine Schumann-Heink, and two brothers who played cello and piano.[6] These years witnessed his first major work, *In Praise of Johnny Appleseed* for bass-baritone, chorus, and orchestra (1938) to poetry by, significantly, another troubadour of the Midwest, Vachel Lindsay. Three years earlier, in 1935, Kubik had turned quite literally to the troubadour repertory in *Variations on a 13th-Century Troubadour Song* for orchestra.

During World War II, Kubik advanced his sort of nationalism in a number of film scores to important war documentaries. It was expressed, too, in a *Folk Song Suite* for orchestra (1945), a work that used the cowboy tune, "Whoopee-ti-yi-yo," in the first movement; two Billings hymns in the second; and Foster's "Camptown Races" in the third.

After the War, Kubik emerged the full-fledged Americanist. There was a folk opera, *Mirror for the Sky* (1946), based on the life of John Audubon, and choral arrangements of numerous folk tunes, as well as Foster's "Jeanie." He once again used Foster, this time "Oh, Susanna," for a choral work, *Pioneer Woman,* dedicated to his mother. The same year saw choral settings of Stephen Vincent Benét's portrayals of *Miles Standish, Theodore Roosevelt,* and *Woodrow Wilson.* "Yankee Doodle" turned up slyly in two works from the 1950s: "A Gay Time" from *Celebrations and Epilogue* for piano (1950) and the *Divertimento I* (1959).

In 1961 Kubik returned to Vachel Lindsay for, essentially, a rewriting of *In Praise of Johnny Appleseed.* The kinship with Lindsay had survived many years, perhaps because they shared a similar profile: they both possessed charm and compassion, but lacked, perhaps, a certain depth and poise. And as with Lindsay, Kubik's populism seemed motivated by more than just idealistic motives, for he showed at times a distinctly commercial turn of mind.[7] He certainly made a nice income from his music, enough to buy a villa in France, to need to teach only intermittently, and to support a number of former wives (his four marriages—in 1938, 1946, 1952, and 1970—all ended in divorce). But his work always displayed high standards, and his populism withstood drastic changes in fashion. There was, for instance, the 1970 *A Record of Our Time,* a "protest piece" for narrator, chorus, vocal soloist, and orchestra to texts from the Bible, Twain, Yeats, Vanzetti, John Jay Chapman, and an anonymous Negro spiritual, all pulled together with the help of novelist Henry Swados. One of his last major works, it was premiered in Manhattan, Kansas, with Ray Milland as narrator. Although by this time interest in Kubik had largely waned, Kansas still appreciated its native son. It seemed, in fact, that much of Kubik's estate, including an important collection of tapes, would wind up at Kansas State University in Manhattan, Kansas, not at Scripps College in Claremont, California, where he had served for a number of years as composer-in-residence before being forced to retire.

Kubik's music, whether or not it used programs or folk tunes (and indeed, there were a number of abstract works, including three symphonies—1949, 1955, 1956), breathed Americana with each note. The energetic fast movement suggested folk music and jazz; the quiet slow movements evoked the pastorale and the chorale.[8] At every turn the melodic bits recalled cowboy tunes, country waltzes, parlor songs, hymns, and vaudeville routines. The textures were sparse, the rhythms vigorous, and the orchestrations bright. Major and minor modes clashed, and Kubik showed special preference for bluesy snippets that outlined the minor third. In all this he owed much to Copland and Piston, whose music he loved.[9] Like them, Kubik felt the profound impact of the French, and he even placed his *Second Symphony* in the tradition of Roussel.[10] And like them, too, the French influence helped him forge, paradoxically, a distinctly American style.

Accordingly, these American styles seemed to accommodate only so much of the French tradition, its charm and irony, for instance, but not very often its sensuousness. In fact, the Americanists tended toward the severe. Kubik took this tendency to provocative extremes. He rarely wrote long, legato lines, favoring instead an endless flow of brittle staccati and accents. Boulanger, a devoted admirer, remarked that the music "tinkles, titters, toddles or runs at high speed";[11] Mel Powell, less sympathetic, called for "something nobler than flecks and flimflam."[12] Kubik's textures were certainly thin, often radically so, tending towards single lines supported by unisons, octave doublings, crisp ostinati, and simple triads in closed positions. A striking example was the slow movement of the *Symphony Concertante* for orchestra (1951, revised 1953), wherein the trumpet and viola soloists were often in unison, accompanied by a single-note ostinato in the piano (the orchestra, for the most part, mute). Kubik also liked registral extremes; as Frederick Sternfeld observed in a review of *Gerald McBoing-Boing* (1950), there was "comparative absence of the middle range."[13] This naturally gave his music a sparse, open quality. Finally, Kubik's orchestrations were very bright, sometimes even shrill: trumpet, flute, clarinet, xylophone, glockenspiel, and piano parts made extensive use of their high registers. Donald Mitchell thought the scoring of the *Violin Concerto* (1940, revised 1951) "excessively brash."[14] The end result was an austerity and clarity not unlike that of the "sharp-focus" painters of the time, especially Grant Wood, considering, too, Wood's relationship to the Midwest. Like Wood, Kubik's austerity had a delicate charm, a broad wit, and a piety that bordered on mysticism. Indeed, their regional sensibilities dovetailed with Europe's medieval legacy, a correspondence made famous by Wood's *American Gothic,* but likewise evident in Kubik's early *Variations on a 13th-Century Troubadour Song,* as well as in the later *Scholastics: A Medieval Set* for a cappella chorus (1972).

Kubik's rural ambiance notwithstanding, there was nothing primitive about his music. When the *Symphony Concertante* won the 1952 Pulitzer Prize, the work must have seemed very chic as well as very American. Kubik elicited warm praise from Edward Steuermann as well as Boulanger.[15] The latter had helped teach him his craft, as did Bernard Rogers (1930–1934), Leo Sowerby (1935–1936), and Walter Piston (1937–1938), "who had a lasting influence on him,"[16] according to Boulanger. Kubik's assimilation of features derived from both Sowerby and Piston was probably unique. He dedicated his favorite, and most lasting, early piece, the 1941 *Sonatina* for piano, to Piston; wrote Kubik, "I had studied with Walter Piston two years earlier, and its economy of expression, its lean texture reflect, I think, something of his influence."[17]

The *Sonatina* was Kubik's art in a nutshell: energetic, clear, "metallic" (as he writes at one point in the score), and "brittle" (as he writes at another). Nothing he wrote later was very much different. The "polytriadic" textures that permeated Kubik's mature work, as described by Roland Jackson,[18] were evident enough here. The opening phrase, untypically long and smooth for Kubik, though not without a few telling jerks, outlined, in the upper voice, E minor, B minor, A major, and F# minor triads, followed by a C# major scale that came to rest on a B#; against this, there was an accompaniment of G major, F# major, and E major triads (Ex. 10). These kinds of triadic clashes, or "polytriadic" harmonies as Jackson called

Example 10. Gail Kubik, *Sonatina* for piano, I (Mercury Music, 1942).

them, characterized the entire work, one would even say
systematically, but this would do injustice to the variety with
which these harmonies were used, not to mention the many
passages that did not use them at all. One noted, nonetheless,
a habitual juxtaposition of triads a half or whole step apart.
Less common, but found, were like juxtapositions at the
third, the fourth, and the tritone. Perhaps the most effective
instance of polytriadic harmony in the *Sonatina* was in the last
movement at measure 41, where the lydian theme, now in C
and in the bass, was countered above by a vigorous ostinato in
B♭ major (Ex. 11). It was a moment reminiscent of Prokofiev
("roughly, savagely" writes the composer), and such bite and
vigor were to have special usefulness in the war effort, as we
shall see. The additional touch of the sostenuto pedal,
frequently encountered in Kubik's piano music, was identified by Steuermann as particularly American.[19]
  The most controversial aspect of Kubik's music was its
coherence. In the modernist tradition, Kubik's approach was
organic; that is, the musical material was logically integrated,
largely through motivic transformation and contrapuntal
manipulation. There seemed to be some question, though, as
to how well the composer carried it off. Boulanger, for
instance, asserted that "each audition (of his music) will
disclose new details: meaningful, savory, ingenious, amusing,
expressive—all conspiring to bring to light the whole in its

unity."[20] Many, however, found the relation of Kubik's finely etched details to his larger whole hard to perceive.[21] Such criticism seemed understandable, especially regarding the larger works. The frenetic activity of Kubik's fast movements, for instance, had little forward thrust; periodically, the music came to an unsettling halt by way of a big internal cadence, often in the tonic. In the *Sonatina's* first movement, such a cadence at m. 51 made the rest sound slightly redundant, while in the last movement at m. 15, it made the preceding material seem merely preparatory. Similar cadences were also found at m. 274 of the first movement of the *Symphony Concertante;* at m. 41 of the first movement of the *Second Symphony,* where it played a more structurally cohesive role; and at m. 125 of the last movement of the *Divertimento I,* "Burlesque," where it was meant as a joke. Slow movements had their weak joints, too, leaning heavily on canonic and ostinato techniques to keep going. Kubik was best when epigrammatic, as in the *Sonatina's* middle movements, or in the piano pieces written between 1938 and 1950, collectively called *Celebrations and Epilogue.* The big, sprawling works— like the symphonies—tended to meander.

These traits—the rural atmosphere, the nationalist vigor,

Example 11. Gail Kubik, "Toccata," *Sonatina* for piano (Mills Music, 1942).

and the episodic forms comprised of trenchant bits—lent themselves well to the pressing needs of war documentarians with the onset of World War II. Between 1940 and 1945, Kubik scored some of the period's finest documentaries, including *Men and Ships* (1940), *Paratroops* (1942), *The World at War* (1942), *Twenty-One Miles* (1943), *The Memphis Belle* (1944), and *Thunderbolt* (1945). Unlike more experienced Hollywood composers under contract to the commercial studios, Kubik was free to devote his time to this specific genre. More importantly, his style perfectly suited the depictions of battle scenes and military operations that were the stuff of the Domestic Branch of the Office of War Information (in contrast to the portrayals of American peace and democracy put out by its Overseas Branch, who wisely turned to Copland and Thomson among others).[22] In fact, in 1942, at age twenty-eight, Kubik was made Director of Music for the Domestic Branch, in part due to his score to *The World at War,* which won a citation from the National Association for American Composers and Conductors. This government appointment left one U.S. senator wondering, "Did the Administration think Hollywood music not good enough for its films? Was it necessary to use a highbrow modernist? Wasn't the old familiar music good enough?"[23]

A "modernist" work like the 1941 *Sonatina,* dedicated to Piston and reflecting "something of his influence," eloquently answers the senator's questions. For the *Sonatina* contained music that could well accompany the principal kinds of scenes that characterized the films of the Domestic Branch: pastoral (for pre-war peacefulness), violent (for battles), plaintive (for war devastation), satiric (for American isolationists and the Axis powers), and heroic (for the Allied forces and domestic industrial production). The bimodal clashes, brittle textures, and changing meters of the *Sonatina's* finale, for instance, could suit violent and heroic moments, while the same features, as used in the second-movement scherzo, could fit satirical ones. And the slow movement had the sort of plaintiveness (first theme) and pastoral quiet (second theme) that could fill out documentary needs.

Perhaps no aspect of the war documentaries so required something altogether novel than did the pervasive sounds of airplanes. A reviewer of *Earthquakers* even complained that the music "was quickly obliterated by an airplane propeller."[24] The extensive use of air warfare was so startingly new and dramatic that documentaries often made this a focus, either in horror at German use of it (*The World at War*) or in defense of Allied retaliation (*The Memphis Belle*). Kubik effectively used loud, dissonant, detached chords to match the sounds of exploding bombs, and ostinati, long-held notes, violin trills, and cymbal and drum rolls to match the sounds of airplanes in flight. (Mark Evans even reported that the piano ostinato in the second movement of the *Symphony Concertante* was intended to substitute for an airplane motor hum heard in the film score to *C-Man* from which the music was adapted.[25]) In the more familiar tradition of Hollywood, Kubik occasionally dotted his scores with quotations of the "Marseillaise" or "God Save the Queen." There was also, in *The World at War,* a paraphrase of Brahms's "Lullaby" against an ominous ostinato to depict sleeping Nazi soldiers, an effect singled out by Paul Bowles for its humor.[26]

The only other film genre of the 1940s to gravitate toward the modernist idiom was the animated cartoon, so it was not surprising that Kubik made a contribution here as well, by way of his 1950 score for *Gerald McBoing-Boing* (pronounced in onamatopoeic fashion, "boyng"). One connection between such contrasting genres as the documentary and the cartoon resided in their feverish energy, as if the animated film transformed the violence of contemporary life into comic fantasy. Ingolf Dahl, who composed cartoon scores himself, noted how the cartoon composers of the 1940s were encouraged to write more daringly in response to new rhythmic asymmetries found in the cartoons themselves.[27] Roy Prendergast pointed specifically to the connection between 1940s cartoons and neoclassicism, writing, "The neoclassical style, with its articulation of phrase and form that gives a work the character of a series of distinct events, was what the cartoon composer instinctively looked to."[28] Prendergast further argued for an aesthetic network that included cartoons, neoclassicism, Picasso, ballet, and opera buffa. Most writers credited composer Scott Bradley with pioneering this field, but Kubik's contribution often was cited as one of the best of such scores.

Only eight minutes long, *Gerald McBoing-Boing* was based

on a Dr. Seuss story about a small boy, Gerald, who cannot talk but can produce all kinds of noisy sound effects—hence, the title. An annoyance to his parents, classmates, and doctor, Gerald runs away from home and is discovered by a radio announcer, who makes him a star, thereby reconciling him with his parents for a happy ending. The UPA animation, once heralded for its refreshing modernity, today seems at least as synthetic as the Walt Disney cartoons for which, at the time, it was seen as a kind of antidote. The music, however, has retained a perky, fresh humor that is quintessential Kubik. And there is also a poignant passage, dramatically textured by major sevenths, for Gerald's departure from home. Following a precedent established by Bradley, Kubik wrote the score prior to animation, and consequently adapted it easily for concert purposes by substituting percussion solos for sound effects. In this concert version, Gerald becomes a percussion virtuoso, and instead of a display of sound effects at the climactic radio show, there is an extended percussion "concerto" for solo percussion utilizing an enormous battery.

Kubik's film scores, especially those for the war documentaries, were no less important to motion picture history than the documentaries themselves. For much as postwar directors of feature films learned from the documentaries how to break through studio restrictions, so did their composers begin to incorporate small chamber combinations, dissonant harmonies, changing meters, and other "modernist" features. By the 1950s, feature film music had caught up with styles long familiar to war documentaries and cartoons, and Kubik himself composed a few such scores, including those for *Two Gals and a Guy* (1951), *The Desperate Hours* (1955), and *I Thank a Fool* (1962). The most successful of these, *The Desperate Hours,* concerned a group of escaped convicts (headed by Humphrey Bogart) who take hostage an Indianapolis family (headed by Frederic March); it required two principal moods at which Kubik excelled—brutal violence and small-town tranquility. Director William Wyler, with whom Kubik had worked on war documentaries, even gave the composer prominent billing on the credits, just before his own name. Surprisingly, in what seemed an overcompensation for Hollywood's typical indulgences, the movie used only about five minutes of music. Passages like that depicting the youngest convict's death nonetheless deserved comparison with Bernstein's music for *On the Waterfront*.

An intricate relation existed between Kubik's film scores and his concert music. Many of the concert works were, in fact, adapted from film scores: *Memphis Belle: A War Time Episode* (1944) from *The Memphis Belle* (1943); *Boston Baked Beans* (1950) from *The Miner's Daughter* (1950); *Symphony Concertante* (1951) from *C-Man* (1949);[29] *Thunderbolt Overture* (1953) from *Thunderbolt* (1945); and *Scenario for Orchestra* (1957) from *The Desperate Hours* (1955). According to Mark Evans, the *Piano Sonata* (1947) and the *Third Symphony* (1956) were based to some degree on film music as well.[30] In fact, the first work we have identified as mature Kubik—the 1941 *Piano Sonatina*—was written one year after his first documentary, so it is probably as true to say that Kubik's style was shaped by his experience scoring documentaries as it is to say that his style suited the needs of the war documentarians. In any case, the close ties between Kubik's motion picture scores and his concert music helped to explain the latter's vivid realism and episodic forms.

One of the best of the concert works was the 1947 *Sonata* for piano, dedicated to Frank Glazer. It was a big, colorful work somewhat preclassical in feel. Here the animated jolts and bumps so characteristic of its composer were given coherent, artful expression. The first movement comprised an idiosyncratic but convincing sonata form; the second-movement scherzo alluded to popular idioms, especially boogie-woogie; the third movement presented three variations on a hymn tune; and the dynamic finale echoed preceding material, notably the hymn tune. Like similar contemporary works by Carter, Barber, and Shapero, it was yet another contender for the great American piano sonata. Indeed, the keyboard writing of the slow movement, including silent depressions, seemed to reflect some familiarity with Carter's *Sonata*.

Kubik's three big symphonies were less successful: they offered unrestrained scope for the composer's tendency to ramble. And their orchestrations, while expert and bright, seemed lusterless compared to his two divertimenti from the late '50s: *Divertimento I* for thirteen players (1959), dedicated to Ingolf Dahl; and *Divertimento II* for eight players (1958), dedicated to Aaron Copland. Here again, in his attempts to revive the wit and poignance of Copland's *Music for the Theatre,* Kubik was at his most delightful and most inimitable. The *Divertimento II,* which demonstrated the advantages of having the composer's melodic bits overlap with one another rather than being separated by rests, was especially appealing.

Kubik produced relatively little in his last twenty-five years. His final film, *I Thank a Fool* (1962), proved an undistinguished vehicle for Susan Hayward. The late concert works included another divertimento, this one entitled *Five Theatrical Sketches* for violin, cello, and piano (1971), and subtitled "Divertimento No. 3." The unison violin-cello melody against a piano ostinato in its first movement, "Tragedy," recalled the war documentaries, but in general the work seemed to harken back even earlier, to the adventures of the touring Kubik ensemble. *A Record of Our Time* (1970) was a plea for sanity, as was, in its own way, *Prayer and Toccata* for organ and chamber orchestra (1968). *Scholastics* for a cappella chorus (1972) consisted of five settings, the central one being a very long satire of the medieval scholasticism of Duns Scotus. A final effort, *Symphony for Two Pianos* (1979), was an arrangement of the *First Symphony.* In many of these late pieces, Kubik's vigor, wit, and bucolic serenity gave way to weariness, sarcasm, and nostalgia. The demoralizing events of the 1960s and '70s seemed to take a particularly heavy toll on Kubik; certainly anyone who took seriously the propaganda of the war documentaries had to be appalled at America's conduct in Vietnam. Kubik retired more and more into himself, and died a largely forgotten man.

From the perspective of style and technique, John Vincent and Gail Kubik were almost antithetical. Vincent wrote long, modal melodies that were bland in their details, and that formed beautifully satisfying wholes. Kubik, on the other hand, composed little tonal bits that were placed in vividly chromatic contexts and that engendered highly episodic forms. Furthermore, Vincent's textures were as lush as Kubik's were severe.

But they shared a love of their country, especially its remote, rural areas, that was deep and far-reaching: Vincent's shaped by his Southern background, with its modal folksongs, and later by the glamour of his adopted Los Angeles; Kubik's by his Midwestern roots, with its austere hymns, and later by the vigor of the war effort. Both styles descended from Franco-American traditions; and both proved particularly serviceable, either directly or indirectly, to Hollywood's needs. By the mid-1960s, their sensibilities seemed, perhaps, quaint to a new generation of listeners. They carried on regardless, sometimes retreating into an almost medieval piety. By their life's end, their relevance appeared dim indeed. But future listeners may well be won over by the elegance and charm of their best music.

Notes

1. Vincent, *The Diatonic Modes in Modern Music* (Berkeley: U. of California Press, 1951), p. vii.
2. Vincent, p. vii.
3. Vincent, p. 253.
4. Vincent, p. 285.
5. Thomson, liner notes to Vincent's *Quartet No. 1 in G,* Contemporary Records M6009.
6. David Ewen, "Gail Kubik," *Dictionary of American Composers* (New York: G. P. Putnam's, 1982), p. 395.
7. Kubik, "London Letter," *Modern Music* 21 No. 4 (May–June, 1944), pp. 240–243.
8. Edward Steuermann, liner notes to Kubik's *Piano Sonata,* Contemporary Composers Series M6009.
9. Kubik, "An American in Paris—and Elsewhere," *Opera News* 32 No. 4 (November 4, 1967), p. 10.
10. Kubik, preface to the *Symphony No. 2 in F* (New York: G. Ricordi, 1958).
11. Boulanger, liner notes to Kubik's *Divertimenti,* Contemporary Composers Series M6013.
12. Powell, review of some Kubik scores, *Notes* 15 (March, 1958), p. 255.
13. Sternfeld, "Kubik's McBoing Score," *Film Music Notes* 10 No. 2 (November–December, 1950), p. 11.
14. Mitchell, "London Music," *Musical Times* 95 (1954), p. 382.
15. Steuermann, liner notes; Boulanger, liner notes.
16. Boulanger.
17. Kubik, quoted by Boulanger.

18. Jackson, liner notes to Kubik's *Symphony for Two Pianos,* Orion ORS 80372.
19. Steuermann, liner notes.
20. Boulanger, liner notes.
21. Arthur Cohn, "Rogers, Diamond and Others at Rochester," *Modern Music* 19 No. 4 (May–June, 1942), p. 269; Mitchell, "London Music"; Powell, review.
22. Arthur Knight, *The Liveliest Art* (New York: Macmillan, 1957), pp. 253–254.
23. Kubik, "Composing for Government Films," *Modern Music* 23 No. 3 (Summer, 1946), p. 189.
24. Lawrence Morton, "On the Hollywood Front," *Modern Music* 21 No. 4 (May–June, 1944), p. 265.
25. Mark Evans, *Soundtrack* (New York: Hopkinson and Blake, 1975), p. 272.
26. Bowles, "Films and Theatre," *Modern Music* 20 No. 1 (November–December, 1942), p. 58.
27. Dahl, "Notes on Cartoon Music," *Film Music Notes* Vol. 8 No. 5 (1949).
28. Prendergast, *Film Music, A Neglected Art* (New York: Norton, 1977), p. 174.
29. When the *Symphony Concertante* won the Pulitzer Prize in 1952, it became, in a sense, the second film score to do so, Virgil Thomson having won the 1949 Pulitzer Prize for Robert Flaherty's *Louisiana Story.* Thomson, *American Music Since 1910* (New York: Holt, Rinehart, and Winston, 1970), p. 9, mistakenly thought his own achievement unique.
30. Evans, pp. 270–273.

4. CLASSICISM PURSUED: EVERETT HELM AND ELLIS KOHS

PISTON HELPED IMBUE HIS STUDENTS with a belief in the relevance of the classical tradition, provided it was balanced by an individual sensibility. His own music—a sort of Hindemithian "neue Sachlichkeit" thoroughly distinguished by a jazzy rhythmic verve and a delicate yet resilient lyricism—suggested but one such persuasive argument. The possibilities were numerous, of course, and the solutions, in fact, were many. Anderson, as we have seen, accommodated classicism to a new form of popular entertainment—the orchestral "pops" concert; Vincent and Kubik gave it a regional drawl and twang; Fine, Berger, and Shapero, as we shall see, aimed for something like Stravinsky's balletic clarity and grace; while Carter and Bernstein enlarged it in remarkable ways. The two subjects of this chapter, Everett Helm and Ellis Kohs, perhaps came closest to Piston's kind of "neue Sachlichkeit" (Piston's broad assimilation of many elements allowed fruitful contact with all kinds of styles), but they, too, created music of distinctive strength and integrity.

Everett Helm, born in Minneapolis on July 17, 1913, earned his BA degree from Carleton College in 1934, and his MA from Harvard in 1936. A recipient of the Paine Traveling Fellowship, he "dumbfounded" the Harvard faculty by choosing to study with Malipiero rather than Nadia Boulanger.[1] During the years 1936–1938 he worked not only with Malipiero, but with Vaughan Williams, acquiring from both a love for Baroque and Renaissance music, and something of a contempt, it might be added, for 19th-century vulgarities and banalities. Helm returned to the States to earn a Harvard doctorate for the dissertation *The Beginnings of the Italian Madrigal and the Works of Arcadelt* (1939), which showed, too, the influence of his studies abroad with musicologist Alfred Einstein. In 1942 he studied with Milhaud and Sessions in California, and subsequently taught in several schools, heading the music department of Western College in Oxford, Ohio, from 1944 to 1946. In 1950 he settled in Europe as a free-lance writer, journalist, and composer.

If Helm was known at all, it was sooner as a writer than as a composer. These writings included a handsome source book on Liszt and a breezy biography of Bartók;[2] surveys of Brazilian and Yugoslavian composers;[3] and three seminal articles in English on Malipiero.[4] For four years (1960–1964), he served as chief of *Musical America*'s European bureau, and, for a few months in 1963, as the magazine's editor-in-chief. Helm also wrote a series of books that took a long view of music, covering such topics as music education, mass media, new music, and music festivals. The first of these was simply entitled, *Music,* and was part of a series of *Vocational and Professional Monographs.*[5] The best-known was the worldly *Composer Performer Public. A Study in Communication.*[6] With *Music and Tomorrow's Public,*[7] commissioned by UNESCO, Helm's reporting took on global dimensions.

Although many of these assignments were workaday, Helm distinguished himself by his ability to write clearly and intelligently about music. *Composer Performer Public* and some other efforts had, furthermore, a liveliness like Virgil Thomson's. And the Bartók biography and the Malipiero articles featured vivid portraitures and deep insights as well. The Malipiero articles, written over a twenty-year span, naturally benefited from Helm's long and intimate friendship with the composer (though references to Malipiero's life under fascist rule, aside from the mention of a close association with D'Annunzio, were avoided).[8] Helm also wrote, in 1963, a persuasive defense of Hindemith, "one of the great musical craftsmen of our time."[9] In still later writings, he observed the work of Stockhausen and similar composers with some skepticism.

Helm's evaluation of American music was given broad and influential expression in a chapter on the subject for the English version of the *Larousse Encyclopedia of Music* (Hamlyn, 1971), pp. 433–444. In many ways, his discussion spoke not only for himself, but expressed the mature viewpoint that prevailed among his generation of Harvard graduates. The article shows little enthusiasm for American music predating 1920, though there is some admiration for Foster's minstrel songs and for Ives. Among composers from the 1920s and '30s, Copland, Thomson, Harris, and Piston are singled out. Copland is "one of the most gifted composers America has produced to date." Thomson is "the prime American exponent of Neo-classicism." Harris's *Third Symphony* is warmly remembered. Helm's assessment of Piston is the most conflicted; given the nature of this study, a full quotation is in order:

> Walter Piston displayed a continuing enchantment with classicism that has been the undoing of his extremely well written, but in the last analysis, academic music. One admires the fine writing and the economy of means, the clever play of rhythms and the balanced proportions of many of his works—not to mention the dry wit of others. But it is cultivated, unimpassioned, easily-forgotten music—even the best of it, which would include the second, fourth and seventh symphonies and the ballet music, *The Incredible Flutist*.

Although Piston's *Fourth* and *Seventh Symphony* date from the postwar period, Helm more or less implies that none of these four composers sustained their importance after 1945. This is in some contrast to Sessions, Ruggles, and Riegger, composers, who were, for the most part, older than the aforementioned four composers, but whom Helm discusses later in his survey; the impression is one of some sort of chronological development, whereas it actually reflects the changing tastes of Helm and the times in general.

Writing of a later, "second generation" of contemporary composers, Helm mentions a number of Piston's students in complimentary fashion, including Carter, Bernstein, Shapero, Fine, Wyner, and Layton. In fact, Helm considers Fine's early death "a great loss to American music." (The omission of Berger seems significant, perhaps related to Helm's indictment of neoclassicism as "as easy escape from musical reality.") Helm also holds the work of Barber and Schuman in esteem, and says respectful things about Gershwin, Rodgers, and jazz. As for still later developments, Helm takes a serious, but guarded interest in Foss and Schuller, while dismissing the "pseudo-oriental" music of Cage, and not even mentioning Babbitt. So much of this—the enthusiasm for Copland, Thomson, Harris, and Piston followed by a reassessment favoring Sessions, Ruggles, and Riegger; the ambivalence concerning Piston, in particular; the respect for the hardier traditions of Ives and Broadway over the more genteel music of MacDowell and Menotti; the interest in Piston's students and those in their general orbit (like Schuller and Foss), and the dismissal of Cage and Babbitt—reflected the mature tastes and sensibilities of many Harvard graduates from the 1930s.

As a composer, Helm probably was better known in Europe than in America, for his mature work was written there, and further, his major publishers were the German firms of Schott, Simrock, and Bote & Bock. Most of his music was small in both scale and scope, typically chamber works in short movements. The only major undertaking seems to have been the 1956 opera, *The Siege of Tottenburg*. Like his prose, Helm's music was not particularly passionate; but it was never trite either, and showed at all times real elegance and a special sort of technical control.

Little is known of Helm's early music. One of his first works to be reviewed, a *Requiem-1942* for chorus and orchestra, already was recognized by Milhaud as the composer's "most important achievement" to that date.[10] Only with the 1943 *Sonata Brevis* for piano did Helm make his presence felt on the new music scene.

The *Sonata Brevis* displayed many of the basic earmarks of the composer's mature style. Its first movement's pastoral lightness, second movement's contemplative serenity (Ex. 12), and third movement's vigorous energy all proved characteristic: a similar dynamic unfolded in such later works as the *Sonata* for flute and piano (1952), the two *Piano Concertos* (1951, 1956), and the *Sinfonia da Camera* for chamber orchestra (1961).

Example 12. Everett Helm, *Sonata Brevis,* II (Hargail Press, 1946).

Here in the *Sonata Brevis* was found, too, Helm's most salient stylistic trait, namely, his strong emphasis on the soprano melodic line, undoubtedly related to his inclination toward such Italian models as Palestrina and Malipiero. These strongly vocal melodies were often propelled by the insistent repetition of smaller bits; in a later work like the *Second Piano Concerto,* this was even done systematically, each repetition picking up a new note (this technique was the legacy of earlier neoclassicists, who often used some variety of it; see, for example, the scherzo of Piston's 1935 *Piano Trio*). Also characteristic were the florid melismas of the *Sonata*'s first movement, looking ahead as they do to the cadenzas of the *Concertos,* as well as the "Nocturne" from *New Horizons,* a collection of piano pieces with strong pedagogical leanings published in 1964. With all these melismas, the influence of

Chopin was pertinent, as Helm himself admitted in preface notes to *New Horizons*. But also important was Milhaud's observation, "Helm can scarcely be disassociated from his wife Helen, who has a voice like a nightingale."[11]

While Helm's melodies, as epitomized by the *Sonata*'s slow movement (see Ex. 12), aimed for a sustained smoothness like Hindemith's, their cramped chromaticism gave such lines a more angular edge. In *New Horizons* and other works from the 1960s, Helm consequently could accommodate the vogue for 12-tone music without much change in style. While Helm's angularity was intriguing in terms of its sophistication

Example 13. Everett Helm, "Aria," *Flute Sonata.* © Schott & Co., Ltd., London, 1952. © renewed. All rights reserved. Used by permission of European American Music Distributors Corporation, sole U.S. and Canadian agent for Schott & Co., Ltd.

and relative daring, more appealing, perhaps, were those fairly diatonic movements whose themes resembled German folksong—the "Aria" from the *Flute Sonata* (Ex. 13); the finale to the *Second Concerto;* and the first movement of the *Woodwind Quartet,* published in 1962.

The preeminence of melody in Helm's work was due more to the reticence of his accompanimental textures than to the strength of his melodies per se. Aside from canon—and indeed the *Second Concerto* was particularly rich in highly skilled canons—there was little in the way of intricate counterpoint; the composer typically supported his melodies with octave doublings, parallel thirds, and simple triads. Very often Helm's textures had a bitonal coloring, including bright clashes of tonalities a tritone or minor second apart; a favorite device entailed the juxtaposition of two triads in closed first or second position. This extensive use of bitonality owed something to Milhaud, as well as to Piston, but it took on utterly different aesthetic aims: Helm's intention was not so much to revive some contrapuntal ideal as to provide a rich, elegant background to his dominant, soprano lines.

Perhaps the most appealing feature of Helm's music overall was its beautiful sonorities, especially in orchestral works like the *Piano Concertos* and the *Sinfonia da Camera.* Helm's orchestrations were animated by the idea of distinct orchestral choirs, an idea he felt regrettably absent in Elgar's mixed pallette;[12] in his own orchestral works, the composer sharply contrasted the coolness of the winds, the lushness of the strings, and the brilliance of the piano. Here again one felt the impact of Piston; certainly the composer of the slow movements of the *Second Piano Concerto* and the *Sinfonia da Camera* must have admired Piston's *Piano Concertino.*

Another impressive aspect of Helm's music, namely, its special kind of formal procedures, probably owed more to Malipiero than to anyone else. These procedures eschewed the schematic and the obviously symmetrical in favor of highly spontaneous and instinctive transformations of thematic material, including contrasting episodes within movements, and reappearances of material from previous movements. Helm's description of Malipiero's forms, "that kind of free association of the musical material encountered in

Vivaldi, Domenico Scarlatti and other old Italian masters,"[13] spoke for his own formal principles as well.

Finally, there was the question of Helm's national identity. At the outset, in the *Sonata Brevis,* for instance, there was no question of a link to American contemporaries like Carter and Kubik, not only in the work's stylistic traits, but in its alternately pastoral, mournful, and vigorous moods. Another work from the early 1940s, Helm's *Comments on Two Spirituals,* reminded Lawrence Morton of "the vigor and wit of the Copland school."[14] But after Helm immigrated to Italy, his music naturally enough took on a greater European overlay, thereby providing a sort of litmus test for the Americanisms of his contemporaries, much as Noël Lee was to do for a slightly later generation of American composers. There was, it is true, some snazzy, almost Gershwinesque moments in, say, the last movement of the otherwise very Bartókian *Second Concerto* that, it would appear, only could have been written by an American. But all in all, his music turned out to be less brilliant and shrill, less percussive and brassy, and less spacious and energetic than was typical of his American colleagues. Indeed, in its high refinement and understatement, Helm's music proved, after all, rather unique.

Ellis Kohs had more of an impact on the American musical scene than did Helm, thanks in part to more than thirty years at the University of Southern California, and a series of well-known textbooks: *An Aural Approach to Orchestration,*[15] *Music Theory* (two volumes),[16] *Musical Form,*[17] and *Musical Composition.*[18]

Kohs was born on May 12, 1916, in Chicago. His family soon thereafter moved to San Francisco, where Ellis spent two years at the San Francisco Conservatory (1926–1928), learning enough piano to accompany his mother, an amateur violinist. They subsequently moved to New York City, where he attended James Madison High School and the Institute of Musical Art (1928–1933). Kohs proceeded on to the University of Chicago, earning both BA and MA. His principal teacher there was Carl Bricken, whose great interest in Bach made a lasting impression.[19] Bricken's taste in modern music, however, did not go beyond Sibelius, and Kohs found himself studying, on his own, Stravinsky's *Rite,* Schoenberg's *Fourth Quartet,* and the Bartók quartets, which he heard performed by the Pro Arte Quartet. After graduation, he spent one year (1938–1939) at Juilliard studying the Beethoven piano sonatas with Wagenaar, and two years (1939–1941) at Harvard, where he attended lectures by Bartók and Stravinsky, took classes with Apel and Leichtentritt, and had private lessons with Piston. Kohs went to Harvard specifically because he admired Piston's music, "which seemed very sane and well-organized, sprightly, healthy, and at the same time not without melodic interest. . . . The classical stance, the tight musical organization, the capacity to communicate directly to a musically informed audience, balance between intellectual thought and 'romantic' feeling, accorded with my own dispositions." He found, too, that in a quiet, unobtrusive way, Piston "helped to reinforce what I already felt to be true, beautiful, and right for me." After several years of service as a bandmaster in the armed forces (1941–1946), and a few more years at various colleges, Kohs, in 1950, joined the faculty at USC.

Kohs's national reputation rested primarily with the two-volume *Music Theory,* which was used widely for some time. The work derived largely from the harmony texts of Piston and Sessions, though it was intended for a less advanced student. Like Piston, the author was concerned with harmony as a component of form and rhythm; like Sessions, he composed musical examples to illustrate certain theoretical points. Where Kohs felt he had superseded both Piston and Sessions was in his discussion of modal, chromatic, and non-functional 20th-century harmonic progressions from the viewpoint of common tones.[20]

As for Kohs's own music, it was only his work prior to 1952 that established something of a following (in this, he resembled his Harvard classmate, Harold Shapero). His first acknowledged works, the *String Quartet No. 1* (1940) and the *Concerto for Orchestra* (1941), both written at Harvard, earned the admiration of Milhaud, Ross Lee Finney, and others for their boldness and vigor.[21] During military service, Kohs wrote a few works meant primarily as entertainment for his fellow servicemen: *Life with Uncle Sam* for orchestra or band (1942); *The Automatic Pistol* (1943) for a cappella male chorus; and the *Sonatina* for bassoon and piano (1944). Only the *Sonatina* survived the occasion. With a return to civilian life came an outpouring of new compositions: *Legend* for oboe and strings (1946), *Passacaglia* for organ and strings (1946), *Piano Variations* (1946), *Etude in Memory of Bartók* for piano (1946), *Variations on l'homme armé* for piano (1947), *Sonatina* for violin and piano (1948), *A Short Concert* (String Quartet No. 2; 1948), *Chamber Concerto* for viola and nonet (1949), *First Symphony* (1950), *10 2-Voice Inventions* (1950), *Sonata* for clarinet and piano (1951), and *Three Chorale Variations on Hebrew Hymns* (1952). Most of these works were published, some won prizes, and a few were recorded.

Whereas Helm only flirted with the trends of the 1940s, Kohs seemed to embrace them all. In his work there was, above all, a close affinity to the neobaroque aesthetic of Hindemith's *Reihe Kleiner Stücke:* one typically found long, lively, chromatic lines; forms like the passacaglia and the toccata; and two- and three-part counterpart every bit as dissonant as Hindemith at his most acerbic. Beginning with the *Passacaglia* and the *Piano Variations,* both from 1946, Kohs also availed himself of the 12-tone technique, a technique that he never adopted in any orthodox sense, but which he nonetheless used extensively for the remainder of his career. (Kohs' particular usage showed somewhat the influence of Piston's early 12-tone works, especially the *Chromatic Study on the Name of Bach* for organ, written in 1940 while Kohs was at Harvard.) Kohs also reflected the influence of Bartók, not so clearly in the *Etude in Memory of Bartók* for piano, which actually sounded more like Prokofiev, as in as early a work as the 1941 *Scherzo* for piano. Still other works, like the *Violin Sonatina,* had jazz harmonies and Latin American rhythms reminiscent of Copland. In *Legend* and in some passages of the *Passacaglia* was a romantic nostalgia like Barber's and Fine's; while in the *Short Concert,* there was a classical elegance like Piston's.

Little wonder, then, Gilbert Chase labeled Kohs an "eclectic,"[22] along with Leonard Bernstein, whom Kohs knew and admired at Harvard. In fact, Kohs played the percussion part in Bernstein's incidental music for a Harvard Classical Club production of *The Birds.* Bernstein's "adroit mixture of elements drawn from Piston, Stravinsky, and jazz," recalled

Kohs, "were sympathetic to my own interests, though the influence of the latter is sublimated in my own music almost to the point of non-existence." The assimilation of Stravinskian elements, apparently, was likewise sublimated, whereas in many works, connections with Piston, and also Hindemith, were fairly overt.

Those works that were most Hindemithian, which included the majority of the keyboard works, tended to date least well. They often had a labored, academic air, as if the composer were exclusively concerned with compositional problems. This was most evident in a work like the *Inventions,* in which the composer addressed certain performance problems (such as playing with one hand alone) and listed "structural motives" like footnotes (Ex. 14). Such works, moreover, shared a number of stylistic features: they were chromatically thick with vague tonal goals; they were frequently constructed from some unusual scale, be it a 12-tone row, an altered mode, or a pentatonic scale; and they were severely

Example 14. Ellis Kohs, "Invention #2 for left hand alone in C#," *Inventions* (Composer's Facsimile, 1954). Used by permission of ACA.

contrapuntal. It was not these traits in themselves, but the manner in which they were used, that gave Kohs's music, at times, a heavy-handedness: the ultrachromatics were rarely playful or sensuous; the artificial scales were employed with academic literalness; and the counterpoint tended to obscure rather than illuminate individual melodic lines. At best, these works merely seemed to challenge the listener with lofty intellectual ideals. The *Chorale Variations* to some degree fit this description as well, but it deserved special attention, for its Bach-like settings of traditional Hebrew melodies had real usefulness, and, further, suggested little-explored possibilities in the area of Jewish liturgical music.

At the same time, Kohs wrote music of greater allure and emotional impact. In such works—the piano *Scherzo* and *Etude,* the *Legend,* the two *Sonatinas,* the *Short Concert,* the *Chamber Concerto,* and the *First Symphony*—the composer's chromaticism was relieved by diatonic passages; his asymmetrical phrase lengths underscored by sequences and 8-measure phrases; and his dark moods offset by humor and wit. The *Sonatinas* might be singled out for their charm, elegance, and depth of feeling, as well as for a lively American spirit reminiscent of both Piston and Copland.

The *Short Concert* (1948) and the *Chamber Concerto* (1949), while perhaps not as polished as the *Sonatinas,* represented Kohs at his peak: they were expertly crafted, imaginative, and at times gripping, with a dark, shadowy quality as characteristic of the late '40s as was "film noir." Both works owed profound debts to, above all, Piston. The *Short Concert*'s first movement, for instance, had the kind of motor rhythms, varied textures, changing meters rooted in $5/8$, grand pauses, and overlapping contrapuntal waves (see the "meno mosso") that were almost inconceivable without the example of Piston's own string quartets; Kohs only seemed indifferent, in this sprawling movement, to Piston's kind of formal tautness. Similarly, the *Concert*'s ensuing dance movements reminded one of Piston's *Incredible Flutist,* not least in their modal haziness; in the case of the lovely "Sarabande" (Ex. 15), Kohs achieved something of Piston's poignance as well. As for the *Chamber Concerto,* it, too, was highly suggestive of Piston, especially the last movement's chromatic passacaglia theme.

Both of these works echoed other composers as well:

Stravinsky in the *Concert*'s first-movement ostinati; Hindemith in the same work's "Gigue"; and Bartók in some passages from the more adventurous *Chamber Concerto.* The composer seemed most himself in the concluding movement of the *Concert,* entitled "Dreams:Recollections." Here, in this eloquent, Beethovenian ode, one discovered a forceful, intense lyricism possibly related to Jewish chant. (In its Beethovenian idealism, and perhaps too in its relation to Jewish chant, one discovered yet another similarity to Harold Shapero.)

After 1952, Kohs devoted much of his time to vocal music. This included, above all, two full-length operas: *Lord of the Ascendant* for eight solo dancers, seven solo voices, chorus, and orchestra (1955) after the Legend of Gilgamesh; and *Amerika* (1969) after Kafka's novel of the same name. Kohs's other vocal music from the 1950s showed, as did *Lord of the Ascendant,* a great interest in various antiquities, including settings of *Psalm 23, 3 Songs from the Navajo, 3 Greek Choruses,* and *3 Medieval Latin Student Songs,* all from 1957.

None of this music helped to consolidate Kohs's reputation: Chase's 1966 edition of *America's Music* dropped the composer from its pages. Nor were the operas ever fully staged. A recorded excerpt from *Amerika* suggested that this was regrettable; the work was emotionally powerful, in the tradition of *Cardillac* and *Mathis,* though Kohs's extensive use of speech, in addition to song, provided a distinctively melodramatic edge.

Kohs continued to write instrumental music as well. One such work, the 1979 *Concerto for Percussion Quartet,* exemplified the composer's pedantic impulse: the work originated as an extended textbook example from the author's *Musical Composition.* The reader was thus privy to the lengthy and elaborate precompositional decisions that went into this work, as well as its composition in 29 "steps." These procedures, while not without interest, and while certainly pertinent to any study of Kohs's music, smacked suspiciously of, say, art manuals that give stroke-by-stroke instructions for painting a mountain landscape. As it turned out, this *Concerto,* like the composer's contemporary setting of Gertrude Stein's *Men* for voice and three percussionists, was surprisingly adventurous, showing some assimilation of elements derived

Example 15. Ellis Kohs, "Sarabande," *A Short Concert* for string quartet (Composer's Facsimile, 1964). Used by permission of ACA.

from the Californian avant-garde, as represented by Lou Harrison, while at the same time retaining a characteristic vigor.

The *Violin Concerto* of the following year, 1980, was even more appealing. (Consistently, Kohs seemed to write his best music for the violin, the instrument played by his mother.) The work remained close to such violin concerti from the 1930s as Berg's and Piston's, but was updated to allow for such ideas as musical exchanges between the soloist, solo saxophone, and percussion battery. In fact, other than Piston himself in the 1970s, few adapted such new sounds to this kind of neoclassical sensibility. Characteristically, the forms tended to meander, but, overall, the workmanship was exemplary, and the brooding lyricism emotionally charged.

The careers of Helm and Kohs demonstrated that the "classical stance" cultivated by young composers at Harvard in the 1930s permitted unique and personal artistic expression, partly because Piston's tutelage encouraged such individuality. With Helm, the result was a thoroughly refined and sophisticated art of considerable sensuous appeal and melancholy delicacy, in the tradition of Chopin and Malipiero; with Kohs, it was grander and more intense, in the tradition of Beethoven and Hindemith.

What the "classical stance" represented was actually an orientation to such general principles as textural clarity, rhythmic vigor, the retention of tonality, and, vaguer still, aesthetic principles like restraint, humor, craftsmanship, and objectivity. The limitations and pitfalls of such an aesthetic were clear enough: how close restraint could come to mere civility; humor to coyness; craftsmanship to academicism; and objectivity to impersonality. But at their best, Helm and Kohs dodged such limitations to create finely crafted works that are still valuable, moving, and, in their own way, original.

Notes

1. Helm, "Gian Francesco Malipiero—An Introduction with Catalogue of Works," *Soundings* 1 (1970), p. 12.
2. Helm, *Franz Liszt in Selbstzeugnissen und Bilddokumentum* (Hamburg: Rowohlt, 1972); *Bartók* (London: Faber & Faber, 1971).
3. Helm, "Inter-American Review," *Modern Music* 23 No. 2 (Spring 1946), pp. 131–133; "Music in Yugoslavia," *Musical Quarterly* 51 (January, 1965), pp. 215–224.
4. Helm, "Gian Francesco Malipiero," *Musical America* 72 (April 1, 1952), p. 8; "Gian Francesco Malipiero—An Introduction," pp. 6–22; "Malipiero in Retrospect," *The Music Review* 36 (1975), pp. 70–71.
5. Helm, *Music* (Boston: Bellman Publishing, 1940).
6. Helm, *Composer Performer Public* (Florence: Olschki, 1970).
7. Helm, *Music and Tomorrow's Public* (New York: Heinrichshofen, 1981).
8. Helm, "Gian Francesco Malipiero—An Introduction," p. 11.
9. Helm, "Editor's Choice," *Musical America* 83 (May, 1963), p. 20.

10. Milhaud, "Through My California Window," *Modern Music* 21 No. 2 (January–February, 1944), p. 94.
11. Milhaud, p. 93.
12. Helm, "The Elgar Case: Ruminations pro and contra," *Music Review* 18 (1957), p. 103.
13. Helm, "Gian Francesco Malipiero—An Introduction," p. 15.
14. Morton, "Los Angeles Interprets Genesis," *Modern Music* 23 No. 1 (Winter 1946), p. 60.
15. Kohs, *An Aural Approach to Orchestration,* reprinted from an article for *Musical Mercury.*
16. Kohs, *Music Theory,* Vol. 1 and Vol. 2 (New York: Oxford, 1961).
17. Kohs, *Musical Form* (Boston: Houghton Mifflin, 1976).
18. Kohs, *Musical Composition* (Metuchen, NJ: Scarecrow Press, 1980).
19. This and other information gained by a series of personal letters from Kohs dated October 14, 1977; March 15, 1985; March 28, 1985; and April 6, 1985.
20. See, for example, the analysis of the opening measures of Scriabin's *Poëme, Music Theory,* Vol. II, pp. 100–104.
21. Milhaud, "Through My California Window," p. 95; Finney, review of the *First String Quartet, Notes* 9 (December, 1951), p. 162.
22. Chase, *America's Music* (New York: McGraw Hill, 1955), p. 544.

5. NEW FORMS, NEW MEANINGS: THE MUSIC OF ARTHUR BERGER

ARTHUR BERGER (b. 1912) WAS ONE OF THE MOST representative composers of his generation. An eminent champion of "neoclassicism" in the 1940s and '50s, he became an equally well-known proponent of "serialism" after 1955. As a critic, Berger was more often spokesman than observer. In fact, he began his career in the early '30s as a pamphleteer for a circle of young New York composers that included Vivian Fine, Israel Citkowitz, and Paul Bowles. "I was supposed to fill the role of Cocteau, or Paul Collaer, the person who would do the propagandizing for them," he recalled.[1] In the mid-'30s he started a journal, the *Musical Mercury*, that provided a forum for himself and other young artists and critics. In later years, in his writings for *Modern Music*, the *Herald Tribune*, the *Saturday Review*, and numerous other magazines and newspapers,[2] Berger viewed the accomplishments of Hindemith, Schoenberg, Stravinsky, Ives, and others from the particular vantage point of his own generation. This was true, too, of his book on *Aaron Copland*.[3] Berger's charge as spokesman was particularly evident in articles like "Stravinsky and the Younger American Composers"[4] and "The Postwar Generation in Arts and Letters."[5] In the 1960s he helped found another journal, *Perspectives of New Music*, which also was representative of current trends, and whose tone Berger hoped to help set[6] (though by the 1970s he admitted that *Perspectives* had developed a character at some odds to his own[7]).

Berger's music itself was highly representative in that it

teetered between the influence of Schoenberg and Stravinsky, finally aiming to reconcile them. Moved by Schoenberg's piano music, and even more by a 1930 performance of
Die Glückliche Hand, the young Berger, still in his teens,
wrote some 12-tone pieces, becoming one of the first
Americans to do so.[8] With the exception of *Two Episodes* for
piano from 1933, this early 12-tone music was later sup-
pressed. After a silent period of six years, during which time
he studied with Piston, Boulanger, and others at Harvard,
Berger resumed writing music, now strongly influenced by
Stravinsky's contemporary work. He remained a Stravinsky
enthusiast, as a number of articles testified,[9] and in 1971 still
regarded him as "the greatest composer of our time."[10] In the
early 1950s, however, he reevaluated Schoenberg on the
basis of that composer's post-1945 works, works which, for
Berger, reaffirmed Schoenberg's importance and relevance.[11]
In 1956 Berger wrote *Chamber Music for 13 Players,* which he
described as "neoclassic twelve-tone."[12] This work was still
much closer to Stravinsky than to Schoenberg; in fact, Berger
originally intended to use the flute solo from Stravinsky's
"Musick to Heare" as the theme for the *Chamber Music's*
opening variation movement.[13] But with the 1958 *String
Quartet* and in subsequent works, Berger achieved a fairer
balance between the influences of Stravinsky and Schoenberg, a goal, he once claimed, that typified the better
composers of his generation.[14]

Reviewing an all-Berger concert in 1973, Donal Henahan
accordingly described it as "a time capsule report" on the
"postwar American academic establishment."[15] This description, while in its own way accurate, was a bit misleading.
Berger, after all, reflected trends that by no means were
limited to the "American academic establishment." His
temperament, in fact, was even somewhat anti-academic. As
a young man, he rebelled against his teachers at City College
and New York University, and he similarly found Boulanger
overly dogmatic and didactic.[16] Later, he decided against
completing his graduate work in musicology at Harvard. For
much of his career, he was a journalist, teaching only
intermittently before joining the Brandeis University faculty
in 1953, when he was forty-one-years old. He balked at being

grouped with what he thought of as the highly academic "Princeton crowd," by which he meant especially Sessions, Babbitt, and Carter. He also disapprovingly noted academic strains in some music by Hindemith and Barber.[17]

Furthermore, many listeners detected a "unique character"[18] in Berger's music, agreeing, above all, that it was charming. Critics wrote of an "individual shy grace,"[19] an "awkward charm and genuine innocence,"[20] a "convivial lyricism,"[21] "great wit, flow and charm,"[22] and a "just-barely-concealed sidewalks-of-New-York-charm."[23] One reviewer called Berger's *Ideas of Order* "as simple and charming as a Haydn symphony."[24] Berger's entire oeuvre tended to be described as charming, witty, polished, and refined. Only a rare observer like Irving Fine, who, although loving the music, saw this as a limitation.[25] Most others seemed relieved that Berger's music was as ingratiating as it was, considering how difficult and thorny it was in other respects.

To some extent, these difficulties were similar to those posed by Berger's stylistic models, especially Stravinsky: dissonant counterpoint, refined textures, syncopated rhythms, and contradictory harmonies. Listeners at home with Stravinsky's *Octet* and Schoenberg's *Piano Pieces, Op. 11* would find little stylistically novel in Berger's music. But Berger's formal procedures were more personal, and often elicited special comment. Early on, Lou Harrison, for instance, noted, "Mr. Berger's work bears the surface evidence of a thoroughgoing devotion to Stravinsky, but he has taken that composer's devices into a farther land where the broken items of discontinuity are evenly distributed throughout the design."[26] In a review of Berger's *Capriccio* (1945), Harrison again observed that the work's thematic structure was limited mostly to two-note groupings "put through the mill with thoroughness, tonally and rhythmically," adding, "Berger appears somewhat embarrassed by the prospect of melodic continuity."[27] This "discontinuity" justified, according to Milton Babbitt, the use of the phrase "diatonic Webern" to describe Berger's *Duo for Cello and Piano* (1951).[28] Even after Berger adopted the 12-tone method, his formal procedures remained essentially idiosyncratic. Wrote Sheila Silver on the

Five Pieces for Piano (1969), "This is music whose pitch organization works from the detail outward, not from the larger unit of twelve chromatic tones inward. The manipulation of several cells, which will probably include all or most of the available twelve tones, is the primary concern. . . . The pairings, the order, and the degree of repetition of certain cells (or pitches) are neither systematic nor consistent."[29]

The coherence of Berger's forms, when not flatly dismissed by a conservative critic like Charles Warren Fox as "unwarrantably loose,"[30] often challenged and perplexed listeners. John MacIvor Perkins stated:

> . . . despite the lucid, consistent, and relatively unbewildering surface of his music—or perhaps because of it—it is by no means easy to hear and follow large-scale structures. The parts, united by a common tightly defined style, bear a superficial but sometimes irrelevant and distracting resemblance to one another: there are no full-fledged themes to use as points of reference; contrasts are not gross; oppositions and other interactions may be very intricate.[31]

Peggy Glanville-Hicks wrote that Berger's music demands "utter concentration; there are no filler parts, few silences, no obvious sequences or repetitions where the mind can momentarily rest and re-gather its powers of concentration, and it may be that it is this demand for total attention that makes his music tough going for some listeners."[32] George Perle suggested that the success of Berger's music depended heavily on the performing musicians, writing, "It is Mr. Berger's misfortune that unless the strong feeling for musical continuity that binds the extrinsic details is firmly grasped by the performers their musical effect is lost."[33]

Making a similar observation, Henry Cowell concluded, however, that this was the composer's problem, not the performer's or the listener's; discussing the quasi-serial technique of *Ideas of Order,* Cowell wrote, "The inevitable result of such treatment, however, is the appearance and development of so many different forms of the original motif that it is hard to relate them on first hearing, and one feels that some further schematization, beyond that of relationship to the original form, is needed to give a sense of solid structure for the integration of so many elements."[34] Elaine Barkin and Benjamin Boretz in a review, or rather "post impressions," of Berger's *Trio for Guitar, Violin, and Piano* (1972), saw fit to address Berger's formal complexities by attempting to match them with discontinuities and ambiguities of their own, Barkin concluding:

> The Trio's piecehood emerges, simply, from the plausibility of every direction taken, of every corner turned, as every (re)shaped twist and (re)twisted shape refers to within itself, neither growing nor going but turning inward, regenerating its own unmistakable flavor and feel as it both pursues and submerges—catching up with and dipping into—without ever really preparing us (but without never preparing us) for what is next to come. Nor for what does not come next.[35]

While Berger occasionally resorted to traditional forms like the sonata, as in the *Woodwind Quartet,* and theme and variation, as in *Chamber Music,* his work on the whole did tend to avoid any obvious "schematization." Was there indeed some formal principle behind his intricate manipulation of tiny cells? To help answer this question, a close analysis follows of two piano pieces by Berger: "Bagatelle No. 1" from the 1946 *Three Bagatelles* (Ex. 16) and "Piece No. 1" from the 1969 *Five Pieces* (Ex. 17).

Berger composed "close to the piano,"[36] and aside from the relatively early, masterful *Woodwind Quartet,* his piano work represented perhaps his most distinctive and innovative accomplishment. Whereas the Bagatelle was in a sparse, spiky idiom derived from Stravinsky (as the attenuated style of his jazz contemporary, Thelonious Monk, was related to his predecessors), the Piece featured the kind of arpeggiated sweeps, registral leaps, and rich chords associated with Schoenberg. In addition, this piece, like the 1961 *Three Pieces for Two Pianos* that preceded it, showed, too, the impact of John Cage, for it called for plucked and stopped strings and prepared notes (the piano's uppermost B requires a piece of rubber split down the center and placed around its middle string, while the G above middle C requires a metal screw 1¼ inches long which is inserted between the two upper strings about an inch behind the damper). Such contrasting pieces were selected so that continuities of formal procedure that possibly stand apart from the specifics of Berger's stylistic evolution can be considered.

The Bagatelle exemplifies how fastidiously the composer worked with but a few basic cells, in this case, little two- and three-note bits from the piece's first measure. These include the ascending minor triad and descending major third in the right hand, and the ascending minor third-minor second and descending minor second in the left hand. Along with their

Example 16. Arthur Berger, *Three Bagatelles,* 1 (Edward B. Marks, 1948).
Used by permission of ACA.

inversions, major and minor thirds remain prominent
throughout, giving the piece its rather mellow sound. The
minor second is important, too, especially (as in the first
measure) for the bass line. Fourths, fifths, and, above all,
tritones are used more sparingly. These intervallic preferences tended to characterize Berger's music as a whole.

Tracing but one of these opening motives, E-G-B, for
example, we find it transformed in m. 4 in the bass to G#-E-B,
a transformation found, too, in the treble at m. 6, and then,
with the original G♮ replacing the G#, at mm. 9, 12, and 19.
In mm. 27–28, the motive is ornamented with an auxiliary
note (B-E-A-G#), resulting in a series of fourths that is

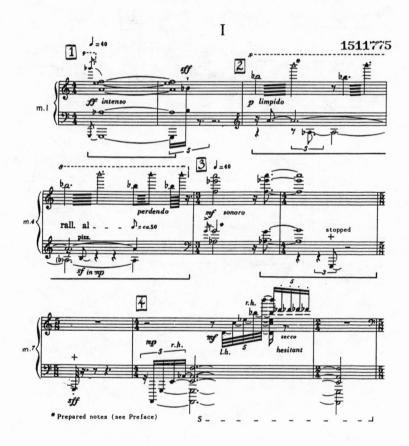

\# Prepared notes (see Preface)

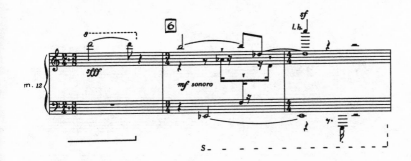

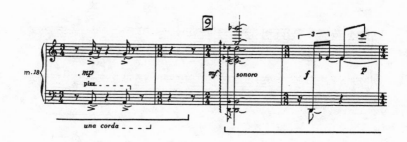

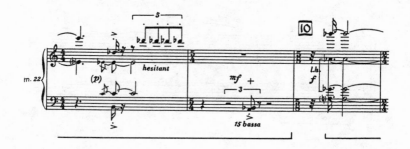

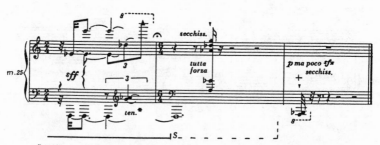

\# While the pedal sustains the total sonority, depress the F again without re-attacking it
So that it continues to sound alone in m.26. Then re-engage it with the middle pedal.

Example 17. Arthur Berger, *Five Pieces* for piano, I (Henmar Press, 1975).
Used by permission.

further explored in mm. 29, 30, 34, 36 and 37. Each and every note of the piece participates in some such transformation and variation.

Similarly, the Bagatelle's opening measure contains the straightforward trochees, dactyls, and, in the bass, repeated notes that generate the work's basic rhythmic character. (The 16th-note motive in the second measure is also important, and occurs throughout in shifting metrical positions.) The opening measure's two-part writing, with its occasional octave doubling, likewise determines the work's texture. Finally, the first measure immediately sets forth the work's distinctively modal flavor.

How are these details shaped? For the most part, Berger's tiny cells fall into well-defined, single-measure units. Further, these units combine into two- and four-measure groupings. What could be neater? And yet, a closer look reveals subtle ambiguities.

Consider the work's opening phrase. The first three measures rock between the tonic, C, and its dominant, before settling, unexpectedly, in B, suggesting a half-cadence in E minor. (Actually, the F#-A# dyad that closes each of the opening three measures looks forward to this tonal shift.) These opening three measures, in fact, are so alike that one can move them about without jeopardizing the music's logic. (Try, for example, switching measures two and three.) Hierarchical relationships are further obscured by having the various musical elements contradict one another: this opening phrase, for instance, might be described as aaab from the perspective of contour and tonality, but abbb in terms of the rhythm of the upper part, or aabb in terms of the rhythm of the lower part. Other elements like dynamics and texture can further contradict expected formal relations, as we shall see.

On a larger level, the piece as a whole operates much like this opening phrase, with the individual phrases interacting in contradictory ways much as the individual measures of the first phrase were shown to do. These phrases, for the most part, are as clearly set off from one another as are the individual measures of the first phrase. This is accomplished

by an articulated cadence or rest, or by changes in texture or
rhythm. Below is an attempt to identify and label them:

mm.	phrase
1–4	1
5–8	2
9–18	3
19–22	4
23–26	5
27–28	6
29–30	7
31–32	8
33–36	9
37–40	10
41–43	11
44–47	12
48–51	13 (tag)

To understand the complex interrelationships of the phrases,
it is helpful to isolate each of the musical elements and note
their distinctive patterns.

Melody. As regards *phrase length,* phrase 1 provides the
norm (it is four measures long), while phrase 3 deviates from
it most dramatically (it is ten measures long). But the first
phrase's *melodic structure,* that is, its use of single measure
units, gives way, in phrase 3, to two-measure groupings as the
basic unit. Also, the principal motive in phrase 1 does not
recur in the course of the piece, except for a subtle, inverted
echo in phrase 11. On the other hand, the third phrase's
opening motive (reminiscent, by the way, of the contemporary popular song "Misty") reappears in phrase 4 and, slightly
altered, in phrase 12. These three phrases, but most especially
phrases 4 and 12, are the only phrases that share a *melodic
identity,* although phrases 2 and 5 also resemble one another
to a degree. As for the more subjective matter of *melodic
quality,* some of the phrases can be said to be more vocal,
more thematic, as it were, while others are more developmental or transitional. Phrases 1, 2, 3, 4, 12, and 13 fall into the
first, more expository category, while phrases 5, 6, 7, 8, 9, 10,
and 11 belong to the latter group.

Rhythm. The Bagatelle's most dramatic rhythmic articulation is at m. 18 where a whole note and decreased rhythmic activity are followed by an eight-note rest, forming an important break between phrases 3 and 4. Also noteworthy is the faster rhythmic motion of phrase 9, and the increased use of syncopation in phrases 3 and 10. The prominent 3/4 meter is contrasted occasionally by 4/4 time: found in phrases 2, 3, 11, and 13, the 4/4 meter only really makes itself felt in phrases 2 and 3.

Tonality. The Bagatelle apparently begins and ends in C, although E minor is suggested at both spots as well: at the opening, through modal inflection; at the end, by unusual spacing. Phrases 3 and 4 are also in C. Other tonal centers include B (end of phrase 1), E♭ (phrase 2 and the start of phrase 5), E (phrase 6), A (phrases 7 and 8), D (phrases 9 and 10), and F# (phrase 11). None of these centers, however, is established long enough to really counterbalance the C. Moreover, the modulations, the progressions, and even the individual dyads, are determined primarily by the interval of the third, rather than the fourth or the fifth, giving the tonal fabric an ambiguous quality. The clearest cadences are at the ends of phrases 1, 8, and 13. Finally, the section from phrase 5 to phrase 11 emphasizes, in contrast to the surrounding music, a minor rather than a major modality; it is also the area of greatest tonal activity.

Harmonic rhythm. The Bagatelle's harmonic rhythm can be interpreted as falling into two categories: harmonic changes within the measure (phrases 1, 2, 5, 7, and 9), and harmonic changes equal to or greater than the measure (phrases 3, 4, 6, 8, 10, 11, 12, and 13).

Texture. Except for the last phrase, the texture is two-voiced. Occasionally, however, a voice is doubled at the octave. This happens in phrases 1, 3, 8, 9, 10, and 11. Throughout, the ranges of the two voices are fairly limited (the work, in fact, originated as a *Duo* for viola and cello). The piece's highest pitch is the high E in phrases 3 and 11, the second of which is a resolution of the high D# in phrase 8. The shift to unison in phrase 6, and the rich expansion to as much as 6-voiced chords in phrase 13, constitute particularly striking textural changes.

Touch. Each phrase tends to use legato, staccato, and accent markings distinctively. Especially noteworthy is the use of long legato lines in phrase 3, and the use of accent marks in phrases 3, 10, and 11.

Expression marks, dynamics, pedaling. The Bagatelle shows careful attention to these elements, but they do not seem to contribute to any larger formal pattern. This is partly because they tend to fluctuate within the phrase, and partly because they tend not to reinforce any of the patterns suggested by other elements. Very important, nonetheless, are the fortissimo markings in phrases 8 and 11 (according to Berger, the opening phrase should read forte, not fortissimo).

When these various musical elements are taken together, they form surprisingly distinct patterns that can be summarized as follows:

> *element: phrases*
> cadence: 1, 2–8, 9–13
> meter: 1, 2–3, 4–13
> melodic structure: 1–2, 3–13
> phrase length, legato: 1–2, 3, 4–13
> tonal center: 1–2, 3–11, 12–13
> melodic identity: 1–2, 3, 4–11, 12–13
> rhythm, range: 1–3, 4–13
> accents: 1–3, 4–11, 12–13
> modality, tonal activity: 1–4, 5–11, 12–13
> harmonic rhythm: 1–4, 5–6, 7–8, 9–13
> melodic quality: 1–4, 5–11, 12–13
> texture: 1–5, 6, 7–12, 13
> dynamics: 1–7, 8–10, 11–13

The presence of so many contradictory patterns suggests why Berger's forms baffled even his most conscientious listeners.

One could simply think of the Bagatelle as a "continuous variation," and let it go at that. But the hierarchical implications, as elusive and contradictory as they are, cannot be ignored. Berger, in fact, intended phrases 1–2 as an introduction; phrase 3 as the theme; phrase 4 as the combined theme and introduction; phrase 5 as a modification of the introduction's second phrase; phrases 6–10 as a development section;

phrase 11 as a transition to the return; phrase 12 as a return; and phrase 13 as a coda. These schematic intentions, however, are purposefully contravened by the composer in numerous ways. And so the result is an ordered, balanced hierarchical form full of subtle and ambiguous meanings.

A similar situation prevails in the first of Berger's *Five Pieces for Piano,* notwithstanding the fact that the music, which smartly incorporates elements from both Cage and Boulez, is wholly different stylistically. Silver's observation, "This is music whose pitch organization works from the detail outward," is as clearly applicable to the early Bagatelle as it is to these late pieces that Silver is describing. The piece, it is true, makes ostensible use of the 12-tone method, but not, as Silver points out, to demarcate phrases or any other formal unit. Rather, Berger employs what he called "harmonic fields"[37] in which notes freely repeat and establish a sort of tonal norm. The most clear-cut example of this is found in mm. 1–7, in which Berger limits himself to the pitches E♭, E, F, G♭, G, A♭, A, B♭, and B. These harmonic fields are a key factor in establishing the piece's vague but suggestive tonality. It seems, for example, that D♭ might be a tonal center, and the prominent A♭ in the work's first few measures, a kind of dominant. But even if D♭ were, in fact, the work's tonic, this would not go far in explaining the work's form, for as in the Bagatelle, the tonic here acts rather statically, without any important counterforce.

Once again, an investigation of phrase provides a good means for understanding form. The piece's phrases are highly compressed: the first phrase (mm. 1–2) consists of just two events. Such phrases, however, are fairly well separated and articulated, primarily through the use of silence, though also through dynamics, touch, register, timbre, and pedaling marks. The first phrase, for instance, closes with a short, accented, loud (sff), and dissonant dyad.[38] As the piece progresses, this motive is transformed into other articulated gestures: the pizzicato sforzando at m. 4; the stopped sforzando at m. 7; the secco repeated notes at m. 8; the triple sforzando at m. 12; and so forth.

The result is a pattern of 10 phrases of about equal length:

mm.	phrase
1–2	1
3–4	2
5–7	3
8–9	4
10–12	5
13–14	6
15–16	7
17–19	8
20–23	9
24–27	10

As in the Bagatelle, these phrases are well unified intervallically, although here the minor second, not the major third, predominates (most often in the form of the major seventh or minor ninth). More specifically, the opening six-note sonority contains two identical trichords (G-Ab-A and E-F-Gb) that color much of the Piece, and that in general characterize the sound of Berger's late work. Berger once even compared his use of these chromatic trichords to Debussy's use of the whole-tone scale.[39]

As for the relationships between the phrases, one discovers the same intricate web of cross-references and contradictions as in the Bagatelle. Similar harmonic fields and pianistic gestures, for instance, argue for the following formal design: 1–3, (4), 5–6, 7–8, 9–10. (Phrase 4 poses special problems: its chordal spacing looks back to phrase 3; its sweeping arpeggiation, and its introduction of the trichord C-Db-D, look ahead to phrase 5; while its repeated notes look even further ahead to phrases 8 and 9). But how do these larger divisions relate? One can argue, most simply, for a plan of abcd, but there is evidence to suggest such other designs as abac, abba, and abca. It might be argued, too, that the piece is a kind of ternary form, with phrases 5–8 comprising a short development.

The structural complexities of individual movements like the first of the *Three Bagatelles* or the first of the *Five Pieces* were compounded when one considered the music in its total context. For the movements of such works were bound not only by intricate motivic relationships, but by connections of a more subtle order. In the *Three Bagatelles,* for instance, the ambiguous C tonality that concluded the first Bagatelle was resolved at the start of the second Bagatelle, which ended, however, in F. The third Bagatelle moved conversely from F to C. This tonal fluidity minimized the separateness of the individual movements, and suggested further formal complexities on a still higher level.

In later years, Berger altogether avoided the classic fast-slow-fast format found in such early works as the *Three Bagatelles* and the *Woodwind Quartet.* He already had written in 1944 the *Serenade Concertante,* a large, single-movement work that fluctuated in tempo and mood. This was a form that came to characterize a number of the composer's works from the 1950s, including a series of chamber duos, as well as two orchestral compositions: the delightful *Ideas of Order* (1952) and the more severe *Polyphony* (1956). There were also two-movement works that were curiously balanced. More unusual was the 1947 *Partita,* a five-movement work whose last three movements were to be played "attacca." A similar design was employed for what possibly was Berger's most complex and ambitious undertaking, the six-movement *String Quartet* (1958). In this work, whole passages from earlier movements turned up in later ones, and in a manner far more subtle than mere romantic reminiscence. In Berger's music from the 1960s, including the *Five Pieces,* contrasts between individual movements were even less distinct. Further, Berger showed a certain casualness about the ordering of such movements. Discussing the origin of the *Five Pieces,* pianist Robert Miller, the work's dedicatee, wrote:

> The piece composed as number 1 became number 2, and 2 became 1, then 3 became 4, and 4 became 3. Five was added almost as an afterthought; it was like an inspiration; it ends up being the most beautiful . . . A problem in performance, or course, is that the fourth piece ends "largo," so the question is how to make sure that the fifth piece isn't redundant.[40]

Berger's individual movements, consequently, were much like his measures and phrases: their interrelationships were logical and exhaustive, but their internal structuring and external placement were ambiguous and highly spontaneous. The daring of his phraseology was extended to the highest levels.

Important to any discussion of Berger's forms was some consideration of an article the composer wrote in 1945, "Form is Feeling."[41] It argued that form, that is, the technique of putting notes together, was the same thing as expression, meaning, and content. "The struggle for a key may seem a prosaic matter," Berger writes, "yet the overtones of all past struggles in our experience may crowd into this presumably abstract material." In fact, Berger argued that the more abstract a work is, the more "the whole unconscious is given free play," and consequently, the more profound and expressive the music. This argument was supported, and in turn was vindicated, by the alleged superiority of 18th-century music over that of the 19th century. The article's equation of form and content reduced, it is true, to mere tautology. But it helped to explain the composer's preoccupation with the complex and contradictory manipulation of tiny cells.

Berger's delight in the abstract play of musical motives, and his revival of 18th-century ideals, were related to his enthusiasm for Stravinsky,[42] Piston,[43] and Copland (especially the *Piano Variations*),[44] as well as to his academic work with Boulanger, and, more importantly, D. W. Prall, his aesthetics professor at Harvard.[45] And like these mentors, he balanced such concerns with a respect for the spontaneous, unplanned aspects of the creative process, in one interview citing Valèry and E. M. Forster on the subject.[46] Consequently, he proved equally aloof from both "aleatoric music" and "total organization."[47]

Our analysis of Berger's music, however, makes clear that while this balance of rational detachment and inspired spontaneity was in the neoclassical tradition, formally, Berger represented, if not a more progressive development, then at least a more idiosyncratic one. His approach was closest, it seems, to Stravinsky's collage-like methods. But there was in Berger little of the long lines, contrasting themes, dramatic modulations, big climaxes, in short, the poised forms of Stravinsky. While his models seemed to be gazing at the stars, Berger seemed to be peering through a microscope: little cells wriggled and bounced, creating the most lively and improbable designs. In this sense, Berger sooner warranted comparison with his only slightly younger contemporary, Gail Kubik, than with certain other composers with whose names his is usually linked, namely, Irving Fine and Harold Shapero.

It was probably no coincidence that both Berger and Kubik were particularly drawn to motion pictures. In his essay on "Copland and Hollywood,"[48] Berger showed not only a familiarity with Copland's movie scores, but a lively interest in the subject in general: he noted the influence of Delius, Tchaikovsky and Strauss on early Hollywood composers; the debt David Raksin and Hugo Friedhofer owed to Copland; the weakness of George Antheil's movie music as compared to his other work; and the overall superiority of the film scores of Louis Gruenberg and Bernard Herrmann (Herrmann, along with Berger and Jerome Moross, another distinguished Hollywood composer, were all students of Vincent Jones at NYU in the early '30s, and discovered New York's avant-garde world together[49]). On at least two occasions (in discussing Ives's *Central Park in the Dark*[50] and Schoenberg's *Erwartung*[51]), Berger suggested that certain musical works could profit from a motion picture accompaniment. He also sometimes evoked movie scores in discussing concert music, comparing, for instance, John Alden Carpenter to "the scores for the smart, fluffy films that were in vogue in Myrna Loy's hey-day,"[52] and Schoenberg to TV mysteries from the 1950s.[53] No doubt this was partly done to engage a readership more familiar with movies than with modern music, but it revealed, nonetheless, a spirited and close involvement with the art of motion pictures.

This involvement ostensibly left a profound mark, not only in terms of the content of Berger's music—for there was a sort of Chaplinesque pathos to his work—but in terms of its unusual formal approach, which was close, after all, to film's unique and startling combination of continuous flow and jagged cutting. In fact, a fair analogy could be drawn between the basic components of film—frame, shot, and sequence— and Berger's use of measure, phrase, and movement. Some critics, significantly, have used quasi-cinematic terms in discussing Berger, such as Silver[54] and Barkin,[55] who both

referred to his music as moving in and out of focus, and David
Stock, who wrote of the *Septet,* "There is, among other things,
a constant interplay between the layers of sustained and
fragmented textures, creating a sense of shifting perspective
between foreground and background."[56] Berger's forms
arguably were related to movies much as Mozart's were to
opera and Stravinsky's were to ballet. Perhaps it was worth
noting that whereas older composers like Piston experienced
the motion pictures as adults, and younger ones like Shapero
grew up with the more traditionally theatrical talking pictures, Berger, like Kubik, came of age amidst the radically
novel, flickering images of the silent movies.

The silent movies were more demonstrably crucial to one
of Berger's closest friends and associates, poet and writer
Delmore Schwartz. Schwartz, a year younger than Berger,
also did some undergraduate work at NYU (though by the
time he transferred there in 1933, Berger already had left),
where, like Berger, he became something of a disciple of
Meyer Schapiro,[57] the well-known advocate for abstract
painting. Berger and Schwartz met as graduate students at
Harvard where they both "rallied around Prall."[58] In early
1936 Berger invited Schwartz, along with Paul Goodman, to
contribute to a Prallian symposium on "The Nature of Music"
for *Musical Mercury.* During the school year 1936–1937,
Berger and Schwartz rented rooms at 94 Prescott Street,[59]
and their close friendship continued long after both left
Harvard. In 1982, Berger paid tribute to his old friend with a
choral setting of the poet's *O Love Sweet Animal.*

Even before entering Harvard, Schwartz had written his
most famous story, "In Dreams Begin Responsibilities," but it
was not published until 1937, when it made a sensation as the
lead piece of fiction for the first issue of the *Partisan Review.*
In the story, a young man dreams that he is seated in a motion
picture theater watching, as if in an old silent movie, his father
court and propose to his mother on a summer day in 1909.
The movie terrifies the young man. He shouts at the
audience, is then scolded and dragged out by an usher, and
finally wakes up "into the bleak winter morning of my 21st
birthday, the window-sill shining with its lip of snow, and the
morning already begun."[60] The point to be made here is the

way in which silent film provided the story with its setting (a motion picture theater), images (such as, "one flash succeeds another with sudden jumps"), characters (screen actors, the audience, an usher), form (six episodes occasionally interrupted by breakdowns with the projector), and symbol (time's irreversibility). Saul Bellow, in a biographical novel about Schwartz, called him "movie-mad,"[61] and his biographer wrote of his "fanatical absorption in the movies that dated from his forlorn youth, when the darkened theaters on upper Broadway had been a second home to him."[62] The story "In Dreams Begin Responsibilities" was indebted to Eliot and Kafka, much as Berger's music was indebted to Stravinsky and Schoenberg; but the silent movies provided a catalyst to an art that was more disjointed and surreal (as well as one that caught the flavor of contemporary America). This blend of modernism and the motion pictures was epitomized in another of Schwartz's stories from the '30s, "Screeno," in which the protagonist recites T. S. Eliot in a garish movie house. Even Schwartz's stories that did not deal specifically with the movies, such as "The World Is a Wedding," were highly cinematic in their collage techniques.

Collage technique also was cultivated by yet another contemporary Harvard graduate student associated with Prall, the painter Robert Motherwell (1913–1991), who, like Berger and Schwartz, left Harvard before completing his PhD.[63] Motherwell met and befriended Berger in Paris and took the composer's advice to study with Meyer Schapiro in New York,[64] where he subsequently fell in with Schwartz and the Trotskyite *Partisan Review* crowd. In the collages that brought him fame in the 1940s and '50s, Motherwell combined spontaneous automatism and learned deliberation in ways that resembled both Schwartz and Berger. In later years he created collages specifically inspired by Schwartz ("In Plato's Cave") and Stravinsky ("Stravinsky").

The network of influences that bound Berger, Schwartz, and Motherwell—the modernists, the silent movies, Prall, Schapiro, Freud, Trotsky, and so on—sheds some light on the distinctiveness of Berger's forms, and on their meanings. It suggested that Berger's complex and contradictory approach to form was not simply an act of individual willfulness, or a

mere affirmation of certain musical traditions, but a reflection
of modern trends in philosophy, psychology, politics, and
popular culture. And it was precisely these ties, rather than
any stylistic or formal detail, that made Berger so representative of his times.

Notes

1. Jane Coppock, "A Conversation with Arthur Berger," *Perspectives of New Music* 17:1 (Fall–Winter 1978), p. 44.
2. See Pamela Jones, "A Bibliography of the Writings of Arthur
   Berger," *Perspectives of New Music* 17:1 (Fall–Winter 1978), pp.
   83–89.
3. Berger, *Aaron Copland* (New York: Oxford University, 1953).
4. Berger, "Stravinsky and the Younger American Composers,"
   The Score 12 (June 1955), pp. 38–46.
5. Berger, "The Postwar Generation in Arts and Letters,"
   Saturday Review 36 (March 14, 1953), pp. 17–18.
6. Berger and Benjamin Boretz, "Editorial Notes," *Perspectives of
   New Music* 1:1 (Fall–Winter 1962), pp. 4–5; also, Berger,
   "Problems of Pitch Organization in Stravinsky," 2:1 (Fall–
   Winter 1963), pp. 11–42; and "New Linguistic Modes and the
   New Theory," 3:1 (Fall–Winter 1964), pp. 1–9.
7. Berger, "Some Notes on Babbitt and his Influence," *Perspec-
   tives of New Music* 15:1 (Fall–Winter 1976), pp. 32–36. Berger
   also expressed doubts about the music of his colleague Martin
   Boykan, personal interview, February 11, 1984.
8. Coppock, p. 45.
9. See especially Berger, "1943 the Stravinsky Panorama," *Igor
   Stravinsky,* Edwin Corle, ed. (New York: Duell, Sloan and
   Pearce, 1949), pp. 105–114; and "Music for the Ballet,"
   Stravinsky in the Theatre, Minna Lederman, ed. (New York:
   Pellegrini and Cuday, 1949), pp. 41–69.
10. Berger, "Neoclassicism Reexamined," *Perspectives of New
    Music* 10:1 (Fall–Winter 1971), p. 79.
11. Berger, "Spotlight on the Moderns," *Saturday Review* April 28,
    1951, p. 64; November 24, 1951, p. 80; June 27, 1953, p. 59;
    November 28, 1953, pp. 72, 86–87; February 27, 1954, p. 71;
    and April 24, 1954, pp. 56–57. See also, "King David and
    Reforestation," *Saturday Review* 35 (March 29, 1952), p. 48;

and "The Later Schoenberg," *Saturday Review* 36 (July 25, 1953), p. 52.

12. Perkins, "Arthur Berger: The Composer as Mannerist," *Perspectives on American Composers*, Benjamin Boretz and Edward Cone, eds. (New York: W. W. Norton, 1971), p. 232.

13. Berger, record liner notes to *Chamber Music for 13 Players*, CRI SD 290.

14. Berger, "The Postwar Generation," p. 17.

15. Henahan, "Arthur Berger: A Retrospective of His Music," *New York Times*, April 3, 1973.

16. Berger, interview with Margaret Fairbanks, c. 1967, Rodgers and Hammerstein Archive of Recorded Sound, Music Division, New York Public Library.

17. Berger, "Scores and Records," *Modern Music* 23 (1946), pp. 66–68.

18. Karl Kohn, review of *Three Pieces for Two Pianos*, *Musical Quarterly* 50 (1964), p. 229.

19. Donald Fuller, review of the *Quartet for Woodwinds*, *Modern Music* 19 (1941–1942), p. 117.

20. Irving Fine, review of the *Partita for Piano*, *Musical Quarterly* 38 (1952), p. 481.

21. Henry Cowell, review of *Ideas of Order*, *Musical Quarterly* 39 (1953), p. 431.

22. Eric Salzman, review of *Chamber Music for 13 Players*, *New York Times*, February 12, 1964. And in a review of Berger's *Three Pieces for Two Pianos*, Saltzman referred to the work as "music of infinite adroitness and charm," *New York Herald Tribune*, April 6, 1966.

23. Virgil Thomson, *American Music Since 1910* (New York: Holt, Rinehart and Winston, 1970), p. 123.

24. Jay S. Harrison, *New York Herald Tribune*, April 13, 1953.

25. Fine, review of the *Partita*.

26. Lou Harrison, review of *Three Pieces for String Orchestra*, *New York Herald Tribune*, January 27, 1946.

27. Harrison, "New Music in Recital and Symposium," *Modern Music* 23 (1946), p. 51.

28. Babbitt, review of the *Duo for Cello and Piano*, *Saturday Review* 37 (March 13, 1954). Peggy Glanville-Hicks and Henry Cowell also drew comparisons between Berger and Webern. Berger once admitted to being influenced by Webern (Fairbanks interview), but to a "lesser extent" than he was by Stravinsky and Schoenberg.

29. Silver, "Pitch and Registral Distribution in Arthur Berger's

Music for Piano," *Perspectives of New Music* 17:1 (Fall–Winter 1978), p. 73.

30. Fox, review of the *Serenade Concertante, Modern Music* 23 (1946), p. 63.

31. Perkins, p. 239.

32. Glanville-Hicks, "Arthur Berger," *ACA Bulletin* Vol. 3 No. 1 (Spring 1953), p. 2.

33. Perle, review of the *String Quartet, Musical Quarterly* 46 (1960), p. 521.

34. Cowell, p. 431.

35. Barkin, "Arthur Berger's Trio for Guitar, Violin and Piano (1972)," *Perspectives of New Music* 17:1 (Fall–Winter 1978), p. 37.

36. Fairbanks interview.

37. Fairbanks interview.

38. This sort of abrupt articulation was highly characteristic. Already evident in the *Partita* (see mm. 1–4), it became more and more integral to Berger's concept of phrase (see, for example, the *String Quartet* or the *Septet*). Its origin could even be perceived in some of the clipped phrases of the Bagatelle.

39. Personal interview.

40. Quoted by George Gellis, record liner notes to *Five Pieces for Piano,* New World Records, NW 308.

41. Berger, "Form is Feeling," *Modern Music* 22 (January–February 1945), pp. 87–92.

42. Berger, "Stravinsky and the Younger American Composers."

43. See Berger, "Walter Piston," *Trend* (January–February 1935), pp. 210–212, and a review of Piston's *First Symphony* for *Modern Music* 23 (1946), p. 135, in which he wrote, "It is a joy to discover how everything fits into place in this elaborate constellation of tones." In the 1980s Berger was teaching Piston's *Passacaglia* to his students at Brandeis, personal interview.

44. Berger, "The Piano Variations of Aaron Copland," *Musical Mercury* 1 (August-September 1934), p. 85, wrote, "I know of no other native piano work which manifests the economy of means, the discrimination, the careful workmanship and at the same time the frankness, originality and vigor." In his book on *Copland,* Berger used this particular work as a "focal point."

45. See Berger's review of Prall's *Aesthetic Analysis, Musical Mercury* 3 (June 1936), pp. 20–27, and his introduction to a reprint of the same work (New York: Thomas Crowell, 1967), pp. ix–xxvii.

46. Fairbanks interview.

47. Fairbanks interview.

48. Berger, *Copland,* pp. 85–90.

49. Fairbanks interview. Herrmann also helped Berger found *Musical Mercury.*

50. Berger, "Spotlight on the Moderns," *Saturday Review* 33 (December 30, 1950), p. 46.

51. Berger, "Spotlight on the Moderns," *Saturday Review* 35 (June 28, 1952), pp. 46–47.

52. Berger, "Spotlight on the Moderns," *Saturday Review* 35 (May 31, 1952), p. 43.

53. Berger, "Spotlight on the Moderns," *Saturday Review* 39 (April 28, 1956), pp. 56–57.

54. Silver, p. 74.

55. Barkin, p. 24.

56. Stock, "New Music," *Perspectives of New Music* 7 (Fall–Winter 1968), p. 143.

57. James Atlas, *Delmore Schwartz. The Life of an American Poet* (New York: Avon, 1977), p. 242.

58. Berger, introduction to *Analysis,* pp. x–xi.

59. Atlas, p. 84.

60. Schwartz, *In Dreams Begin Responsibilities and Other Stories* (New York: New Directions, 1978), p. 9.

61. Bellow, *Humboldt's Gift* (New York: Avon, 1973), p. 13.

62. Atlas, p. 303.

63. Motherwell and Schwartz were both students of philosophy; Berger was a student of musicology.

64. H. Harvard Arnason, *Robert Motherwell,* second edition (New York: Harry N. Abrams, 1982), p. 227.

6. EXPANDING THE MODERNIST TRADITION: ELLIOTT CARTER AND LEONARD BERNSTEIN

ELLIOTT CARTER'S SECOND STRING QUARTET of 1959 and Leonard Bernstein's *West Side Story* of 1957 were so new, so original, and so unalike that it was surprising to recall that twenty years earlier the tastes, sensibilities, and even the musical styles of these two composers were, while not indistinguishable, very similar. The similarities were in part shared by other composers who studied at Harvard before the War, and in part unique to themselves.

The central fact of this closeness circa 1940 was a basic orientation toward what was already an American modernist tradition as represented, above all, by Stravinsky, Hindemith, Copland, and Piston. This meant an allegiance to the ideals of formal and textural clarity, of tonal sophistication and rhythmic vigor, of contrapuntal finesse, of an ironic, objective tone, and of a sensibility that could accommodate popular styles and everyday needs.[1]

To an extent, Carter and Bernstein held these ideals even more vigorously than their elders: the rise of Nazism, and their own strongly anti-fascist feelings, made any taint of emotional bombast or aristocratic privilege, let alone the tradition of German Romanticism, distasteful. This was more or less documented by the reviews they wrote for *Modern Music* in the 1930s and early '40s, reviews which similarly revealed a profound admiration for the aforementioned modernists, and a concurrent dislike for anything apprehended as soggy, messy, or overly romantic.[2] Carter, for example, deprecated Schoenberg, blasted Ives's *Concord*

Sonata ("Behind all this confused texture there is a lack of logic which repeated hearings can never clarify. . . ."), and ridiculed modern dance (as opposed to modern ballet). Bernstein, for his part, observed structural lapses in the music of Carpenter, Harris, and Schuman, writing of the latter, "Too much love and too much conviction dull his sense of proportion."

Both men in large part acquired these tastes at Harvard, where Carter studied in the late '20s, Bernstein in the late '30s, both under Piston's supervision. Indeed, both had come to Harvard with strong attachments to late Romantic styles, especially Scriabin and Rachmaninov, respectively[3] (orientations that eventually reasserted themselves, as we shall see). How much their modernist sympathies were shaped or influenced by Piston himself, as opposed to, say, other students and faculty, or just simply by growing up in the 1930s, is hard to say. But some evidence suggested for Piston an important role. Carter greeted Piston's eightieth birthday by stating that the composer "was a ray of light at the Harvard of my time, when the contemporary was considered not teachable in any of the arts."[4] And in his classic 1946 article on Piston, he recalled that Piston's music had "dazzled" him and his Harvard colleagues "by their remarkable command."[5] As for Bernstein, for whom Piston's class in fugue was as close as he ever came to actual lessons in composition, he wrote, "Everything he [Piston] taught me has stuck—especially the example of his highly refined ear, and his non-pedantic approach to such academic subjects as fugue. . . . I loved his own music (and still do) although I cannot say that I was particularly influenced by it stylistically (as I was by Copland)—except in the matter of the highest standards of craftsmanship and clarity of sonic intention."[6] Such standards set a high ideal that, for the moment, Bernstein and Carter agreed was to be found only in a small number of contemporary composers.

Not surprisingly, their music from this period, with its strong ties to Copland, Piston, Hindemith, and Stravinsky, took on a similar profile. In the following passages—the first from Carter's 1940 *Pastoral* for viola and piano (Ex. 18), the second from the closing movement of Bernstein's 1942

Example 18. Elliott Carter, *Pastoral* for viola and piano (New Music Society, 1945).

Sonata for clarinet and piano (Ex. 19)—the relation to Piston and Copland (and to each other) was particularly marked, not least in the slightly nervous 5/8 rhythms, in the clear, open intervals, and in the way vaguely modal melodies outlined triads. The extreme delicacy of both passages—Carter's through the restrained use of both piano staves in treble clef, Bernstein's through the piano's pianissimo staccati occasionally breaking out in Baroque-like mordants—pointed specifically to Piston, for his kind of delicacy was rare even among the modernists; Carter, in fact, referred to the *Pastoral* as his "Walter Piston piece."[7] What is intriguing is not so much the accumulated debts, but the individual voices so prescient of later, highly characteristic works. Carter and Bernstein, in other words, did not explode on the musical scene; their developments were evolutionary. Considering works like these, one was reminded of, say, the young Beethoven finding his way among the legacy of Haydn, Mozart, and Clementi.

Carter's *First Symphony* (1942) and Bernstein's *First Symphony* ("Jeremiah," 1943) were the major achievements of this early, apprenticeship period. In the Carter work, there was a robust passion already his own (though in its busy moments there was some similarity to David Diamond's remarkable work from the 1930s); still, the contrapuntal sophistication, the textural elegance, the pastoral sweetness, and the subtle modulations pointed alternately to Copland and even more so, Piston. Bernstein's *Symphony*—a stunning accomplishment for a 24-year-old—opened with the obvious imprint of Harris's *Third Symphony* (some listeners also might think of Barber); but as the work progressed, the technical control and textural finesse pointed to lessons learned from Piston and Copland. Partly this had to do, as with Carter, with the use of modulation and tonality to create satisfying and interesting rhythmic designs.

In the tradition of Copland and Piston, these early works

Example 19. Leonard Bernstein, *Sonata* for clarinet and piano, II (Warner Bros., 1943).

were also related, more or less, to jazz. Wrote Carter, "I have always felt that my music derived from jazz of the late Thirties and Forties, particularly the jazz of 'Fats' Waller."[8] The influence of Fats Waller was most evident in Carter's *Piano Sonata,* with its strong rhythmic energy, its wild riffs, its extraordinary pianistic effects, and its use of the blues scale. But the influence of jazz was also noticeable in other Carter works, for instance, in the syncopations in the "Torture of John Smith" from *Pocahontas* (1936); in the ragtime-like "Giacoso" sections of the *Pastoral;* and in the Benny Goodmanish clarinet solo near the close of the *First Symphony.* Bernstein's involvement with jazz was even more intimate. At Harvard he wrote a senior honors thesis on "The Absorption of Race Elements into American Music" (1939). Later, he transcribed the music of Earl Hines, Coleman Hawkins, and others for Harms Music, and played boogie-woogie for servicemen during the War.[9] This involvement drew deep response in all of his early scores, but most notably in the ballet *Fancy Free* (1944).

It was precisely this involvement with jazz that highlighted a difference between the older generation of modernists and younger composers like Carter and Bernstein, for jazz itself had evolved. No longer the ironic and earthy art of the 1920s, swing was at once more exuberant and more sentimental. Carter, Bernstein, and their contemporaries paralleled this development. A comparable exuberance was found in these composers' fast movements, which were often quite frenetic, with jagged melodies supported by driving rhythms. A comparable sentimentality was captured in their slower paced music: the trumpet solos, for instance, in works as different as Bernstein's *Fancy Free,* Berger's *Serenade Concertante,* and the slow movements of Carter's *First Symphony* and Shapero's *Symphony for Classical Orchestra,* all breathed a similarly romantic air, one that was in some contrast to the more restrained and brittle atmosphere of the older modernists.

There was a related difference between the two generations of modernists, namely, a political one. Swing, after all, emerged in the '30s and reflected contemporary worldwide tensions. The older generation, whatever their individual politics (and they did indeed vary), tended toward the Enlightenment ideal of agrarian liberalism: individual liberty, limited government, rural life,[10] and peaceful and profitable international relations. The younger generation, on the other hand, rallied around the New Deal, the urban proletariat, and the anti-fascist front. In this Carter and Bernstein were no exception.[11] As young men, they were moved by Eisenstein's *Potemkin* in more ways than one,[12] and as adults, both were glad to lend their talents to Lincoln Kirstein's dream of an American ballet for the common man.[13] Carter found a congenially dissident temper in the poetry of Herrick, Gay, Whitman, and Crane; his setting of Herrick's "Harvest Home" was thought by Paul Rosenfeld to be "one of the best of leftist chants."[14] Bernstein never published a cycle of anti-fascist songs undertaken in 1943,[15] but the *Jeremiah Symphony* of the same year spoke related sentiments. He also gently poked fun at bourgeois music-making in the 1943 song cycle, *I Hate Music!* In 1944 Carter commemorated the liberation of Paris in the *Holiday Overture,* while Bernstein celebrated the breezy vivacity of the American sailor in *Fancy Free.* Carter and Bernstein may have learned their fundamental respect for the common man from the older modernists, but the times encouraged a more radically left-wing outlook.

If it were only a matter of the new jazz and leftist politics, Carter and Bernstein would not have differed too much from such contemporaries as Berger and Fine, composers once dubbed by Copland as America's "Stravinsky school." But Carter and Bernstein deviated from the modernist tradition in other ways as well, and, moreover, in ways that were similar insofar as they tended toward romanticism. This was most clearly seen by the enormous role that literature played in their work. Carter actually had majored in English at Harvard, where Bernstein also studied languages and literature extensively. Carter initially was known as a composer of songs and choruses, and Bernstein always was best known for his theatrical works.[16] Nor were their literary tastes exclusive: both, for instance, had special admiration for Hart Crane[17] and Auden.[18] Of course, the older modernists were quite literary, and Stravinsky especially well-known for his text settings and theatrical works. But the romantic impulse behind Carter and Bernstein manifested itself through their tendency to attach literary ideas to instrumental works, something eschewed, if not actually scorned, by the older

modernists.[19] Even their first symphonies, modernist though
they were in so many respects, were animated by literary
ideas. Carter's *Symphony* was inspired by the landscape and
cultural heritage of New England;[20] one could hear the
chirping of birds at the close of the first movement (much as
one could hear the shrieking of gulls in the much later
Symphony for Three Orchestras), the singing of hymns in the
second movement, and the stomping of country fiddlers in
the finale. The three movements of Bernstein's *Jeremiah
Symphony* were likewise descriptive, though the composer
noted, "The intention is . . . not one of literalness, but of
emotional quality. Thus the first movement ('Prophecy') aims
only to parallel in feeling the intensity of the prophet's plea
with his people. . . ."[21] In the course of their careers, Carter
and Bernstein were as ready to disclaim literary meanings in
their work as they were to suggest them. Carter was especially
ambivalent in this regard, subtly invoking, as the case might
be, Joyce (the *Cello Sonata*), Mann (the *First Quartet*),
Theophrastus (the *Variations for Orchestra*), Beckett (the
Second Quartet), Lucretius and Pope (the *Double Concerto*), Job
(the *Piano Concerto*), and Mallarmé and William Carlos
Williams (*Night Fantasies*).[22] In addition, both wrote a few
works which, if not as literal as, say, Richard Strauss, were at
least as descriptive as Liszt or Debussy, namely, Carter's
Concerto for Orchestra (after St. John Perse) and *Symphony for
Three Orchestras* (after Hart Crane); and Bernstein's *Age of
Anxiety Symphony* (after Auden) and *Serenade* (after Plato).
Bernstein went a step further: he put words to instrumental
portions of *Fancy Free* ("Big Stuff"), *Facsimile* ("After-
thought"), and the *Mass* ("Things Get Broken").[23]

Their early work evidenced a certain romanticism in purely
musical terms as well. The harmonies were rich and somber,
the melodic lines were twisted and restless, and the forms
were spontaneous and evocative, with melodies transformed
from movement to movement somewhat in the spirit of the
Wagnerian leitmotif. Often the resultant romanticism had a
brooding quality closer to Harris than any other of the older
modernists, or to Diamond and Barber, as mentioned.
Harris's influence was particularly keen in Bernstein's *Jeremiah Symphony* and in some passages in Carter's *Holiday
Overture*. Significantly, Carter and Bernstein, like Harris,

were serious students of Renaissance music. Carter and Bernstein even surpassed Harris by occasionally writing music that was frankly neo-Renaissance, Carter in his early career, Bernstein later on. This included songs in the manner of Dowland (Carter's "Tell Me Where Is Fancy Bred" and Bernstein's "It Must Be So" from *Candide*) and choruses in Renaissance style (Carter's "To Music" and Bernstein's incidental music to *The Lark*). The "Pavanne" from Carter's *Pocahontas* and the finale from Bernstein's *Jeremiah Symphony* (especially that music used afterwards as an "Anniversary" for Natalie Koussevitzky) were among some of their instrumental music that appeared to look back to the Renaissance.

In addition to this interest in Europe's remote past, they shared an enthusiasm for exotic music.[24] This found a picturesque outlet in the American Indian dances from *Pocahontas* and the Jewishness of the *Jeremiah Symphony*, but may have been related more generally to their musical styles, for instance, in their marked preference at times for pentatonic melodies and unusual meters. In fact, Carter's "metric modulation" can perhaps best be viewed in the context of classical Indian music.

In short, the early works of Carter and Bernstein shared basic affinities, both in their debt to modernism and in their deviations from it, that were not necessarily evident in their mature work. But quite early on, Carter and Bernstein also revealed highly individual temperaments. This individuality crystallized around 1944 with the former's *Holiday Overture* and the latter's *Fancy Free*.

The *Holiday Overture* stood at the crossroads of Carter's development. It opened in a jaunty idiom like Piston's and proceeded to an intensity like Harris's, but as the piece progressed, it grew more powerful and intense: the lines became more frantic, the harmonies more dissonant, the rhythms more intricate, and the textures more daring. Finally, there was a brief, tumultuous climax, featuring the brass, and a tonal conclusion that was as much a revelation as it was a resolution. The work was clearly an act of self-discovery.

Fancy Free was no less important for Bernstein. The work's distinctive personality—the romantic tenderness, the soaring lyricism, and the prankish humor—overshadowed its obvious debt to Copland and Stravinsky. Moreover, it made effective use of the styles and orchestrations of American popular music. In part inspired by Jerome Robbins's comparable blend of Balanchine's modernism and Broadway's razzle-dazzle, this kind of popular modernism proved thoroughly winning.

As the 1940s wore on, Carter and Bernstein continued to stretch the limits of modernism. In addition to some lighter efforts, Carter wrote two thorny, remarkable works, the *Piano Sonata* (1946) and the *Cello Sonata* (1948), that gave incredible punch and vitality to the modernist tradition, and that rightfully placed him in the forefront of the new music scene. Bernstein, for his part, successfully adapted *Fancy Free* for the Broadway stage (*On the Town,* 1944) and wrote a glittering piano concerto-cum-symphony, the *Age of Anxiety Symphony* (1949), that supported the popular contention that he was a sort of American Shostakovich. But it was not until around 1950 that Carter and Bernstein really went beyond the realm of the modernist tradition.

Carter's *8 Etudes and a Fantasy* for woodwind quartet (1950) was a decisive turning point in his career. It was written, significantly, less as a concert work than as a compositional exercise, each etude exploring a different compositional challenge: textural contrasts (Etude I), musical stasis (Etude II), color changes (Etude III), intervallic mini-malism (Etude IV), registral extremes (Etude V), idiomatic techniques (Etude VI), dynamic changes (Etude VII), and octave displacement (Etude VIII). (Carter similarly had explored purely rhythmic problems in his *Eight Pieces* for solo timpani from the preceding year.) This intense, somewhat abstract concern for color, register, dynamics, and rhythm stood in contrast to the older modernists who, while not insensitive to these elements, used them to delineate form, not as primary subjects in their own right. In fact, it was their revisionist attitude toward the color principle of late Roman-ticism that had helped define their aesthetic in the first place. In contrast to the modernists, the formal structure of the *8 Etudes,* especially the larger form, was of secondary impor-tance: Carter even prefaced the score with "suggestions for incomplete concert performance." Each etude stood on its own as a little, independent sonic adventure. These adven-tures were quite visceral, and often suggested a novel dimension of musical time and space. In Etude II, for instance, each voice, like a part of a mobile, repeated the same phrase in ever-changing contexts (Ex. 20); Etude IV was compared by the composer to a mosaic (Ex. 21). This exploration of musical time and space suggested some relation to the avant-garde as represented by Boulez; but Carter was less interested in 12-tone methodology, or, for that matter, any "organization." His basic impulse was more impressionistic, closer to Varèse than to Webern. And, like Varèse, who was a boyhood enthusiasm and whose music Carter had begun to rediscover, the *Etudes* were suggestive of modern urban life. Etude VII, the famous study on a single pitch, was like the void of a telephone dial tone; Etudes VI and VIII were like the jumble of city traffic, or like a tape recorder in reverse. The *Etudes* were as poetic as those Carter works prefaced by literary excerpts.

The *8 Etudes,* however, did not represent a total break from the modernist tradition: for all its novelty, the work was cool, concise, and polished. Etude V (Ex. 22a), in fact, recalled the second of Piston's *Three Pieces* for flute, clarinet, and bassoon, written in 1925 (Ex. 22b). (Years later, in 1978, Carter requested that this early Piston work be played at a concert honoring his seventieth birthday.[25]) There were also connections with jazz, for example, Etude IV with bebop (see Ex. 21), and Etude VII with Charlie Parker's "sheets of sound." Furthermore, all of these little pieces were streamlined. Etude I, for instance, presented an elegant ABA design whose middle section (mm. 8-15) featured the oboe and clarinet in long notes. In the more complex Etude II, articulation was provided by moments of repose at measures 2-3, 8, 13-14, and 21-22 (see Ex. 20); while in the mosaicked Etude IV, the fortissimo unisons functioned as a sort of ritornello (see Ex. 21). Even the Etudes using only a single pitch (Etude VII) or triad (Etude III) showed careful attention to formal balance. Although the *Etudes* were often harmonically intricate (this was Carter's first work, significantly, to do without a key signature), there was throughout a firm sense of tonal tension and resolution. This combination of old and new was epitomized by the Fantasy that concluded the work. Here all the sound innovations of the preceding Etudes were incorporated into a fugal form that included augmentation, diminution, and stretto. It well exemplified Carter's call for "a new universe of emancipated discourse" that does not sacrifice "a knowledge and feeling for the high standards of coherence and meaning which the musical tradition has brought to great subtlety."[26]

"A new universe" was an apt metaphor for Carter's aspirations. The works that followed the *8 Etudes and a Fantasy* were more and more fluid and open-ended, reflec-

Example 20. Elliott Carter, *8 Etudes and a Fantasy*, II (Associated Music, 1955).

IV

Example 21. Elliott Carter, *8 Etudes and a Fantasy,* IV (Associated Music, 1955).

tive, arguably, of the new "space age" in which they were written. These works displayed a special fondness for opposing heterogeneous elements, for instance, the *First Quartet* (1951), whose slow movement pitted the earthy cello and viola against the celestial violins; the *Sonata for Flute, Oboe, Cello and Harpsichord* (1952), with its color contrasts; the *Variations for Orchestra* (1955), which simultaneously developed three separate ideas; the *Second Quartet* (1959), in which the individual parts were set off from one another by their character and intervallic content; and the *Double Concerto* (1961), which opposed "two contrasting worlds of musical expression"[27] and whose opening Carter compared to the

V

Example 22a. Elliott Carter, 8 *Etudes and a Fantasy,* [This example is just 8 *Etudes and a fantasy,* V.] First 3 measures of No. 2, first 5 measures of No. 4, first 3 measures of No. 5. Copyright by Associated Music Publishers, Inc. All rights reserved. Used by permission.

formation of the universe as described in Lucretius's *De rerum natura.*[28] Eventually there were works that juxtaposed movements (the *Third Quartet,* 1971), ensembles (the *Symphony for Three Orchestras,* 1976), and even texts (*Syringa,* 1978). These works pulsed and quivered with a sort of primal, organic quality. And yet there was, too, a well-developed feeling for "high standards of coherence and meaning." Carter's amazing flux and diversity always was based on some chord or melody or interval, and it was, indeed, easier to perceive the underlying unity in his work than in much contemporary 12-tone music that was "totally organized." Especially impressive was the way in which Carter reached those remarkably complex climaxes that capped most of his music since the *Holiday Overture.*

In his music from the early '50s, Carter's cosmic or mystic urge remained tempered by modernist criteria. The balance of daring and eloquence in, for instance, the *First Quartet* placed that work more or less in the tradition of Beethoven, Brahms, and Piston. In the *Sonata for Flute, Oboe, Cello and Harpsichord,* sound innovations served, as they had in the *Etudes,* a rather formal grace and wit; and in the *Variations for Orchestra,* textural complexities helped define and enliven its classical structure. In all these works, the modernist tradition was still evident in the use of long melodic lines, thematic sequences, motor rhythms, imitative techniques, jazz elements, and tonal cadences. But then came a silence of four years and, finally, in 1959, another Carter landmark, the *Second Quartet.*

In this work, the remnants of modernism all but disappeared: spontaneity, suspense, and ambiguity were now distinctly favored over form, elegance, and clarity. The *Quartet,* it is true, was divided into four movements bridged by cadenzas, a form Piston himself was to use for his *Clarinet Concerto;* but the whole was rounded by an introduction and conclusion that gave the work an air of mystery. Further ambiguities arose from thematic cross-references, such as the use of the first movement's main theme in the cadenza connecting the third and fourth movements. The work's tonal language, like its formal logic, tended toward the evocative. In the composer's opinion, the work's most noteworthy feature was its absolute differentiation between the parts.[29]

Example 22b. Walter Piston, *Three Pieces* for flute, clarinet, and bassoon, II (Associated Music, 1933).

Like Ives, and indeed inspired by Ives, Carter likened his *Second Quartet* to four people conversing. He even outdid Ives in textural complexity: there was not one simultaneous attack in the *Quartet*'s slow movement, and one theorist counted forty-six vertical combinations in just one measure at the work's climax.[30] There was consequently a loss of the central, cohesive voice of, say, the *First Quartet*. The work reflected certain contemporary trends in Europe, especially the work of Boulez, but perhaps was understood best as a response to certain literary ideas and techniques, especially those of Joyce, Kafka, and Proust, the writers Carter most often cited. The *Quartet* indeed seemed to express something comparable to Joyce's stream-of-consciousness, Kafka's ironic detachment, and Proust's psychological subtlety.

The *Second Quartet* represented, arguably, the high point of Carter's career. Listeners were impressed especially with the work's originality. Paul Henry Lang, for instance, wrote, "The music is cleansed of all neo-classic motorism, post-impressionistic sunlamp glow, quasi Baroque muscle-flexing, and grim dodecaphonic dice-throwing. Nor does it flirt with jazz or with exotic cantillation."[31] The work was awarded the 1960 Pulitzer Prize, the 1960 New York Music Critics Award, and the 1961 UNESCO First Prize. It solidified Carter's international reputation and established the course he was to follow in later works.

While Carter's artistic development in the 1950s unfolded in a series of quartets, Bernstein's largely took place in the theater. Following the success of *On the Town,* he collaborated once more with Adolph Green and Betty Comden for another Broadway hit, *Wonderful Town* (1952). Both musicals had great charm and vitality—the movie version of *On the Town* became a classic of its genre—but they were not the real Bernstein, as represented by *Trouble in Tahiti* (1952), *Candide* (1956), and *West Side Story* (1957). Their books and lyrics gave little scope for much depth or originality. Both were romantic tales about provincial Americans in New York City, vehicles that were nicely suited for sentimental remembrances of "Main Street" and "Ohio," and tourist snapshots of "New York, New York" and "Christopher Street."

Trouble in Tahiti, a one-act opera that explored the conflicts and illusions of a suburban couple named Sam and

Dinah, was more personal and complex. Bernstein wrote the libretto himself; Sam, significantly, was his father's name. The work's opening number for jazz trio, in the role of Greek chorus, was detached and ironic, closer to cool jazz than to swing. In a bit of self-mockery, Bernstein even set the word "suburbia" to the principal motive from *On the Town*'s "New York, New York." The irony intensifies as Sam and Dinah make their appearance, at which point the slick tribute to suburbia, transposed to minor, underscores a bitter domestic quarrel which explodes into an instrumental interlude suggestive of a commuter train, as Sam rushes off to work (Ex. 23). In this attempt to capture the tensions and frustrations of postwar urban life, the composer reached out into new terrain. This new urban realism—vibrant, breathless, and violent—was to find an especially suitable vehicle with *West Side Story*, set as it is in the slums of New York City. Especially noteworthy in this regard was *West Side Story*'s instrumental music, with its innovative use of snapping fingers, bongos, police whistles, and shrill brass. In his score to Elia Kazan's

Example 23. Leonard Bernstein, *Trouble in Tahiti* (G. Schirmer, 1953).

1954 *On the Waterfront,* Bernstein introduced this hard-edged tone to Hollywood as well; here the New York harbor was no longer *On the Town*'s port of call for sailors on a spree, but rather the setting for vice, corruption, and labor union struggles. The urban realism of all these works was as influential in contemporary film music and musical theater as Carter's psychological realism was in contemporary chamber music.

While Bernstein's urban realism may have been the most compelling aspect of his stage works, it was not the only one. *Candide,* in fact, made no use of it; and in *Trouble in Tahiti* and *West Side Story,* it served primarily as a backdrop, depicting characters only in moments of stress, as in the aforementioned duet from *Trouble in Tahiti,* or "Cool" and "A Boy Like That" from *West Side Story.* Indeed, most of Bernstein's songs had a warmth that was very different from the cold violence of his city landscapes, and very often they had, too, a special kind of humor.

Bernstein's humor was closer to the broad satire of Sullivan than to the sensuous elegance of Strauss and Lehár, or the whimsical irony of Porter and Gershwin. The operetta *Candide,* with its young lovers, its ridiculous baritone, and its crusty old contralto, was especially reminiscent of Gilbert and Sullivan. The work parodied a wide range of styles, including the pastorale ("Oh, Happy We"), the cabaletta aria ("Glitter and Be Gay"), the Jeanette MacDonald-Nelson Eddy movie musical ("You Were Dead, You Know"), and 12-tone composition ("Quiet"). Bernstein's other stage works also, to some extent, engaged in parody. *Trouble in Tahiti* satirized radio jingles in its "Prelude," and movie musicals in "What a Movie"; *West Side Story* made comic use of Latin music in "America," and vaudevillian shenanigans in "Officer Krupke." These parodies used the time-honored techniques of exaggerating a musical style, or using an incongruous text, or both. But where Bernstein differed from older traditions was in sometimes making commercialism and bad taste, not the character per se, the principal object of parody. In fact, the characters were often in on the joke. This was most explicit in "What a Movie," in which the sophisticated heroine admits that the movie musical she fervidly describes to her hairdresser is "escapist Technicolor twaddle" (Ex. 24). (Fur-

Example 24. Leonard Bernstein, "What a Movie," *Trouble in Tahiti* (G. Schirmer, 1953).

ther ambivalence was suggested by the fact that the "twaddle" faintly resembled *South Pacific,* a work Bernstein held up as a theatrical model;[32] moreover, at the phrase, "There's a legend," the melody punned, intentionally or not, "Cheek to Cheek" by Irving Berlin, whom he also admired.) A similar sort of humor characterized much of *Candide,* for example, "Glitter and Be Gay," in which Cunegonde slyly satirizes the melodrama of Verdi's "Sempre libera"; or "I Am Easily Assimilated," in which the cosmopolitan old lady wittily spices her tango with East European inflections. In "Officer Krupke," the music-hall idiom that was lightly, even quaintly, satirized in *On the Town,* is here facetiously used by city hoodlums to deride the liberal establishment. In these and like examples, the wit reflected an urbane and modern sensibility that was known as "camp" humor. Very often this sort of humor eluded the male characters[33]—"Officer Krupke" presented something of an exception—and it is worth noting that such humor, in large part, originated and thrived in gay circles. Bernstein's use of it proved as new and innovative as his urban realism, and probably more important in terms of the history of the American musical comedy. Susan Sontag explained the attraction of camp by observing, "The traditional means for going beyond straight serious-ness—irony, satire—seem feeble today, inadequate to the culturally oversaturated medium in which contemporary sensibility is schooled. Camp introduces a new standard: artifice as an ideal, theatricality."[34]

There was yet another dimension to the Bernstein stage works—a yearning for a return from the violence and "camp" of contemporary life to some peaceful state of innocence, sometimes having utopian overtones. This was expressed in two principal ways: as a sort of wistful idealism ("There Is a Garden" and "Long Ago" from *Trouble in Tahiti;* "Eldorado" and "Ballad of the New World" from *Candide;* and "Something's Coming" and "One Hand, One Heart" from *West Side Story*) and as a more sober and realistic hope for the future ("Is There a Day" from *Trouble in Tahiti;* "Make Our Garden Grow" from *Candide;* and "Somewhere" from *West Side Story*). There were notable differences among all these songs, however. The wistful ones tended to be rather intimate, but "There Is a Garden" and "Long Ago," as well as "One Hand, One Heart," specifically evoked Satie; "Eldorado" and "Ballad of the New World" had the elegant lyricism of Piston's *Incredible Flutist;* while the more vigorous "Something's Coming" was closer to Copland. The more sober songs, which provided these three stage works with their finales, were, accordingly, grander and more dramatic; they typically outlined a sweeping minor seventh, and were treated canonically, often over a tonic pedal. In "Make Our Garden Grow," the minor seventh comprised two perfect fourths, in the tradition of Piston and Copland (a melodic gesture also found in "A Boy Like That" from *West Side Story,* as will be discussed in chapter 8). In "Is There a Day," the minor seventh—here descending—was part of a four-note motive (Ex. 25a) that recalled the Stravinsky *Octet* (Ex. 25b); this particular transformation of a chic and amusing '20s idea to an expression of desperate hope, epitomized both Bernstein's debt to modernism, and his success in giving it new, urgent meanings. "Somewhere" was even more thoroughly his own.

West Side Story was probably the most important of Bernstein's stage works. It subordinated all the aforementioned elements in the interest of a large, compelling dramatic form. Moreover, it addressed the racism, alienation, and violence that tore through postwar life, though its portrayal of

Example 25a. Leonard Bernstein, "Is There a Day," *Trouble in Tahiti* (G. Schirmer, 1953).

Example 25b. Igor Stravinsky, *Octet,* III (Boosey & Hawkes, 1947).

a social underclass had, like Gershwin's *Porgy and Bess,* an artificiality that some found disconcerting. (In later years, the work's lyricist, Stephen Sondheim, commented wryly on his naiveté in writing a Noel Cowardish lyric, "I Feel Pretty," for Maria.) According to the composer, the work's main significance was in its potential as a model for the development of the American musical theater; he hoped the work might prove a turning point comparable to the role of Mozart's "Singspiel" in the history of German opera.[35] Its success in this regard remained an open question. But there was no doubt that the work took the ideals of *The Magic Flute* very much to heart: it represented a brilliant synthesis of popular and serious elements. This was especially evident in its more operatic moments: Tony's recitative and aria, "Maria"; the love duets; the ensemble, "Tonight"; and the duet for Anita and Maria, "A Boy Like That," which here takes its Verdi rather seriously. And as in Bernstein's 1949 *Prelude, Fugue and Riffs* for jazz band, there was also a masterful fugue in jazz style. At a time when "third stream" was a portentous slogan for some avant-garde intentions, Bernstein fulfilled like aspirations with consummate skill and ease.

Considering the similarities between Carter and Bernstein in their early years, were works like the *Second Quartet* and *West Side Story* also somehow related? It appears that both composers forged their mature styles about 1950; clearly, the limits of modernism could not meet their needs for a new, postwar style, but neither could the prevailing fashion for serial and chance music. With their highly literary impulses, both attempted to capture the newness of postwar life in vivid, poetic ways. Carter was intrigued with the sights and sounds of the city, the discoveries of modern science, and the flux and subtlety of ordinary conversation; Bernstein was intrigued by the violence, humor, and moral despair of contemporary life. Carter, in other words, proved more the phenomenologist, finding chamber music the best forum for his ideas; Bernstein, more the sociologist, preferred the bold strokes of the theater.

That there was still an underlying bond was nowhere better illustrated than in two later works: Carter's 1969 *Concerto for Orchestra* (which Bernstein, incidentally, premiered, and to whom it was dedicated) and Bernstein's 1971 *Mass*. Both were clearly reactions to the chaos of the late 1960s.[36] Carter's inspiration was St. John Perse's poem about America, "Vents," whose winds ". . . having exposed to the air the attrition and drought in the heart of men in office, Behold, they produced this taste of straw and spices, in all the squares of our cities. . . ." Perse's ubiquitous wind metaphor encouraged Carter to extend his search further for spontaneous, fluid forms and new orchestral sounds. Bernstein's *Mass,* inspired at least to some extent by the composer's friendship with the antiwar activist Father Berrigan, interrupted its Latin text with denunciations of "you people in power" and confessions of anger and emptiness. For this work, Bernstein accommodated an even wider range of styles, including aleatoric music, rock, "folk" music, and "rhythm and blues." In both works, then, the force of nature—whether the "very great winds" or the "word of the Lord"—triumphs over the day's cataclysmic events and encourages new stylistic adventures.

If Carter and Bernstein were a bit like the opposite sides of the same coin, then this was highly symptomatic of the times. In painting, for instance, there was abstract expressionism and pop art, two movements that were obviously related, and yet very different in impact. Carter, in fact, described his aims as comparable to those of the abstract expressionists,[37] while Bernstein's stage designs for *Trouble in Tahiti* anticipated pop art by a number of years.[38] In poetry there was a similar relationship between the "confessional" and the "beat" poets. Significantly, Carter set the poetry of Elizabeth Bishop and went to work on a cycle of poems by Robert Lowell,[39] while

Bernstein, for his part, set poems by Frank O'Hara and Lawrence Ferlinghetti; his *Kaddish Symphony,* furthermore, suggested some kinship with Allen Ginsberg's poem of the same name. These lines were not hard and fast, as evident from Carter's setting of Ashbery's "Syringa," and Bernstein's consideration of some poems by Robert Lowell for his *Kaddish Symphony.*[40] Rather, they formed the complex web of postwar American modernism.

And what of the older modernist tradition? Did it survive in the mature work of Carter and Bernstein? To be sure, Carter and Bernstein reevaluated the music of the 19th century, toward which they showed much more sympathy: Carter found particularly helpful inspiration in Schumann, Debussy, and Scriabin; Bernstein in Verdi, Satie, and Mahler. Both, furthermore, were instrumental in bringing Charles Ives to public attention, though they were attracted to Ives for different reasons.[41] They also traced histories for themselves that had little to do with modernism: Carter in "Expressionism and American Music,"[42] Bernstein in "American Musical Comedy."[43] But they continued to hold Copland, Piston, and Stravinsky in high esteem, and although they placed less emphasis on design and clarity than did the older modernists, their works never wanted for elegance or expert craftsmanship. Further, in the spirit of American modernism, they continued to cultivate a jazzlike rhythmic vigor and freedom along with a Baroquelike contrapuntal finesse and discipline. This was evident in works as late as Carter's 1965 *Piano Concerto,* with its concertino, and his 1976 *Symphony for Three Orchestras,* with its antiphonal textures, as well as in Bernstein's 1971 *Mass* and his 1980 *Divertimento* for orchestra. Most importantly, they strove to interpret their complex world as truthfully as they could for the benefit of their fellow man. In this they were truly successors of the modernist tradition.

Notes

1. Such concerns expressed themselves in Hindemith's chamber works for amateurs, Copland's music for high school students,

Piston's ballet for the Boston Pops, and Stravinsky's music for the circus.

2. Carter's reviews for *Modern Music* are reprinted in *The Writings of Elliott Carter,* compiled, edited, and annotated by Else Stone and Kurt Stone (Bloomington: Indiana University Press, 1977); Bernstein's reviews for *Modern Music* can be found in Vol. 15 (pp. 103–106; 239–241), 16 (pp. 182–184), 19 (pp. 97–99), and 23 (pp. 10–11).

3. For Carter, see Allen Edwards, *Flawed Words and Stubborn Sounds* (New York: W. W. Norton, 1971), p. 40, and Carter, "Charles Ives Remembered," *Writings,* p. 258; for Bernstein, see David Ewen, *Leonard Bernstein* (New York: Chilton Company, 1960), p. 18, and John Gruen, *The Private World of Leonard Bernstein* (New York: Viking Press, 1968), p. 39.

4. "Happy 80th Birthday, Walter Piston," *Boston Globe,* January 20, 1974, A-9.

5. Carter, "Walter Piston," *Musical Quarterly* 32 (1946), pp. 354–375.

6. Bernstein, personal letter, October 5, 1977.

7. David Schiff, *The Music of Elliott Carter* (New York: Da Capo Press, 1983), p. 109. Schiff writes, "Piston's influence on Carter, however, should not be underestimated. Not only did Piston encourage him to go and study with Nadia Boulanger, but his music, which Carter began to know in the 1920s, forcefully illustrated the strengths of the new classicism." Carter, unfortunately, destroyed much of his music from the 1930s, including a 1934 *Flute Sonata,* and two *String Quartets* (1935 and 1937), works that well may have documented further debts to Piston. Concerning Bernstein's *Sonata,* its first movement, in some contrast to the second, was more decidedly like Hindemith. Hindemith remained an important influence: strains of *Mathis,* for instance, are heard at the very end of *Candide* (where it is neatly complemented by the coda of Stravinsky's *Firebird*) and, more pervasively, throughout much of the *Kaddish Symphony.*

8. Leighton Kramer, "Elliott Carter," *Saturday Review* (December 1980), p. 42.

9. Ewen, *Bernstein,* p. 48.

10. This was seen in works like Stravinsky's *Les Noces,* Piston's *The Incredible Flutist* and *Three New England Sketches,* Copland's *Appalachian Spring* and *The Tender Land,* and Harris's *Kentucky Spring.*

11. For Carter, see the interview at Oberlin College, February, 1973, a tape of which is in the Rodgers and Hammerstein

Sound Archive, Music Division, New York Public Library, and
Edwards, *Flawed Words,* p. 53n; for Bernstein, see Thomas
Cole, "Can He Really Be 50?," *New York Times,* August 18,
1968.

12. For Carter, see Edwards, *Flawed Words,* p. 99; for Bernstein,
see Irving Fine, "Young America: Bernstein and Foss," *Modern
Music* 22 (May–June 1945), p. 238.

13. This included Carter's music for *Pocahontas* (1936) and *The
Minotaur* (1947), and Bernstein's score to *Fancy Free* (1944).
Neither Carter ballet was a success. *Pocahontas* was too somber
to rival Copland's *Billy the Kid* or Thomson's *Filling Station,*
though its importance was not lost on Hunter Johnson, who
wrote to Carter after seeing the ballet, "I hear you, and my
country suddenly takes on stature" (letter from Johnson to
Carter, June 8, 1939, Carter Collection, Music Division, New
York Public Library). *The Minotaur,* a still better score, might
have become a classic if Balanchine had choreographed it as
originally intended. *Fancy Free,* on the other hand, was an
instant and enduring hit.

14. Rosenfeld, "The Newest American Composers," *Modern Music*
15 (January–February 1938), p. 158.

15. Unidentified newspaper clipping, Bernstein file, Music Division, New York Public Library.

16. In the course of his career, Carter set Greek fragments
(including Sappho and Aeschylus), Homer, Plato, Ovid, Rabelais, Shakespeare, Gay, Herrick, Dickinson, Whitman, Joyce,
Frost, Crane, Van Doren, Tate, Bishop, and Ashbery. Bernstein, for his part, set portions of the Psalms and Jeremiah, the
Latin Ordinary, chanson texts, and cookbook recipes, as well as
lyrics by Rilke, O'Hara, Ferlinghetti, Burgos, Whitman,
Hughes, Jordan, Bradstreet, Stein, Aiken, Corso, Millay, Poe,
Betty Comden and Adolph Green, Richard Wilbur, John
LaTouche, Dorothy Parker, Lillian Hellman, Stephen Sondheim, Stephen Schwarz, and Alan Jay Lerner; very often he
wrote his own texts, too.

17. For Carter, see Edwards, *Flawed Words,* p. 106; for Bernstein,
see "Bernstein Talks of his '76 Salute," *New York Times,*
October 1, 1974.

18. For Carter, see "Introduction to a Poetry Reading Session by
W. H. Auden," *Writings,* pp. 256–257; for Bernstein, see his
Norton lectures, *The Unanswered Question* (Cambridge: Har-
vard University Press, 1976).

19. Copland and Piston occasionally wrote what might be called
picturesque works, such as the former's *El Salòn Mèxico* and the

latter's *Tunbridge Fair*. But, for the most part, the modernists, especially Stravinsky, took pains to disassociate their instrumental music from literary interpretations.

20. Carter, record liner notes to the *First Symphony*, Louisville Records, LOU 611.
21. Bernstein, record liner notes to the *Jeremiah Symphony*, Columbia Records, MG 32793.
22. See the respective liner notes for these works in Carter's *Writings*, and Schiff, pp. 197, 315.
23. In *The Unanswered Question*, Bernstein used Chomsky's work in linguistics as a model to explain musical meaning.
24. For Carter, see Edwards, *Flawed Words*, p. 41; for Bernstein, see *The Unanswered Question*, p. 7.
25. Schiff, p. 110.
26. Carter, "A Further Step," *Writings*, pp. 186, 190.
27. Carter, "Music and the Time Screen," *Writings*, p. 353.
28. Carter, "Double Concerto," *Writings*, p. 329.
29. Carter, "Music and the Time Screen," p. 353. Carter's discussions of his own work, however, displayed an intellectual rigor that was not entirely borne out by the music itself, according to Rudolf Kompanek, *A Study of Elliott Carter's Double Concerto for Harpsichord and Piano with Two Chamber Orchestras*, MA Thesis, Eastman School of Music, 1972.
30. Eugene Schweitzer, *Generation in String Quartets of Carter, Sessions, Kirchner, and Schuller*, PhD thesis, Eastman School of Music, 1965, p. 41.
31. Lang, "Juilliard String Quartet," *Herald Tribune*, March 26, 1960. Similar tributes were forthcoming from Ross Parmenter (*New York Times*, December 22, 1960), Eric Salzman (*New York Times*, May 7, 1961), and Harold Taubman (*New York Times*, April 3, 1960), whose review was subtitled, "With Completion of New Work in the Form, Elliott Carter has Proved Himself to Be a Major Creative Artist."
32. Bernstein, "Whatever Happened to That Great American Symphony?," *The Joy of Music* (New York: Simon and Schuster, 1959), p. 51.
33. Candide, it is true, sings some parodistic duets with Cunegonde, but as her dupe. In "Oh, Happy We," for instance, Candide takes the pastoral ideal seriously while Cunegonde muses incongruously on aristocratic pleasures. Similarly, in their romantic duet à la Jeanette MacDonald and Nelson Eddy, Candide guilelessly asks, "Dearest, how can this be so? You were dead you know. You were shot and bayoneted too," to which Cunegonde replies, "That is very true. Ah, but love will

find a way." In other words, Candide is the object of straight satire, whereas Cunegonde knowingly satirizes various musico-dramatic conventions.

34. Sontag, "Notes on 'Camp'," *Against Interpretation and Other Essays* (New York: Delta, 1966), p. 288.

35. Gruen, *Private World*, p. 25.

36. Both composers remained politically active during this period, although Carter's persistent efforts on behalf of I Sang Yun, the South Korean composer accused of espionage by his country, were far less publicized than Bernstein's support of Martin Luther King, Father Berrigan, Eugene McCarthy, and the Black Panthers (the last of which inspired Tom Wolfe's satirical commentary, "Radical Chic," *New York Magazine*, June, 1970). Both Carter and Bernstein also actively supported the cause of dissident artists in the Soviet Union.

37. In "Current Chronicle: Italy," *Writings*, p. 178, Carter com-pared the use of time by composers like himself with the use of space by the abstract expressionists. Leonard Meyer objected to such comparisons in *Music, the Arts, and Ideas* (Chicago: University of Chicago, 1967), p. 251, while Schiff gave them serious consideration (pp. 24, 134–136).

38. In discussing "our friend Larry Rivers" with Bernstein, John Gruen (*Private World*, p. 151) comments that the painter combined "Pop, nostalgia, and the political," a remark that arguably could have described Bernstein as well.

39. Kramer, "Carter," p. 42.

40. Bernstein told Gruen, "he (Lowell) actually wrote three poems for it, three beautiful poems, but they're lyric poems of a certain obscurity which would not have served the purpose of immediacy needed in the concert hall," *Private World*, p. 40.

41. Carter arranged performances of *The Unanswered Question* and *Central Park in the Dark* in 1946, and Bernstein premiered Ives's *Second Symphony* in 1951. Carter was most impressed with Ives's polyrhythmic textures and his optimistic transcen-dentalism ("Charles Ives Remembered," *Writings*, p. 267), while Bernstein emphasized Ives's humor and charming use of Americana (record liner notes, Ives's *Four Symphonies*, Colum-bia Records, D3s 783).

42. Carter, *Writings*, pp. 230–243.

43. Bernstein, *Joy of Music*, pp. 152–179.

7. ADVENTURES IN WONDERLAND: IRVING FINE AND HIS MUSIC

BY PRODUCING A BODY OF WORK that uniformly was technically expert, stylistically sophisticated, and immediately accessible, Irving Fine (1914–1962) came about as close to the achievement of one of his favorite composers, Ravel, as did any American composer of his time. In this, too, he resembled Samuel Barber, whom he also admired (probably more than did many of his friends and colleagues). In the years following his early death, most of his music was regularly revived, if not a part of the standard concert repertory itself; in this latter category would belong most of his choral and vocal works, the *Partita* for wind quintet, the *Fantasia* for string trio, and *Serious Song* for string orchestra. All of his twenty major works were recorded,[1] only in small part due to his wife Verna's long association with CRI records. Fine scholarship and criticism were not quite as plentiful. Perhaps most insightful were informal remarks by such friends as Copland, Berger, and Bernstein. Also helpful were three dissertations from the mid-1960s that discussed single works by Fine in some context or another.[2]

Fine's career spanned only the twenty years from 1942 to 1962. He began writing music in the mid-1930s as an undergraduate at Harvard, where he studied theory and composition with Piston, orchestration with Hill, music history with A. Tillman Merritt, and choral conducting with Archibald Davison. He had already learned enough piano from Frances Grover to become the accompanist for the

Harvard Glee Club, and to make some money playing popular music and accompanying silent movies.

Most of his student compositions were, in fact, written for piano, including three works found in the Fine Collection at the Library of Congress: *Preludium and Fuga, Passacaglia,* and *Thing.* The *Preludium and Fuga,* which Fine entered in a Bohemian Club contest, was a scholarly exercise in the style of Bach. *Passacaglia* and *Thing* were neobaroque, too, but in a more contemporary, Hindemithian way. The *Passacaglia,* with its ultrachromatic theme and its accompaniment of chromatic major thirds, vaguely looked ahead to the mature Fine, while *Thing,* an atonal concoction aptly titled, was more clearly an experiment. Fine also wrote several canzoni and ricercari, a *Suite,* and a *Pastorale,* all for piano;[3] they do not seem to have survived, but their titles suggest preoccupations similar to those of the extant works. An early *Violin Sonata* also appears to be lost.[4] Two other student projects, however, have survived: the sketches for a neobaroque orchestral work reminiscent of Piston's *Concerto for Orchestra;* and the Gilbert and Sullivanish score to a musical comedy, *The Christmas Sparrow or Double or Nothin',* written in collaboration with fellow classmate John Horne Burns, and performed at Dunster House on December 16, 1936. This last contained songs like, "I am the Queen of the Biddies."

John Horne Burns, incidentally, went on to a career much like Fine's. His three moody, delicately crafted novels—*The Gallery* (1947), *Lucifer with a Book* (1949), and *A Cry of Children* (1952)—with their evocative blend of irony and elegy, were analogous to Fine's work, and they earned him a comparable critical reception. As with Fine, Burns's early death—in 1953 at age thirty-six—was mourned as a tremendous loss to American arts and letters. There is considerable evidence to suggest that David Murray, the pianist-composer protagonist of his last novel, *A Cry of Children,*[5] was modeled, in fact, after Fine. Murray's character—somewhat finicky, but more than redeemed by a gentility of manner—seemed to fit, as did the fact that he entertains friends by playing Jerome Kern at the piano (p. 29); loves Mozart and Debussy (pp. 58, 79); and performs, in recital, works by Stravinsky, Bach, Scriabin, and some modern Americans (p. 136). Some of the story's homosexual tensions also apply, for Burns was attracted to Fine (who, however, turned down his advances). The clincher is the premiere of a *Sinfonia concertante* by Koussevitzky in Symphony Hall, for the book was written shortly after Koussevitzky premiered Fine's *Toccata concertante*. This fictional composer's assessment of his work, that "it was like Vivaldi in 1952, with none of the meretriciousness of Stravinsky," was, however, sheer projection on the author's part, for Fine revered Stravinsky.

Fine graduated from Harvard cum laude in 1937 and took his master's degree the following year, studying with Piston at Harvard and with Nadia Boulanger, visiting professor at Radcliffe. In June, 1939, he left for Paris to continue his work with Boulanger, studying harmony and counterpoint. He also began a piece for cello and piano under her tutelage. In the course of the summer, he wrote often to his parents, telling them about Paris's rich concert life, a charming Algerian restaurant, "boring" Versailles, and the pride and solidarity of the French worker.[6] Fine had hoped to stay in Paris for at least a year, but the War forced him to return in October.

Back in Boston, Fine began a ten-year career at Harvard, first as a tutor at Radcliffe (1939–1940); then as a tutor and teaching fellow at Harvard (1940–1942); then as an instructor, assistant conductor of the Glee Club, and the conductor of the Naval Training School Glee Club (1942–1945); and finally as an assistant professor (1945–1950). When the U.S. declared war, he enlisted as a Naval officer, but before his commission came through, he was drafted and classified as 4-F; he failed the Army's neurological test because of irregular brain waves, the result of a teenage head concussion.[7] He nonetheless supported the war effort by writing a few patriotic things: two songs (the satiric "My Name is Mussolini" and the unfinished "When men of war roll ashore in Cambridge Town"); a choral piece, "It's the Navy," for the Naval Glee Club; and a choral arrangement of Stowe's "The Battle Hymn of the Republic" for a large rally in Boston in 1944.

On June 25, 1941, Fine married Verna Rudnick, whom he described as follows:

> My wife Verna has more than enough vivacity and charm to pull me out of the torpor that I occasionally find myself in, usually as a result of the sheer contempla-

tion of hard work—especially creative work. She also is very practical and orderly, has a positive genius for figures and accounts and taxes, adores luxurious living, but chiefly away from home—which means that she rarely gets it.[8]

Verna introduced Fine to a young lyricist, Maynard Kaplan, and in 1942 the two men collaborated on a number of songs: "This is Heaven," "A Letter from Paris," "A Kiss from Mister Liszt," "There'll Come a Day," "What Is this Warm Feeling," "Springtime," and "It's Funny Honey."[9] According to Verna Fine, their motive was simply to make some money, but they never found an interested publisher. (Fine's financial needs were better met by a piano piece, "Interlude," commissioned by Newsong Fabrics for a magazine advertisement.) The songs might have sold with better lyrics; even Fine's melodic gifts could do only so much for a line like, "Springtime is ringtime for Margie, Betty, and Jo, so, why can't it be for me?" But they were awkward musically as well, especially when it came to setting up the return of the main tune. Most of the songs, including the best one, "This Is Heaven," was in the tradition of Rodgers and Hart (Ex. 26); "A Letter from Paris" was more like Vernon Duke. The up-tempo numbers, "It's Funny Honey" and "A Kiss from Mister Liszt," were as close as Fine ever came to jazz: the former had a boogie-woogie bass, and the latter had a bluesy melody that quoted *Les Préludes.* Fine never again attempted to compose quite in this vein, but he continued to have some appreciation for such

Example 26. Irving Fine, "This Is Heaven."

styles; he thought Rodgers's "If I Loved You" the kind of melody he would have liked to have written, and he loved Bernstein's *West Side Story*.[10] There were, in any case, links between all these early popular songs and Fine's serious work, especially the vocal music.

During the War, Fine also wrote some music for two theatrical productions: one of Lorca's *Doña Rosita, the Spinster* (performed by the Harvard Dramatic Club on April 28, 1943) and Eva LeGallienne's adaptation of Carroll's *Alice in Wonderland* (performed at the Erskine School on May 22, 1942). For the Lorca production, Fine wrote two songs that were somewhat like da Falla: "What the Flowers Say" and "Because I Caught a Glimpse of You." For the latter, Fine dismissed Lorca's specific instructions for a polka, writing instead a languorously romantic tune. In contrast, "What the Flowers Say" had a more folklike vigor.

Fine needed to write many more songs as well as incidental music for the *Alice* production, and to meet the deadline, he called on the help of a young Harvard student, Allen Sapp. The show was a local success, and G. Wallace Woodworth, conductor of the Harvard Glee Club, suggested that Fine arrange some of his songs for mixed chorus. Fine selected "The Lobster Quadrille," "The Lullaby of the Duchess," and wrote a new "Father William," based on some of the music from the chorus, "It's the Navy" (Ex. 27).[11] These choruses, especially "Father William," quickly became great favorites with the Harvard Glee Club and with choral groups around the country. Fine orchestrated the set in 1949. In 1953 he arranged another three songs from the show, "The Knave's Letter," "The White Knight's Songs," and "Beautiful Soup," this time for women's voices alone.

Unlike those musical settings of Lewis Carroll that tended to sentimentalize the author, Fine's songs combined childlike innocence and sophisticated irony in ways that brilliantly matched their texts. Because this very blend was found in so many of Fine's later compositions, the *Alice* songs were better regarded as emblematic and seminal rather than as a mere commission. Rhythmically, for instance, the use of the chant ("Lobster Quadrille," "Knave's Letter") and the march ("Father William," "Beautiful Soup")[12] to impart a childlike vigor, and the lullaby ("Lullaby of the Duchess," "White Knight's

Example 27. Irving Fine, "Father William," *Alice in Wonderland* (M. Witmark, 1943).

Song") to suggest a childlike gentleness, looked ahead not only to the little children's piano pieces, *Victory March of the Elephants* and *Lullaby for a Baby Panda,* but to such serious works as the *Notturno* and the *Fantasia.* Melodically, the use of wavering major and minor thirds (explicitly related to children's taunts in "Father William") and drooping minor seconds (meant to evoke crying infants in "Lullaby of the Duchess") was similarly typical of the composer's style. Harmonically, too, the music's simple triads, thirds and sixths, triadic ostinati, and diatonic textures, all employed with childlike directness, proved characteristic.

In Carroll's kind of childlike playfulness, Fine found a sensibility akin to his own. Like Carroll, Fine's sophisticated, almost pedantic erudition complemented a breezy, charming ingenuousness. Alongside musical sketches, for instance, he would jot down risqué limericks set to baby tunes. He also indulged in childish fantasies to those close to him, such as his sister, to whom he once wrote, "I'm your leedle brudder Itzick, the boy with hair on his pipick, who is incidentally married to a noodnick nee Rudnick."[13] He gravitated toward Carroll naturally enough, much as he selected from the *New Yorker Book of Verse*,[14] for his *Choral New Yorker* for mixed chorus (1944), four poets who, whether or not he realized it, also happened to be writers of children's literature: Peggy Bacon, Isabel MacMeekin, David McCord, and Jake Falstaff. Fine returned once again to McCord for a 1956 work for men's chorus that proved very successful, *McCord's Menagerie*.

Fine himself wrote the equivalent of children's literature: the two aforementioned pieces for beginning pianists; *Homage à Mozart* for intermediate pianists (1956); and *Diversions for Orchestra* (1960), written for a Boston Symphony Children's Concert, and which returned in part to the original *Alice* score, this time to its incidental music. His one television score, the 1959 *One, Two, Buckle My Shoe* put out by the Green Shoe Manufacturing Company, set the mood for the rompings of a small girl. And Fine's two sets of *Childhood Fables for Grownups* for medium voice and piano (1954, 1955) had obvious similarities to *Alice*, including a cast of personalized animals. In fact, the number of animals found throughout Fine's work was extraordinary.[15] As a freshman at Harvard, he even had thought seriously about entering the field of zoology, but scientific inquiry eventually gave way to artistic fantasy.

The child's world that colored Fine's work was coupled with such wit and refinement that one was reminded of a much earlier generation of composers—of Americans like John Alden Carpenter and E. B. Hill, and French composers like Satie, Debussy, and Ravel. The straightforward musical materials as described were always highlighted by sophisticated stylistic references. "The Lobster Quadrille," for instance, combined the simple scalar patterns of a student exercise with the subtle harmonies of the Americana style then in vogue; while in "Father William," the popular children's taunt, "nah-nah-nah-nah-nah," was given a dainty setting somewhere between Mendelssohn and the Andrews Sisters. There were other like combinations in *Alice:* the wails of a baby and those of a blues singer in "Lullaby of the Duchess"; wide-eyed excitement and Broadway chic in

"Beautiful Soup." There was neither cynicism nor alienation in these parodies, but rather some hoped for harmony between child and man. Often this dialectic worked itself out through polytonality, as in "The Knave's Letter." Other times, there was a lustrous diatonicism, as in "The White Knight's Song," whose use of a Scottish folk idiom brought it close to Brahms's "Intermezzo" No. 1, Op. 117—a fitting allusion considering that Brahms and Carroll were exact contemporaries. In every case, Fine's music was marked by emotional detachment and expert technique, including elegantly spaced chords, sure harmonic flow, independent, lively bass parts, and felicitous, idiomatic writing. (Copland apparently was cognizant of these virtues when he asked that his *Old American Songs* for mixed chorus be arranged by Fine.) Such detachment and craft enabled him to be tender and nostalgic without being coy or saccharine.[16]

Fine's emotional detachment was strenuously cultivated. As early as 1934, he wrote to his parents, "I am certain now that solitude, and solitude only is conducive to any productiveness. One must have friends but not see them too much—at least when one is trying to develop himself."[17] In 1952 he wrote to his wife:

> I have been noticing that whenever I write something romantic and lyrical in a major key I get tense and rather depressed but that when I discover material of a powerful yet rather impersonal nature I feel quite elated. Don't know which comes first—the music or the mood. In the end I usually prefer the impersonal music. . . .[18]

And in some notes to himself, he wrote:

> The initial musical impulse must be strengthened by practice. It must be freed of anxiety. Only then can it leap forward. *Music is only notes.* Only by working at it with a playful, constructive attitude can we provide groundwork for inspiration. *God helps those who help themselves.* Outside help is a bonus. Let the mind attach itself fully, completely and without reservation, and without thought to self to that which is outside of it. Complete and total surrender—complete commitment

> is necessary. The presence of self in music is a flaw. That
> music which concerns itself least with self expression
> contains the richest personality.[19]

Fine nurtured this "playful, constructive attitude," by, for
example, improvising at the piano on tunes based on friends'
telephone numbers.[20] His sketchbooks revealed yet other
ways: he might develop some music from "Happy Birthday"
or some ditty, or he might assign a pitch to each letter of the
alphabet and create melodies derived from the names of
friends. These games were not ends in themselves; rather,
they were manipulated until the composer found what he
wanted. This attitude, which eventually had recourse to the
12-tone method, contained certain similarities to Carroll's use
of a chess game in *Through the Looking-Glass*.

How Fine's sensibility—in particular, his combination of
childlike directness and emotional detachment—was related
to his own childhood was a question the composer thought
best left to psychologists.[21] But he often reflected, nonetheless, on his troubled childhood. His parents, George and
Charlotte, were unhappily married; Fine once returned home
from school to find his mother attempting suicide.[22] Fine
frequently fought with his father, especially while at college,
and harbored resentments against his sister, Audrey.[23] He
wrote of his "constant sympathy" with his mother: "I would
like to have identified with my father," he confessed, "but I
identified really with my mother."[24] Fine's music occasionally
addressed such issues, as in "My Father" from *Mutability*.
There were, indeed, numerous depictions of parents in Fine,
including the sadistic Duchess and contemptuous Father
William from *Alice;* the murderous Caroline Million in *The
Choral New Yorker;* the loving mothers in "An Old Song" and
"Lenny the Leopard"; and the pathetic couple from Stephen
Crane's *Maggie,* on which Fine planned a musical: the
composer could undoubtedly relate to *Maggie*'s conflicts
between husband and wife, brother and sister, and father and
son.

Fine's need for an identifiable father was met in different
ways by Piston, Stravinsky, and Copland. Piston introduced
the young Fine to the world of modern music, and may have
helped him decide on a career as a composer. Fine adored

both the man and his music,[25] writing, "At times he is capable
of writing extremely abstract-sounding music, music which
reminds one of nothing else, and at other times he can
compose slow movements of a longing tenderness. He has a
special knack for turning out sparkling final movements that
bubble and bounce along with catching gaiety."[26] In a review
of Piston's *Prelude and Allegro* for organ and orchestra, Fine
found that its "clarity and nobility of expression" distinguished it from like works by Porter, Hanson, Poulenc, and
Sowerby.[27] Piston, for his part, was very fond of Fine, and
wrote on the occasion of Fine's death, "It is a tremendous loss
for all of us. He was a true friend as well as a most cultured,
sensitive, and gifted person."[28] Piston resigned from the
Harvard Musical Association in 1948 when one of its
members blocked Fine's nomination because he was Jewish.[29]
Fine, however, held Piston to some account when after ten
years of service he was denied tenure by Harvard, and his
bitterness over this may have colored his subsequent opinion
of Piston, who, Fine decided in 1957, "no longer offers us any
surprises."[30] In striking contrast to earlier statements, Piston's slow movements now "seem too long and stretched out"
and his finales "seem too short and almost perfunctory." Then
again, this sort of reassessment of Piston was characteristic of
the times.

Fine never suffered any disillusionment with Stravinsky. In
his mature view, Stravinsky's *Symphony of Psalms* stood with
Mozart's *Così fan tutte* and Beethoven's late quartets as an
example of musical perfection.[31] Fine's devotion to Stravinsky dated back to 1939 when the composer came to
Harvard to give the Norton Lectures; Fine, entrusted to
chauffeur Stravinsky about and to undertake the first translation in English of *Poétique musicale*,[32] became very
attached.

It was also at Harvard that Fine became friendly with
Copland, who came there in 1944 to teach Piston's classes.
The two performed Copland's *Danzón cubano* in April of
1944, and later in the year Fine traveled to Washington, D.C.
to hear the premiere of *Appalachian Spring*. Fine loved the
music, but was wary of following imitatively in its wake. After
the War, Fine and Copland spent many summers together at
Tanglewood;[33] their extensive correspondence only hinted at

their close friendship, for they communicated most often by telephone. Copland was more like an older brother to Fine than a father; Fine's three daughters, in fact, knew him as "uncle Aaron." Fine often wrote of Copland's "key position" in American music,[34] and especially admired the *Emily Dickinson Songs*.[35]

Fine's love for the music of Piston, Stravinsky, and Copland was exceptional in the context of his general views, which tended to be quite severe. In his reviews for *Modern Music* from the 1940s, he found fault with works by Fauré, Hindemith, Schoenberg, Prokofiev, Shostakovich, Villa-Lobos, and Martinů. When discussing still lesser composers, he could be barely tolerant, as in the following review of a Boston Symphony concert:

> Among the pieces heard here for the first time were Gretchaninov's *Elegy,* Opus 175, an agglomeration of the eclecticism of Glazunov and Rachmaninov, which, although completed in 1945, could have been written in 1880; John Ireland's *The Forgotten Rite,* written in 1913 and as pale and ineffective a piece of musical landscape as has been heard here in many a decade; Sir Arnold Bax's turgid, hybrid *Tintagel* of 1917 which Koussevitzky's good taste has spared us up till now; and Anthony Collins's *Threnody for a Soldier Killed in Action,* a hoax upon the public sympathies and a work whose musical substance is zero.[36]

Fine's tastes overlapped with a group of contemporary composers who were sometimes referred to as a "Stravinsky school,"[37] but whom Fine simply called a "later group of neoclassicists."[38] This group was the subject of a well-known article by Arthur Berger, who listed as its most important members Louise Talma (b. 1906), himself (b. 1912), Ingolf Dahl (1912–1970), Alexei Haieff (b. 1914), Fine, Harold Shapero (b. 1920), and Lukas Foss (b. 1922).[39] They were as much a Stravinsky school as were France's "Les Six," that is, a loose association of contemporary composers who admired Stravinsky's revitalization of tonality, pulse, textural clarity, and formal finesse. And like "Les Six," the more derivative features of their early works matured, in time, into greater and greater individuality, if they were ever that alike to begin with. Dahl, for instance, had a seriousness brought from his native Germany, and, similarly, Haieff had a brilliance inherited from his native Russia. Shapero early on made the sort of blatant references to Viennese Classicism that were rare in this circle, despite its "neoclassicist" label. Berger's brisk, distinctive personality was his own, as was Talma's. And Foss proved to be the most adventurous and unpredictable of the lot.

Fine, in fact, explored some of these particular stylistic differences in his two sets of *Childhood Fables* for voice and piano, for each of its songs was a sort of portrait of the composer-friend to whom it was dedicated:[40] Berger, Shapero, Haieff, and Foss (especially as represented by his opera, *The Jumping Frog of Calaveras County*) were successively parodied by "Polaroli" 's wide leaps and accented staccati (Ex. 28), "Tigeroo" 's ferocious energy (Ex. 29), "The

Example 28. Irving Fine, 8 measures from "Polaroli," from *Childhood Fables for Grownups.* Copyright by G. Schirmer, Inc. All rights reserved. Used by permission.

Example 29. Irving Fine, 9 measures from "Tigeroo," from *Childhood Fables for Grownups*. Copyright by G. Schirmer, Inc. All rights reserved. Used by permission.

Duck and the Yak" 's colorful drama,[41] and "The Frog and the Snake" 's youthful wit. In addition, there was a song dedicated to Bernstein, who, as close as he was with this group, was never quite accepted as one of them, as suggested by his omission from Berger's article. Fine tried not to make the song, called "Lenny the Leopard," "too sentimental" (Ex. 30).[42]

That Fine would undertake these sophisticated yet loving parodies suggested what was no doubt true: that he was attached to a fair number of fellow composers much as his music established contact with theirs. For even in those early instrumental works most reminiscent of Stravinsky—the *Sonata* for violin and piano (1946), the *Toccata Concertante* for orchestra (1947), the *Music for Piano* (1947), and the *Partita* for wind quintet (1948)—one found echoes, resemblances, and foreshadowings of these younger friends, especially Shapero. At the same time, their childlike joy, exuberance, and sadness, and their bittersweet combination of wit and

Example 30. Irving Fine, 5 measures from "Lenny the Leopard," from *Childhood Fables for Grownups*. Copyright by G. Schirmer, Inc. All rights reserved. Used by permission.

nostalgia, were wholly distinctive, not only among the so-called Stravinsky school, but on the American scene in general.

As with the *Alice* songs, these instrumental works were usually cast in unambiguous 2/4, 3/4, or 4/4 meters, with rhythms reminiscent of the march or lullaby. Also like the *Alice* songs, the melodies featured small fragments within the compass of a second or third, often insistently repeated in changing harmonic, registral, and metrical contexts. More expressive ideas outlined the minor or major seventh, and music in a major mode (which included most of Fine's early work) showed a special fondness for two successive fourths built on the tonic or the dominant (this was not Fine's trademark, but rather a melodic emblem for his whole generation, derived from such works as Piston's *Second Symphony* and Copland's *Fanfare for the Common Man:* see Bernstein's setting of the phrase, "(love him) forever," from *West Side Story*'s "A Boy Like That," for one of its more popular incarnations). The predominantly homophonic textures of Fine's music further contributed to an immediate grasp of these melodies, as did the harmonies themselves, which although piquant and imaginative, had perceptible roots that moved slowly and rather conventionally. The result was a very vocal ambiance.

In the classical spirit, Fine organized his attractive melodies into clearly defined phrases that formed hierarchical patterns. The "Prelude" from *Music for Piano,* dedicated to Nadia Boulanger, offered a particularly clear example of this. The piece opened, like most of Fine's music, with two phrases (the first found in Ex. 31) that formed an antecedent-consequent paragraph. The succeeding six phrases formed three more antecedent-consequent paragraphs. Each of these eight phrases, most of which were four or five measures long, were themselves divided into balanced halves. The movement's larger design was ABA; the A sections were in E^b, while the four quasi-developmental phrases that comprised the B section unfolded a symmetrical tonal pattern: C, A^b, A^b, C. Fine often used this sort of ABA design for shorter pieces, while for longer movements he tended toward sonata structures of the Scarlatti or Haydn variety.

Notwithstanding this classical restraint and symmetry, there was a noticeable absence of the sort of dramatic contrast characteristic of high Classicism, and emulated by, say, Shapero. Fine even seemed to avoid any modulation to the dominant; his "Prelude" was typical in its move to the subdominant and submediant. When he did modulate to the dominant, as in the "Theme" from the *Partita,* the effect was uncharacteristically strong. Another unusually strong mo-

Example 31. Irving Fine, "Prelude," *Music for Piano* (G. Schirmer, 1949).

ment occurred at the start of the last movement of *Music for Piano,* where there was a big buildup on the dominant (one, incidentally, that was strikingly like that which opened Shapero's *Symphony*); yet characteristically, the main theme began on the submediant, thereby undercutting the arrival of the tonic, which did not appear until a few measures later.

Fine also avoided pronounced thematic contrasts. In the "Interlude" from the *Partita,* for example, the development of a single idea totally eclipsed its tiny ABA design. Even in his sonata movements, secondary themes arrived without much fuss, and developments unfolded without much tension. Nor were there dramatic recapitulations; very often main themes returned only at a movement's end. In the "Gigue" from the *Partita,* a formal reprise was dispensed with altogether, the first theme merely returning as accompanimental figuration. Significantly, many of his sonata movements had Baroque titles like "Gigue," or *Toccata concertante,* indicating the composer's aim for a very thoroughgoing unity. The initial measures of any work were apt to generate all the music that followed; Fine did not exaggerate when he wrote that the entire five-movement *Partita* "is evolved out of two melodic fragments."[43] He worked slowly and painstakingly to emphasize connections between each and every detail, and in this sense, his later adoption of the 12-tone method proved very congenial.

Fine's sort of neoclassicism initially showed the influence of Piston even more than Stravinsky. This was especially true of his student compositions and his first acknowledged works, for example, the *Violin Sonata,* his only work, incidentally, to comprise a fast-slow-fast format, or to contain a fugue. Fine's subsequent work became more individual as he allowed his distinctive lyricism to find its own kind of formal expression. The resultant style, with its elegant and refined lyricism, and its detached, restrained emotions, had a closer precedent in the gallant style of J. C. Bach than in some of the more exalted works of the 18th century. Many also noted a Gallic strain in his mature style: Thomson was reminded of Sauguet,[44] and Berger was reminded of Poulenc and Auric.[45] And while he was not an old-fashioned Francophile like E. B. Hill, Fine had special admiration for Satie, Debussy, Ravel, and Milhaud,[46] and a concurrent dislike for most German expressionist art.[47]

Fine's love of French music took him back to Paris as a Fulbright fellow in 1949, ten years after his studies there had been interrupted by the War. He spent the year composing the *Notturno,* as well as researching the current French musical scene. For *The New York Times,* he provided an enthusiastic review of three Milhaud operas,[48] and a cool account of new trends.[49] This latter piece, "Composers in France," emphasized the influence of Messiaen and Leibowitz on the work of "brilliant" young composers like Serge Nigg, Maurice Le Roux, Pierre Boulez, and Jean-Louis Marinet, and commented with surprise on the Parisian vogue for Brahms, Bruckner, Mahler, Schoenberg, Berg, and Webern. In the course of his stay, Fine became friendly with Milhaud and Leibowitz, as well as Pierre Schaeffer and Pierre Henry, the creators of "musique concrète."[50] Fine's initial reaction to "musique concrète" was "humorous, frightening, and visceral," but he came to understand its aim of liberating "the music inherent in concrete objects."[51] Back in the States, his sympathetic lectures on dodecaphony and "musique concrète" aroused the skepticism of such friends as Lukas Foss and Arthur Berger.[52] He even arranged for the American premiere of the Schaeffer-Henry collaboration, *Symphony for One Man,* which was presented at Brandeis in 1952 with dancing by Merce Cunningham.

Given these new discoveries and experiences, it was not surprising to find a new kind of daringness in Fine's *Notturno* for strings and harp (1950–1951). Not that the *Notturno* signaled a break with the past. Even some of its more progressive features could be found in an earlier work like the *Partita,* especially that work's "Coda," which, incidentally, had the same tonal center as the *Notturno,* B♭. Further, the work clearly belonged to the tradition of Stravinsky's *Apollo* and *Orpheus,* and Fine, in fact, played the work for Balanchine in the hope that he might choreograph it (Balanchine was "courteous but uncommunicative"[53]). But the *Notturno* brought to the fore certain previously repressed romantic impulses. There was a new sensibility expressed even with the work's opening phrase (Ex. 32); this newness was evident in the wide intervals of the seventh, octave, and ninth; the syncopations and triplets that obscured the 4/8 meter; the lush tonal motion from an ambiguous B♭ minor to a cadence, via an E♭ minor pivot chord, in E minor; and the novel textures, including a kind of "Klangfarbenmelodie" for the strings, heterophonic doubling between the harp and the first violin, and unusual part-crossing. Not all of the *Notturno* was as evocative as this opening phrase, but there were other moments of similar daring, such as the last movement's dense, rich chords; and the second-movement passage at m. 107, in which the first violins were accompanied by pizzicati, harmonics, glissandi, and perpetual motion in the other strings.

Also unusual was the *Notturno*'s form, including its slow-fast-slow format. The opening movement put forth an antecedent-

Example 32. Irving Fine, *Notturno* for strings and harp (Boosey & Hawkes, 1952).

consequent paragraph in B♭ minor (mm. 1–12), a variation in D♭ (mm. 13–27), an extended variation in F (mm. 28–54), and a return, via a fuzzy A minor, to the original B♭ minor, with a concluding B♭ major seventh chord (mm. 55–71). But the music made a more lyric, less schematic impression than this outline suggests; the four sections combined to form the introduction, antecedent, consequent, and conclusion of an instrumental song. This effect was even more pronounced in the last movement which, although telescoping the identical tonal motion of the first movement, sounded essentially like a recitative and aria. Since this last movement begins where the first movement leaves off, it was even more simply like a cadenza or coda to the first movement. On another level, the last movement, like the second-movement scherzo, was a variation of the first movement. These structural ambiguities added much to the *Notturno*'s evocative atmosphere. In fact, this lush, somewhat troubled score proved to be Fine's most romantic work, at once looking back, at least in its scoring, to the "Adagietto" of Mahler's *Fifth Symphony,* and ahead to the work of Ned Rorem.

Fine returned to this slow-fast-slow format for his most important instrumental music to come—the *Fantasia* and the *Symphony;* hence, its seminal importance. The *Notturno*'s figuration suggested that the idea of opening with a slow movement was related not only to nocturnal reflections, but to Beethoven's *"Moonlight" Sonata.* The *Fantasia* and the *Symphony* may have been likewise nocturnally inspired; Fine, indeed, referred to part of the *Symphony*'s first movement as "a kind of night music."[54] And it was at night, in fact, when Fine, for the most part, composed. In any case, the composer's mature preference for a slow-fast-slow format helped explain the somewhat puzzling dynamic of his 1952 song cycle, *Mutability,* for its songs formed a similar pattern of pastoral romance ("I have heard the hoof beats of happiness," "My father," "The weed"), whimsy ("Peregrine," "Orpheus") and elegy ("Mutability").

The adoption of the 12-tone method in Fine's next work, the *String Quartet* (1952), disconcerted some of his admirers,[55] but in the end may have helped earn the work some prestigious awards.[56] In later years, this development was assumed to be the result of Stravinsky's influence,[57] but this was implausible, as Fine's 12-tone works predated Stravinsky's. More likely influences were his recently acquired French contacts, and some American associates who had already experimented with the method, including Piston, Sapp, and above all, Copland, whose 12-tone *Piano Quartet* of 1950 shared with Fine's *Quartet* the conspicuous flavor of whole-tone melodies and augmented harmonies. In any event, the idea of achieving melodic and harmonic unity through a predetermined arrangement of the chromatic scale was quite consistent with Fine's general principles.

Fine's actual use of the 12-tone method in the *Quartet,* as in later works, was extremely personal, and had only oblique relation to the Schoenbergian model. The row (C-F#-A-F-Bb-G#-B-E-G-Eb-C#-D) and its transformations, for instance, were rarely spelled out as self-contained ideas; only once, in fact, did the row generate a melodic phrase, and that was at the very end of the two-movement work, where it was found in the first violin, "declamando, quasi lamentoso." More typically, the row was broken up into fragments repeated over and over: see, for example, the four pitches that comprise the first violin's opening twenty-four measures; the wavering thirds found later in this movement; and the recitatives on a single pitch in the "Adagio" movement. Fine's penchant for insistent melodic repetitions, noted in the *Alice* songs, was never more apparent, only here adapted to a more chromatic context.

Furthermore, Fine was not inclined to keep to strict orderings of the row. To take but one small detail, the *Quartet* sketches indicate that Fine originally intended to begin the work with the falling tritone, C-F#, the first two notes of the row; but he later decided to add a Db pick-up, an addition that cannot be explained in terms of the row. The sketches also reveal that Fine liked to make up his own orderings of the row, for example, 1-3-5-7-9-11-2-4-6-8-10-12. These orderings reached cabalistic proportions with the 1962 *Symphony,* for which Fine wrote out pages and pages of rows involving such permutations as the inversion of 1-4-7-10-2-5-8-11-3-6-9-12. Not surprisingly, Fine's 12-tone procedures often eluded theorists.[58]

In addition, all the Schoenbergian dicta about tonality, triads, octave doublings, repeated notes, and the like were totally rejected. The *Quartet* as a whole, wrote Fine, "is frankly tonal, C being the prevailing tonality."[59] According to

Fine's sketchbooks, the row itself suggested a C tonality to the composer, as did two other forms of the row, RI° and R^{11}. And indeed, the row's one clear exposition was supported by a harmonic progression from C to E^b to E and back to C (note the unabated preference for harmonic motion by thirds). Furthermore, the row was further designed to comprise familiar chords, specifically, a progression in E minor: ii° (1, 3, 2), bV^7 (5, 6, 4), i (7, 9, 8). (This progression, transposed to G minor, opened the "Adagio.") The conflict between C and E inherent in the row assumed formal significance as the piece progressed.

As for the work's emotional content, it seemed likewise removed from Schoenberg, though it did have a brooding, intense quality of its own. Some precedence for its two movements could be found in two songs from Fine's 1949 choral setting of six Ben Jonson poems, *The Hour-Glass,* namely, "Against Jealousy" ("Wretched and foolish Jealousy, How cam'st thou thus to enter me") and "Lament" ("Slow, fresh fount, keep time with my salt tears"). The *Quartet* reminded Wilfred Mellers of Berg: "The tender fine-spun lyricism of his slow movements suggests a Berg reborn in the clear New England air; if some of the Viennese 'morbidity' has gone, so has some of the strength."[60] (This observation, incidentally, echoed remarks made by Robert Evett concerning the *Notturno:* "It's quite possible that Fine has lost quite a lot of the expressiveness of expressionism and of the clarity of classicism in his effort to fuse elements of the two attitudes. . . ."[61]) The *Quartet* prompted Mellers to place Fine, along with Kirchner and Imbrie, in a sort of Sessions tradition. This context was a bit unusual, but at least had some validity (unlike one discussion that grouped Fine with Varèse, Babbitt, and other "experimentalists"[62]). Fine grew to appreciate Sessions more and more, claiming in 1957 that "Sessions and Copland have exerted the strongest influence upon the younger generation."[63] The impact of Sessions on Fine's 1962 *Symphony* was clear enough. But the *Quartet* still looked back to Piston's kind of refinement. And, in any case, the work was not that characteristic; the composer himself was displeased with the work's "morbidity,"[64] and he never again attempted a work with so many fluctuations of tempo.

The morbidity of the *Quartet,* such as it is, was possibly

related to Fine's growing concerns about his psychological
health (as well as the health of the nation: he spent the
McCarthy hearings glued to the television). Fine long had
been fascinated by psychology. He read much on the subject,
including the writings of his friend Abe Maslow, and he
shared with Copland the notion that had he not become a
composer he would have liked to have been a psychiatrist.[65]
Fine's two sets of *Childhood Fables* were as much psychological
studies as they were stylistic parodies,[66] and it was regrettable
that he never gave this gift larger scope, as in opera. His
letters very often made psychological observations: Roy
Harris "possesses a megalomania that passes comprehen-
sion";[67] Dika Newlin is "one of those 'I myself' types—a
young female Leichtentritt";[68] and Irene Orgel (whose poetry
Fine set) is "very neurotic."[69] And he was every bit as critical
of himself; writings scattered among his sketchbooks reveal a
man haunted by insomnia, hypochondria, depression, and anxiety, a perfectionist tortured by a sense of inferiority.[70] This
melancholy worsened throughout the 1950s, only somewhat
relieved by therapy with Harvard's eminent John Nemiah.

His nighttime anxieties and fantasies notwithstanding, Fine
performed brilliantly in his important and pressing duties as
teacher, administrator, and impresario for Brandeis University. In a tribute to Fine, one colleague wrote, "Irving's way
was to share the burden of our weaknesses. Where we
faltered or stood bemused, he was there, actively unraveling
the tangle of our indecisions, exactly as though his problems
were not ours but his."[71] And a former student recalled, "As
an advisor, he brought to people's problems the understanding of a skilled psychologist—intuitively."[72]

When Fine joined the fledgling university in 1950, the only
other music teacher on the faculty was musicologist Erwin
Brodky. Fine soon was appointed chairman of Brandeis's
School of Creative Arts, and in the decade that followed, he
faced the challenge of creating and administering not only the
department of music, but the departments of art and theater.
In his twenty-fifth anniversary report to Harvard, Fine took
no credit for the fact that the Brandeis Music Department "is
regarded very well nationally" and that there are "some
genuinely creative people in fine arts and theatre"; rather,
with typical modesty, he discussed personal regrets:

> Whatever frustrations I have had at Brandeis were at least in part due to my own lack of professional experience and contacts outside my own field and in part the natural consequence of building a school and attempting to establish its reputation. I might have wished at times that our administration were less impressed with yesterday's headlines; that our publicity were better informed; that our architects would resist certain cliches as well as the temptation of being creative at other people's expense; that some artists I know were more tolerant of their older confreres and that others were less fearful of competition from younger men; and finally, that art and music historians were less concerned with academic respectability.

This relative indifference toward "academic respectability" encouraged Fine to hire practicing artists in lieu of scholars per se, and within two years he brought Arthur Berger, Harold Shapero, and, for a while, Leonard Bernstein to Brandeis, quickly establishing the school as a musical center of international standing.

Fine's position also allowed him to implement strongly held educational views, most importantly, the belief that musical activity was at least as important as academic musical instruction. Fine benefited in this regard from his participation in the curriculum reforms at Harvard, where he was placed in charge of the newly established Basic Piano Program.[73] But to his mind Harvard did not go far enough, and he aimed for the sort of balance between Ivy League academicism and Big Ten vocationalism that one found in a few women's colleges.[74] He promoted courses that emphasized practical musicianship, including participation in musical ensembles. He also thought it important that college students know the music of their time,[75] and to this end he offered courses in modern music, and arranged concerts of contemporary music, including an annual series of Festivals of Creative Arts (produced from 1952 to 1957). The 1952 Festival featured the world premieres of Blitzstein's version of *The Three-Penny Opera* (later to become a Broadway hit) and Bernstein's *Trouble in Tahiti;* the American premiere of *Symphony for One Man,* as mentioned; a performance of *Les Noces;* and works by Copland, Britten, Fine, Weber, and

others. Later Festivals included the American premiere of
Poulenc's *Les Mamelles de Tirésias* and a production of
Copland's *The Tender Land.*[76]

Fine also served Brandeis as a composer. He undertook a
film score for Sam Slosberg's Green Shoe Company at least in
part in appreciation of that philanthropist's commitment to
the school. He wrote a refined, spirited marching song,
"Blue-White," and later gave it a flashy orchestral setting,
Blue Towers, somewhat reminiscent of Piston's festival overtures. He began, but presumably never completed, a "Hymn
for Brandeis." Finally, and most ambitiously, he embarked on
a musical based on Crane's *Maggie: A Girl of the Streets* that
was to be produced by Brandeis. His principal collaborator on
the project was Gertrude Norman, who had written the lyrics
for *Childhood Fables.* The musical was to include a prologue
and three acts, including a beer hall scene with a prepared
piano playing "honky tonk." In his youth Fine detested opera
for its elitism and conservatism, but he revised his opinions in
the light of operatic productions at Tanglewood, especially
the legendary American premiere of *Peter Grimes* in 1946.[77]
The aforementioned productions at Brandeis probably further encouraged him to write a work of musical theater
himself. In 1954 he found a "nice story by Bret Harte that
might make an opera,"[78] but he eventually decided on
Maggie. In many ways this was an excellent choice, what with
its small number of principals, its anonymous crowds of boys,
factory girls, and pleasure seekers, its high-pitched emotions,
its ethnic flavor (Irish New York), and its eerie tavern and
music-hall scenes. The two songs that Fine completed, the
nostalgic "I Wonder" for Maggie, and the cynical "Tell It to
the Worms" (Ex. 33) for Pete and Jimmie, showed too that
the story could accommodate the traditions of Weill and
Blitzstein. But a major problem was in writing a convincing
book, for *Maggie* was, ironically, a study in tragic inarticulate-
ness: Maggie herself rarely speaks in the novella, and the
other characters mostly just curse. The University, citing
problematic cross purposes between the songs and the dialog,
decided not to support the project.

Works like the *Childhood Fables,* the unfinished *Maggie,*
and the beautiful *Serious Song. A Lament for String Orchestra*
(1955), showed that Fine's adoption of the 12-tone method in

Example 33. Irving Fine, "Tell It to the Worms," *Maggie: A Girl of the Streets.*

the *Quartet* did not signal a "conversion" to dodecaphony. But he did return to the 12-tone method for his final major instrumental works: the *Fantasia* for string trio (1956), the *Romanza* for wind quintet (1958), and the *Symphony* (1962).

Least well-known, the *Romanza,* a personal tribute to Verna Fine, was not performed until after the composer's death, and never began to rival the popularity of the earlier *Partita.* The *Fantasia,* on the other hand, became one of Fine's most successful chamber works. In three movements, the *Fantasia* combined the slow-fast-slow format of the *Notturno* with the 12-tone technique of the *Quartet.* Its outer movements were quite short, almost epigrammatic; its first movement was a fugato whose six statements formed a binary design, and its third movement was a ternary piece whose outer tranquil sections were contrasted with an agitated recitative for the violin at its center. The larger, more complex middle movement dominated the work. It began with a "scherzo" (mm. 1–132), followed by a variation-cum-trio, followed, after m. 200, by a free variation that seemed more like a coda or a development than a return. The movement finally dissolved into the finale. Fine's formal daringness again seemed related to Beethoven, for the *Fantasia*'s very opening recalled the opening of Beethoven's *Quartet,* Op. 131. Fine's daringness was also evident in the work's chromaticism, greater here than in the *Quartet,* yet still anchored in tonality; the work, in fact, abounded with familiar chords (especially minor triads) and extended ostinati of one or two pitches. There was even a lengthy passage in the first movement (mm. 26–44) in which a 12-tone duet for violin and viola was supported by a rocking V-i progression in E minor (a similar passage could be found in the song "Mutability," which was also 12-tone). Much of the *Fantasia* hovered about E^b and B, though the work finally came to rest on a surprising A minor chord.

The *Symphony,* also in slow-fast-slow format, and also 12-tone, was like a magnified version of the *Fantasia.* While the earlier *Toccata* had been written for Koussevitzky and the Boston Symphony,[79] this *Symphony* was written for the same ensemble under Munch. These were Fine's only works for orchestra, not counting orchestral arrangements of one sort or another.[80] Fine's reluctance to write for orchestra stemmed from regrets that he had studied orchestration with Hill and not Piston, and consequent doubts about his abilities as an orchestrator.[81] He also found orchestrating "a real bore as well as a chore."[82] Nonetheless, the *Symphony*'s orchestration, like that of the *Toccata,* was thoroughly expert and imaginative. The pronounced use of heterophony, polyrhythms, extreme registers, and other textural intricacies gave this later work a complexity that deserved comparison with Sessions's *Second Symphony* and Carter's *Variations for Orchestra.* There was also a certain glassy quality to the music, due in part to the prevalence of the piano, harp, celesta, trumpet, and glockenspiel. Fine's comment, "I was applying the finishing touches to the orchestration on February 20, 1962, nervously watching the television set out of the corner of one eye when the news of Colonel Glenn's return from outer space was announced,"[83] consequently seemed quite telling, for the *Symphony* itself was an exploration into a new sonorous universe, and its glassy sounds had a weightless quality about them. In other respects, the *Symphony,* with its motto theme of six notes, was in the older tradition of Roussel, Piston, and Stravinsky (Fine's renewal of these traditions had a French parallel, perhaps, in the work of Dutilleux). The first movement even seemed to be in sonata form,[84] though Fine described it simply as "a kind of choreographic action." As a whole, the *Symphony* was distinctively tense and unremitting, and revealed, according to Copland, "a restless and somewhat strained atmosphere that is part of its essential quality."[85]

The *Symphony,* for all its novelties and complexities, looked back to the *Alice* songs, indeed, seemed to summarize Fine's entire oeuvre; for the mock-innocence of its first movement, the ironic humor of its second movement, and the elegiac sorrow of its third movement were final expressions of moods and feelings the composer had explored throughout his career. In the wake of one disaster after another—his mother's suicide attempt, his father's rejection, the anti-Semitism of the Harvard Club and the Harvard Musical Association, his dismissal from Harvard, the McCarthy trials, and so on—the composer's dreadful anxieties found some solace in the poignant dichotomy of innocence and experience; he was an heir not only to Carroll but to Wordsworth and Blake. Indeed, Blakean well might describe the *Sym-*

phony's awful progress from its opening childlike march to its final dismal dirge, a life story told, ironically, just months before the composer's death.

On August 23, 1962, eleven days after he conducted the *Symphony* at Tanglewood, Fine died suddenly and unexpectedly of a heart attack. He was forty-seven years old. Given the grandeur and daring of the *Symphony,* friends naturally mused about what Fine might have accomplished had he lived. Martin Boykan wrote:

> Conversations I had with him during the course of last year suggested that the *Symphony* was meant to be the last in this series of twelve-tone works. He felt that he had said all he could with the serial technique, and in the early part of the summer, he began work on a violin sonata in a free chromatic idiom. It is likely that he was reaching out toward a new style, and if so, this represents a tragic loss for American music.[86]

Fine was already well under way on a five-movement *Partita on an Israeli Theme* for orchestra; it presumably would have opened with the modal Israeli theme in the trumpet, accompanied by the strings in what might be called a "free chromatic idiom." Also planned was a choral work based on Biblical excerpts from Exodus, Kings, Ezekiel, Isaiah, and Daniel. Both projects suggested that Fine was growing increasingly interested in his Jewish heritage, an inference further supported by his last letters.[87] Most likely Fine would have continued to write in a variety of styles as he always had done. But what the composer left behind was great enough: inimitable music of innocence and experience that is still played and loved.

Notes

1. A major work is defined as a composition in the Fine catalog over five minutes in length (most are around fifteen minutes). This excludes only three pieces for chorus ("A Short Alleluia," "In grato jubilo," and "An Old Song"), three little piano pieces (*Lullaby for a Baby Panda, Victory March of the Elephants,* and *Homage à Mozart*), and a piece for orchestra (*Blue Towers*). Two

majors works—*Music for Piano* and *Diversions for Orchestra*—were recorded only in part.

2. Maurice Ivan Laney, *Thematic Material and Developmental Techniques in Selected Contemporary Compositions* (Ph.D thesis, University of Indiana, 1964); Lawrence Gould Rickert, *Selected American Song Cycles for Baritone Composed since 1945* (DMA thesis, University of Illinois, 1965); Ronald Eugene Wise, *Scoring in the Neoclassic Woodwind Quintets of Hindemith, Fine, Etler, and Wilder* (Ph.D thesis, University of Wisconsin, 1967).

3. Leonard Burkat, "Current Chronicle," *Musical Quarterly* 35 (1949), p. 282.

4. Fine, letter to his parents, July 23, 1939, Fine Collection, Library of Congress, Washington DC. This early *Violin Sonata* possibly evolved into the *Violin Sonata* of 1946.

5. Burns, *A Cry of Children* (New York: Harper, 1952).

6. Fine, letters to his parents, July 13, 1939; July 23, 1939; and August 14, 1939, Fine Collection.

7. Verna Fine, personal interview, May 16, 1982.

8. Fine, *25th Anniversary Report Harvard Class of 1937*, pp. 346–347.

9. These songs, and other unpublished songs and sketches mentioned in this chapter, are in the Fine Collection.

10. V. Fine.

11. Only minor adjustments were needed to make the words, "You are old, Father William, the young man said," fit the music to "It's the Navy! the Navy! Our ships on the sea." The latent patriotism of "Father William" may have contributed to its enormous success.

12. "Beautiful Soup" is perhaps more of a Charleston than a march, but demonstrates, in any event, the closeness between these two styles.

13. Fine, letter to Elaine (Barbara) Katz, February 25, 1944, in the possession of Verna Fine (V. Fine Collection).

14. *New Yorker Book of Verse* (New York: Harcourt Brace, 1935).

15. This list includes the auk, beaver, black bird, canary, cat, clam, condor, crab, crow, dog, donkey, duck, elephant, fawn, flamingo, fly, frog, goose, gerbil, hawk, hen, kangaroo, Koko (Fine's poodle), leopard, lobster, mole, monkey, mouse, panda, pig, polar bear, porpoise, rat, sheep, snail, snake, spider, swan, tiger, whitney, worm, and yak.

16. Leonard Bernstein pointed this out in preface notes to the published score of Fine's *Diversions:* "In these four brief pieces we can behold a personality: tender without being coy, witty without being vulgar, appealing without being banal, and

utterly sweet without ever being cloying. Such a man (and such a work) is rare enough to cause rejoicing."

17. Fine, letter to his parents, March 8, 1934, Fine Collection.
18. Fine, letter to his wife, July 2, 1952, V. Fine Collection.
19. Fine, undated note from c. 1955, Fine Collection.
20. V. Fine.
21. Privately noting some trends in academia that displeased him, Fine wrote, "Composers try to be scientific—Musicologists become social scientists," c. 1955, Fine Collection.
22. V. Fine.
23. The relationship between Fine and his father resembled, to some extent, Burton Bernstein's account of Leonard Bernstein and his father ("Personal History. The Bernstein Family," *The New Yorker,* March 22, 1982, pp. 53–127, and March 29, 1982, pp. 58–121). Both involved the classic conflict between a strong, self-made father and a rebellious, artistic son. And although Fine's parents, unlike Bernstein's, were born in America, their conflicts with their fathers similarly reflected the gap between Jews from Eastern Europe and their better-educated, more assimilated children. One way they dealt with this conflict was through humor, by creating a comic language, called "Rybernian" by Bernstein, that made sophisticated and cheeky use of immigrant syntax, vocabulary, and pronunciation (see the aforementioned letter from Fine to Barbara Katz). The similarities between these two composers gained even greater resonance when one considered that they were in high school and college together, and that their mothers were close friends.
24. Fine, personal note, c. 1955, V. Fine Collection.
25. V. Fine.
26. Fine, "The Story of Twentieth-Century Music," *Book of Knowledge,* E. V. McLoughlin, ed. (New York: Grolier, 1948), p. 357.
27. Fine, "English in Boston; Stravinsky's Symphony," *Modern Music* 23 (1946), p. 211.
28. Piston, letter to Verna Fine, August 24, 1962, Fine Collection.
29. This episode almost became a cause célèbre, as it would have exposed anti-Semitic elements among Boston's old guard. With the exception of A. Tillman Merritt, the Department's fund-raiser, the entire Music Department, including Edward Ballantine and G. Wallace Woodworth, who had nominated Fine in the first place, resigned from this organization which, ironically, was meant in part to serve the needs of the Harvard Music Department. To prevent this breach with the Harvard

faculty, and to avoid public scandal, the Association eventually reversed its decision. Fine uneasily accepted the membership and quietly resigned the following year. It was the second such humiliation he had suffered at Harvard; in 1937 he was denied entrance to the Harvard Club because he was Jewish, although as vice-president of the Glee Club he was automatically entitled to Club membership. When Harvard denied Fine tenure in 1950, he and many of his supporters understandably assumed that his religion had been held against him.

30. Fine, "American Composers—Older Generation," unpublished lecture given at Tanglewood, 1957, V. Fine Collection.

31. Fine, "Education for Youth in the World of Today and Tomorrow," lecture for the New York Chapter of the Brandeis National Women's Committee, c. 1955, V. Fine Collection.

32. V. Fine.

33. Fine happened to be with Copland when the latter accidentally killed an angus steer while driving his Studebaker, and was able to testify that Copland was not speeding. "Composer Fined $35 After Car Kills Angus Steer," *Berkshire Evening Eagle,* August 15, 1949.

34. Fine, "Story," p. 357; also, "American Composers - Older Generation."

35. Fine, review of Copland's *Dickinson Songs, Notes* 11 (December 1953), pp. 159–160.

36. Fine, "English in Boston," p. 209.

37. This phrase, coined by Copland, was taken up by Gilbert Chase, *America's Music,* revised second edition (New York: McGraw-Hill, 1966), pp. 559–564; and by H. Wiley Hitchcock, *Music in the United States* (Englewood Cliffs, NJ: Prentice Hall, 1969), p. 227.

38. Fine, unpublished lecture, 1957, V. Fine Collection, was referring to himself, Berger, Shapero, Foss, Talma, and Smit.

39. Berger, "Stravinsky and the Younger American Composers," *The Score* 12 (June 1955), pp. 38–46.

40. The only exception is "Two Worms," which bears a dedication to Arthur Cohn. According to Verna Fine, this one dedication was decided upon only after the song's completion, and has nothing to do with its style, though possibly its content.

41. Some commentators have confused Haieff's influence with Stravinsky's. In liner notes to a recording of some of the *Fables,* New World Records (NW 300), George Gelles wrote, "This debt [to Stravinsky] is most evident in 'The Duck and the Yak,' whose declamatory style, accompaniment figurations, and

harmonic spectrum inevitably bring the neoclassical *Rake* to mind."

42. Fine, letter to his wife, January 17, 1955, V. Fine Collection.

43. Fine, program notes, V. Fine Collection.

44. Thomson, in a review of Fine's *Toccata, New York Herald Tribune,* January 16, 1949, wrote, "Aside from a certain genuine prettiness of material, its chief news value, as I see it, is having introduced for the first time into American composition the direct influence of Henri Sauguet." Thomson repeated this association twenty years later, writing, "Oriented towards French neo-Romantic art of the 1930s, his music seems to remember without really resembling it the music of Henri Sauguet." *American Music Since 1910* (New York: Holt, Rinehart and Winston, 1970), p. 142. Fine met Sauguet in Paris in 1949, and well may have admired his music, but Thomson's remarks seemed to be, more than anything else, a plug for his French friend.

45. Berger, "Stravinsky," p. 43.

46. V. Fine. Fine, in fact, devoted most of "The Story of Twentieth-Century Music" to Debussy, Ravel, Roussel, Satie, and Les Six, pp. 350–352.

47. Fine had mixed feelings about Schoenberg. He thought the *Second Quartet* "beautiful, if neurotic music"; and he thought the *Ode* "exciting melodrama," but he questioned the purposefulness of "Sprechstimme," "Bartok's New Koussevitzky Number," *Modern Music* 22 (1944–1945), p. 116. He was more critical about lesser expressionist art, such as the music of Fartein Valen, "Reviews of Records," *Musical Quarterly* 41 (1955), p. 411, or the paintings of Lukas Foss's mother. V. Fine.

48. Fine, "Milhaud at Home," *New York Times,* January 8, 1950. Writes Fine: Milhaud's compositions for the lyric theater "contain his most important music and form some of the finest pages written in our time."

49. Fine, "Composers in France," *New York Times,* June 4, 1950.

50. V. Fine.

51. Harold Rogers, "Musique Concrète for Brandeis Festival," *Christian Science Monitor,* June 4, 1952.

52. Arthur Berger, "'Concrete Music,' New Fad, Causes Stir at Tanglewood," *New York Herald Tribune,* August 6, 1950. Foss's skepticism was directed toward dodecaphony, Berger's toward concrete music.

53. Fine, letter to his wife, January, 1952, V. Fine Collection. The

work was eventually performed as a ballet, but not until after the composer's death.

54. Fine, program notes, V. Fine Collection.

55. Arthur Berger, review of the Fine *Quartet,* the *Boston Herald Tribune,* February 19, 1953.

56. The *Quartet,* like the *Partita,* was given a citation by the New York Critics Circle, and came very close to winning their 1954 Award (partisans for Bloch's *Third Quartet* won out). The work also received an Award from the Society for the Publication of American Music (SPAM), and probably prompted Fine's Award from the National Institute of Arts and Letters in 1955.

57. In *Music in the United States,* Hitchcock states, "At the same time that Stravinsky approached row-composition (via Renaissance counterpoint) in his *Cantata* (1952) and turned definitely to dodecaphony in the mid-1950's, these composers [Fine, Berger, Talma, and Dahl] began to espouse the twelve-tone idea" (p. 227).

58. According to sketchbooks, the *Symphony*'s basic set is D-E-F-E♭-D♭-B♭-G-F♯-A-C-B-A♭. Two reviewers, Martin Boykan in *Musical Quarterly* 48 (1962), pp. 385–387, and David Epstein in *Perspectives of New Music* 3 (1965), pp. 160–164, quite understandably identified different rows based on the score; while the tritone is a dominant interval throughout the work, it does not even appear in the basic set.

59. Fine, program notes, V. Fine Collection.

60. Mellers, *Music in a New Found Land* (London: Barrie and Rockliff, 1964), p. 144.

61. Evett, review of Fine's *Notturno, Notes* 11 (September 1954), p. 608.

62. Ronald Davis, *A History of Music in American Life,* Vol. III (Malabar, Florida: Robert Krieger, 1981), p. 238.

63. Fine, "American Composers—Older Generation."

64. Fine, letter to his wife, January 17, 1955, V. Fine Collection.

65. V. Fine.

66. Each song humorously depicted a salient trait of its dedicatee: Berger's fastidiousness (this song is ironic), Shapero's irritability, Bernstein's insecurity, Foss's mischievousness, Cohn's loneliness, and Haieff's despondency.

67. Fine, letter to his wife, July 2, 1952, V. Fine Collection.

68. Fine, letter to his wife, June 3, 1947, V. Fine Collection.

69. Fine, letter to his wife, July 9, 1952, V. Fine Collection.

70. A Freudian description of Fine's character as anal would find plentiful justification in his limericks, which often joked about

behinds, as well as in a bizarre fantasy in the aforementioned letter to Barbara Katz about Nazi carrier-pigeons that defecate on a Jewish middle-class family.

71. Edwin Burr Pettet, "A Sublime Selflessness," *The Justice XV,* No. 5, October 30, 1962.

72. Richard M. Finder, "A Student Recalls," *The Justice* XV, No. 5, October 30, 1962.

73. Fine, "Elementary Theory in Music Curriculum at Harvard University," *Music Teachers National Association, Volume of Proceedings for 1948* (Pittsburgh: Association, 1950), pp. 210–217.

74. Fine, "The School of Creative Arts," unpublished lecture, May, 1952, V. Fine Collection.

75. Fine, "The Composer and His Audience," unpublished lecture, December 6, 1956, V. Fine Collection. Fine also warned composers against being too obscure and of resembling avant-garde poets when music was essentially a dramatic and theatrical art.

76. For more on Fine and Brandeis, see Abram L. Sachar, *A Host at Last* (Boston: Little, Brown, 1976).

77. V. Fine.

78. Fine, postcard to his wife, August 4, 1954, V. Fine Collection.

79. Fine was one of Koussevitsky's last protégés. The conductor was also responsible for bringing Fine to Tanglewood to teach "harmonical" analysis.

80. These included arrangements of the *Alice* songs, *Music for Piano,* "Blue-White" (*Blue Towers*), and the piano pieces that comprise *Diversions,* as well as Fine's contribution to an orchestral cantata in honor of Koussevitzky, "In grato jubilo."

81. V. Fine.

82. Fine, letter to his wife, June 10, 1947, V. Fine Collection.

83. Fine, program notes, V. Fine Collection.

84. One can argue for an exposition (mm. 1–33), a development (mm. 34–110), and a recapitulation (mm. 111–155). The work's tonality needs careful scrutiny, but it seems to center around B, and furthermore, seems to move to the dominant at the close of the "exposition." Whether or not the oboe melody at m. 20 is intended as a second theme is also hard to say, but it is worth remembering that the *Toccata*'s second theme was given to the oboe.

85. Copland, liner notes to Fine's *Symphony,* Desto DC 7167.

86. Boykan, "As Composer," *The Justice* XV, No. 5, October 5, 1962.

87. Fine, in a letter to his parents, August 1, 1958, V. Fine

Collection, wrote that a synagogue in Casablanca left him "terribly moved . . . for me it was like seeing a miniature version of the Market Street or East Boston schules"; and to his daughter Claudia, in a letter dated April 3, 1961, Fine described a visit to Maimonides's home in Cordova, and praised Seville's Jewish quarter.

8. A MIDCENTURY MASTERWORK: HAROLD SHAPERO'S *SYMPHONY FOR CLASSICAL ORCHESTRA*

I N THE 1940S, STRAVINSKY AND COPLAND agreed that Harold Shapero (b. 1920) was very likely the most gifted of America's many young composers.[1] During these years, in fact, Shapero often was mentioned in the same breath as Piston, Copland, and other older, more established figures. Only in his twenties, he was producing a series of chamber and orchestral works, each one longer and grander than the last, a series that climaxed with the 1947 *Symphony for Classical Orchestra.*

Shapero's earliest works only vaguely foreshadowed his greatest accomplishments. In his teens he studied composition with Slonimsky (1936–1937) and Krenek (1937), under whose tutelage he wrote a 12-tone string trio (1938). At Harvard (1938–1941), however, he began to write music more like Piston, his principal teacher there. This included his first published work, the 1939 *3 Pieces for 3 Pieces,* which, significantly, was, like Piston's first published work, a set of three small pieces for flute, clarinet, and bassoon. Not surprisingly, there were similarities of style as well, though whereas Piston's 1925 composition was the mature debut of a late bloomer, Shapero's work was the tentative effort of a precocious nineteen-year-old. His next work, the 1940 *Trumpet Sonata,* also echoed Piston, this time the latter's 1930 *Flute Sonata.* The first of its two movements had the sort of long, solo arioso accompanied by icy, chromatic chords in the piano's upper register found in the *Flute Sonata*'s slow movement, while its second movement had the Baroque-like vigor of the *Flute Sonata*'s finale. It was to Aaron Copland, however, that Shapero dedicated the *Trumpet Sonata,* and his influence was detectable too, especially in the finale.

Shapero's 1941 *String Quartet* likewise was indebted to Piston, in particular, to Piston's early string quartets; one found similar kinds of quartal harmonies and jazzy rhythms. As with his earlier works, the *Quartet* possessed little of Piston's calm and humor, projecting rather Shapero's own darker, more agitated personality. But he, nonetheless, approximated Piston's marvelous balance of novel sound and traditional finesse, something that few contemporaries were either inclined or able to do. Shapero dedicated this work to Piston.

Shapero looked up to Piston without any special coaxing. He sought out Piston's scores on his own, and wrote his undergraduate thesis on the music of Piston and Stravinsky, finding Piston's the more difficult to reduce to systematic principles. In private sessions, however, Piston was exasperatingly cool and evasive. In one instance, Shapero excitedly brought to class his newly completed *9-Minute Overture* for orchestra (1940); Piston, looking over the score, merely pointed to one spot in the music, saying, "Well, if it were mine, I'd put two bassoons *there.*"[2] Piston may well have been astonished at how close this particular work came to his own kind of elegance and dash. In addition, there were aspects related to Harris and Shostakovich; and further, the work was historically interesting in the way it anticipated and possibly influenced Bernstein. In later years, Shapero agreed with critics that the literalness of the work's sonata form made its last few minutes seem redundant. But the work won the prize it set out to win, namely, the "Prix de Rome."

During the summers of 1940 and 1941, Shapero continued his studies with Hindemith, who proved quite the opposite of Piston; he amazed Shapero by rapidly rewriting the young composer's work before his very eyes. Once, after having a series of original melodies rejected by Hindemith as unacceptable, Shapero, in desperation, passed off as his own the slow cello theme from Piston's 1937 *Piano Concertino.* Hindemith liked the tune, which he called "Frenchy," but rewrote it anyway. When Shapero returned to Harvard, he slyly offered to show Piston Hindemith's "corrected" version, to which Piston replied, "Well, I could change one of his, too."

Another major influence on Shapero's early work was contemporary jazz and popular music, which the composer knew well as a dance band arranger and pianist. And, indeed, some jazz or popular strain often was discernable in the rhythmic, melodic, and harmonic details of Shapero's work. But as with Piston, they were subordinate to neoclassical criteria: subtle contrapuntal textures, long melodic lines, motor rhythms, and organic forms constructed from a few key intervals. The jazz and popular elements in the *Trumpet Sonata* were particularly pronounced, especially in the opening slow movement, with its muted trumpet writing, its bluesy melodic line, its cool chromatic chords, and its improvisatory feel. There perhaps was a special connection to George Gershwin, not only in the movement's quasi-song form, but in its suave harmonic progressions.

The connection between these jazzy, Pistonian works and the music of Leonard Bernstein, as alluded to above, deserves some amplification. Shapero and Bernstein had been good friends since the late 1930s, and even roomed together at Tanglewood during the summer of 1940.[3] Shapero dedicated his 1941 *Sonata for Piano 4-Hands* to "Bernstein and myself," and they premiered it together; this was another particularly jazzy work, one, moreover, highly inventive in its form and piano writing. Shapero's work from this period (1939–1941) quite generally foreshadowed the somewhat older Bernstein, whose first recognized work was the 1942 *Clarinet Sonata.* Some of the orchestral and harmonic details of the *9-Minute Overture,* as mentioned, looked ahead to Bernstein's symphonic work. Similarly, the finale to the *Trumpet Sonata* alternated 2/4, 7/8, and 4/4 meters in ways that would become associated with Bernstein. Moreover, this same finale used a four-note motive that years later turned up in waltztime as, "I Feel Pretty." But Shapero's work with Nadia Boulanger subsequent to the *Trumpet Sonata* steered him in a somewhat different direction, leaving Bernstein, more or less, to fulfill these kinds of early aspirations.

The initial result of his work with Boulanger, with whom

Shapero studied at the Longy School in 1942 and 1943, was to bring him closer to Stravinsky, as evident from his 1942 *Sonata* for violin and piano. Stravinsky, it is true, was very much in the air, especially at Harvard, where his 1939 Norton Lectures and his 1940 *Symphony in C* had made a profound impression. Piston's 1941 *Sinfonietta* and Berger's 1941 *Woodwind Quartet* were only two works that gave evidence to this. Indeed, the *Violin Sonata*'s modal shadings, for instance, its simultaneous suggestions of C major and E minor, reminded one of certain tonal ambiguities in contemporary works by Piston and Berger. But Shapero came closer to Stravinsky in the *Sonata* than did most any other American, not only in terms of certain mannerisms, but in its brilliance and daring and passion. This must, in part, be attributed to Shapero's close study of Stravinsky's music under Boulanger. Significantly, Shapero's 1945 *Serenade* for orchestra, full of Stravinskyisms, was dedicated to Boulanger and inspired by her teaching.[4]

But it was Boulanger's analyses of Mozart, Haydn, and Beethoven, especially her fiery performances of the Beethoven string quartets at the piano, that really made a "devastating impression." This was partly because Shapero was actually less familiar with these composers than he was with Stravinsky. Such revelations led him, in a 1946 symposium of neglected modern works, to include Mozart's *Divertimento in B♭*, K. 289, in a list along with works by Stravinsky, Hindemith, Copland, and Piston, "because to my ear he is a most modern composer."[5] Shapero began restudying 18th-century counterpoint and harmony, and better familiarizing himself with that century's literature. The first fruit of this undertaking was the *3 Piano Sonatas* from 1944, a work that "takes its inspiration from the keyboard music of Scarlatti, K. P. E. Bach, and Haydn."[6] The freshness, wit, and sophistication of these *Sonatas* made them one of Shapero's most immediate, and as it turns out, lasting successes. Encouraged, he gave his classicism greater scope in the *Serenade,* which was closer to Mozart (and, as mentioned, to Stravinsky), and, finally, in the 1947 *Symphony for Classical Orchestra,* which was closer to Beethoven.

Just prior to the *Symphony,* Shapero wrote an article, "The Musical Mind," that shed some light on his work from the mid-1940s, and the *Symphony* in particular.[7] Partly an objective account of the creative process, partly an artistic manifesto, it argued that "the musical mind is concerned predominantly with the mechanism of tonal memory"; that is, we absorb "a great percentage" of our musical experiences, we submerge them in our unconscious mind, and we recall them at will, the composer altering them in the process. Shapero acknowledged a connection between this thesis and "the modern emphasis on scientific method," but contended that earlier composers were as concerned, if not more so, with the mechanism of the creative mind, quoting letters by Mozart and Beethoven as evidence. Basic to this mechanism was fundamental musical syntax, especially the melodic phrase, which was "exactly equivalent to the sentence in the syntax of language." And since Haydn, Mozart, and Beethoven "possessed the greatest mastery of musical phraseology," unlike later composers who replaced phrase groupings with the "concept of organic form," the composer was advised to become intimate with their melodic procedures. Shapero outlined some different ways in which this could be done. One way was through daily imitation of the classic masters, through which the composer "will be surprised to find that along with the thousand subtleties of technique he will absorb from his models, he will discover the personal materials of his own art." The article concluded that this sort of conditioning does not prevent inspiration, as it is in accordance with the "natural functions of the musical mind," unlike the systems of Schoenberg and Hindemith, which warp such natural functioning. This line of reasoning received its most persuasive argument, however, with the composer's own *Symphony for Classical Orchestra* of the following year.

Commissioned by the Koussevitzky Foundation, the *Symphony* was a large work in traditional format: there was an opening sonata allegro (in B♭ major), a slow sonata movement (in E♭ major), a scherzo (in G major), and a sonata finale (in B♭ major). As its title indicated, the work called for forces smaller than the modern orchestra, though its exact instrumentation was found in only one classical symphony, namely, Beethoven's *Fifth*. This particular connection was emphasized by the fact that Shapero, like Beethoven, reserved the piccolo, the contrabassoon, and the trombones for the final movement.

Shapero's actual orchestration, however, contained many novel touches. The work began, for example, with a held note on the tonic, as does many a classical symphony (Shapero probably had the Beethoven *Fourth* in mind), but it is scored just for winds and brass, and, further, with the oboe and clarinet in their high registers, and the flute in its middle register, a colorful and fairly novel sound. Noteworthy, also, was the pronounced and expressive role given to the first trumpet, not only in this introduction, but throughout. The work's orchestration, in general, was distinctively bright and brassy, and undoubtedly derived a fair amount from Piston and Copland, as well as from the composer's experience as a dance band arranger; indeed, the prominent first trumpet, which often had the flavor of a Baroque obbligato part, had, at the same time, the aura of a Harry James-like solo.

The "Adagio" introduction to the first movement opens with the motive Bb-A-Bb in 32nd-note triplets, like the inverted mordant that might begin a Bach toccata. This motive colors much of the first movement, often, as at first, as 8-7-8 (see 1 m. after 11), but also as 3-b3-3 (see 7) and 5-#4-5 (see 22). This motive undergoes octave displacement four measures after 26, a displacement that, stretched out, becomes the opening gesture of the slow movement's main theme. It appears in the last two movements as well, where it is found, among other places, in the scherzo at 222 (here as 4-3-4) and at the start of the finale (as b7-6-b7 as well as 8-7-8). This motive is not an important thematic idea, but rather a simple ornamental device that helps articulate a specific tonality and unify the work's varied textures.

Inspired by Beethoven, Shapero, throughout the work, shapes his tonal gestures into big, sharply etched strokes, something that gives the work its impressive spaciousness. These big strokes often involve the kind of heightened dramatic conflict between tonic and dominant characteristic of the 18th century. In the "Adagio" introduction, for instance, Shapero puts forth a phrase in I (to 1); an answer with a triplet tag in V (to 2); a cadence in I with a triplet tag that closes in the tonic minor (to 5); another triplet tag in V for one measure; a cadence in the tonic minor that settles into a luminous tonic major triad; and a wispy return to V that leads into the "Allegro," whose first five pages are a dominant preparation for the first theme, at 11, in the tonic. This dialog between tonic and dominant achieves freshness not only through interesting rhythms and sonorities, especially the wonderful contrast between the cold, processional winds and the warm, "dolce" strings, but through extensive use of flatted thirds and sevenths, modal inflections derived from native traditions in both popular and concert music. The form of the introduction itself, with its slow harmonic rhythm and its three cadences in the tonic, faintly suggests a "blues" strophe, a suggestion that further contributes to the music's distinctively earthy character. Even Shapero's use of the major mode is smartly modern, often forming colorful ellipses, as at one measure after 1, where the winds are in the tonic while the strings are in the dominant.

The first movement's main theme illustrates yet another distinctive feature: the composer's ability to write not only an attractive melody, but one particularly suited for symphonic development (Ex. 34). This melody is neatly constructed, consisting, as it does, of a phrase in the tonic played by the strings and completed by the winds in the subdominant, followed by a consequent phrase in the subdominant played by the strings and completed by the winds in the tonic. This sort of symmetry also characterizes the movement's two other important themes: the harmonic structure of the second theme (see 26) is i-V-i-V-i, that of the closing theme (see 44), I-bVII-bVII-I. The second theme (Ex. 35) is in F minor, the dominant minor; a jazzy melody for flute and clarinet, it features the sort of ambiguous tragic-comic pathos found too in the opening of Shapero's 1948 *Piano Sonata,* also in F minor. A fragment from this second theme is used later in the development as the basis for a fugue subject.

Shapero achieves another kind of unity throughout this movement, and throughout the whole work for that matter, by joining thematic ideas in counterpoint: an introductory fragment at 7 becomes an ornamental countermelody to the first theme; a slightly transformed first theme, played by the violas, subtly supports the second theme (see Ex. 35); and the development's fugue subject sounds high above the climactic

Example 34. Harold Shapero, *Symphony for Classical Orchestra,* I (Peer-Southern, 1965). Used by permission.

return of the first theme (see 85). Again Shapero presumably is thinking of Beethoven's *Fifth,* and the way in which that work's motto theme underscores the first movement's second theme.

Yet another Beethovenian feature is the way in which Shapero paces himself, alternating long passages in the tonic and the dominant, with fast, dramatic modulations often reserved for transitions and developments. In general, key relations are close and direct, and Shapero has no hesitation in moving by fifth. It is not until the development's fugue that Shapero finds his way in this opening B♭ major movement to the remote regions of B, E, and F♯ minor. Further, modulations are typically prepared by the dominant. There are some nice surprises, like the return to B♭ from a shortly established D major at 18, but nothing really startling. Although the

Example 35. Harold Shapero, *Symphony for Classical Orchestra*, I (Peer-Southern, 1965). Used by permission.

model, again, is ostensibly Beethoven, there are many touches that more emphatically recall Schubert: the minor modality of the second theme, the tonal deviations in the second theme group, the long stretch of D major at the start of the development, and similarly, the stretch of G♭ major, functioning as a spacious augmented chord, in the coda. But whereas Shapero's key design and tonal rhythm are reminiscent of the classic repertory, his rhythmic and contrapuntal textures are pungent and vibrantly modern, offering an alluring variation on traditional rhetoric.

Like the slow movements from the *Serenade* and the *Piano Sonata*, the *Symphony*'s "Adagietto" elicited special praise from critics, and on occasion was performed by itself. Francisco Moncion choreographed it in 1966 for a ballet called *Night Song*. The mood is warm, tender, and romantic, its poised calm attained through its leisurely 8/8 meter, its spacious sonata form, and its placid harmonic movement. The opening phrase (133–134), for instance, moves surely and slowly against a I-IV-V-I progression in the movement's tonic key, E♭ major (Ex. 36). After this opening phrase, there is a consequent phrase (134–136) that smoothly moves through the dominant, B♭, to a cadence in G. The theme's second half (136–139) moves from C minor back to E♭ major after first cadencing in C major (1 m. before 138). The theme itself, played by the first violins, is classically balletic, with supple rhythms, graceful turns, sighing fourths, and sweet appoggiaturas and suspensions. An occasional large leap gives the theme an added expressive edge, especially the impassioned jump of a minor ninth at 136. The theme's supporting texture is more Baroque than Classic: the second violins provide an intertwining duet, the violas some rhythmic activity, and the basses a firm harmonic support. Shapero subsequently varies the texture, but the idea of the duet is retained throughout much of the movement.

The quasi-variations that follow are organized according to the sonata principle, so they consequently deviate from the theme to varying degrees. The first variation (139–145), in which the fragmented theme modulates against Beethovenian hammerstrokes in the first violins, provides a transition to the

Example 36. Harold Shapero, *Symphony for Classical Orchestra,* II (Peer-Southern, 1965). Used by permission.

dominant, B^b, and the second theme, variation two (145–151). This second theme is indeed quite new, a delicate theme that recalls the original theme only subtly, as in, for example, its inverted major seventh, here falling peacefully into the subdominant rather than straining upwards in the tonic. The melodic writing, scoring, and harmonic progressions of this section are slightly reminiscent of Mahler, slightly because Shapero's sensibility is more delicate and restrained. Variation three (151–153), which combines the movement's opening viola figure, the hammerstrokes of the first variation, and the chord progression of the opening phrase, provides the "exposition" with a short, hearty conclusion in the dominant.

The fourth variation (153–163) is at once a development section and a variation in minor. Not only does it restlessly and dramatically modulate, but it recalls thematic fragments from the preceding variations, most emphatically the second theme, which appears in the winds above the busy strings with the nobility of a chorale theme in some polyphonic setting by Bach. Toward the end of this development section, Shapero, wavering between E^b and A^b, settles into the first theme, variation five (163–168), in A^b, the subdominant. It is a beautifully ornamented reprise, like a florid da capo. Only the original theme's first half is recapitulated, and Shapero moves quickly after a brief arrival in C (166) to prepare for a restatement of the second theme in the tonic, variation six (168–175). The second theme is here rescored and rewritten, with a surprising excursion into A, the tonic's tritone. The recapitulation's closing section, variation seven (175–177), is also in the tonic, although there is a short, unexpected shift to A^b at 176. The movement's coda (177 to the end) offers an appropriately romantic conclusion, what with its echoes of previous variations, its chromatic wanderings, its short cadenza for the first violins, and its fluctuations in tempo.

While the 8/8 meter of the "Adagietto" gives that movement a certain suspended feeling, the extremely fast 3/4 meter of the scherzo ("Vivace," and conducted "a due battute" and, at one point, "a tre battute") gives this movement an energetic, even hectic quality. The "battute" indications naturally suggest the influence of Beethoven's *Ninth Symphony,* but the scherzo theme itself (Ex. 37a) points

Example 37a. Harold Shapero, *Symphony for Classical Orchestra*, III (Peer-Southern, 1965). Used by permission.

more directly to the *Third;* Shapero updates Beethoven's two-note idea (Ex. 37b) to include a jazzy flatted third. The movement contains other Beethovenian features: ghostly chromatics (186), a sort of peasant stomping (189), and a generous sense of humor, sometimes quite broad, as at the surprising major III chord at 216. The scherzo is in G, the *Symphony*'s submediant, an unusual relationship, but not unknown to the classical repertory.

The trio section (213–236), itself tripartite, is in E major, with a C major middle section. The trio's outer sections feature a jazzy theme for the clarinets. Again, the jazz flavor reminds one of Bernstein, but Shapero submits his theme to the rigors of symphonic development in a more thoroughgoing manner. While the trio's outer sections have a traditional pastoral lightness, its middle section has the sort of urgency

Example 37b. Ludwig van Beethoven, *Symphony No. 3,* III.

and poignancy occasionally encountered in Mozart's trio
sections. In this middle section (222–229), the flutes and the
oboes have expressive, legato lines, while the cellos, staccato,
keep up the joke by (three times out of four) foiling harmonic
expectations and cadencing in C major rather than E or A
minor. Despite these changes of mood, the scherzo's three
main themes are essentially variations of the same idea. This
unity is emphasized with the return of the scherzo, at which
point Shapero combines the scherzo and trio themes in
counterpoint.

The *Symphony* concludes with a rousing 2/2 finale, "Allegro
con spirito." This movement is articulated by four long-held
notes: at the very opening (F), at the start of the development
(E^b), at the start of the coda (D), and at the very end (B^b).
These long notes are usually followed by an introductory idea
(see 269–271, for example) that recalls Beethoven's finale to
the *Seventh Symphony,* but only in rhythm, for its pitches look
back to the opening motto, B^b-A-B^b. The finale's main theme
(271), "leggiero" and in perpetual motion, is more like
Rossini, perhaps, than Beethoven (Ex. 38). It begins in the
subdominant, E^b, setting up an ambiguity (is the B^b cadence
four measures after 271 in the tonic or dominant?) that is
quickly resolved after 272. (This ambiguity between I and IV
is found elsewhere in the *Symphony,* and is at the heart of a
beautiful little children's piano piece that Shapero wrote in

Example 38. Harold Shapero, *Symphony for Classical Orchestra*, IV (Peer-Southern, 1965). Used by permission.

1956, *Song Without Words*.) The finale's first theme group is organized into two large paragraphs (271–278; 278–287), each concluding with a sort of fanfare for the brass. The second of these two paragraphs features a five-note motive (280) that is used prominently in the transition (287–296) and the closing theme (309–314).

The connections between the finale and the preceding movements, especially the first, are numerous, and often rather dramatic. The second theme (296), for instance, is a climactic and impassioned variation of the first movement's main theme, its forceful, conclusive character due in large part to its postponement of a cadence in the tonic, its pedal point, and its emphasis on V rather than on I or IV (Ex. 39). The cellos and basses support this theme with the *Symphony*'s motto, now on the dominant. The links between the first and last movements are not restricted to thematic transformation. The syncopated chords for wind choir in the finale's closing theme (3 before 311) recall the rhythm, harmony, and orchestral writing of a particular passage from the first movement (4 before 13) without recalling any melody. Even more subtly, the G^b tonality found at the recapitulation of the second theme looks back to the first movement's coda.

After an initial establishment of E♭ major, the finale's development section (314–360) happily offers something new: an exciting, elegant fugue in the tradition of Piston (318–333). Actually, the fugue subject and its running-note accompaniment are derived, at least rhythmically, from the finale's second and first themes, respectively. But the fugue's chromaticism, its minor modality (the subject's opening outlines a minor seventh chord, like the fugue that concludes Barber's *Piano Sonata* of the following year), and its rapid modulations provide welcome contrast. The latter portion of the development introduces a new, rhythmically trenchant motive (333) that alternates with delicate fragments from the second theme. The return of the fugue subject at 345 adds to the excitement, soon giving way, shortly before the recapitu-

Example 39. Harold Shapero, *Symphony for Classical Orchestra,* IV (Peer-Southern, 1965). Used by permission.

lation, to a climactic cadence in the tonic major, B^b (357). This arrival in B^b naturally sets up the return of the main theme in its original key, E^b; the ambiguity between I and IV now takes on an even heightened tension. This tension is finally resolved by the recapitulation of the second theme, now in the tonic, and, finally, by the coda, a brilliant perpetual motion that begins in G and slowly works its way back to B^b against thematic reminiscences of the entire *Symphony.*

The *Symphony* was premiered by Leonard Bernstein and the Boston Symphony on January 30, 1948. The reviews were highly enthusiastic, Irving Fine calling the work "an extraordinary achievement."[8] Bernstein went on to play the *Symphony*'s "Adagietto" with the New York Philharmonic, and to record the whole work with the Columbia Symphony Orchestra, a recording rough in spots, but whose passion and finesse clearly suited the music. The *Symphony*'s bold vigor, imposing scale, social idealism, and national cut, reflecting deep concerns for folk, popular, and jazz styles,[9] deserved comparison with contemporary works by such outstanding young American artists as Orson Welles and Norman Mailer.

Many listeners, understandably enough, were inclined to regard the work as a cross between Beethoven and Stravinsky, including Lincoln Kirstein and George Balanchine, whose plans to choreograph it never materialized.[10] The connection with Beethoven proved the more troubling. Even admirers like Fine[11] and Berger[12] found fault with, in Fine's words, Shapero's "literalness in adherence to classical formal procedures." Copland qualified his enthusiasm by discussing Shapero's "hero-worship complex—or perhaps it is a freakish attack of false modesty, as if he thought to hide the brilliance of his own gifts behind the cloak of the great masters."[13]

Forty years have not resolved these problems (though the scarcity of live performances and new recordings has not helped), problems concerning questions of tradition and style, especially as far as Beethoven is concerned. Perhaps it is fair to say that the work is to Beethoven what Prokofiev's similarly-titled *Classical Symphony* is to Haydn. Why does Prokofiev's work appear less "freakish" than Shapero's? Is it because a neoclassical symphony is expected to be, in the end, a joke? Because music for chamber orchestra is expected to be light and brisk rather than grandiose and passionate?

One thoughtful response to these questions was provided by Wilfred Mellers in his discussion of the composer:

> The *Symphony in Classical Style* (sic) and the big *Piano Variations* are impressive pieces, remarkable for their very attempt to use Beethoven as (in Stravinsky's sense) a mask. One may still think, however, that the attempt was misguided: for Beethoven's essence is a revelation of identity rather than a manifestation of tradition. Identity can never be emulated, only superseded. This is why the sheer (Bostonian) musicality and facility of Shapero's invention becomes, in these works, almost a liability. Where is Beethoven without the sense of struggle? If Beethoven has won his victory, why fight the fight again?[14]

But what, then, of Schubert and Tchaikovsky, symphonists who did emulate Beethoven, and whose works are antecedents to Shapero's *Symphony?* Is it that such emulation was beyond the pale in the 20th century? For an American? A composer like Sessions, it is true, could successfully abstract the Beethovenian ideal naturally enough; and a composer like Rochberg could stylishly evoke his manner. Perhaps the challenge of Shapero's achievement was in incorporating both Beethoven's ideal and manner within the context of a modern and individual sensibility. To even attempt this required a personality that could at least approach Beethoven's courageous and powerful own. Tragically, it was never allowed to develop, partly because, as we shall see, the 20th century wanted nothing of it.

If it were at all possible, it was perhaps only possible in the 1940s. Beethoven's *Fifth Symphony,* which played a determinant role in Shapero's *Symphony,* right down to its instrumentation, was far from the cliché it appeared to be both before and after the War; it even came to symbolize Allied victory. Beethoven himself had lived through such tremendous upheaval. Other works of the decade—symphonies, for instance, by Piston, Copland, Sessions, and Stravinsky—also had, to varying degrees, Beethovenian aspirations. Indeed, Stravinsky had no qualms about Shapero's *Symphony,* writing to Robert Craft, "I cheer the influence of Beethoven in

Harold Shapero's work."[15] (Stravinsky well might have dismissed objections to such an influence as "intellectual and sentimental."[16]) Not surprisingly, there existed a close kinship between Shapero's *Symphony* and Stravinsky's *Symphony in C.*

The *Symphony's* controversial evocation of Beethoven notwithstanding, there was no doubting the individual voice heard throughout the work, one that was warm, full of tenderness, passion, and, at times, anguish. Its distinctive qualities have engaged many listeners over the years, most recently, André Previn, who successfully revived it in the late 1980s. And, indeed, Previn's interpretation, less mannered than Bernstein's, tended to accentuate not its derivative features, but rather its freshness, its contemporaneity, and its strongly communal sensibilities, with their close ties to various popular idioms.

In any case, Shapero was not daunted, not immediately. Contemporary with the *Symphony* came two additional Beethovenian works, both for piano, the 1947 *Variations* and the 1948 *Sonata in F minor.* The latter, in particular, highlighted the romantic depths of Shapero's personality, evoking, as it does at times, Schubert and Chopin, just as the *Symphony* itself had looked back to a number of 19th-century styles. (The Symphony's blend of Baroque and Classic elements, for instance, often had the flavor of Mendelssohn and Schumann.) Neither work, however, enjoyed the success that greeted the *Symphony;* the *Sonata,* in fact, was hissed at its New York premiere.[17] Even less successful was a 1948 orchestral work originally entitled *The Travelers Overture* after a painting, *The Travelers,* by the composer's wife, Esther Geller, and subsequently retitled *Sinfonia in C minor.*

Shapero composed less music in the years after his twenty-eighth birthday in 1948, than in the eight years prior to this date. Some of these later works, for instance, his two works from 1950, the *Concerto* for orchestra and the *America Variations* for piano, were in a constant state of revision. The *Concerto's* slow movement, simplified, became the 1955 *Credo,*[18] a work reminiscent of the *Symphony's* "Adagietto," but more like its skeletal remains. Its austerity reminded listeners of hymnal moments in Copland, Thomson, and

Cowell. In the composer's words, the *Credo* attempted, "with relatively few notes, to convey religious ideas in which I have been interested for some time."[19]

Shapero's religious ideas also began to take expression in vocal works, including *Two Psalms* for chorus (1952), dedicated to Irving Fine, and related to Renaissance styles; *Hebrew Cantata* after Halevi for soloists, chorus, and small ensemble (1954), whose use of Jewish folk idioms suggested the influence of Bartók; and *Two Hebrew Songs* for tenor and piano (1973) to texts by S. Shalom and L. Goldberg. This interest in religious ideas, and particularly in his Jewish heritage, may have been fostered by his position at Brandeis University, where he taught for more than thirty years.

It was for a 1957 Brandeis University Festival of the Arts that Shapero produced a little oddity, *On Green Mountains* (Chaconne After Monteverdi) for jazz band (arranged for orchestra in 1981). It was part of a concert series devoted to the so-called "third stream," and was premiered along with such works as Gunther Schuller's *Transformation,* Milton Babbitt's *All Set,* Jimmy Giuffre's *Suspensions,* and Charles Mingus's *Revelations,* Part I. Based on Monteverdi's chaconne-madrigal "Zefiro torna" ("Zephyr returns"), Shapero's work was unusual in that it did not so much presuppose some new genre as it did dramatize traditions common to both classical music and jazz, in this case, the recurrent chord pattern. Indeed, its title punned not only Monteverdi's name, but a popular tune also built on a repetitive chord pattern, Richard Rodgers's "Mountain Greenery." Shapero retained Monteverdi's chaconne bass, as well as much of the original melody, which, however, was jazzed up in a way then made popular by the Swingle Singers. In addition, there were opportunities for improvisation, including a "blues" passage that appropriately substituted for the melancholy recitative near the madrigal's end.

With the 1960 *Partita for Solo Piano and Orchestra,* Shapero's only major undertaking after 1950, he explored the 12-tone method. In one of its movements, "Ciaconna," the method was used with idiosyncratic straightforwardness: the row was put forth in unison to a tango-like rhythm, and then provided the foundation for a series of simple triads. The more complex "Scherzo" and "Burlesca" showed an awareness of *Agon,* while the neobaroque "Aria" looked back to Piston.

Shapero produced no new works between 1960 and 1968. In a 1967 interview, he spoke with his characteristic blend of humor and bitterness about the "degraded level of democratization" and the "erosion of aristocratic values" in contemporary life.[20] He showed little sympathy with current trends, including John Cage ("probably misunderstood Zen Buddhism . . . kindergarten philosophy and kindergarten activity"), the Princeton "school" ("an admirable sort of intellectual activity . . . the danger is that you may lose music to numerology . . . in other words, just the order expressed in the numerical design is no guarantee of any musical validity whatsoever"), computer music ("the computer may turn out to be a very poor vehicle for the sublime"), and happenings ("they think they're getting in touch with the absolute spontaneity of the universe, but what actually happens at happenings is an incredible dreary boredom"). And yet he thought Henry Pleasants's *The Agony of Modern Music* ridiculous, saying, "The agony that I sense is something else, is the agony of the whole civilization"; and he found some hope in the example of Stravinsky, and some comfort in Piston's remark, "composition is a very luxurious hobby." Of the things that currently interested him, Shapero mentioned, among others, "the extension of tonality (still); the mixture of tonality and serialism; the poetic content of the musical idea; melody; the possibilities of motoric rhythm; and just the one thing that is considered unsayable: musicality, sentiment."

Although Shapero denied in this interview any "really enormous drive for electronic music personally," at about this time he founded Brandeis's electronic music studio, and began to write a series of pieces for piano and synthesizer: *Three Improvisations in B* (1968), *Three Studies in C#* (1969), and *Four Pieces in B♭* (1970). They were intended as duets for himself and his daughter Hannah, who by age fourteen was playing the Buchla Synthesizer in concert. These and other electronic works hardly were known outside the Brandeis community.

A rare glimpse into Shapero's late work was provided by a

small piano piece published in *Perspectives of New Music* in honor of Arthur Berger's sixty-fifth birthday.[21] Called *A.B. 65,* the work was built on the motive, A-B, and the harmonic intervals of the sixth and the fifth. Stravinskian in its brilliance and elegance, the work's delicate lyricism, nervous tremolos, and strong tonic-dominant tensions were nonetheless pure Shapero.

The restraint and austerity of *A.B. 65* were characteristic of Shapero's music after 1948. The unisons, homorhythms, two-part writing, and simple triads found in his later work betokened a consistent search for greater and greater directness and purity of musical thought. This search had begun long before, with Shapero's emulation of Piston, and then the Viennese Classicists. The search after 1950, however, became so intermittent, so subtle, and so personal that it failed to hold the interest of listeners and critics.

This sort of decline was not unique, especially in the 20th century; but in Shapero's case, it was especially dramatic in that the early works had been so enthusiastically received and so promising. In discussing this decline, Mellers pointed to the harmful influence of Beethoven.[22] Some who knew Shapero suggested that the reasons were of a more personal nature. Then, too, Shapero's decline may have been precipitated by a widespread indifference, if not actual hostility, toward his ideals. Certainly, it is significant that this decline occurred in the late 1940s, when the changing times inspired all kinds of new styles, even from Harvard colleagues: the 12-tone rapprochement of Fine and Berger; the cool jazziness of Bernstein; the sound explorations of Carter. And Shapero, in fact, explored all these trends: in the *Partita, On Green Mountains,* and the electronic pieces, respectively. But no new work met with much success, and no new approach was long sustained.

This decline in no way diminished the glory of such works as the *3 Piano Sonatas* and the *Symphony for Classical Orchestra.* In this respect, Shapero once again resembled such figures as Orson Welles and Norman Mailer more than any musician. For if the expectations of the 1940s were not fulfilled, Shapero's early work constituted, nonetheless, some of the best American art of that decade, indeed, of any decade.

Notes

1. Stravinsky, *Selected Correspondence*, Vol. I, Robert Craft, ed. (New York: Alfred A. Knopf, 1982), p. 226n; Copland, "1949: The New 'School' of American Composers," *Copland on Music* (New York: W. W. Norton, 1963), p. 169.
2. Shapero, personal interview, December 1, 1978. As it turns out, Piston must have been impressed with the work, for he sat on the jury, along with Howard Barlow, Leo Sowerby, Albert Stoessel, and Howard Hanson, that awarded the *9-Minute Overture* a "Prix de Rome." Prior to this, Shapero's two George Arthur Knight Awards from Harvard would have required Piston's approval as well.
3. Joan Peyser, *Bernstein. A Biography* (New York: William Morrow, 1987), p. 81.
4. Shapero, liner notes to a recording of the *Serenade*, MGM E3557.
5. Shapero, "Neglected Works: A Symposium," *Modern Music* 23 (1946), pp. 8–9.
6. Shapero, liner notes to a recording of *Sonata No. 1*, Concert-Disc M-1217.
7. Shapero, "The Musical Mind," *Modern Music* 23 (1946), pp. 31–35.
8. Fine, "Shapero Symphony Given Premiere," *Musical America* (March 15, 1948), p. 14.
9. According to Clive Barnes ("Dance: A Visit by the National Ballet," *New York Times*, March 7, 1966) and Walter Terry ("National Ballet Graded B Plus," *New York Herald Tribune*, March 7, 1966) in reviews of Moncion's *Night Song*, no distinctive national or individual qualities were to be found in either music or choreography. Barnes wrote, "It is curious that one of the most intelligent and powerful performers America has produced should offer this kind of neo-Balanchinian nothingness . . . a drearily pretentious nocturnal ramble in the Balanchine country . . . little helped by the score of Harold Shapero, which sounded wispily like Tchaikovsky in the next room, savored, but little, by a few Stravinskian astringencies."

   Bill Evans, in a modern dance after Shapero's *String Quartet* called *The Legacy* (1972), seemed more successful, or at least more direct, in bringing out Shapero's national profile. *The Legacy*, inspired by photographs of polygamous Mormon families taken during the 1880s, told the unusual domestic drama about a Mormon boy who falls in love with one of his father's wives. The dance was like *Appalachian Spring,* only darker and more thwarted. One need not make too much of this, for the *String Quartet,* an abstract work after all, also met the needs of a 1962 abstract dance by Glen Tetley entitled, *Dance in the Bone House.* But it, nonetheless, demonstrated the kind of distinctive national ambiance Shapero's music was capable of evoking.

10. Stravinsky, *Selected Correspondence,* pp. 266, 290.
11. Fine, "Shapero," p. 14.
12. Berger, "Stravinsky and the Younger American Composers," *The Score* 12 (June 1955), p. 43.
13. Copland, "1949," p. 70.
14. Mellers, *Music in a New Found Land* (London: Barrie & Rockliff, 1964), p. 221.
15. Stravinsky, *Selected Correspondence,* p. 353. At the same time, Stravinsky admitted feeling "more than a little bit embarrassed by his influence in Romain Rolland's work." These reflections, including the statement, "It is wrong that I do not like Beethoven," were prompted by an article by Eric White entitled "Stravinsky as a Writer," *Tempo* (1948).
16. Stravinsky, *An Autobiography* (New York: W. W. Norton, 1962; first published by Simon and Schuster, 1936), p. 115.
17. Upon learning that Shapero's *Piano Sonata in F minor* was hissed at its New York premiere "for daring to attempt a reinstatement of late Beethoven principles, instead of adding to musical evolution with new sonorities," Stravinsky wrote back to Robert Craft, March 22, 1949, "Convey my sincerest sympathy to Harold Shapero," *Selected Correspondence,* p. 360.
18. David Ewen, *Dictionary of American Composers* (New York: Putnam, 1982), p. 590.
19. Shapero, liner notes to a recording of the *Credo,* LOU 56.
20. Shapero, interview with Margaret Fairbanks, 1967, Rodgers and Hammerstein Archives, New York Public Library.
21. Shapero, "A.B. 65," *Perspectives of New Music* 17 (Fall-Winter 1978), pp. 78–82.
22. Mellers, p. 221.

9. A HERITAGE UPHELD: DANIEL PINKHAM

DANIEL ROGERS PINKHAM (B. 1923) bridged the old and the new in strikingly unique ways. He had a distinguished career, in the 1950s, as a harpsichordist, and, in later years, as musical director of Boston's historic King's Chapel and as chairman of the department of early music at the New England Conservatory. In these same capacities, he performed and commissioned many new works. In addition, he produced much music of his own, music that incorporated such modern trends as neo-classical counterpoint, 12-tone melody, electronic media, and aleatoric composition.

Pinkham could not help but be aware of the past. He was the great-grandson of Lydia Pinkham (1818–1883), whose "vegetable compound" (a herbal decoction preserved with alcohol—forty proof!) for "female complaints" (the "catchall nineteenth-century term for disorders ranging from painful menstruation to prolapsed uterus"[1]) had made her name and face a familiar household commodity for over fifty years. It was largely the brilliant advertising campaign staged by her sons that turned Lydia's "compound" into a multi-million-dollar business. Lydia, nee Estes, was descended from the Italian house of Este, but by the 17th century, the American Estes were Quaker and settled in Lynn, Massachusetts. They were a trail-blazing lot. One early American Estes, in around 1687, acquired a songbook in disregard to Quaker injunctions against music, and "refused to see anything wrong in it."[2] Lydia's parents, advocates of Abolition, temperance, progressive education, Swedenborgianism, and woman suffrage, eventually left the Quaker Church. Their friends included some of New England's most famous Abolitionists, including William Lloyd Garrison, Nathaniel Rogers, Wendell Phillips, John Greenleaf Whittier, and Frederick Douglass. Lydia herself taught Douglass's wife to read, and in 1843 she instituted an open forum "which represented the avant-garde of Lynn."[3] (Lydia's forums looked ahead to her great-grandson's late-night concerts at King's Chapel, of which the composer wrote, "at eleven o'clock decent people are in bed. Then we do all the really avant-garde things we want to."[4]) Lydia came to defend Darwin and to hold novel and influential opinions about sex, medicine, and hygiene. Her husband, Isaac Pinkham, was descended from an old Massachusetts family as well; his ancestors included two Revolutionary War soldiers, Daniel Pinkham and Captain Joseph Pinkham, and a victim of the Salem witch trials, Mary Tyler (a relevant bit of family history when considering not only such Pinkham works as *Witching Hour* and *The Descent into Hell,* but the family's irrepressible nonconformity in general). Isaac and Lydia named one son Daniel Rogers (the composer's great-uncle) in memory of both Daniel Pinkham and Nathaniel Rogers; as a state legislator, this Daniel Rogers Pinkham described himself as "a radical democrat with a small d."[5] Their other sons, William and Charles (the composer's grandfather), were early members of the Universalist Church.

Lydia's great-grandson Daniel, also born in Lynn, began piano lessons at age five, and studied organ and harmony with Carl Pfatteicher at Phillips Andover Academy (1937–1940). It was there that Pinkham first encountered E. Power Biggs, his most important organ teacher: "I recall at the time finding Biggs' playing remarkably unlike the reverend and churchy legato playing then considered the decent way to play the organ."[6] Later, at Harvard, Pinkham grew familiar with Biggs's playing by way of weekly broadcasts of old and new music from Harvard's Busch-Reisinger Museum. In 1944 Biggs premiered the young Pinkham's *Sonata No. 1* for organ and strings at one such broadcast. In the following year, 1945, Pinkham studied with Biggs at the Longy School, where he learned "a systematic approach to pedal technique." He later began to substitute for the Busch-Reisinger broadcasts when Biggs was away on tour, and eventually collaborated with Biggs on a recording of Soler's *Concertos* for two organs. By his own admission, however, he never mastered the organ or the piano, a limitation that decided not only the music he chose to perform, but the way in which he wrote for these instruments.[7]

Another important experience at Andover was his stint as school carilloneur. For one thing, this experience provided some impetus to his study of clavichord and harpsichord. In addition, it influenced his own music, not only his two small pieces for carillon, A Song for the Bells (1944) and Dithyramb (1946), but his entire oeuvre. Is there another composer whose work—chamber, choral, and orchestral alike—is so filled with bells, celesta, harpsichord, vibraphone, antique cymbals, harp, guitar, piano, and glockenspiel? When Pinkham took up electronic media in the 1970s, it was in part to surpass the etherealness of even the celesta and the glockenspiel. And his one foray into "musique concrète," The Shepherd's Symphony (1973), used "some clay shepherd bells . . . recorded and then slowed down . . . so it sounds like not very resonant church bells."[8] Pinkham's scoring in general reflected these preferences, for instance, in the frequent mutings for brass.

Pinkham's love of bells had other consequences on his style. Sometimes there were long, sustained notes, or stretches of tonal immobility, that seemed related to bells, for example, in the Easter Cantata's second movement. There were moments in this same movement, as well as in the first movement of the Concerto for Harpsichord and Celesta, that more specifically recalled the tolling of bells. One found, too, in Pinkham's music, evocative harmonies that suggested the undertones or overtones of bells, as in the climax of the First Symphony's first movement (m. 153), and in the little major-second clusters in the St. Mark Passion.

Yet another experience at Andover that had a major effect on the composer was a concert there by the Trapp Family Singers. The Trapp Family, recently emigrated from Austria, had an earthiness and idealism closer to the Pinkham family than to the sentimental portrait they received at the hands of Rodgers and Hammerstein in their 1959 hit, The Sound of Music; they unpretentiously revived and performed works by Dufay, the Elizabethan madrigalists, Bach, and others on harpsichord, viola da gamba, and recorder.[9] To Pinkham, who had assumed that classical music essentially meant Wagner and Brahms, this concert was "the real day of conversion, like Saul on the road to Damascus." He began to read about early music and returned for his senior year at Andover with a German clavichord.

Pinkham decided not to go to Brown University, a family tradition, but rather Harvard, so that he could pursue the study of clavichord and harpsichord in Boston. He studied first with Jean Claude Chiasson (1940–1941), then with Chiasson's teacher, Putnam Aldrich (1941–1942), and finally with Aldrich's teacher, Wanda Landowska (1946). For his lessons with Landowska, he needed to travel to New York City, and pay "the astronomical fee of thirty dollars per lesson."[10] Her knowledge of early music made a lasting impression,[11] and Pinkham wrote an *Homage to Wanda Landowska* for harpsichord (1959) in her memory. In 1948, his harpsichord studies completed, Pinkham formed a violin-harpsichord duo with Robert Brink, a violinist with the Boston Symphony. In the ten years that followed, the Duo concertized frequently in the Boston area and made tours of the United States, Canada, and Europe. From 1950 to 1956 Pinkham also served as harpsichordist for the Boston Symphony. During these years he participated in recordings of many orchestral and chamber works, most from the Baroque, but some modern works as well. Two bad bouts of hepatitis forced him to give up his concert career in 1961, and he rarely performed after that, reserving his energy for composition. Not surprisingly, the influence of early music on his own music was extensive and profound, ranging from forms and texts to rhythms and textures, an extraordinary study in its own right.

Pinkham seriously began to compose at Harvard (1940–1943, BA; 1944, MA), where he worked primarily with Piston. This included Piston's classes in fugue, harmony, orchestration, and at least three semesters of Composition Seminar. At first he disliked Piston, thinking him cold and aloof; but he came to regard Piston as "a little bit shy," and to appreciate the subtlety and wisdom of his dry wit and "crazy off-the-wall comments." He also realized that Piston was not indifferent toward his students, only undemanding; ". . . if students wanted to bring in something to show him, he would look at it with pleasure and give wonderful comments." Pinkham also discovered that in a very quiet way, Piston acted on his behalf by arranging the aforementioned premiere of his *Organ Sonata,* and by doing "many, many kindnesses that resulted in commissions and that sort of thing." The two men never became friends, however, and even when Pinkham taught at Harvard for one year (1957–1958), he could not address Piston by his first name.

Pinkham knew and admired Piston's music. Piston's *Prelude and Allegro* for organ and strings, which he called "a very marvelous piece, entirely accessible and warm, with a joyous allegro,"[12] stood up better, in his estimation, than his own *Sonata* and similar pieces by Harris, Porter, and Hanson.[13] Piston's influence occasionally was felt in Pinkham's handling of irregular meters and modal-chromatic counterpoint, especially in his instrumental music from the 1950s, including the *Concerto for Harpsichord and Celesta* (1955) and the *Cantilena and Capriccio* for violin and harpsichord (1954, 1956),[14] a work indebted to Piston's *Sonatina* for the same medium (Ex. 40).

The influence of Hindemith, while related, was probably greater; Hindemith came closer to the ideals of the Trapp

Example 40. Daniel Pinkham, "Cantilena," *Cantilena and Capriccio* for violin and harpsichord (Ione Press, 1972).

Family. Pinkham early on learned to love Hindemith; at Andover, he listened to a recording of the *Kleine Kammermusik* for wind quintet "until the other side came through." In 1941 he attended Hindemith's classes and lectures at Tanglewood, and learned to admire the man's character as well. Throughout his career he remained devoted to the principles of the "neue Sachlichkeit" (as exemplified by Hindemith, not necessarily by the Bauhaus) and "Gebrauchsmusik," which he defined as "music which has its own integrity as a piece of art but which is not geared only to professionals." As for Hindemith's style, its influence primarily was evident only in Pinkham's very earliest scores, like the 1943 *Sonata*.

Copland tried to steer Pinkham away from Hindemith when he came to teach Piston's classes in the winter of 1944. It was to little avail: Pinkham went on to complete the very Hindemithian *Duo* for violin and violoncello (1945). But perhaps Copland's presence at Harvard helped prompt the ballet, *Narragansett Bay,* undertaken in 1944 and completed in 1946, a work, like Piston's *Incredible Flutist,* that was written for choreographer Jan Veen. Pinkham, however, had little enthusiasm for jazz, folk, or other popular styles. The "Scherzo" from the 1958 *Partita,* a movement slightly reminiscent of Irving Fine, proved a rare excursion into a sort of Americana idiom. This is not to say that Pinkham's modal cross-relations and syncopated rhythms were unrelated to the vernacular; but they served universalist ideals rather than nationalist ones.

Pinkham completed his education during the summers of 1946 and 1947 with lessons with Boulanger, Honegger, and Barber. He regretted that Boulanger's personal fondness for him prevented her from being as demanding as he would have liked. But he learned from her, as he had from Piston, "the importance of the craft of composition. They were always much concerned, not with what musical language you chose, but with the consistency of the style."[15] Boulanger probably brought Pinkham closer to Stravinsky, whose *L'Histoire* and *Octet* he considered as fine an expression of the "neue Sachlichkeit" as anything by Hindemith. He also admired Stravinsky's habit of setting "a new problem for himself in every piece he writes," in contrast to Richard Strauss, who "hit the jackpot with *Rosenkavalier* and . . . tried to keep cashing the same old opera."[16]

Pinkham studied with Honegger at Tanglewood only briefly, but he served the French composer as translator and driver, and came to know him quite well that way. Pinkham spoke with deeper emotion about Honegger than about any other teacher; "a dearer man," he said, "couldn't have existed." He was glad to learn from Honegger certain orchestral tricks, like accompanying an entrance of the low brass with harp, or perhaps pizzicato double basses. An opera written about this time, *The Garden of Artemis* (1948), showed the unmistakable impact of Honegger, according to Warren Story Smith.[17] In general, Pinkham showed a profound love for French composers of classic bent, especially Fauré.[18] He once wrote, "I can confess a certain sympathy for François Couperin who wrote in 'L'art de toucher de clavecin' that he preferred music which touched him to that which surprised him."[19]

After Honegger suffered a heart attack at Tanglewood, Pinkham took some lessons with his replacement, Samuel Barber. "At a time when a songwriter was not taken seriously," Pinkham and his friends William Flanagan and Ned Rorem were excited to find in Barber a composer of stature with whom they could discuss. text setting with seriousness, even passion. Piston, in contrast, had been only cooly sympathetic to songwriting, once commenting, "Writing a song must be like working with watercolors. I'm happier with oils on the big canvas." Pinkham, in contrast, was to make his composerly reputation principally as a writer of songs and choruses.

Pinkham's best-known song was a 1949 setting of Ben Jonson's "Slow, slow fresh fount" (Ex. 41). This song well represented Pinkham's aims, which sought to recreate the elegance and restraint of early music styles, in this case, specifically, the Elizabethan song. The melodic line was understated in its conjunct motion, small compass, and dignified rhythms; it subtly evoked the poem's melancholy through drooping seconds and thirds. The piano accompaniment simply consisted of a series of delicate chords. It was less like the art songs of Barber, Rorem, and Flanagan, actually,

Example 41. Daniel Pinkham, "Slow, slow fresh fount" (C. F. Peters, 1961). Used by permission.

than the neo-Elizabethan songs of Carter, Bernstein, and Fine. In fact, in this same year, 1949, Fine set this same poem in his choral *Hour-Glass Suite.*

Pinkham's kind of neo-Renaissance sensibility, however, had a distinctively romantic coloring. This was most evident in the piano accompaniment, for instance, the D phrygian context for the word "tears"; the move to A^b major for "o faintly, gentle springs"; the surprise cadence in E major, not D^b major, on the word, "sings"; the slowed harmonic rhythm for "Droop herbs and flowers"; the bluesy B^b for the first syllable of "craggy"; and most dramatically, the passionate return at measure twenty, "Drop, drop, drop, drop," and the subsequent move, not to A^b, but, through a poignant dominant B^7 chord at measure twenty-two, to E minor, for "wither'd daffodil." This harmonic palette—restrained yet sensual—helped explain Pinkham's attraction to Fauré. And given, too, the song's refined antiquarianism, the sensibility seemed particularly close to the 19th-century pre-Raphaelites. It was not surprising to find Pinkham in later years setting Christina Rossetti's "Love Came Down At Christmas." In fact, in the course of Pinkham's career, his songs made much less use of old English verse than of 19th and 20th-century poems of agreeable sensibility. A favored poet early on was Robert Hillyer, Pinkham's collaborator for *The Garden of Artemis.* After 1960 he showed a preference for the work of two little-known contemporaries, Norma Farber and Howard Holtzman. His cycle of seven Holtzman poems, *Transitions* for voice and bassoon (1979; later transcribed for voice and piano), demonstrated, not least in its archaic medium, that the ideals of "Slow, slow fresh fount" could accommodate new trends in both music and poetry.

Pinkham achieved greatest fame, however, for his choral music, most of which was for the church. Marlowe Johnson, who wrote a dissertation on Pinkham's choral music, explained its success as follows: "Audiences find immediate appeal in the sonorous harmonies, the striking melodies, and the stimulating rhythms. . . ."[20] Warren Story Smith noted, too, that "these sacred pieces reveal a genuine aptitude for choral writing, a refreshing approach to the matter of instrument support and a true devotional spirit."[21] It was arguably the most important body of Christian choral music by a 20th-century American.

Much of this music was written for Pinkham's own choir at King's Chapel,[22] where he was appointed music director in 1958. Consequently, it was music, in great part, intended for a small group of ten to twenty singers of good, amateur abilities. The texts were usually in English, but there were Latin and Hebrew settings as well. The music was highly sophisticated, and occasionally experimental as well, as with the introduction of electronic media and aleatoric techniques in the choral works of the 1970s. In these and other matters, the liberal leadership of King's Chapel allowed Pinkham utmost freedom.

Like Pinkham's secular works, the sacred works looked back to early musics, but with even greater stylistic explicitness. These works included the joyous *Glory Be To God* for a cappella mixed choir (1955), whose tonal stasis was reminiscent of medieval organum; another a cappella work, the haunting *Agnus Dei,* a work that responded to the Renaissance ideal of Tallis and Byrd, not Palestrina, whom Pinkham thought too predictable; and Pinkham's most successful choral work, *The Christmas Cantata* ("Sinfonia Sacra") for chorus and brass (1957), which came closer to the Gabrielis than did Piston's *Carnival Song.*

Notwithstanding these close ties to European traditions, there was a recognizably American quality to Pinkham's sacred music. There was, for instance, a liveliness and vibrancy that seemed related to jazz. Some melodies, too, bore a relationship to early American hymnody, despite the composer's indifference to the hymn repertory as such. Indeed, Robert Stevenson, in *Protestant Church Music in America,* asserted that Pinkham recreated "in contemporary terms the brisk confidence that has always been a characteristically American trait from its beginnings in Lyon, Billings, Holden, Edson, and Ingalls."[23]

Beginning with *Jonah* in 1966, the year Stevenson's book was published, Pinkham devoted less time to sacred pieces of "brisk confidence" than to large, serious dramatic works on religious themes. They were still characteristically American, perhaps, in their bare, austere religiosity, but they brooded on the subjects of evil, human suffering, and salvation, reflecting something of the nation's changing temper. They were not as popular as the earlier choral works, in part because they were not as useful, but they were among Pinkham's most ambitious and significant works. Besides *Jonah* for solo voice, chorus, and orchestra, there was the *St. Mark Passion* for solo voices, chorus and small orchestra (1967); *Daniel in the Lion's Den* for narrator, solo voices, chorus, two pianos, instruments, and tape (1973); the *Passion of Judas* for solo voices, chorus, instruments, and organ (1976); and *The Descent Into Hell* for solo voices, chorus, brass, percussion, organ, and tape (1980).

The inspiration for many of these big choral works was the high Baroque, especially the oratorios of Handel and the passions of Bach. The most operatic of these works was *Jonah,* subtitled a "dramatic cantata," a composition that the composer called his "one overstuffed work." Its libretto derived from Jonah, the Psalms, Proverbs, and Ezekiel. Some of its more theatrical devices included the use of speakers and divided chorus to depict God's voice; an aria for Jonah's wife; speaking voices that moved across the stage in the harborside scene "to give the illusion of Jonah's progress through the market"; and an exciting storm sequence that, like the work in general, effectively used 12-tone melody.

Both of the Pinkham passions derived from the Bach passions, but with the *St. Mark Passion,* the connections were the more literal, including a tenor evangelist to narrate the passion in recitative; solo singers to represent Pilate, Judas, and Old Testament prophecy; and a mixed chorus to depict the crowd and the chief priests, as well as to contemplate the action. *The Passion of Judas,* on the other hand, was more novel in that it retold the passion from Judas's perspective. One connection with Bach, however, resided in the combined use of Old Testament, New Testament, and contemporary texts, the contemporary texts being two poems (Norma Farber's "Tell me about the mother of Judas" and James Wright's "Saint Judas") and a short play (*Rescue of the Innocents* by R. C. Norris). Both passions also recalled Bach in their occasional chorale-like choruses: see "But be not far from me, O Lord" from the *St. Mark Passion* (m. 117), and "O Lord, who may lodge in thy tabernacle" from *The Passion of Judas.*

The Passion of Judas at the same time had a distinctly

medieval quality, not only because of certain harmonic and melodic features, but because of its delicate and colorful instrumentation for clarinet, viola, harp, double bass, and chamber organ. Even more medieval was *The Descent Into Hell,* with its similar instrumentation, and its allegorical portrayals of Satan, Hell, and the King of Glory as found in *The Apocryphal New Testament.* In addition, the casting of Satan as a woman had medieval iconographical validity, though it was, in fact, a very contemporary rebuke to "some noisy women's lib types" at West Virginia Wesleyan College who insisted that Pinkham change the word "man" to "all" in one line of text.[24] The work's joyous rondo finale suggested a return to the "brisk confidence" of Pinkham's earlier work.

The combination of the old and the new was even more startling in Pinkham's instrumental music than in his vocal music. There were, for instance, new works for old instruments, like the harpsichord and the recorder. One of the grandest of these, the 1958 *Partita* for harpsichord, was moreover, at once a film score and a large concert work. The work was commissioned by WGBH, which originally wanted Pinkham to record some harpsichord music for a TV series called "A Layman's Guide to Contemporary Art," but then agreed with the composer that a new work would be more appropriate. To precisely fill out a needed twenty-nine minutes and thirty seconds, Pinkham wrote a final "Envoi" with four fermatas, five pause marks, and seven retards. The TV series was never released, but the *Partita* became well-known as a concert work.

The success of the *Partita* was due to, among other things, its piquant harmonies, its intriguing counterpoint, its expert writing for the instrument, and its large scope. The first movement alone, with its "Toccata," "Andante," and "Fugue," was tantamount in scale to an entire Bach toccata. And there were five other movements! The second movement, consisting of three two-part "Inventions," looked back not only to the Bach *Inventions,* but to the *Art of the Fugue* (Ex. 42). Couperin, in contrast, was evoked in the third movement, an "Interlude and Rondo," with couplets. The final three movements were titled "Fantasia," "Scherzo and Trio," and "Envoi." The *Partita*'s impressive variety could be attributed in part to the fact that each of its six movements

Example 42. Daniel Pinkham, "Three Inventions," *Partita* for harpsichord
(C. F. Peters, 1964).

was dedicated to a different contemporary harpsichordist.
The work seemed to say all its composer had to say for the
solo harpsichord until the 1971 *Lessons,* another big work,
though not as successful. Both, however, were major 20th-
century contributions to the harpsichord literature.

As for traditional chamber ensembles, Pinkham wrote only
infrequently for these. There were no solo piano works, no
string quartets until 1989, indeed, little traditional chamber
music of any sort. He was very intrigued, however, with the
orchestra, and in the 1950s he scored documentaries and
industrial films specifically to learn "goof-proof" orchestration. (Pinkham's music from the '50s sometimes even
sounded like the stylish movie music of, say, Franz Waxman.)

In the 1960s Pinkham wrote three large orchestral works:
Symphony No. 1 (1961), *Symphony No. 2* (1963), and the *Signs
of the Zodiac* on poems by David McCord, with optional
speaker (1965). Like all of Pinkham's music, these works
blended the very old and the very new, without much
reference to the intervening years. The two symphonies, for
instance, had little to do with the standard symphonic
literature. The *First Symphony,* in fact, originally was called
"Centennial Elegy" in commemoration of the Civil War,
earning its symphonic title only after its completion. The
Second Symphony was similarly more elegy than anything else;
wrote the composer, "The premiere [of the *Second Symphony*]
took place on November 23 [1963], the day following the
tragic death of President Kennedy. The concert program was

fittingly declared a memorial. By coincidence the elegiac mood of my work seemed strikingly appropriate to the occasion."[25] Moreover, the titles of this work's four movements—"Aria," "Three Epigrams," "Ballade," and "Envoy"— pointed specifically to early musics. So did its content, for instance, the first of the "Three Epigrams," which was somewhat like a Renaissance dance.

At the same time, these orchestral works used new and fashionable techniques. The *First Symphony* had chromatic counterpoint and changing meters reminiscent alternately of Piston and Stravinsky (Pinkham called the decade 1955– 1965, his Stravinsky period[26]). The even more adventurous *Second Symphony* used the 12-tone method, and an effective bit of aleatoric writing. Pinkham had shown an inclination toward the 12-tone method at least as early as the 1953 *Prelude and Chaconne* for organ, in which the ground bass was 12-tone. Indeed, much of his instrumental music was richly chromatic. The *Second Symphony*, however, did not sound characteristically 12-tone, in part because the row was supported so often by Renaissance-like pedals and ostinati. Some reviewers even supposed that the reference to the 12-tone method in the work's program notes was meant as a joke. On the other hand, the sparseness and delicacy of Pinkham's textures and rhythms, especially in the latter two "Epigrams," and in some of the *Signs of the Zodiac*, showed some kinship with Webern.

Pinkham's combination of the old and the new was epitomized by those works that used both old and new instruments in concert, such as the *Concerto for Harpsichord and Celesta* (1953). In this work, the venerable, stately harpsichord and the relatively novel, wispy celesta joined in irreverent, unexpected partnership: in playful dialog in the opening 5/8 "Prelude"; in strict counterpoint in the particularly elegant and ingenious "Ricercare"; and a bit more confrontatively in the jazzy "Canzona." Such a work understandably led Wilfred Mellers to speak of Pinkham's "prettified medievalism,"[27] an assessment that squares, more or less, with the notion of Pinkham as a sort of pre-Raphaelite. Pinkham once again combined harpsichord and celesta in the 1954 *Concertante No. 1* for violin and harpsichord soli, strings, and celesta (the work's slow section was an arrangement of the violin-harpsichord *Cantilena* from the same year), and combined organ and celesta in the 1962 *Concertante* for organ, celesta, and two percussionists.

Pinkham's interest in combining old and new sounds was a primary motivation behind his extensive involvement with electronic instruments. This involvement dated from 1970, when Pinkham took a course in electronic music given by his colleague Robert Creely at the New England Conservatory.[28] He subsequently acquired a studio synthesizer, a keyboard unit, a sequencer, and tape decks. He enjoyed experimenting with this equipment, which he likened to improvising on a big, unfamiliar organ. After hearing Richard Felciano's *Gods of the Expanding Universe* for organ and electronic tape (1971), he decided that this particular combination was especially attractive. Furthermore, an electronic accompaniment to an organ could provide added richness to a church's acoustics, something that especially stood to benefit small New England churches, which were often built for speech, not music. Consequently, there followed a series of sacred works that employed organ and tape in some combination or another, including *The Other Voices of the Trumpet* for trumpet, organ, and tape (1971); *Toccata for the Vault of Heaven* for organ and tape (1972); *Mourn for the Eclipse of His Light* for violin, organ, and tape (1973); *For evening draws on* for English horn, organ, and tape (1973); *The Shepherd's Symphony* for organ, one or more soft melody instruments, tape, and optional percussion (1973); and *Liturgies* for organ, timpani, and tape (1974). Pinkham also discovered electronic tape a welcome complement to choruses, and there followed *To Troubled Friends* for mixed chorus, string orchestra, and tape (1972; text by James Wright); *Two Poems of Howard Holtzman* for women's voices and tape; and *Witching Hour* for women's voices, electric guitar, and tape (1975; text by Norma Farber).

The greatest challenge posed by these pieces was in coordinating the performing musicians and the electronic tape. Pinkham soon discovered that any rigid synchronization denied the performer desirable rhythmic liberties, and so he resorted to one of two solutions: nonsynchronization, in which the performer could play at his or her own pace, independent of the tape; or aleatoric devices, in which the performer was further called on to make compositional choices. The latter solution was found in works like *The Shepherd's Symphony* and the second movement of *Liturgies,* works that provided performers with musical fragments that could be played in any order, works that brought Pinkham to the cutting edge of the avant-garde.

The electronic tapes for these works were, for the most part, highly restrained and unobtrusive. They typically provided background hums, buzzes, and, in the pastoral *For evening draws on,* chirps. One exception to this was the *Toccata for the Vault of Heaven,* which originally was intended to be a virtuoso piece for organ with simple tape accompaniment, but which turned out to be just the opposite. Another exception was *Aspects of the Apocalypse* (1972), one of Pinkham's rare efforts for tape alone. Inspired by the Book of Revelations, the work was divided into distinct sections ("aspects"?) of about one minute's length, some sounding like sirens or helicopters, others quite contrastingly resembling Baroque walking basses and toccata figuration. Whatever the tape, it was practically designed for inexpensive playback equipment.

After *Nebulae* for large ensemble and tape (1975), the electronic adventure seemed to wind down. In 1978 Pinkham wrote:

> I think we've seen it as far as tape is concerned. It was certainly an agreeable and interesting phenomenon, and had a lot of people doing things for organ again. The reason I've started doing non-tape pieces is because I've found that the tape pieces were after a while a "cop-out": just too easy to do. And it's much more difficult to control time by putting notes down, because the tape machine will just simply do it for you. . . . It's so easy to get corrupted—seduced—by something like that.[29]

These "non-tape pieces" included *Masks* for harpsichord and organ (1977); they were followed by *Serenades* for trumpet and wind ensemble (1979), a *Brass Quintet* (1984), and many other such works.

Wilfred Mellers, in his book on American music, included Pinkham, along with Griffes, Cowell, Brant, Hovhaness, Harrison, and Varèse, in a chapter entitled "The retreat from the West."[30] Pinkham's *Concerto for Harpsichord and Celesta,* cited by Mellers, was, in fact, dedicated to Cowell; and indeed, this work, like the coeval *Cantilena* (see Ex. 40), could be said to be as much in the tradition of Cowell as of Piston (this particular stylistic merger was probably unique). Then, too, Pinkham and Brink often performed Hovhaness's *Duet* for violin and harpsichord. One could further argue an affinity between, say, Pinkham's *Divertimento* for oboe and strings (1958) and Harrison, or his *Eclogue* for flute, harpsichord and bells (1965) and Brant. On the other hand, Pinkham had little sympathy for Varèse.[31] But there was a larger question with Mellers's evaluation; for if there was a connection between Eastern music and Pinkham's long pedals, melismatic modal fragments, metric subtlety, and bell-like delicacy, it was very much filtered through a deep commitment to early European music, which was not the case with most of these other composers. In fact, far from retreating from the West, Pinkham probed its musical roots with exceptional thoroughness and enthusiasm. In any event, how different Warren Story Smith, who saw in Pinkham's straightforward, accessible craftsmanship a successor to Paine, Foote, Chadwick, Parker, and Converse![32] Or Stevenson, who saw in Pinkham's devotional spirit the legacy of early American hymnodists! All of these contexts had their validity and pointed to the fact that Pinkham was not an easy composer to categorize.

In a very special way, however, Pinkham remained a successor to Hindemith, though he rarely sounded like him (he sounded sooner like Piston or Stravinsky or Honegger). But Hindemith's kind of revival of early music ideals came closest to his own ideals, and perhaps those of the Trapp Family and Landowska as well. Pinkham even surpassed Hindemith by spanning an even vaster time range: from medieval organum and chant to 12-tone, electronic, and aleatoric techniques.

At the same time, Pinkham proved a successor to his illustrious great-grandmother. They both revived the past: she, with herbal remedies; he, as a harpsichordist. They both exploited the newest resources; she, modern advertising; he, all kinds of fashionable musical techniques. They both were eminently practical: she, as a businesswoman and reformer;

he, as a composer of "Gebrauchsmusik." And they both held high ideals: she, improved conditions for women and blacks; he, the spirit of Christianity. It was Pinkham's special accomplishment to find room for this family heritage in the world of 20th-century music.

Notes

1. Sarah Stage, *Female Complaints: Lydia Pinkham and the Business of Women's Medicine* (New York: W. W. Norton, 1979), p. 27. Stage's study rejected the notion that the Vegetable Compound was a simple fraud or, as was sometimes alleged, a harmful one ("at worst, [it] produced an alcoholic haze in women suffering from female complaints," p. 176); rather, she viewed it as emblematic of the relationship between women and medicine (noting connections to contemporary dispensation of valium and other tranquilizers in treating many of the same symptoms, as well as to the reemergence of herbal medications in the 1970s). Stage's sympathetic portrait of Lydia herself was not too different from that found in two earlier biographies: Robert Collyer Washburn, *The Life and Times of Lydia E. Pinkham* (New York: G. P. Putnam, 1931); and Jean Burton, *Lydia Pinkham Is Her Name* (New York: Farrar, Straus, 1949).
2. Burton, p. 8.
3. Burton, p. 22.
4. Michael Corzine, *The Organ Works of Daniel Pinkham* (PhD thesis, Eastman School, 1979), p. 5.
5. Burton, p. 130.
6. Pinkham, "Favorite Memories of a Great Organist," *Boston Globe,* March 20, 1977.
7. Corzine, p. 3; Pinkham, personal interview, February 9, 1984 (all quotations not footnoted are from this interview).
8. Corzine, p. 227.
9. Maria Augusta Trapp, *The Story of the Trapp Family Singers* (New York: J. B. Lippincott, 1949), p. 196.
10. Corzine, p. 2.
11. Wanda Landowska, *Landowska on Music,* collected, edited, and translated by Denise Restout (New York: Stein and Day, 1965).
12. Pollack, *Walter Piston* (Ann Arbor, Michigan: UMI Press, 1981), p. 78.

13. Pinkham, "Favorite Memories."

14. The *Cantilena and Capriccio* originally were intended as separate pieces.

15. Daniel Pinkham, "Interview with Charles Henderson," *Music/ The AGO-RCCO Magazine* 8 (December 1974), p. 21.

16. Daniel Pinkham, "New Problems Enlarge Horizons," *Music Journal* 23 (April 1965), p. 40.

17. Smith, "Daniel Pinkham," *American Composers Alliance Bulletin* 10 (1961), p. 9.

18. Pinkham, "Interview," p. 21.

19. Quoted by Ewen, *American Composers* (New York: G. P. Putnam's, 1982), p. 510.

20. Johnson, *The Choral Writing of Daniel Pinkham* (PhD thesis, University of Iowa, 1968); "The Choral Writing of Daniel Pinkham," *American Choral Review* Vol. 8 No. 4 (June 1966), p. 16.

21. Smith, p. 12.

22. Founded in 1868, King's Chapel was Boston's first Anglican Church, and later in the century, its first Unitarian one.

23. Stevenson, *Protestant Church Music in America* (New York: W. W. Norton, 1966), p. 132.

24. The line in question was, "Now cross that says that *man* shall look/ Upon its form for promise of/ Eternal life in Paradise."

25. Daniel Pinkham, *Symphony No. 2* (New York: C. F. Peters, 1964), p. 2.

26. Pinkham, "Interview," p. 2.

27. Mellers, *Music in a New Found Land* (London: Barrie & Rockliff, 1964), p. 156.

28. Corzine, pp. 191 ff.

29. Corzine, p. 259.

30. Mellers, p. 156.

31. Daniel Pinkham, "Hartt College Workshop," *Music/The AGO-RCCO Magazine* 6 (September 1972), p. 36. This is what Pinkham had to say about *Ionization:* "It proved a shocker in its day and is a monument of its kind. Placed at the end of a long high-octane concert, however, the effect was not much greater than had it been performed by a rhythm band on Orff instruments. It only goes to point up that the more avant-garde a work is the more quickly it becomes dated."

32. Smith, p. 9.

10. FAVORED SONS: ROBERT MIDDLETON AND ALLEN SAPP

THE CAREERS OF ROBERT MIDDLETON AND ALLEN SAPP closely paralleled one another. Born in the early 1920s, they attended Harvard both before and after serving in the Second World War. Excellent pianists, they became friends as students; they also married exceptionally fine pianists, with whom they gave four-hand and two-piano recitals. (In fact, Sapp's *Four Dialogues* for two pianos, occasionally performed by the composer and his wife Norma, was originally composed for Robert and Polly Middleton.) Their early work won a small but appreciative following in Boston and at Harvard, including Piston himself. Both taught at Harvard in the early '50s; after leaving Harvard (Middleton for Vassar, Sapp for a series of positions), they continued to compose, as they really always had done, in fair obscurity, with next to no publications or recordings of their music. They remained friends, sending scores to each other in manuscript. This music, which not surprisingly shared some features, was similarly unworthy of such neglect.

Middleton was born on November 18, 1920 in Diamond, Ohio, on a farm near Youngstown. His first piano teacher was his mother, and he began composing at about age eleven. In 1933, after the death of his father, the family moved to Columbus, where Middleton studied piano with one of Artur Schnabel's first American pupils, Marie Waller, and attended a progressive high school under the auspices of Ohio State University. Middleton profited from the school's fine library and experimental curriculum, as well as from his experiences there as magazine editor, pianist, and composer.[1] Boulanger, passing through town, looked at his music and suggested that he go to Harvard to study with Piston. Middleton, by that time, had learned to like Piston and Hindemith along with Mozart, Brahms, Chopin, Debussy, and Ravel, and left for Harvard with high hopes and a good scholarship.

Except for the friendships formed there with Sapp and other classmates, he found Harvard deflating and tedious, especially in comparison with the University High School. After two years (1939–1941), he quit Harvard to spend a year with Boulanger at the Longy School and with pianist Beveridge Webster at the New England Conservatory. Then came three years of military service (1942–1945), after which he returned to finish his degree at Harvard (1946–1948), enjoying his studies of advanced harmony, fugue, and orchestration with Piston. In 1948–1949 he did more work with Boulanger, this time in France. 1949–1950 was spent in Italy, where he looked up Dallapiccola, with whom he thought he might study; but he finally chose not to, deciding, "I won't be taught by anyone else; I'm on my own now." Middleton subsequently taught at Harvard for three years (1950–1953), and at Vassar for thirty-two years (1953–1985), before retiring to his summer home in New Hampshire.

One of Middleton's first notable works was his *String Quartet,* written in Tremezzo in the summer of 1950, shortly before the composer's return to the States and his post at Harvard. The sunny Italian skies seem to have made an impression, for this was a particularly cheerful work. The first movement was a joyful sonata with warm, lyrical themes (Ex. 43); the second was a tender set of variations; and the finale was a sprightly ternary movement, the middle section more resigned than sad. This last movement was reminiscent of Beethoven, or perhaps even more so, of Haydn's Ländler variety of minuet; but the brilliant, almost strident textures recalled at the same time American folk styles. This subtle blend of classic and national elements in a minuet-finale gave some hint to the composer's rarified and unusual musical personality.

The *Quartet* clearly fell within a tradition nonetheless,

Example 43. Robert Middleton, *String Quartet,* I.

namely, that of Bostonian neoclassicism; or to be more
specific, it was written in the tradition's afterglow. The string
writing and quartet textures derived from Piston; the warm
lyricism suggested Fine; and the vigorous classical idealism
looked back to Shapero and Kohs. One important distinction,
and a characteristic one, was the amount of chromatic activity
and harmonic dissonance, still relatively tame here, but often
greater than in the forenamed predecessors. By this time,
Middleton must have been thinking about 12-tone music, as
evidenced by his near-study with Dallapiccola. Also characteristic was the way in which the work's formal savvy and light
tone seemed to belie the music's surface dissonance; indeed,
it was precisely such objective and elegant use of advanced
materials that suggested in Middleton an heir to Piston.

Middleton's formal control needed detailed study. Here, in
the *String Quartet,* a few characteristic traits could be noted,
especially with future works in mind: the way dissonant
counterpoint stylishly converged on triads (this certainly
related to Hindemith); the pervasive harmonic tension, often
deflected to distant tonal goals, and only really relaxed at ends
of movements or sections; and the use of sequence. This last
was particularly prominent, for the composer frequently

sequenced on multiple levels: from accompanimental bits and melodic motives to whole phrases and even key areas. In some works, he often sequenced a melodic motive four or five times, while tiny bits could be repeated many more times over. This ubiquitous sequencing, which helped explain the composer's admiration for Schumann, imparted a yearning quality; it also helped Middleton successfully shape large forms in an ultrachromatic idiom.

Middleton further enriched his chromatic textures by adopting the 12-tone technique for such subsequent works as *Four Organ Preludes* (1956), the *Piano Sonata* (1957), and the *Inventions on the Twelve Notes* (1961). The result was a 12-tone style that was still richly tonal, and still fairly conservative, at least rhythmically; one that, further, harkened back to Piston's own 12-tone music from the early '40s, and was related more or less to the work of such other Harvard graduates as Fine, Binkerd, and Sapp. The connection with Sapp was perhaps strongest, especially in the *Piano Sonata,* which resembled Sapp's own piano sonatas from the 1950s. Middleton's use of the method was particularly freewheeling, however: sometimes strict, sometimes exceedingly free, sometimes merely accompanimental, sometimes decorative, sometimes dispensed with altogether.

The varied uses of the 12-tone method were matched by a lively stylistic breadth, particularly in the *Inventions on the Twelve Notes.* This work's title referred not only to its occasional use of the 12-tone method, but to the fact that each of the twelve Inventions was centered on different pitches, forming its own 12-note series consisting of pairs of fifths: B-F#-Eb-Bb-G-D-A-E-C#-G#-F-C. The first Invention, "Fantasia," was Schumannesque both in its dreamy main theme (Ex. 44), and in its emotional outbursts (which were, nonetheless, cooly supported by a return of the main theme in the bass). Like the second of the Chopin *Preludes,* the second Invention, "Movement from a Suite," was slow and mournful; the connection with Chopin was emphasized further by Middleton's own performance, in which the melody line often just lagged behind or speeded ahead of the plodding bass. The third, "Toccata," was a stylishly virtuoso perpetual motion, like Ravel. The fourth, "Theme and Variations," featured a legato 12-tone melody with a staccato countermelody; when a second counterpoint entered, the texture was reminiscent of Sapp. The fifth, "Prelude," was like an updated Fauré barcarolle. The sixth, "Fugue," had intricate inversion, stretto, and invertible counterpoint, all within 12-tone procedure. The seventh, "Aria with cadenzas," contrasted a doleful melody over a pedal point, with florid interludes, while the eighth, "Capriccio in thirds and sixths," looked back to the hearty merriment of the *String Quartet*. The ninth, "Sonnetto No. 4," suggested Liszt both in its title and in its pianism, though its principal idea resembled Schoenberg. The tenth, "Chaconne," strove to duplicate the wild bravura of Bach's solo violin writing (going so far as to instruct the pianist to play certain notes like harmonics, or like open string pizzicati, or, at one point, to play a melody

Example 44. Robert Middleton, "Fantasia," *Inventions on the Twelve Notes*.

with the thumb to suggest the intensity of the G string), though its busy activity in the piano's highest register against simple triads held for long durations in the bass, was somewhat like Messiaen. The eleventh, "Double Intermezzo," was like Fine in its bittersweet, lyrical quality, while the last, "Canon," returned to something dreamy and Schumannesque. Despite this stylistic diversity, the *Inventions* made a unified impression, partly because of similarities in its melodic and harmonic materials, partly because of its consistently lush piano textures. Indeed, its kind of variety within a coherent style deserved comparison with similar sets by Bach, Chopin, Debussy, and Hindemith.

In the meantime, Middleton continued to compose for the theater; he initially had established his reputation with a one-act opera performed at Tanglewood on August 13, 1948, entitled *Life Goes to a Party* (1947). The *Boston Herald,* reviewing a 1951 performance at Boston University, described it as an "ingenious one-act allegory" that "employs a number of clever and witty devices to examine the party in terms of Aesop."[2] The libretto was by the composer himself. Middleton went on to write two more operas: another one-act opera, *The Nightingale Is Guilty* (1953) to a libretto by his brother, William Middleton; and a four-act opera, *Command Performance* (1960) to a libretto by his friend of Harvard days, Harold Wendell Smith. Sarah Caldwell directed and conducted the premiere of all three works.

In four acts, *Command Performance* was the most ambitious undertaking of Middleton's career. Based on the historical fact of the gift of an animated organ from Queen Elizabeth I to Sultan Mehmet III, the synopsis is as follows.

Act I. January 24, 1599, the Queen's Presence Chamber. Jack Wilton, a court musician, informs the Queen of his intention to marry her favorite lady-in-waiting, Lady Anne. The Queen, impressed by his boldness, orders him to accompany to Turkey an organ created especially for the Sultan, in the hopes of procuring exclusive trading rights.

Act II. Eight months later, a prison in the Sultan's seraglio. The Sultan, delighted with the organ and Jack Wilton's playing, has taken the musician hostage. Dorina della Corta, a captured Venetian, escapes the Sultan's harem dressed as a janissary, and finding her way to Wilton's quarters, pleads for help. Learning that Dorina can play harpsichord, Wilton devises a plan. If he can teach the "janissary" to play as well as he himself can, will the Sultan free him? The Sultan agrees, preferring a musician of his own race, and gives Wilton one month to train the "Turk."

Act III. One month later, the Sultan's pavilion. Jack and Dorina have fallen in love. She performs brilliantly for the Sultan, who agrees to free Wilton, and sign the trade agreement with England. Wilton suggests that as a personal gift for the Queen, the Sultan release Dorina, who can take the place of a former Italian music teacher. He consents to this too.

Act IV. Six months later, the Queen's Chamber. Anne, uncertain of Jack's fate, has decided to marry Lord Richmond. Jack and Dorina arrive. The Queen is delighted with the trade agreement, angry at the "gift" of Dorina (she was hoping for emeralds), but, in the end, forgiving. A double wedding is planned for the young lovers. Suddenly word comes from the Sultan that the "Turkish" musician cannot be found; he promises his ships against the Spanish fleet if Elizabeth will send Wilton back. The Queen, casting sentiment aside, orders Wilton to return to Turkey, this time as England's Ambassador and accompanied by his Venetian lady.

Conceived on the heels of *The Rake's Progress* (significantly, the first work by Stravinsky that Middleton "warmed up to"), *Command Performance* disclosed affinities with that work, especially Smith's finely honed libretto with its historical flourishes, its rhymed couplets, and its arch one-liners. But the similarities were largely superficial. Unlike Stravinsky's work, this was not a morality tale, but an ironic political allegory about those who wield power and those who do not. Writing during the Cold War, Smith and Middleton perhaps meant the English-Turkish conflict to symbolize contemporary West-East tensions. But the subject of political power clearly fascinated Middleton in general and attracted him to Stendhal's *Charterhouse of Parma,* which he also hoped to adapt as an opera.

Of the opera's characters, Wilton and Elizabeth were the most interesting, indeed, the only characters who showed some true understanding of one another. At first, Wilton appears to play Figaro to Anne's Susanna, but he emerges in

Acts II and III as quite the romantic hero; by Act IV, he is nearly Elizabeth's equal as he amuses her about his escapades. But he ultimately remains a pawn in the scheme of things. Elizabeth's character is even more central: she has some of the regal hauteur of opera's "bel canto" queens, but also a reflective, introspective quality more like Mozart's Countess and Strauss's Marschallin. The other figures were either burlesque caricatures, like the Minister of Trade, and the Organ Builder; or lightly drawn, like Anne and Dorina. The Sultan was fairly uncomplicated as well, more like Rodgers's King of Siam than Mozart's Pasha.

The work's musical setting, consisting as it does of a heightened recitative which flows seamlessly into arias, duets, and ensembles, suggested Richard Strauss. The highlights included, in Act I, a duet for Jack and Anne, and an aria for the Queen; in Act II, an aria for Jack and a trio for Jack, Dorina, and the Sultan; in Act III, a duet for Jack and Dorina; and in Act IV, a quartet for Elizabeth, Jack, Dorina, and Anne. There was some use of leitmotifs, most notably themes for Elizabeth and the Sultan that opened and closed their respective acts. Like Strauss, the music was consistently richly chromatic in a refined way, nicely reflecting the romantic, ironic tone of the book. The style, indeed, was very much the style of the *Inventions,* which almost might be seen as mere sketches for this work.

One outstanding aspect of *Command Performance* was the importance music itself played in it, as epitomized by the title's double meaning, as well as by the work's subtitle, "an opera concerto." Keyboard instruments, both organ and harpsichord, were central to the story (in fact, the work was originally entitled, *Keyboards and Crowns*); new music styles allowed for novel touches: during the cleaning ladies' chorus in Act I, dissonant notes in the harpsichord humorously depicted Wilton at work on the out-of-tune keyboard; and at the top of Act II, harpsichord clusters evoked two Ethiopians feather-dusting the instrument. In addition, music making proper of one sort or another occurred in each of the four acts—most notably, Elizabeth's song in Act I, Dorina's performance at the organ in Act III, and the four-voice madrigal in Act IV. The style for this "Renaissance" music was surprisingly romantic and chromatic (Middleton's 1940

Elizabethan Song Book surely would shed light on this matter),
and not too different, in fact, from the rest of the opera. But
it was different enough to suggest a fantasy world richer and
more profound than the world of power politics. Certainly, it
possessed a special calm and introspection; the opera reached
its most relaxed moment when the quartet arrived in unison
on the madrigal's last line: "The light of love, Defies all
change."

Commissioned for the centennial of Vassar College, *Command Performance* was premiered on November 11, 1961.
After a repeat performance there, it played in Cambridge for
two nights. Local critics and audiences were enthusiastic, but
attempts to promote it with such a likely showcase as the New
York City Opera failed. Its neglect was probably the most
disheartening event in the composer's career.

After *Command Performance* and the *Inventions,* there
followed, among other works, the 1962 *Concerto di Quattro
Duetti* for solo winds and string orchestra, dedicated to
Piston, and the 1965 *Variations* for piano and orchestra.
Then, starting with *Approximations* for viola and piano and
Notebooks of Designs Book I for solo piano, both from 1967,
came a startling development: Middleton began to compose
in an aleatoric and, at times, atonal manner. This new,
adventurous style was further explored in *Notebooks of Designs
Book II* (1968), *Vier Trio-Sätze in romantischer Manier* for
violin, cello, and piano (1970), *vARIAzioni-variAZIONI* for
piano (1970), and *Two Duologues* for violin and piano (1973).
These proved to be Middleton's most daring works.

The composer's use of aleatoric notation and techniques
varied from work to work, but remained consistent in many
particulars. *Approximations,* one of his first such works, and
his only aleatoric work to be published, proved prototypical.
The work completely dispensed with conventional rhythmic
notation—there were no meter signatures, bar lines, or note
values—and instead employed an approximate system in
which "the duration of a note corresponds to the spacing on
the page"[3] (Ex. 45). That some pulse was intended was
suggested by the vertical dotted lines meant to indicate "a
general feeling of downbeat," as well as by the fact that each
of the four movements was headed by a metronome marking

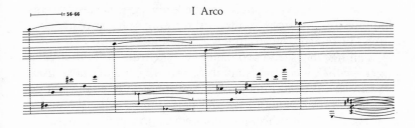

Example 45. Robert Middleton, "Arco," *Approximations* for viola and piano (Edward B. Marks, 1970).

in spatial terms, though this indication "is not to be taken too literally, however, since considerable freedom is desired (except where marked 'preciso')." *Approximations* contained many other novelties, including a system in which dynamics were indicated by the size and shape of the notehead.

Middleton's later aleatoric works used some of these features, though in revised ways. *Approximations'* cumbersome notation of pitch, for instance, gave way to a system in which all whiteheads were natural, and all blackheads were either flats or sharps. Its peculiar dynamic notations also were given up in favor of conventional fortes and pianos. And the use of downbeat indications was vastly minimized, or scratched completely. The two solo piano works had no pulse indications at all, and *Notebooks of Designs,* Middleton's most radical work, experimented with random ordering of events, as well as serial arrangements derived from "the tracing of various geometric designs amongst the numbers within a magic square." (This work, above all, warranted comparison with Cage.) The *Trio* was unusual in that it had many passages that did not specify pitch, giving only general indications about range, contour, and rhythm. *Duologues* also had unpitched passages, but to much less extent.

In all instances, the avoidance of synchronization between voices, which sometimes involved techniques like those used by Lutoslawski and Penderecki, and the lack of any specified rhythmic ratios, which gave the performer a sort of Cagean rhythmic freedom, brought such works in range of the day's most avant-garde trends. Somewhat amazing in the context of the composer's former works, this development certainly distinguished him from most Harvard graduates of his generation.

And yet, for some time, the composer had shown a definite desire to break out from the confines of traditional rhythmic practices, as evident from the numerous cadenzas that dotted his work from the '50s and early '60s. Indeed, for Middleton, the rhythmic adventures of his aleatoric work ultimately were related not so much to Cage, as to the composer's love for Schumann, Chopin, and Liszt. It already was noted that in performance of one of the *Inventions,* the composer's rubato was such that the two voices were often a hair off: perhaps it was just a step (albeit a big step) from there to the kind of nonsynchronization used in the aleatoric works. Certainly, the *Vier Trio-Sätze,* with their Schumannesque movement headings ("Phantasiestück," "Humoresque," "Romanze," and "Novelette"), bespoke a connection with Schumann, and, in fact, the composer, along with Matthew Raimondi, violin, and Luis Garcia-Renart, cello, performed Schumann's *Trio No. 2* on the program with this work at its well-received New York premiere on May 27, 1971. This *Trio,* in particular, seemed to be a plausible outcome of Schumann's rhythmic impulses.

The connection with Schumannesque romanticism to some degree could be found in the score of the *Vier Trio-Sätze* itself—for instance, the parallel tenths for strings against luminous tremolos in the piano—but was further brought out in performance by Middleton, Raimondi, and Garcia-Renart, as was evident from one such taped performance. For example, there was not much in the score to suggest the driving dotted rhythms—clearly Schumannesque—put forth by these three players in this particular performance. Of course, with such music, there was the question: what is the work—the score or the performance? A problem for all notated music, perhaps, it was particularly acute here, where rhythms and even pitches, at times, were not specified. Middleton himself thought the *Vier Trio-Sätze* his best work (and one well could agree from a taped performance), but the composer admitted that when played by others, the musicians would request a tape of the Middleton-Raimondi-Renart performance, and then try to duplicate it. In other words, the effectiveness of the score, as distinct from what was, in large part, a brilliant improvisation by the composer and his friends, was never really tested.

There were no new works from 1973 to 1978, and then, beginning with the 1979 *Four Nocturnes* for clarinet and piano, Middleton began once again not only to compose, but to use conventional notation. Middleton's aleatoric period, coinciding significantly with the domestic turmoil of the late '60s and early '70s, was over. In fact, the *Four Nocturnes* looked back to the clear textures, steady rhythms, and chromatic tonality of a much earlier work like the *String Quartet*. Perhaps the only reflection of the aleatoric adventure was a certain impressionistic shimmer, related also, presumably, to the famous French works evoked by the work's four movement headings: "Les sons ét les parfums," "Barcarolle," "Jeux d'eau," and "Fêtes." A connection with French art was also affirmed in the 1981 *Overture to "The Charterhouse of Parma"*; this orchestral work was intended as "the opening of an imaginary opera based on scenes from the Stendhal novel." Like the *Nocturnes,* the music was stylistically conservative, reminding one listener of Barber and Verdi, and leaving him hopeful for more performances.[4]

About the time of his retirement, Middleton also began to revise earlier works: the 1949 *Violin Concerto* in 1984, the 1965 *Variations* for piano and orchestra in 1985, and the 1962 *Concerto di Quattro Duetti* in 1986. Perhaps in their revised form they would win some more friends. But performances of Middleton's work remained few and far between. It was regrettable that such a strong and refined composer was so ignored. Perhaps it was, to some extent, a problem of self-advertisement. If so, it may have been yet another trait he shared with his friend, Allen Sapp.

Allen Sapp, born in Philadelphia on December 10, 1922,

knew Robert Middleton while a student at Harvard in the
1940s, and as a colleague on the Harvard faculty in the early
'50s, during which time they formed, along with Claudio
Spies, Paul Des Marais, and others, a Creative Concerts
Guild. The Guild sponsored chamber music concerts in the
Boston area that featured new music; it also commissioned
new works, including Dallapiccola's *Goethelieder,* Wolpe's
Saxophone Quartet, and Imbrie's *Second String Quartet.*[5] Both
Sapp and Middleton were as much protégés of Piston as was
anyone. Piston helped them obtain fellowships and the like,
and even invited them to his home for a spaghetti dinner, the
sort of invitation he extended to very few associates.
Certainly their kind of refinement accorded well with his own
temperament.

Sapp went to Harvard in 1939 specifically to study with the
composer of the *Concerto for Orchestra* and the *Piano Concertino.* After the War, he returned there to do graduate work
(1947–1949). He took nearly all of Piston's courses—
advanced harmony, fugue, orchestration, 20th-century materials, composition seminar—and some more than once. In
discussing Piston, Sapp emphasized his slow, quiet classroom
manner ("sometimes one felt that he was struggling with
some mighty problem of conscience"), his inductive rather
than systematic approach, his concern for formal rightness,
and his special fascination with texture that helped make
Fugue his best course. In 20th Century Materials, students
wrote phrases or pieces exploiting such techniques as atonality, nontertian harmonies, and unusual rhythms. In Composition Seminar, Piston never mentioned his own music and was
tolerant of all styles save the "gumdroppy."

Sapp did not consider himself one of Piston's better
students and worked especially hard to win his approval. In
the course of the 1950s, he took less interest in Piston as he
began to feel that the older composer had betrayed, if not
exactly certain standards, then certain ideals: that he had sold
out, after a fashion. But even after leaving Harvard, Sapp
continued to hold Piston's sensitivity to line, texture, and
design a basic feature of his "musical style and musical
philosophy." And he never lost admiration for Piston's work
from the 1930s.

Most of Sapp's work was for piano, either alone or in some

chamber combination. This was partly because of his own talents as a pianist, and those of his wife Norma, whom he had met at Harvard, and who often premiered his works. By the mid-1980s this corpus included eight piano sonatas, four piano sonatas for four-hands, two piano sonatinas, assorted smaller piano works, *Colloquies III* for piano and ten winds (1982), four sonatas for violin and piano, songs for piano and voice, and much more.

One of the earliest of such work was his *First Piano Sonata*, written at Harvard in 1941. More like a prelude and allegro than a real sonata, its sort of neobaroque idiom, with its quartal harmonies, modal melodies, bitonal clashes, and vigorous rhythms, clearly reflected the composer's admiration for Piston. The slightly crude work of a nineteen-year-old student, it nonetheless looked ahead to Sapp's later work, for instance, in its crisp piano writing full of octaves.

The 1949 *Suite for Piano*, on the other hand, was more fully characteristic, and turned out to have some impact on the new music scene at Harvard. Least personal was the first of its five movements; written in a mild Stravinskian idiom, it pointed to Sapp's intervening studies with Boulanger, Fine, and Copland, to whom the *Suite* was dedicated. This first movement, in fact, sounded somewhat like Fine. The *Suite*'s four subsequent movements, however, were more distinctive. Many of its features, further, became characteristic, and therefore deserve some comment.

One characteristic feature found in the *Suite*, for instance, was a preference for very long melodic lines. Here the composer's legato markings often extended to many measures; in later works, they extended to whole staves. This was generally typical of the neoclassicists, but Sapp's long lines were distinctive in a number of respects. First, his phrases did not reach firm or expected tonal goals, which imparted a certain breathlessness to his music. Second, his rhythms were elusive, even when toccata-like and cast in a single meter. And third, the long phrases interacted in novel ways, that is, they did not fall into familiar patterns like the antecedent-consequent or the sequential; this often gave his music a striking asymmetry. A whole movement would be necessary to illustrate such traits, though the opening of the *Suite*'s fourth movement (Ex. 46) provides some inkling of them.

Example 46. Allen Sapp, *Suite* for piano, IV.

This fourth movement, written in one of the composer's favorite meters, 5/8 (the legacy of Piston, perhaps), further documented Sapp's growing inclination toward ultrachromaticism. The opening phrase contained, as can be seen, all twelve pitches; in fact, this work represented a tentative adoption of the 12-tone method. At the same time, the *Suite* also revealed a penchant for simple triads. The opening phrase of the second movement offered an especially good example of this, as six of its thirteen harmonies were either major, minor, or diminished triads (Ex. 47). Example 46 similarly illustrates this predilection for triads; here, the triads provided a fairly clear context for the melody's nonchordal tones. Sapp's use of triads had two unusual aspects, however. First, they emerged in the midst of very advanced harmonies, which made them all the more noticeable. And second, they related to one another, and to the principal melody, in unexpected ways. In Example 47, for instance, the accompanying triads were F major, E minor, and D minor (if we interpret the dyad D-F as such), although the melody suggested a tonal center of A♭ (with modal ♭7 and #4 inflections); the movement even concluded with an E minor triad—and this in a piece whose key signature consisted of three flats!

Finally, there was perhaps the most distinctive feature of Sapp's style, his textures. There was, for example, the simple chordal writing found in the *Suite*'s second movement, a style

that was found, too, in the second theme of the 1957 *Third
Piano Sonata* (a style, furthermore, that was possibly related to
American hymnody). But much more characteristic was a
three-part texture in which a single soprano line was supported by dyads, as in the *Suite*'s fourth movement (see Ex.
46), or, conversely, a series of dyads that were supported by
a single bass line, as in this same work's third and fifth
movements. In either case, the harmonic texture was consequently three-part, while the rhythmic texture was essentially
two-part (such textures, incidentally, were occasionally encountered in Middleton as well, for instance, in his "Theme
and Variations" from the *Inventions,* as mentioned). These
textures may have derived largely from the piano music of
Chopin and Brahms, but there was also a connection to
medieval music, a repertory close to the composer, as we shall
see. Such textures were not typically maintained throughout
an entire piece, but rather represented a favored norm. The
dyads varied in intervallic content, but intervals smaller than
the seventh were preferred, especially thirds and sixths, while
sevenths and complex intervals were used sparingly (and this
although the composer's own span was quite large, if the *First
Sonata* was any indication).

Sapp's work from the 1950s continued along the lines of
the *Suite,* quickly ripening into a fully personal style. The
years 1956–1957, spent in Rome, proved particularly produc-
tive; during this stay abroad he revised the *Piano Sonata No. 2,*
composed *Double Image* for orchestra (1956), and wrote two
more piano sonatas (Nos. 3 and 4, both from 1957). The
aforementioned features said to be characteristic were all
found in these works as well, but used here with greater depth
and subtlety. It was regrettable that such works did not find

Example 47. Allen Sapp, *Suite* for piano, II.

their way into print, for they were of a high order of craftsmanship and imagination. Most accessible was *Double Image,* a short work that contrasted somber, slow sections with jazzy, fast ones. The work effectively combined aspects derived from Harris, Copland, Barber, and, above all, Piston. The slow sections, which possessed a troubled, confessional quality that could occasionally mark Sapp's letters as well, were especially gripping. The work seemed more like the sketch for something potentially grander than a significant achievement in and of itself; one could imagine Koussevitsky taking a fancy to its young composer and asking for symphonies. But the work was not even performed until Lukas Foss played it with the Buffalo Philharmonic in 1963; and there were no symphonies forthcoming, indeed, very little orchestral music of any kind.

Piano Sonatas Nos. 3 and *4,* in contrast, were big works, and had more the feel of repertory status. Furthermore, they enjoyed repeated, expert performances by the composer's wife. They represented, especially *Sonata No. 4,* a continued expansion of the composer's chromatic adventurousness, but they retained a fundamental tonal bearing, and often came to rest on triads.

Both *Sonatas* were in fast-slow-fast format, with the tonal center of the middle movement a diminished fourth away from that of the outer movements. Both works, too, made skilled use of thematic transformation, with ideas from one movement found in some other movement in thoroughly new contexts. The piano writing combined aspects of Debussy's lushness, Bartók's percussiveness, and Schoenberg's jaggedness, an amalgam that brought it close to contemporary piano sonatas by fellow Harvardians Binkerd (1955) and Middleton (1957).

There were important differences between the two sonatas, however. The opening movement of No. 3 had a crystalline formal neatness that included a thoroughly classical development of its dynamic and syncopated first theme, whereas the corresponding movement of No. 4 was more spontaneous in feel, with its rhapsodic second theme announcing the recapitulation. The slow movement of No. 3 had a hymn-like, four-voice first theme, and a marchlike contrasting theme that eventually submitted to Pistonian contrapuntal development, whereas the slow movement of No. 4 featured those characteristic dyads (here providing an almost Straussian shimmer) that in the course of the movement were used as an ostinato for a relaxed, dreamy interlude. The swirling last movement of No. 3 was an act of dissolution, like the ending of the Chopin *Sonata* in B♭ minor, whereas the finale of No. 4 was a witty variation movement full of contrapuntal ingenuity (Ex. 48). It also might be noted that whereas No. 3 was intended for performance by the composer himself, No. 4, "a less aggressive piece" in the composer's estimation, was written to be played by his wife.

Like the aforementioned sonatas by Binkerd and Middleton, these works made use of the 12-tone method.

It was only natural, according to the composer, for someone like himself, who had served the Army as chief cryptanalyst for the Civil Censorship Division, and then as chief of Code Research, to be intrigued with the 12-tone method. Upon release from the Army, his "decodings" of such Schoenberg works as the *Third Quartet* won the respect

Example 48. Allen Sapp, *Piano Sonata No. 4,* III.

of Piston, who by then had used the method himself, but was rather quiet about it. Sapp's analyses may have helped spur the interest of such older friends as Copland, Fine, Binkerd, and Middleton in the technique. His theoretical work also set the stage for Peter Westergaard's senior honors thesis on Schoenberg's *Third Quartet,* a thesis which in turn helped clarify Sapp's thinking on the subject. Sapp himself first used the method in a few movements of the 1949 *Suite,* as we have mentioned, and in his *Piano Trio* of the same year. He subsequently used it in one way or another for every work after that, though he claimed to retain fundamental principles independent of the technique.

Sapp's own use of the 12-tone method seemed fairly inscrutable, for the specific row of any given work was often in question. The row was used, typically, not as a source for melody or even motive, but rather as a vague harmonic resource, which made it difficult to pinpoint the row. In the theme that opened the last movement of the *Fourth Piano Sonata* (see Ex. 48), for instance, the melody's first phrase (mm. 1–3) repeated notes out of some ostensibly 12-tone order, contained no G, and further had only a vague relation to the chromatic hexachord that comprised the left-hand part. This was thoroughly characteristic of the composer's 12-tone procedures. Also characteristic, incidentally, was the jazzy flavor of this excerpt's harmonies, which might be compared, too, to the boogie-woogie inflections in the *Third Sonata's* finale.

The reason for Sapp's lifelong attachment to the 12-tone method was itself somewhat obscure. He obviously did not use it to avoid tonality, as we see from Example 48, which suggested the following progression in D: I (m. 1), bIII (mm. 2–3), I (mm. 3–4), bIII (mm. 4–5), VI (mm. 6–7), bIII (m. 7), and I (first beat, m. 8). He did not use it to create new kinds of forms, favoring as he did in large part the traditional forms of variation, sonata, and suite. He did not use it to replenish an exhausted tonal vocabulary, for his music always had its own sort of lively chromaticism, and, further, he used the method very idiosyncratically, for instance, to create ostinatos and simple triads. Finally, his adoption of the method was not merely a response to fashion, for he anticipated its vogue in America. It seems that the attraction was primarily cryptic, inspired by the symbolic tension between meaning and code.

This, perhaps, was to be expected from an expert crypt-analyst.

Sapp's cryptanalytic orientation was also evident in the quasi-mathematical titles of some of his compositions, such as *Double Image* (1957), *Septagon* (1959), and *Taylor's Nine* (1981). This last work also represented the composer in a particularly avant-garde vein. Initially quiet and sparse, with single notes separated by long silences, the work progressively becomes more active, apparently according to some arithmetic scheme, and concludes loudly and busily. Its harmonic stasis (around F, though the work ends on a startling F#) suggested some connection to Reich and Glass, though its restraint and elegance more forcibly recalled a work like Lukas Foss's *Percussion Quartet* from 1983. Its enigmatic title referred both to the infinite power series named after mathematician Brooke Taylor, and to the change ringing methods discussed in Dorothy Sayers's mystery novel, *The Nine Tailors*. According to the composer, these conceits could be made to dovetail with certain 12-tone rows. To uncover the work's connections with Taylor's series, change ringing techniques, and the 12-tone method doubtless would require nothing less than the acumen of Lord Peter Wimsey himself! For Sapp, the 12-tone method could be caught up quite naturally with all kinds of esoteric codes, old and new.

Notwithstanding the abstract, cryptic features of Sapp's music, it had, too, a refined sensuousness of French cast. This French strain, which the composer felt distinguished him from many American colleagues, stemmed from his long contact with Piston, and could be detected in his music throughout his career. Certainly there was something of Couperin in the piano sonatas, and something of Ravel in the orchestral works. And in a review of Debussy's *Pelléas and Mélisande*, Sapp's most important piece of music criticism, he praised the work's "exquisite taste," a feature "all-important," but, he implied, overlooked in an age like the present concerned about "style, new experiments in technique, systems and counter-systems."[6]

The appeal of hidden codes and exquisite refinement came together in Sapp's interest in medieval art. Some of his most significant efforts were inspired by the Middle Ages, including *A Maiden's Complaint in Spring-Time* for women's chorus and chamber group (1960; to an English translation of an anonymous Latin poem); *Imaginary Creatures* for harpsichord and orchestra (1980; each movement depicting a legendary, mythic animal); and *Crennelations* for tenor solo and orchestra (1982; a setting of Ezra Pound's paraphrase of the provençal poem, "Marvoil"). *Crennelations* was especially allusive of medieval idioms. Even *The Lady and the Lute* for soprano and piano (1952), a setting of eight poems by Robert Herrick, and a work of delicate textures, bell-like sounds, and modal cadences, seemed closer to the Middle Ages than to Herrick's 17th century. In this context, it is significant to note that those features said to be characteristic of Sapp—the long, asymmetrical melodies, the floating triads, the distinctive three-part textures—were also quite characteristic of late medieval and early Renaissance music.

Sapp's interest in medieval music surely was guided at Harvard by such scholars as Davison, Apel, and Gombosi; significantly, other Harvard students from Sapp's time, including Binkerd, Pinkham, Adler, and Kohn, also incorporated medieval elements in their work. The 1950s in general looked favorably on medieval music: for one, some of it was coming to light in new, authentic performance; for another, the resources of 18th-century models were felt to be somewhat exhausted. Sapp's medievalism was distinctive, however. Pinkham and Adler, for instance, cultivated, somewhat like Hindemith, a communal and ritualized medievalism, based on their deep involvement with the ancient traditions of church and synagogue, respectively. Binkerd's medievalism was more Gothic, with closer ties to Protestant metaphysics and in the tradition of Bruckner and Brahms. Kohn's medievalism tended to be at once visceral and detached, and was related to Stravinsky as well as to Hindemith. For his part, Sapp's medievalism was sensual and esoteric, and more like Debussy's *Pelléas*. Significantly, works like *Lady and the Lute*, *A Maiden's Complaint*, and *Crennelations*, with their sad reflections on absent love, established contact with, above all, the troubadour repertory.

Between *A Maiden's Complaint* of 1960 and the *Imaginary Creatures* of 1980, Sapp composed only sporadically, one example being the 1978 *Nocturne* for cello and piano. This was due to administrative preoccupations, first at the State University of New York at Buffalo, and later at Florida State University at Tallahassee. Then, too, having to leave his position at Harvard may have been a wrenching experience, as it was to varying degrees for Fine and Spies and Moevs. But after settling in Cincinnati (where he served as dean for the University of Cincinnati) in the 1980s, Sapp produced a flood of new works, of which *Imaginary Creatures, Taylor's Nine,* and *Crennelations* were but samplings. Further, this music was more sprightly and vigorous than ever: it was as if two decades of pent-up creative energy finally exploded. There were new things in these later works—not only the experimental number play of *Taylor's Nine,* or something like "Halcyons" from *Imaginary Creatures,* which had some relation to Messiaen's bird music, but a denser, more complex rhythmic texture, found, for instance, in a number of more abstract works, including piano sonatas (up to No. 10 by the early 1990s), violin sonatas, and so forth. At the same time, these more classical works, in particular, bore the imprint of Piston's ideals. It was hard to imagine Piston as gritty as Sapp (Sapp himself guessed that Piston would have thought his mature work "coarse"), but on the other hand, there were few works of the 1980s that seemed to carry forth Piston's kind of elegance and craftsmanship so convincingly.

In the meantime, the works from the '40s and '50s were enjoying some successful revivals, to the point that the composer quipped, with the sort of irony Piston would have appreciated, that he had some hope that he might be rediscovered "like a Janáček or a Nielsen."

The similarities between Middleton and Sapp were more a matter of sensibility than of specifics of style and technique, though there was that, too. This sensibility entailed a chromatic palette that was bold yet elegant, rhythms that were strong yet supple, and textures that were dramatic yet restrained. They integrated refinement, daring, and high ideals into cohesive and balanced forms that helped revitalize the great Western traditions even in the most trying times. It was this that undoubtedly earned them Piston's special admiration.

Notes

1. Robert Middleton, personal interview, November 9, 1984.
2. R. S. T., *The Boston Herald,* April 21, 1951.
3. Middleton, preface to *Approximations* (New York: Marks Music, 1970).
4. M. F. Heresniak, "Philharmonic opens on good notes," *Poughkeepsie Journal,* October 19, 1985.
5. Sapp, a series of personal letters, September 23, 1977; August 1, 1984; August 10, 1984; August 13, 1984; August 25, 1984; and August 30, 1984.
6. Sapp, review of a recording of *Pelléas and Mélisande, Musical Quarterly* 39 (1953), pp. 310–314. Sapp admitted, though, that the subject of taste was "indefinable and elusive."

11. IN BARTÓK'S WAKE: JOHN BAVICCHI, NICHOLAS VAN SLYCK AND NOËL LEE

N THE LATE 1940S AND EARLY '50S, Bartók enjoyed the sort of vogue at Harvard that Hindemith had enjoyed before the War, and Stravinsky during it. According to Allen Sapp, it was Otto Gombosi "who brought a sense of Bartók" to Harvard during these years,[1] though a lively interest in Bartók characterized the immediate postwar years in general. Not that Harvard's new young composers imitated Bartók to the extent that their earlier counterparts had modeled themselves after the neoclassicists. For one thing, Bartók was no longer a living presence, as Stravinsky and Hindemith had been in the 1930s, and, in fact, still were. Also, for Americans, Bartók was more resistant to imitation, given his close association with Eastern European folk styles. But the impact of Bartók on the young composers of the postwar years was nonetheless profound, and reflected itself in many ways. With young composers from Harvard, it often blended and mingled with styles and ideals related to other well-favored composers, including Piston.

These young composers, most born in the early 1920s, included John Bavicchi (b. 1922), Nicholas Van Slyck (1922–1983) and Noël Lee (b. 1924). In time, Bavicchi won a local reputation in Boston as a conductor; Van Slyck, a national one as an educator and administrator; and Lee, an international one as a pianist. As composers, Lee had, perhaps, greatest prestige, especially among the artistic elite of New York and Paris. Van Slyck, for his part, established a following among music educators. But of the three, Bavicchi's music was most widely disseminated across the American mainstream, thanks in part to the patronage of Oxford University Press.

Bavicchi's 1956 *Sonata No. 1* for unaccompanied clarinet not only epitomized his own musical style, but the way in which his generation of Harvard composers drew upon both Piston and Bartók. The little groupings of two and three eighth notes in the first movement's opening phrase (Ex. 49), for instance, was reminiscent of Piston, but the systematic regularity of such groupings, as indicated parenthetically alongside the meter signature, showed the influence of Bartók. (An even more pointed example of this sort of thing could be found in the first movement of one of Bavicchi's earliest works, the 1951 *Trio* for viola, clarinet, and piano, Op. 4, in which the 7/8 meter was subdivided fairly consistently into units of 2-2-2-1.) The second movement opened with a long, sustained, pliant melody like Piston (Ex. 50), but grew more rhapsodic in ways closer to Bartók. Similarly, the opening of the giguelike finale, with its snazzy syncopations (Ex. 51), was in the tradition of the Piston *Oboe Suite,* while later on, the insistent repetition of a simple, cascading figure had more of a Bartókian flair. (Both these features—the preference for dance rhythms like the gigue, waltz, and march, and the predilection for repeating certain rhythmic figures in an almost trancelike way—were characteristic of Bavicchi's music.)

As for pitch material, the neatly designed phrases (often coming to rest on a cadence), the smooth modulations, and the modal inflections all bespoke a derivation from Piston, as well as Hindemith. But the increased chromatic tension and

Example 49. John Bavicchi, *Sonata* for unaccompanied clarinet, I (Oxford University Press, 1970).

Example 50. John Bavicchi, *Sonata* for unaccompanied clarinet, II (Oxford University Press, 1970).

modal ambiguity suggested the influence of Bartók. Does the rising, chromatic line in the first two measures of the first movement (see Ex. 49) suggest a tonal axis of D, G, or some other pitch? (As it turns out, the movement ends in G.) In measure four, is there a fleeting arrival in C, in D♭? Is E established at the end of the phrase? Note, too, in the other examples, how the tonal movement appears to shift: in Example 50, from F to F♯; and in Example 51, from E to G, reversing the motion of the first movement's opening phrase. Such richness and ambiguity colored entire movements, including the final affirmation of some or another tonal center. Even when Bavicchi concluded with a simple major or minor triad (which, in fact, happened quite often) the effect could be jolting.

Finally, in the matter of form, Bavicchi tended toward poised, sectional forms that showed a relation to the neoclassical models of Piston and Hindemith. But again, an added level of ambiguity and complexity was also entertained, pointing to Bartók's kind of formal freedom. This could be

Example 51. John Bavicchi, *Sonata* for unaccompanied clarinet, III (Oxford University Press, 1970).

seen best by a close look at a representative work, such as the *Trio* for violin, clarinet, and piano, Op. 33 (1958), which in its version for violin, clarinet, and harp (Op. 33a) was recorded by CRI.

In liner notes to this recording, Bavicchi described the *Trio's* three movements as in "pyramid form," "ABA mold," and "ternary form."[2] It was, however, somewhat difficult to perceive these forms as such, because Bavicchi's continuous development of small motives gave more the effect of a mosaic than of some schematic design. The first movement's introduction (mm. 1–8), for example, followed seamlessly into its A section (mm. 9–25). There were, in addition, more subtle kinds of ambiguities. In the first movement, ABCDCBA in form, the music grew progressively more complex as themes from one section reappeared juxtaposed with others, until all four principal themes were put forth simultaneously in the final A section—a cumulative effect. In this same movement, the return of section B was disguised to resemble a piano (or harp) cadenza, though, in fact, it recapitulated material quite literally. Then, too, all the material up to rehearsal letter D, the movement's midpoint, was cast in contrasting time signatures, while everything after it, excepting the coda, was in 2/4, a rather asymmetrical scheme. All these ideas—the cumulative, the quasi-cadenza, and the asymmetrical—contradicted and obscured the poised "pyramid form" that is the work's basic structure.

The *Trio's* ABA slow movement was much more straightforward, a work of neoclassical finesse, with poised cadences in B^b, D, and D^b. And yet there were features here, too, that slightly jarred its classic balance, such as the expansion of the consequent phrase in section A, the trancelike repetitions in section B, and the overpowering countermelody at the reprise of section A.

The last movement was formally the most adventurous. According to the composer, it "is built on a formal principle or device which is exciting to work with, and, to my knowledge, original in concept. The fundamental idea is one of expanding 'elements' of musical material, which is certainly not unique as a developmental device; but here I have attempted to use it as a formalistic principle." There were four of these "elements," each comprising a single, self-contained measure: the first and third were in 3/4; the second and fourth, in 6/8 (Ex. 52). They were put forth side by side, and eventually in counterpoint as well, and although they were clearly related to one another, they were distinct enough so that the effect was, once again, like a mosaic, or in what is perhaps a more apposite metaphor, like the whirl of atoms. The real novelty, as Bavicchi himself pointed out, was the way in which these elements were developed. This development was most systematic in the first A section: after an initial exposition (mm. 1–4), the elements expand to comprise two measures each (mm. 5–13), then three or four measures (mm.

Example 52. John Bavicchi, *Trio* for violin, clarinet, and harp, III.

14–29), and finally five or six measures (mm. 30–52). By the slower B section, the elements were expanded to the point that a single statement of each comprised the entire section. The return of the A section was wholly rewritten, consisting, as it does, of a kind of free-for-all in which the systematic rigor of the preceding sections was given up for kaleidoscopic juxtapositions and trancelike repetitions that become increasingly wilder, capped, finally, by a cadence in D major. Here again, as in the first and second movements, a basic ternary scheme was complemented and obscured by other, more novel ideas. More than any formal detail, such as pyramid form, or quasi-mathematical progressions, it was this simultaneity of formal levels—between the mosaic and the hierarchical, and between other contradictory formal ideas—that pointed to the influence of Bartók.

Bavicchi's penchant for abstract, technically smart, quasi-mathematical forms might have stemmed, too, from his background in engineering, a background he shared with Piston. During high school in Dedham, he studied trombone and piano, wrote a few pieces, including a work for orchestra, and began his lifelong attendance of Boston Symphony concerts. His father, a contractor, pressured him to study civil engineering at MIT. When the War came, he joined the Navy and completed his engineering studies at Naval training programs in Newark, New Jersey, and Cornell. From 1943 to 1946 he served the naval civil engineering corps on Guadalcanal and Okinawa, and in Tokyo. In all these places Bavicchi sought out native musical groups. This interest in Eastern musics found overt expression only in a setting of *Six Korean Folk Songs,* Op. 35 (1959), undertaken as a commission from a Korean singer who supplied the tunes, and a subsequent *Fantasia on Korean Folk Tunes,* Op. 53 (1966). The influence of Asian music, however, may have taken more subliminal expression, in the composer's modal inflections and in his mesmerizing repetitions.

On his return to civilian life, Bavicchi worked for a few years as a structural steel designer, but then took advantage of the GI Bill to enroll in the New England Conservatory, where he studied composition with Carl McKinley and Judd Cooke. He also learned enough viola to play middle-period Beethoven quartets. By the time he graduated in 1952, he had begun his long list of opus numbers (his opus 1, a *Divertimento* for violin, clarinet, and trombone, dated from 1950), and had determined, more or less, his musical tastes, which took as their two principal criteria formal command of material and consistent stylistic development. These criteria were met best, he allowed, by Bach, Beethoven, Schumann, and Bartók (eventually he would teach courses on the string quartets of Beethoven and Bartók, and make something of a specialty conducting Schumann's choral music). He also came to prefer Haydn to Mozart, Schoenberg's *Pierrot Lunaire* and *Erwartung* to his *String Quartets Nos. 3* and *4,* Hindemith to Webern, and in time, Hartmann to Hindemith. Other loves included Renaissance choral music, the operas of Wagner and Strauss, and the music of Berg and Piston.[3]

It was because of this admiration for Piston that Bavicchi entered Harvard as a graduate student in musicology, where he studied composition with Piston (1952 to 1956), choral music with Davison, medieval music with Gombosi, and counterpoint with Merritt. Piston was an evasive teacher, but he was responsive to questions, and "knew more about instruments than anyone I've ever met." His criticisms could be barbed. After the premiere of Bavicchi's *Second Cello Sonata,* Op. 25 (1956), which ended with a fugue, Piston told the composer, "If you left off the last movement, it would be a great piece." Once he pointed to an orchestral spot where Bavicchi had written different rhythms for the cellos and double basses, and called it "a lot of mud." This kind of admonition against cluttered orchestral textures stayed with Bavicchi throughout his career.

Of the more than eighty works in Bavicchi's catalog by his sixtieth birthday, only a few, however, were for orchestra. Most were for chamber ensembles, including a series of trios for unusual combinations, such as the aforementioned *Trio* for violin, clarinet, and piano (harp). These trios and many other works often featured the clarinet, so that by 1975, the editor of reviews for *The Clarinet* could write, "In terms of number, variety, and significance, few living composers can rival John Bavicchi's output of music for the clarinet. From virtuoso pieces to an extremely diverse ensemble repertory, there is at least one work suitable for players at most any kind of advancement."[4] The novelty of Bavicchi's chamber combinations, and the variety of their uses, suggested yet more connections to Bartók. Certainly the *Trio*, Op. 33 was a descendent of Bartók's *Contrasts* for the same instrumental combination.

Unlike Bartók, Bavicchi had little interest in folk music. Aside from the aforementioned arrangements of Korean tunes, the only other work to use folk material would seem to be the *Fourth Violin Sonata;* in this case, the use of Lithuanian melodies apparently was related to the fact that the work was commissioned by a Lithuanian immigrant, Izidore Vasyluinas (and perhaps reflected as well Bavicchi's close friendship with the Lithuanian-American composer, Jeronimas Kacinkas, whose *King Minelaugas's Mass* he arranged in 1980). He was little attracted to jazz either, but admitted a fondness for waltzes and marches.

According to the composer, his career fell more or less into three periods: a "formative" period (1950–1955, Op. 1–15); a "romantic" period (1955–1961, Op. 16–43); and a "late" period (after 1961). The major work of the first period, the *Concerto* for clarinet and string orchestra, Op. 11 (1954), was written during his first years with Piston. Its lively rhythms and sophisticated harmonies notwithstanding, the work had a certain roughness and awkwardness that helped explain the label "formative." A similar rawness characterized the *Trio* for clarinet, cello, and piano, Op. 13, of the same year.

The "romantic" works, including the two works we have examined—the unaccompanied *Clarinet Sonata,* Op. 20, and the *Trio No. 4,* Op. 33—as well as the *Six Duets* for flute and clarinet, Op. 27, and the *Oboe Sonatina,* Op. 30, exhibited a lighter, more controlled touch, and pointed unmistakably to Piston's influence. These were probably Bavicchi's most accessible works, especially the *Six Duets* (1957), which represented a charming addition to an undersized repertory. These little duets extended Piston's polymodality and contrapuntal liveliness in "romantic" directions, sometimes in ways reminiscent of Carter's *8 Etudes.* As for the *Trio,* its romanticism resided in its occasional use of the whole-tone scale, and in its lush colors in the version for violin, clarinet, and harp.

Even in these "romantic" works, Bavicchi never renounced a natural predilection for the rough and bold, as evidenced, too, by his unwavering enthusiasm for Michelangelo, Turner, and Kandinsky. Now, in his "late" works, such as the *Festival Symphony* for concert band, Op. 51 (1965), and the *Sonata* for clarinèt and piano, Op. 57 (1969), the appropriation of 12-tone ideas gave his bite an even greater severity, sometimes even a ferocity. Bavicchi always had favored long, chromatic melodies that reached repose only after a certain arduousness; now the difficulties had a grittiness that could set one's teeth on edge: the textures were dense with major sevenths, often in parallel motion. Further, the more expressive lines leaped about in surprising ways. In other respects, there was little change: the composer still exhibited rhythms based on Bach and popular dances, fast-slow-fast formats of a kind of "neue Sachlichkeit" coolness, and big, frenetic codas. The influence of Bartók was found most clearly in the faintly impressionistic slow movements, which were night pieces of a sort; while in the slow movement from the *Festival Symphony,* with its hymn tune and chorale setting, there was little doubt that the composer also had Berg's *Violin Concerto* in mind. The end result was a style that was often forbidding, but not without an impressive originality and earnestness.

Nearly all of Bavicchi's music was performed at least once. He won, in addition, a few commissions and, in 1959, a major award from the National Institute of Arts and Letters. But earning an obscure and precarious living as a free-lance copyist, bookbinder, teacher, and conductor, he found performances of his music hard to come by. Around 1958 he joined Nicholas Van Slyck, Allen Sapp, Jeronimas Kacinkas, and Boston Symphony trumpeter Roger Voisin in forming a sort of league to promote composers in the Boston area. They organized concerts in Brookline and Cambridge, and eventually a whole series at Boston's Nova Art Gallery, the Nova Concerts, that lasted for about four years. After Sapp left Boston in 1961, Bavicchi and Van Slyck formed a similar sort of forum for a few more seasons.

An appointment in 1964 with the Berklee School of Music finally provided Bavicchi with some economic security and institutional support. Journalists never warmed up to Bavicchi's music, noting its grimness sooner than its ingenuity or sophistication or occasional charm. His most loyal friends included clarinetists Felix Viscuglia, Sherman Friedland and conductor John Corley, who premiered many of Bavicchi's later works with the MIT Band. He remained close friends, too, with Van Slyck, who often spent an evening at Bavicchi's home, always well-stocked with rum, to listen to recordings of their favorite composers, including Bartók.

Nicholas Van Slyck, born in Philadelphia in 1922, earned both bachelor's and master's degrees at Harvard (1944, 1947). During his lifetime, his reputation rested primarily on his work with community schools. His obituary in the *Boston Globe,* for instance, hardly mentioned his more than one-hundred compositions.[5] This involvement with community schools included Boston's South End Music Center, which he directed from 1950 to 1962; the Longy School, which he directed from 1962 to 1976; and finally, the Cambridge New School of Music, which he founded and directed until his death on July 3, 1983, from cancer. His success rested in part on his high idealism, his good looks, and his talented oratory, traits Bavicchi and Sapp were glad to enlist for the cause of new music, although they agreed that Van Slyck's own music was not sufficiently original. Van Slyck's dedication to community education led to his dismissal from the Longy School, whose trustees wanted for their school the more high-toned prestige of the New England Conservatory. Van Slyck went on to found the New School, where he was free to lower fees, abolish age requirements, institute the Suzuki method, and start outreach programs into poor neighbor-hoods.[6] His obituary said that he believed "music can be part of everyone's life."

In his response to varied community needs, Van Slyck was what so few other of Piston's students were—a sort of populist. Whether his long involvement with community schools shaped his aesthetic aims and convictions, or vice versa, was difficult to say (and analogous, perhaps, to the relationship of Kubik's musical style to his film work). In any case, one found in his catalog piano pieces of graded difficulty that could meet his own pedagogical needs, such as *Finger Paints* (1958) and *Six Sonatinas* (1956–1968). In addition, there were etudes, rounds, and other works for choruses; sonatas for woodwind instruments; an *Encore March* (1969) for the Boston Pops; a song cycle on words by Whitman, *Sea*

Drift (1965); a ballet based on *The Legend of Sleepy Hollow* (1963); and a setting of Longfellow's "Salem Farms," entitled *Judgement in Salem* (1974). But there were, as well, serious instrumental works, including a series of piano sonatas, the *First* (1947), incidentally, dedicated to Noël Lee, and the *Third* (1952) to John Bavicchi. After 1957, his more ambitious work was written mostly for his second wife, pianist Trudi Salomon. For her, and for the two of them, he wrote fairly demanding pieces for solo piano, piano four-hands, two pianos, and piano and orchestra.

Of all these works, the pedagogical works like *Finger Paints* were most successful. Such works were as likely to turn up at workshops for piano teachers as in music libraries, let alone in scholarly publications, and helped earn him the 1982 Composer of the Year Award by the Music Teachers National Association.[7] And, indeed, something like the two volumes of *Finger Paints* were still useful in the 1990s: they introduced the beginning pianist to such "progressive" (to quote from its subtitle) features as clusters, dissonant counterpoint, bitonal harmony, in short, to the kind of stylistic advances represented by Prokofiev and Bartók. Nor were these little pieces undistinguished, especially some from Volume II, such as "Landscape" (Ex. 53) and the final "Vanishing Horizon." The picturesque titles were aimed at stimulating beginning musicians so that their "perception become artistically finer," according to introductory notes by the composer. Although some of these titles were vaguely abstract, like "Portrait," or simply precious, like "Valentine for Tina," others often suggested some vivid association that could help put over Van Slyck's ideas.

Example 53. Nicholas Van Slyck, "Landscape," *Finger Paints* for piano, Vol. II (General Music, 1980).

Titles aside, *Finger Paints* clearly followed in the footsteps of Bartók's *Mikrokosmos,* along with children's pieces by Prokofiev. One found these dual influences merged in Van Slyck's more ambitious music from the time as well, as David Witten noted in liner notes to his recording of one such work, the *Capriccio No. 3* (1957). Here it was the Bartók of the *Piano Sonata* and the Prokofiev of the *Seventh Sonata* whose marks were felt. At the same time, underpinning the biting syncopations was the kind of vigorous, marchlike rhythms that were very American in spirit: indeed, in the work's grim sort of cheerfulness, *Capriccio No. 3* represented a late spin-off of American neoclassicism. This Prokofievan brand of classicism reminded one of Gail Kubik, only here the connection with Piston was even more remote.

Not surprisingly, when Van Slyck began to employ the 12-tone technique in the 1960s, it was in a particularly accessible and conservative way. In *12 Cadenzas: Preludes in All Keys in a Brilliant Style* (1966), for instance, each Cadenza had its own row, put forth like a principal theme, to be freely supported harmonically and developed motivically. Indeed, the harmonic writing was as triadic as ever, whether or not triads were written into the row, and the style in general was even more retrogressive than Prokofiev, looking back to such transitional styles as Rachmaninov, Ravel, and Busoni. This did not stop it, however, from being one of Van Slyck's most effective works.

Van Slyck's adventurousness took a new turn in 1970 with *Pantomime,* a "Fantasie" for piano four-hands written for himself and Trudi Salomon. It ingeniously combined the traditional spirit of the piano duet with imaginative explorations of new piano sounds: the second piano not only was expected to pedal, as custom decreed, but to make all sorts of sounds using the inside of the piano. Only the fourth of its five movements (entitled "Scene-setting," "Procession," "Monologue," "General Dance," and "Curtain") did not call for such techniques. "Procession," a march, made especially smart programmatic use of the inside of the piano in its suggestions of crashing cymbals and pounding drums. Once again, here in the work's evocation of an old world of simple, slightly burlesque entertainment, Van Slyck seemed to continue along the lines of Gail Kubik.

And later still, in "Will-o'-the-Wisp" from *Seven Short Mysteries* for piano (1976), the composer showed some awareness of still newer trends in the piece's faintly oriental ostinato, its Victorian title notwithstanding; the unlikely result was a sort of minimalist MacDowell. One was curious about the other six mysteries!

All of these works, virtuosic and pedagogical alike, exhibited a classic restraint related to the composer's love of Bach and his many years of study with Piston. In an article that argued that the second book of *The Well-Tempered Clavier* was, to a certain extent, a conscious improvement on the earlier volume, though yet still another stepping stone to the *Art of the Fugue,* he wrote, "more than any other composer in history, he [Bach] had the greatest control of all the elements that make up the art of music."[8] Van Slyck, in fact, arranged the *Art of the Fugue* in 1972 so that he and Trudi could play it at the piano, and in the following year, concluded a piano suite entitled *Gardens of the West,* with a "Meditation on the Art of the Fugue." Other titles that suggested some connection to Bach included a *Fugue Cycle* for organ (1968), *12 Cadenzas: Preludes in All Keys in a Brilliant Style* for piano (1966), *Nine Inventions* for piano (1969), and a *Prelude and Fugue* for chorus (1972). But nearly all of Van Slyck's work, for instance, enjoyed some canonic development of material. Even in the flashy *Cadenzas,* two of the twelve pieces were fugues, the second built on an inversion of the first fugue's subject.

Nor was Van Slyck's enthusiasm for the Baroque limited to Bach. For harpsichordist Irma Rogell, who was also the recipient of two *Suites* for harpsichord (1970, 1972), he wrote *Diferencias* (1966), a set of variations on the "La Folia" theme used by Corelli and Handel, as well as a work entitled *La Tomba di Scarlatti.* And, indeed, Van Slyck's sense of the Baroque was not the streamlined, linear conception associated with Piston and Hindemith, derived almost thoroughly from Bach, but something more improvisational, ornamental, dramatic, and lush. Significantly, other Harvard composers born in the early 1920s, such as Pinkham, Middleton, and Sapp, for all their differences, shared that kind of sensibility. The neobaroque sensibility of Van Slyck's *Cadenzas,* for instance, could be compared with Middleton's even more brilliant and ornate *Inventions on the Twelve Notes* for piano, written a few years earlier in 1961.

But Van Slyck's easy-going congeniality stood apart. One of his last works—*Piano Partners* for two pianos (1977–1980)—was perhaps at times cloying in its whimsy, but, all in all, a delightful contribution to the genre (Ex. 54). It was refreshingly modest in its technical demands too; although it was yet another work written for his second wife and himself, it did not necessitate their expert skills. In this work in particular, Van Slyck came close to the one contemporary composer he regarded as highly as Bartók and Prokofiev, namely, Frank Martin. This close relationship with Martin—unique, perhaps, among American composers—would be further illuminated once other works were better known, such as the two *Piano Concertos,* which Trudi Salomon considered among her husband's most important work.

Example 54. Nicholas Van Slyck, "Opening Moves," *Piano Partners* (General Music, 1982).

In the scholarship of 20th-century American music, few omissions were as glaring as in the case of Noël Lee. Here was a pianist whose more than one-hundred recordings included classic performances of Schubert, Debussy, Ravel, Stravinsky, and Bartók, and who was an excellent composer in his own right. And yet he received no mention in *Grove's VI, Baker's, Vinton's,* or most other reference texts. Indeed, published material on the composer was limited mostly to record liner notes.

Lee was born in Nanking, China, on Christmas day, 1924, the son of American professors later to settle in Lafayette, Indiana, where he grew up. He began composing at age six. From 1942 to 1943, and then from 1946 to 1948, he attended Harvard, graduating with a BA cum laude. At Harvard he benefited from Irving Fine's friendly counsel, but vacillated under Piston's laissez faire. After settling in Europe, Lee realized:

> Young Americans live in a society where they are told that anything and everything is possible. Be this true or not, the idea sometimes prevents students from making decisions. Young Europeans, living in a more closed society, often have fewer choices, therefore less indecision.[9]

Lee, nevertheless, held Piston, along with Copland, in special regard among American composers. They, in turn, admired him: Piston arranged a scholarship so that Lee could work with Boulanger in Paris; Copland singled him out in 1959 as an outstanding young American writing in a conservative vein, and in years after had other complimentary things to say.[10] With Boulanger, Lee found more the sort of direction he was looking for, less so with Boris Blacher, with whom he briefly studied in London. His European studies completed, Lee decided to settle in Paris, later traveling to the States to concertize as well as to teach at Cornell and other universities.

As a composer, Lee won a local fame comparable to Bavicchi and Van Slyck, the difference being that the locality was Paris, not Boston. As with them, his music earned him a few awards, including the 1953 Prix Lili Boulanger, a 1959 National

Institute of Arts and Letters Award, and the 1986 Prix Arthur Honegger. He did not have an originality like Bavicchi's, or an accessibility like Van Slyck's, but he had an eloquence and command greater than theirs. Like Bavicchi and Van Slyck, he was strongly attracted to Bartók; indeed, he recorded many of Bartók's major piano works, and wrote a piano etude, "On a rhythm by Bela Bartók." But while the influence of Bartók was tempered in Bavicchi's case by an objectivity like Hindemith's, and in Van Slyck's case by a populism like Prokofiev's, with Lee it seemed to accommodate a polish and refinement reminiscent, alternately, of Stravinsky, Copland, and Piston.

These varied influences were all evident in one of Lee's earliest works, the *Variations* for harpsichord, flute, violin, and cello (1952), commissioned by a Parisian department store for a fashion show. The influence of Piston was felt immediately in the siciliana-like theme upon which the *Variations* are based (Ex. 55), resembling, as it does, the "Siciliana" from *The Incredible Flutist.* Throughout the work, the controlled harmonic tension, the artful sequences, and the refined counterpoint often recalled Piston, especially the quasi-fugal Variation V, and Variation III, parts of which resembled Piston's *Flute Quintet.* The very openings of Variations I, III, and VIII, on the other hand, recalled Stravinsky, while Variation VII was more like Copland.

At the same time, the *Variations* had some features that suggested the influence of Bartók. The theme itself (see Ex. 55), which Lee described as lydian-mixolydian, comprised a new mode that included the tritone and flatted seventh, a

Example 55. Noël Lee, *Variations* for flute, violin, cello, and harpsichord.

mode reminiscent of Bartók: D-E-F#-G#-A-B-C. The supporting counterpoint was derived from this mode as well, and gave rise to subtle harmonic implications: measures three and four in the harpsichord, for instance, pointed to F# minor, but the F# that arrived in the bass at measure five supported a D major triad in first inversion. These and like modal inflections cast a dark shadow upon the music, especially Variation VI, which had a brooding, rhapsodic quality like Bartók's.

The work, however, was no mere pastiche, no mere assemblage of undigested influences. All of its derivative elements served a fine, individual imagination, for example, Variation IV, with its ghostly march for pianissimo violin, flute, and cello intriguingly spaced against toccata-like activity in the harpsichord. A similar idea characterized the second of Lee's *Deux Mouvements* for violin, cello, and piano, a beautiful work from 1959 that exhibited a yet more personal and mature profile.

Another work from 1959, the *Sonatine* for piano, put Lee's individuality into even greater focus. It possessed the elegance, clarity, and charm of the *Variations* without the latter's more mannered and derivative features. Its first movement was constructed from two principal ideas: a three-note motive, C#-B-D, and a four-note scalar fragment that outlined a fourth. The texture was contrapuntal, though in a highly restrained way: three levels of melodic interest often coexisted, but one usually predominated. The form honored traditional sonatina conventions, not only in its modest scale, but in certain particulars: there was an opening antecedent-consequent phrase in A (mm. 1–11); a second theme in the dominant (mm. 12–17); a development of sorts (mm. 18–50), which modulated to such distant centers as D# and G#; and a return of both themes in the tonic, though in inverted order (mm. 50–69). This form, however, did not appear schematic because of its playful, spontaneous approach, as in the proportionately over-large "development." Also, the movement's classic tonal design was offset by certain harmonic ambiguities. An example of this was the very opening, which pitted a D-minor seventh chord against the tonic A major, causing a dualism not unlike that noted in Bavicchi's unaccompanied *Sonata* for clarinet. There were other sorts of polymodal and polytonal touches, for example, the Stravinskian conflict between E major and G# minor at measure twelve; and the simultaneous arrival of G#

and A at the climax at measure fifty. Another distinctive feature of the *Sonatine* was the work's elegant, limpid piano writing, which nicely matched the composer's own velvety sound. In later years, Lee's piano writing could get quite thick, even to the point of clusters to be played with the palm, but it always remained highly idiomatic and refined.

Lee called his *Sonatine,* "frankly neo-classic . . . a piece for summer; the clouds, if there are any, do not last long."[11] One only faintly felt a connection with Bartók, for example, in the first movement's descending fourths, or in the second movement's "tranquillo" melody—perhaps these were the passing clouds. Lee's *Dialogues* for violin and piano, written in the previous year, 1958, was, in contrast, much closer to Bartók (Ex. 56). Significantly, the work was described by its composer not as "a piece for summer," but rather in terms of silhouettes vaguely espied in "the moist greyness" of an "early Spring mist."[12] The dark silhouettes were evoked by a very Bartókian concept, a chromatic tetrachord that "appears throughout the work in 353 shapes and forms—horizontally, vertically, diagonally, octagonally, maybe elliptically or spherically?" The tonality was misty too, decidedly in B, but only really confirmed at the very end, when the four-note motive, B-C-D-C#, crept up in the violin, pianissimo, to the D# of a poised B major. The work was schematic to a degree (it comprised eight variations), and as with Bavicchi, the combination of through-composition, variation form, and arch design suggested Bartók. Finally, *Dialogues* displayed a Bartókian rhythmic flair, including rhapsodic moments that dispensed with barlines and meter signatures. The work was dedicated to violinist Paul Makanowitzky, who frequently concertized with Lee, and whose poetry Lee set to music.

Lee's national identity was elusive. He liked titles that were the same in English and French, such as *Dialogues,* or *Convergences,* a work from 1973 for flute and harpsichord. Othertimes, there were English titles like *Four Etudes* and *Commentaries,* and French titles like *Sonatine* and *Deux Mouvements.* Similarly, there were text settings in both languages: the English settings included the Bible (*Rhapsodies* for mezzo-soprano, chorus and orchestra), Shakespeare (*Devouring Time* for mixed chorus and piano concertante), and Makanowitzky (*Three Intimate Songs* for tenor and piano); the

Example 56. Noël Lee, *Dialogues* for violin and piano (Theodore Presser, 1958).

French settings included Valéry (*Paraboles* for tenor solo, chorus, and orchestra, 1954), Lorca, translated by André Bélamich (*Five Songs on Poetry by Federico Garciá Lorca* for soprano, flute, and guitar, 1955), Catherine Pozzi (*Four Ballades* for soprano and orchestra, 1956), and Baudelaire (*Quatre Chants sur Baudelaire* for voice and piano, 1971). One was reminded of the French-American composer Loeffler, who made the same transatlantic move in reverse. Lee more properly belonged in the context of a new generation of American expatriates that included James Baldwin, Gore Vidal, and Ned Rorem. Rorem's many books and diaries provided too little a glimpse into their interactions, though Lee is mentioned as "the favorite of us all,"[13] and one of a group of friends that cried with him over a performance of Ravel's *L'Enfant et les sortilèges*.[14] Lee's emigration to France might have helped shape his mature taste in American music, but did not seem to lessen it. He recorded piano works by, among others, Griffes, Ives, and Copland, and even composed works in homage of the latter two: *On Chords from Charles Ives* for piano (1967) and *Commentaries on a theme from Aaron Copland* for trumpet, clarinet, and piano (1966). Lee once spoke of the "American flavor" of his *Sonata* for piano (1955),[15] which he perhaps thought of as somewhat ominous, obstinate, almost inelegant.

In the 1950s, Lee began to use the 12-tone method. The first work to do so was the 1955 *Five Songs on Poetry by Federico García Lorca* for soprano, flute, and guitar, a work which won first prize in the 1961 Arthur Shepherd Composition Contest. A sumptuous work, with highly effective use of Spanish color, the *Five Songs* deserved the kind of popularity accorded the more famous, but very different, Lorca cycles by George Crumb, for which it may have been an inspiration. Each song had its own 12-tone row, except the last, which used them all, doubtless in response to the fact that this last poem echoed themes and images found in the preceding ones. Lee spelled out the individual rows at the start of each song, a practice reminiscent of Robert Middleton, who occasionally spelled out a row at the end of a piece, not to mention Schumann, who wrote out the motive ASCH in the score to *Carnaval.* (Lee later omitted the rows.) *Carnaval,* in fact, was quoted in another of Lee's 12-tone works, *Caprices on the Name of Schönberg* for piano and orchestra (1975), in what was a slightly esoteric pun on the Schumann motto (ASCH) and Schoenberg's name (A. SCHBEG).[16] Both the *Five Songs* and the *Caprices* accommodated the 12-tone technique to a distinctively rich, tonal language.

Lee's music after 1960 became more and more daring, especially regarding new kinds of sound material. Some of the *Etudes* for piano (1961, 1967) required the performer to play the inside of the piano; *Convergences* for flute and harpsichord (1972) required the keyboardist to knock on the instrument's wood; and the forementioned *Caprices* (1975) called for both. In addition, the harmonic and rhythmic textures became thicker and less traditional. By the time of *Chroniques* for solo piano (1977), Lee's style included the absence of barlines, unusual rhythmic proportions, a fairly atonal harmonic language, and a wealth of new piano techniques including clusters, unmeasured repeated notes, prepared strings, silently depressed keys, and aleatoric notation. In all these later pieces, the use of colorful harmonies in the piano's highest register created glassy sonorities of decidedly French cast, which pointed to a degree of closeness to Messiaen and Boulez. These works were novel from the standpoint of form as well, especially *Caprices,* with its seven contiguous sections that suggested the broad outline of a classical four-movement design.

Caprices well demonstrated the breadth of the composer's mature style. Appropriate to the work's full title, there were textures and orchestral touches reminiscent of Schoenberg's Op. 16. But more to the fore were features related to Lee's Franco-American identity: the French features would include those rich harmonies in high registers; the American ones would include the rhythmic liveliness and crispness of certain passages, especially when accompanied by xylophone and cymbals. Then, too, there was Lee's particular penchant for soaring, nostalgic lines that at times gave *Caprices* the chic of a particularly sophisticated motion picture score. Even the very daring *Chroniques* exhibited balanced phrases and expressive melodies, while its unstemmed splashes of notes, as performed especially by Lee, had some relation to Chopin's ornamental figuration. These later works did not, perhaps, have the charm and appeal of the composer's earlier music— there was even an almost willful eccentricity about them—but they nonetheless were distinguished by a graceful elegance and a cool grandeur.

Lee's individuality in his later works was such that any former debt to Bartók was subtle, though evident enough in the "cantando" section of *Chroniques* (Ex. 57). More generally it was felt in the handling of new sounds and forms. Certainly for Lee, as for Bavicchi and Van Slyck, Bartók was a major, seminal figure, if not the greatest composer of their century. There was possibly a sentimental component in this genera-

Example 57. Noël Lee, *Chroniques* for piano.

tion's attachment to Bartók (as there was, perhaps, with the parallel vogue for Webern), the feeling that the lofty and noble Bartók had suffered neglect and hardship in the United States as well as in Europe. But the closeness Lee, Van Slyck, and Bavicchi felt toward Bartók was deeper than mere sentimentality, and survived the vagaries of fashion; like Carter and Kohs slightly before them, they found in Bartók the exemplary compromise between the classicism they admired in Bach, Schumann, and Piston, and some newer trends, such as tonal ambiguity, percussive instrumental writing, and unusual superimpositions of traditional formal principles. Some of Bartók's social ideals, especially his interest in writing music that suited the most varied uses, including the pedagogical, were also reflected in their work to varying degrees.

Where Bavicchi, Van Slyck, and Lee differed most dramatically from Bartók was in the small role that folk styles and traditions played in their work. Consequently, they stood in relation to Bartók as some of their more avant-garde contemporaries stood in relation to Webern: more in the matter of technique than in spirit. As for the latter, here they inherited, more tellingly, perhaps, something of Piston's classical ideals. This common bond of Bartók and Piston, with its richly dialectical overtones, was indeed a primary one for young composers coming out of Harvard in the late 1940s and early '50s, not only for these three, but for Allen Sapp, Gordon Binkerd, and many others.

Notes

1. Sapp, personal letter, August 13, 1984.
2. Bavicchi, liner notes to a recording of the *Trio No. 4,* Op. 33, CRI 138.
3. Bavicchi, personal interview, February 8, 1984; also, "Five Questions: Fifty-Five Answers," *The Composer* 7 (1976–1977), pp. 16–25.
4. James Gillespie, "The Clarinet Music of John Bavicchi," *The Clarinet* 2 (February 1975), p. 26.
5. "Nicholas Van Slyck, 60, headed Boston, Cambridge Music Schools," *Boston Globe,* July 3, 1983, p. 27.

6. Trudi Van Slyck, personal interview, September 28, 1984.
7. "MTNA 1982 Composer of the Year," *American Music Teacher* 32 (April–May 1983), p. 5.
8. Van Slyck, "Bach's Second Chance," *Clavier* 19 (December 1980), pp. 17–21.
9. Lee, personal letter, March 16, 1978.
10. Copland, "1959: Postscript for the Generation of the Fifties," *Copland on Music* (New York: Norton, 1963), p. 178. See also Copland's liner notes to recordings of Lee's music, Fona 122 and 130, for which he wrote, "It is a pleasure to lend oneself to music so clearly conceived and so beautifully controlled. One can always follow his line of musical thought—it represents a refreshingly honest approach to the art of composition. Here is a composer who writes his music with his eyes open, and with a kind of cool intensity that defines his personality."
11. Lee, liner notes to a recording of the *Sonatine,* Fona 122.
12. Lee, liner notes to a recording of *Dialogues,* Fona 130.
13. Rorem, *Critical Affairs* (New York: George Braziller, 1970), p. 182.
14. Rorem, *Setting the Tone* (New York: Coward-McCann, 1983), p. 291.
15. Lee, liner notes to a recording of the *Sonata,* Fona 122.
16. Lee, liner notes to a recording of the *Caprices,* CRI 408.

12. THE CENTER HOLDING: GORDON BINKERD

LTHOUGH FOUR YEARS OLDER than Harold Shapero, Gordon Binkerd (b. 1916) stood in relation to the 1950s
much as Shapero did to the 1940s, that is, as one of
America's freshest and most powerful voices working in a
neoclassical idiom; and, indeed, works like the *Cello Sonata*
(1952), *Symphony No. 1* (1955), *Piano Sonata* (1955), *Symphony No. 2* (1957), and *String Quartets Nos. 1 and 2* (1958,
1961) had an elegance and sophistication that suggested in
Binkerd a successor to Piston as well as to Shapero. As with
Shapero, the ensuing years brought a long period of neglect.
But unlike Shapero, Binkerd, teaching at the University of
Illinois from 1949 to 1971, and living quietly on his farm,
"Three Acres," outside Champaign-Urbana, continued to
produce a large body of work, including six symphonies and
four piano sonatas. Though this later music was not as
well-known as his music from the '50s, much of it was
published by Boosey and Hawkes, and regularly performed.
And it furthermore won serious scholarly attention.[1]

One trait that emerged prominently in portraits of the
composer by Dorothy Veinus Hagan[2] and Rudy Shackelford[3]
was Binkerd's attachment to the land. Hagan wrote:

> He is a man who delights in making things grow. He has
> a small farm of good, black Illinois soil, and his
> gardening runs the gamut from red and white potatoes
> to wild flowers and trees. He is a strongly built,
> energetic man who is fond of chopping wood in
> moments of relaxation. In fact, his nature is the exact
> opposite of 'Bohemian.' "[4]

Shackelford's portrait included a poem about Binkerd written by Etta Blum, who had met him at the MacDowell Colony; called "A Chopper of Trees," it read in part:

> He sits at the piano and ponders.
> It is his turn to make music now.
> The hut sings, stilling the birds
> who have never before heard such
> sounds in these fortunate woods.[5]

Not surprisingly, Binkerd's music teemed with observations of the natural world; there were reflections on mice and sheep, running waters and white fields, evening moons and spring afternoons. The *First Symphony*'s "Adagio," to take one example, was inspired by the song of the Alder Flycatcher.[6]

Binkerd's love of nature dated back to his childhood in the Sandhills of Nebraska and the Black Hills of South Dakota. His grandparents on both sides had homesteaded in Nebraska in the 1860s, and he was born in Lynch on a Ponca Indian reservation. While in high school, his family moved to the Rosebud Sioux Reservation in Gregory, South Dakota.[7] His contact with the Indian population on these reservations was slight, but he felt sympathy for their plight. In later years he became an admirer of Marie Sandoz, the noted Indian writer, and was glad to learn of an Indian tribe that had decided not to celebrate Columbus Day.

A pianist, Binkerd studied music at South Dakota Wesleyan University, where he worked with Russell Danburg and Gail Kubik, who was only two years his elder, and in whose footsteps he was more or less to follow. Graduating in 1937, he "came out of college into a world smothering in dust and seemingly dying of the Great Depression."[8] He taught for one year at a junior college in Garden City, Kansas, and for two years at Franklin College in Franklin, Indiana, before a windfall of $600 won on a Bank Night at a local motion picture show enabled him to pursue his studies at the Eastman School. There he studied piano with Max Landau, "whose wisdom and perception meant more to me than I can say." He also had "the great fortune to be in three classes of Bernard Rogers."

In 1941 Binkerd moved to Chicago and "went on the bum," working in a Hardings Restaurant, and ushering concerts at Orchestra Hall, where he was thrilled by the Chicago Symphony Orchestra under Frederick Stock. The following year he enlisted in the Navy, serving for four years, including time spent in the Pacific.

After his release in 1946, he immediately enrolled in Harvard as a doctoral student, studying three years with Piston, Kinkeldey, Davison, and others, and assisting Irving Fine as a teaching fellow.

Binkerd's work with Piston proved decisive. He once told a panel of music theorists, "The study of Bach fugues and the Gedalge fugue book with Walter Piston proved the most important single factor in my preparation as a composer."[9] Binkerd took Piston's class in fugue three times, classes which transmitted "a kind of unspoken standard very difficult to define," and which Binkerd described as follows:

> It is difficult to say in what way Piston contributed to this experience. He was an extremely taciturn man, hardly ever wrote anything on the black board, corrected our fugue papers with minimal notations, seemed most of the time just to sit still in the classroom. And yet it was there that it became possible for me to become a composer. He took us through the Gedalge fugue book, never even bothering to ask if we could get hold of a copy or could read its French if we did. We went through the Art of the Fugue, with himself performing a different fugue each time the schedule called for it, always from the "full" score, perhaps wishing to amaze us a bit by his ability to read four-part counterpoint in open score set in C-clefs.[10]

Piston's composition and orchestration seminars were less memorable. The composition classes, remembered Binkerd, had no organization of any kind:

> We brought things to this class as we had something ready. We played it on the piano as best we could. Remarks by him were very few. Pressures came from fellow members of the class.

As for the seminar in advanced orchestration, Binkerd
presumed that it was not as rewarding as Piston's undergraduate class in orchestration, for which players from the Boston
Symphony gave demonstrations on their instruments.

Piston's own music also proved to be quite influential. This
could be seen by comparing Binkerd's *Poem after Thomas
Wolfe* for baritone and orchestra, written at Eastman in 1941,
with his *Sonatina* for flute and piano, written at Harvard in
1947. The former, a dark musical landscape, suitably depicted
its romantic, nocturnal text with rippling triplets and tremolos, impressionist harmonies, and the sort of piquant orchestration one might expect from a student of Bernard Rogers.
The *Sonatina,* in contrast, was in a lean, neobaroque style,
with quartal harmonies and sprightly rhythms, including a 5/8
finale, that pointed directly to Piston. The work's mood,
however, was the composer's own, and not so different from
the *Poem after Thomas Wolfe* after all. In fact, the *Sonatina's*
dark shade of classicism betrayed a special kinship to Brahms,
one that foreshadowed the more overtly Brahmsian works of
Binkerd's later years. Piston, it would seem, suggested ways
in which Binkerd's individual temperament could be reconciled to a classical sensibility.

An orchestral work written soon after Binkerd joined the
faculty of University of Illinois, *Sun Singer* (1952), suggested
that the composer's individuality was related to his regional
background. While the work showed some indebtedness to
Piston, especially in the coda with its changing meters, and to
Harris, too, the work's national ambiance stood in some
contrast to Piston's New England, or Harris's Far West, or
even to Kubik's Midwest, evoking rather Binkerd's native
Northern Plains. The work's antiphonal textures and modal
melodies suggested Lutheran Church music, and its vigorous
rhythms and repeated snippets, Indian ceremonial music. The
work's regionalism bore some resemblance to a work like the
Prairie Symphony by his colleague on the Illinois faculty,
Eugene Weigel, not to mention that other symphonist from
Nebraska, Howard Hanson, of whom Binkerd also could be
seen as something of a successor. But Binkerd's classical
eloquence had no room for the picturesque or sentimental,
and his kind of dark, romantic regionalism probably was

matched sooner by the novels of Willa Cather than by the symphonies of Hanson or anyone else. In any event, Binkerd's regionalism was of a particularly subtle and refined order, and, perhaps, was seen best in the light of various classical models.

The title *Sun Singer,* in fact, did not refer to an American subject but rather to a 1928 sculpture by the Swedish Carl Milles, a replica of which was housed in the University's Robert Allerton Park in Monticello, Illinois. The possible connection with the regional traits mentioned above might reside in the heavily Scandinavian makeup of America's Northern Plain states. The choice of this bronze 12-foot streamlined torso of a male nude as an inspiration was significant in any case. First, sculpture provided a good metaphor for Binkerd's forms, which were likewise solid, organic, and compact. Second, Milles, best known to Americans for his sculptures for Radio City Music Hall, created out of Gothic, Jugendstil, and other elements a sensuous, decorative, and mythic art that was analogous to Binkerd's work. And finally, Binkerd's responsiveness to Milles showed his independence of thought, as the sculptor had fallen out of favor during the postwar period.

In the same year, 1952, Binkerd wrote his first work to bring him national recognition, the *Sonata* for cello and piano. For this work, Binkerd employed the 12-tone method, which he had investigated at Harvard with fellow student Allen Sapp through analyses of Schoenberg's *Wind Quintet* and *Third String Quartet.* Binkerd's application of the method was strikingly straightforward, with the row (G-E-G#-C-B-Bb-F-F#-D-A-C#-Eb) and its transformations spun out melodically throughout the work. The opening cello statement, for instance, clearly defined the basic parameters of the row by putting forth, like Schoenberg's *Variations,* and Piston's *Chromatic Study,* its principal forms: P, R, I, and RI (Ex. 58). Sometimes the row was used as a self-contained motive or phrase; other times it was used with greater flexibility, as in mm. 8–9, where 6-7-8-9-10 of I was poignantly answered by 11-12(I)-2-3-4(R). But in any case, the row was used essentially as a melodic rather than as a harmonic resource, and the few more chordal passages, such as six measures after 10 ("brillante"), arose from strict contrapuntal activity, in this

Example 58. Gordon Binkerd, *Sonata* for cello and piano, I (Boosey & Hawkes, 1971).

instance, the simultaneous presentation of the four basic row-forms of a new, subsidiary row introduced at 9.

Some liberties from 12-tone orthodoxy were indulged nonetheless, often in ways reminiscent of Schoenberg himself. Notes and little melodic bits were sometimes skipped or repeated. Special fondness was shown for row-forms that shared a common first or last pitch, and that, consequently, enabled the composer to smoothly elide one row-form to another, a technique that proved something of a mannerism in the course of the work. Binkerd's principal deviation from 12-tone orthodoxy, however, resided in his use of subsidiary rows; there was one, as mentioned, in the first movement at 9, and three in the last movement: at measure one (the piano figuration), at 13 (the cello melody), and at 20 (the piano part, "furibondo").

All things considered, however, the *Sonata*'s use of the method was surprisingly rigorous and uncompromising, surprising because the work made a fairly conservative impression. For one thing, there was a strong tonal coloring to the work, due not only to the choice of the row, with its thirds and fifths, but more specifically to the way in which these intervals were articulated. Moreover, there were dramatic thematic contrasts and returns. The individual movements, in fact, suggested in no small way classical forms—sonata, ABA, and rondo, respectively. Binkerd accommodated these classic forms to the 12-tone method by substituting what might be called "row-form areas" for tonal areas. For instance, in the first movement, Binkerd introduced I^7 and RI^7 at 3 to help signal the arrival of the "second theme," and further, when this "second theme" was restated in the recapitulation (at 16), it put forth I^4, the row-form that was a fourth higher than I^7. Similarly, Binkerd used an increased number of row-forms, and introduced a new one, in this movement's "development section." Even the *Sonata*'s larger form reflected traditional practice: the outer movements basically used the same row (the finale's row is the RI of the first movement's row), while the middle movement used a contrasting one.

Even more conservative were the *Sonata*'s neobaroque stylistic features. The long, graceful melodies, the lean textures (often two- or three-part), the motor rhythms, and the lively counterpoint, including extensive use of canon, augmentation, and diminution, looked back to the Baroque, in particular to the keyboard works of Bach. (Significantly, the composer, throughout his career, transcribed music, principally organ works, by such composers as Bach, Buxtehude, Redford, Weckmann, Frescobaldi, Pachelbel, and Walther.) When the piano part occasionally burst forth, it was still reminiscent, as in the first movement, of such classical models as Brahms (see 11 mm. after 9) and Piston (see 6 mm. after 1). Indeed, the *Sonata*'s kind of conservative and yet uncompromised use of the 12-tone technique came close to Piston's own use of the method, at least in those 12-tone works of his from the early '40s. But as with the earlier *Flute Sonatina,* the truer kinship was with Brahms: it was through Piston that Binkerd revitalized the tradition of Brahms, as it was through Piston that Shapero rediscovered Beethoven.

Binkerd's *Cello Sonata* was a breakthrough, much as Carter's was for him. And as with Carter, the breakthrough came in finding a new and personal voice within the context of classical poise and refinement. According to the composer, the 12-tone method had worked "like a charm." But unlike

Carter, who pushed further and further into new ground, Binkerd began to retreat almost immediately. He used the 12-tone method once again, more freely this time, for the first two movements of the 1955 *First Symphony;* but he remembers "between the second and third movements, I suddenly experienced an intense revulsion away from the system. I gave it up and have returned to it only briefly, and in a sense casually."[11] Binkerd's 12-tone adventures revealed to him his own ultrachromatic voice, but giving up the system allowed him to put forth an equally personal expression of diatonic and modal materials. In this sense, Binkerd's artistic development was less like that of his own generation of composers, who often adapted the 12-tone method to some already established style, than to those composers of a later generation, whose first distinctive works were 12-tone, and who afterwards renounced the method in favor of more traditional procedures.

Composed in the same year as the *First Symphony,* Binkerd's *First Piano Sonata,* which earned high praise from Herbert Elwell,[12] William Flanagan,[13] and others, also used both 12-tone and non-12-tone materials, not in separate movements, however, but rather for formal contrast within movements. In the first of its four movements, the first theme group was 12-tone, while the lyrical second theme was more diatonic. A similar dichotomy occurred in the scherzo movement, which contained a freely chromatic scherzo and a 12-tone trio. The work's broad range of tonal materials was matched by an impressive variety of textures, which ranged from the very delicate, even wispy, to the bold, dramatic, and sensuous. While Binkerd's characteristic leanness and clarity were still evident, the work had too an impressionistic glow, so that if neobaroque was still an applicable label, it was more the neobaroque of Debussy's *Pour le Piano* than of Stravinsky's *Piano Sonata.*

A similar blend of impressionist and classical features characterized the *First* and *Second Symphonies* as well; indeed, this was far more evident than any debt to Viennese expressionism, the influence of the 12-tone method notwithstanding. The *First Symphony,* for instance, opened with a taut, urgent movement full of Stravinskian energy, featuring an exhaustive treatment of the motive of a rising semitone,

and sharply defined contrasts between the strings, winds, and
brass. (Its technique of reiterating bits of the row was
something Binkerd might have picked up from Fine's 12-tone
music.) The second movement, reminiscent alternately of
Bartók and Piston, was a sensuous, romantic nature piece that
exhibited the composer's more impressionistic side. The last
movement, a robust finale, had the kind of healthy vigor
characteristic of American neoclassicism, but brought more
up-to-date—like Bernstein or Shapero. Considering the first
movement's tonal center of A, this movement's B♭ tonality
neatly reflected the *Symphony's* principal motive, A-B♭.

The 1957 *Second Symphony,* a two-movement work, was
considerably different, though Piston was again evoked,
especially in the concerto grosso-like first movement, which
looked back to Piston's *Concerto for Orchestra.* The vigor of its
main theme (Ex. 59), however, was grittier than Piston, and
was even reminiscent of leftist anthems from the 1930s. Also
unlike Piston was the way in which elements began to break
apart to create a more disjointed style, looking ahead, as it
turns out, to the mature work of Karl Kohn. The second
movement, which featured long solos for the alto flute, was,
like the slow movement of the *First Symphony,* apparently

Example 59. Gordon Binkerd, *Symphony No. 2,* I (Boosey & Hawkes, 1970).

inspired by nature. Here, the music echoed Stravinsky's *Rite,* and also, once again, Piston, especially at those more intimate and nostalgic moments after 6. But Binkerd's pastoral mood, at once peaceful and dark, was distinctive: such music reminded one of the composer's later settings of Thomas Hardy. It was also distinctive to conclude the work with this long, poetic slow movement.

Both symphonies, in short, balanced traditional and personal elements in persuasive, moving ways. Neatly formed, full of rhythmic life and contrapuntal vitality, beautifully scored, they represented as fine a continuation of the Pistonian classical ideal as was to be found in the 1950s, in a way that William Schuman convincingly continued the Harris symphonic tradition. (Binkerd, in fact, dedicated his next symphony, the *Third* from 1959, to Piston.)

In a review of these two symphonies from the 1950s, David Cohen claimed that the combination of tonal and nontonal materials, and the use of "referential" rather than "functional" harmony, placed Binkerd in the "radical center" of postwar concert music.[14] By "referential" harmony, Cohen meant the use of traditional harmonies, including simple triads, in untraditional, posttonal contexts. Cohen expressed some concern about the eclecticism of such a procedure, especially as found in the *First Symphony,* with its "structural use of key relationships in the Finale" coming, as it does, on the heels of two 12-tone movements. Shackelford countered these concerns by pointing out certain thematic motives and orchestral textures that unified the entire work.[15] He might have mentioned, too, the fact that the finale's B^b tonality resolved the tonal expectations of the preceding movement, that traditional harmonies were found throughout the work, and that, in any case, a partial use of the 12-tone method could have a dramatic resonance all its own, as Bernstein also demonstrated in his *Kaddish Symphony* from about the same time. Cohen and Shackelford agreed that simultaneous inversion, tonal "poles" a tritone apart, and antiphonal orchestration were all important aspects of Binkerd's two early symphonies, and of the composer's style in general.

While Cohen, Shackelford, and others considered Binkerd's music, in some sense, tonal, close tonal analysis of whole works proved highly problematic. This was seen in one of the

few notable attempts to do so, in Howard Smither's review of
the *Second String Quartet* (1961).[16] For each of the work's
seven movements, Smither identified one or two tonal
centers, centers that formed a neat pattern of ascending
fourths: A (I), D (II), G (III), C and F (IV), B^b (V), E (VI), and
A (VII). He further observed:

> In each movement the presence of these tonal centers
> can be demonstrated by analysis, and they are clear to
> the listener part of the time, particularly at beginnings
> and endings of movements and of smaller structural
> divisions. But the harmonic language is so complex that
> it will probably obscure the tonality frequently for many
> listeners.

Smither paid special attention to the third movement, "the
clearest movement of the quartet . . . from the standpoint of
tonality"; although measure numbers were not given, Smither
probably meant to suggest the following scheme: G (m. 1)—C
(m. 22)—B (m. 26)—E (m. 33)—A^b (m. 38)—D (m. 44)—G
(m. 46). The criteria for such an analysis, however, was
disquietingly vague, consisting as it did of an occasional
diatonic snippet, a fleeting triad, or a sustained bass note.
Only twice did this movement seem to head for a cadence in
G (at measures 21 and 52), and in both cases, a resolution was
frustrated. The beginning and end of the movement, far from
being clear, are probably heard in F$^\#$ or B sooner than in G.
Such ambiguities and multiple tonal meanings characterized
the work's other movements as well. Smither himself heard
the opening of Movement V, allegedly in C, as being in
A—one could as easily say, perhaps, E or D.

These ambiguities and complexities did not in any way
deter Smither from recommending the *Second Quartet* as "an
exciting, highly concentrated, and immediately communicative work, particularly interesting for its variety of textures
and sonorities."[17] Perhaps the work's most startling and
impressive feature was the fact that its last three movements
were, with only minor adjustments, retrograde versions of its
first three movements. Such ambitious use of retrograde
technique even surpassed similar efforts by Hindemith and
Piston. While Binkerd's result was no mere stunt, the work as
a whole was probably less affecting than his dark and dramatic

First Quartet of 1958. Both quartets, in their brilliant string writing and evocative textures, showed the influence of Piston and Bartók, and perhaps Carter as well.

These two string quartets were the composer's last instrumental works to win widespread attention. This drop in popularity was not that surprising: as trends became more experimental and radical, Binkerd's music became more finished and conservative; he was not to go the way of Karl Kohn, after all. And yet, it was at the same time too personal and sophisticated to appeal to old-fashioned tastes. David Cohen, in the aforementioned review for a 1964 issue of *Perspectives of New Music,* observed this sympathetically, but with some defensiveness, not to say misgivings. Singers and choral directors, it is true, continued to find much that was interesting and useful in Binkerd's vast body of vocal works. But all in all, the composer's day seemed all too brief; fame came too late for inclusion in Chase's 1955 survey and was over by the time of its 1966 revision.

Binkerd became, moreover, a surprisingly outspoken critic of new music, as in a 1972 article for *Music and Artists,* in which he noted the inability of listeners to respond to new music, writing, " . . . the fault is not in themselves, but in their 'stars.' Generally the product is not pleasing. Beauty is banished. The very search for beauty is banished."[18] The only 20th-century symphonists who "reach the heart," he wrote, were Vaughan Williams and Sibelius; the only composer after Debussy "with a genuinely personal piano style" was Rachmaninov; and the only work that "maintains a place for opera" in the 20th century was Hindemith's *Mathis der Maler.*

Such remarks could easily be misunderstood. What they primarily attested to was the composer's desire to renew certain past ideals, especially regarding the composer's relationship to his public. This concern strongly demonstrated itself in Binkerd's music after 1960, for instance, in a series of moderately difficult piano works like *Entertainment for Piano* (1960) and *Piano Miscellany* (1969), works reminiscent of the "album-blätter" of Grieg or MacDowell: picturesque pieces that could be played for one's own enjoyment, or for a few friends, or in concert. Then there were song cycles and choral works that met a variety of secular and sacred needs. And there were a few works for children, including *The Young*

Pianist (1969), a stylish collection of easy piano pieces, and a choral work, *An Evening Falls* (pub. 1978), for a unison children's chorus and piano, the piano part a transcription of blues pianist Jimmy Yancey's "How Long, How Long Blues," the text by the 19th-century poet James Stephens. But at the same time, these later works did not compromise the high level of stylistic sophistication and technical brilliance achieved in the 1950s. They exhibited, perhaps, only a greater warmth, calm, and elegance.

If it were not clear from all this that Binkerd's ideal was Brahms (especially the late Brahms), a few specific works gave no doubt of it. In one of these, the 1975 *Suite* for piano, the three middle movements were arrangements (or "Intermezzi," as the composer called them) of three Brahms Lieder. The first two of these "Intermezzi" merely combined the original voice part and piano accompaniment, but texturally rearranged through octave displacements and doublings so as to become Binkerd's own. In the opening measure of the "Intermezzo on 'Meine Lieder,'" for example, Brahms's drooping minor second was changed to the daring leap of a major seventh. Consequently, both "Intermezzi" proved stunning examples of how music could be profoundly altered solely by means of texture and register. The third "Intermezzo" was freer in its approach, with changed notes, and even some variations of the composer's own.

Even freer was the arrangement of Brahms's "Intermezzo" Op. 118, No. 1, which comprised the first of Binkerd's *Essays* for piano (pub. 1976). The composer called it a "recasting" of the original. In this work, Binkerd adhered somewhat to Brahms's formal and tonal design, and even to some occasional melodic or harmonic gesture, but the whole was so rearranged that the composer doubted "very much whether it is perceptible as having any relation to the original."[19] For example, Binkerd's first four measures (Ex. 60a) clearly derived from Brahms's opening two measures (Ex. 60b): both began with an upbeat gesture; they contained the same pitch content; and Brahms's principal melodic idea, C-Bb-A, was even echoed. But Binkerd's thinned-out texture, repeated notes (Bb-A-G-E), and snazzy triplet upbeat had more the atmosphere of boogie-woogie than of 19th-century Vienna. As the piece progressed, Binkerd freely contracted and

Example 60a. Gordon Binkerd, "Intermezzo," *Essays* for the piano (Boosey & Hawkes, 1976).

Example 60b. Johannes Brahms, "Intermezzo," Op. 118, No. 1.

expanded material: the section from measures 18–32 corresponded to only two measures in the original (mm. 8–10). Further, there were overlapping motives that created dissonances foreign to Brahms's style. As with certain works by Stravinsky and Picasso, this little piece paid homage to a past master while highlighting its own author's individuality. See especially the G major harmony with an added sixth at measures 51–52, which, in its particular arpeggiated configuration, and in its harmonic context (that is, in the midst of a passage in A minor), was pure Binkerd.

Given the subtlety of this "recasting," there well might have been other such parodies of Brahms or others. But in any case, the impact of Brahms was evident enough in many other of the composer's later works, including the "Capriccio" and "Rhapsody" from the *Suite for Piano,* and two other pieces from the *Essays,* "Adagietto" and "Allégresse." One critic noted the influence of Brahms, too, on the slow movement of the *Fourth Symphony*[20] (a work later recalled, though this movement was salvaged as an independent work, namely, *Movement for Orchestra*). The influence of the Brahms Lieder, and the 19th-century German song repertory in general, was felt in much of Binkerd's vocal repertory as well, for example, in his two extremely elegant song cycles for soprano and piano, *Shut Out That Moon* (1968) and *Four Songs for High Soprano* (1976). Binkerd, in fact, called "A Bygone Occasion" from the former work, his "Bruckner motet."[21]

The Brahmsian quality of these songs was suggested also by the fact that transcriptions for solo piano of three of them were found in the same collection of pieces that contained the recast "Intermezzo," and the very Brahmsian "Adagietto" and "Allégresse." For the most part, these transcriptions, unlike Binkerd's transcriptions of the Brahms Lieder, omitted the vocal line; the bare piano parts proved satisfying pieces in their own right. These transcriptions also pointed to the fact that throughout the composer's career, his vocal and instrumental works were particularly interdependent. The slow movement of the *First Piano Sonata,* for instance, served as the basis for a choral setting of Blake's *The Lamb* (pub. 1971). In the same *Sonata,* one detected other resemblances, between, for instance, the first movement's second theme and a choral setting of Christina Rossetti's *O Sweet Jesu* (pub. 1974); and between the finale and a choral setting of e.e. cummings's *and viva sweet love* (1948).

Some instrumental works, like the *Sonata* for violin and piano (1977) and the *Third* and *Fourth Piano Sonatas* (1982, 1983), represented a somewhat different strain in the composer's late years, one that was less Brahmsian and romantic, but no less effective. They continued more along the lines of the composer's neobaroque style from the late '40s and 1950s. In the two-movement *Piano Sonata No. 3,* for instance, the first movement suggested Scarlatti not only in its binary form, but in the delicate brilliance of its piano writing. The second movement, also in binary form (reversing the larger tonal plan of III-i to vi-I), combined toccata and fugal elements. The brittle textures of these sonatas often sounded particularly spiky due to a prevalence of exposed tritones, sevenths, and ninths. But there was always great vitality and forward-going momentum. There was also often the suggestion of popular idioms: hymnlike in the slow movements, waltzlike (or something even more bucolic) in the faster ones. In much of all this, Binkerd carried forth the tradition of

Piston, especially the Piston of the *Violin Concerto* and the *Violin Sonatina*. Binkerd's own sensibility, alternating between gloom and a broadly acerbic wit, seemed a kind of American counterpart to late Shostakovich.

Binkerd's prodigious vocal output deserved special attention. There were over one-hundred such works, including settings of English and Latin sacred texts, not to mention the verse of at least thirty-eight poets.[22] They all revealed very high artistic standards, and often were of considerable length. Roger Scanlon appreciatively surveyed, principally for the benefit of voice teachers, those Binkerd songs available to him, concluding:

> Binkerd's vocal lines encompass wide ranges and are smooth or disjunct, depending on textural implications. There is frequent use of word painting achieved by embellished poetic extensions. In many instances the vocal lines are an integral part of the imitative texture and are not doubled in the accompaniment. The music is rhythmically active and involves the use of shifted accents, asymmetrical phrases, and changing meter signatures. . . . The majority of them call for a finished technique and a command of the elements of music.[23]

Binkerd's choral music was even more imposing and varied than his songs. Some choruses had the neo-Renaissance delicateness of Thompson, some the jazzy chromaticism of Piston, and some the modal elegance of Fine (Binkerd dedicated a 1962 choral setting of Crashaw's *The Recommendation* in memory of Fine). All, however, had a novelty and intensity that was distinctive, most evidently, as with the instrumental works, in the province of texture. Consider, for example, the rich five-part writing in his 1970 SATBB setting of Henry Vaughan's *Jesus Weeping,* or the conclusion of his 1969 SATB setting of Thomas Hardy's *In a Whispering Gallery,* where the chorus, divided to create a nine-voice harmony, sang the word "whisper" repeatedly, triple pianissimo, with the basses in falsetto, and a solo soprano holding a long, high D^b "al niente" (Ex. 61). (The magic of a moment like this, however, resided not only in its evocative texture,

Example 61. Gordon Binkerd, *In a Whispering Gallery* (Boosey & Hawkes, 1969).

but in the way it climaxed and resolved the motivic and harmonic material that preceded it.)

At such moments, the composer's intention clearly was to make audible the transcendentalism of the text at hand. In his profile of Binkerd, Shackelford drew attention to a "metaphysical strain" in the composer's work, as evident by his preference for Herrick and Hardy.[24] One, indeed, could detect a metaphysical strain in even the instrumental works. In this sense, Binkerd, for all his classicism, was something of an heir to Ives and Emerson. His romantic and fanciful portraits of starry nights and warbling birds reminded one, too, of the Midwestern painter Charles Burchfield, whose direct descendancy from Van Gogh and Cézanne found some parallel in Binkerd's connection to Brahms and Debussy. Both men similarly transformed the rather austere prairie landscape into visions of shimmering, spiritual loveliness. Such work, somewhat eccentric in style, somewhat mystical in content, was too personal to fit any trend or label conveniently. But for those who sought beauty, individuality, and depth, rather than labels in art, such work seemed destined to hold its own.

Notes

1. This includes four dissertations: Loyd Furman Hawthorne, *The Choral Music of Gordon Binkerd* (DMA, University of Texas at Austin, 1973); Eugene Miller, *A Stylistic Study of the Songs of Gordon Binkerd* (D. Mus. Ed., University of Oklahoma, 1974); Patricia Griffith, *The Solo Piano Music of Gordon Binkerd* (DMA, Peabody Conservatory, 1984); and D. A. Saladino, *The Influence of Poetry on Compositional Practices in Selected Choral Music of Gordon Binkerd* (DMA, Florida State University, 1984).
2. Hagan, "Gordon Binkerd," *ACA Bulletin* 10 (September 1962), pp.1–6.
3. Shackelford, "The Music of Gordon Binkerd," *Tempo* 114 (September 1975), pp. 2–13.
4. Hagan, p. 2.
5. Shackelford, p. 9.
6. Shackelford, p. 4.
7. Shackelford, p. 2; Binkerd, personal letter, August 18, 1984.
8. Binkerd, liner notes to a recording of the *Cello Sonata,* CRI 289.
9. Binkerd, "The Professional Music Theorist—His Habits and Training: A Forum," *Journal of Music Theory* 4 (April 1960), p. 78.
10. Binkerd, personal letter, November 23, 1977.
11. Shackelford, p. 4.
12. "Concert Hall," *ACA Bulletin* 5 No. 3 (1956), p. 16.
13. Flanagan, "Reviews of Records," *Musical Quarterly* 52 (October 1966), p. 537.
14. Cohen, "Music from the 'Radical Center,' " *Perspectives of New Music* 3 (Fall–Winter 1964), pp. 131–135.
15. Shackelford, p. 4.
16. Smither, "Current Chronicle," *Musical Quarterly* 49 (1963), pp. 237–240.
17. Smither, p. 237.
18. Binkerd, "Contemporary Music," *Music and Artists* 5 (June–July 1972), p. 5.
19. Shackelford, p. 7.
20. Bain Murray, "Composer's Exchange," *Musical America* 82 (January 1962), p. 128.
21. Shackelford, p. 8.
22. These poets included Thomas Beddoes, Béranger, William Blake, Elizabeth Browning, Robert Burns, Thomas Campion, Gutierre de Cetina, Gilbert Chesterton, William Cowper,

Adelaide Crapsey, e.e. cummings, Babette Deutsch, Emily
Dickinson, John Dryden, Jean Garrigue, Pauline Hanson,
Thomas Hardy, Robert Herrick, Rudyard Kipling, Carlton
Lowenberg, Thomas Moore, Edwin Muir, Sean O'Casey,
Ambrose Philips, Ezra Pound, Rainer Maria Rilke, Christina
Rossetti, Rudi Shackelford, James Stephens, Edward Taylor,
Alfred Tennyson, Spencer Trash, Henry Vaughan, Jones Very,
Neal Weiss, Richard Wilbur, William Carlos Williams, and
Walt Whitman.

23. Scanlon, "Spotlight on Contemporary American Composers,"
    NATS Bulletin 31 (May/June 1975), p. 27.
24. Shackelford, p. 8.

13. A LIFE IN MUSIC: THE SYMPHONIES OF SAMUEL ADLER

SAMUEL ADLER (B. 1928) was one of the most prolific American composers of the 20th century. His hundreds of compositions included not only small choral works, but chamber, orchestral, and stage works of considerable size. He composed fluently and daily, without having to wait for motivation or inspiration. Some were skeptical about such fluency: that it was more appropriate to feudal Europe or contemporary Hollywood than the modern world of concert music. But Adler himself regarded such productivity as a professional obligation, if not an actual moral imperative, and he encouraged his students, above all, to write, write, write. That his own music grew continuously more polished, sophisticated, and daring gave weight to such urgings.

To keep up with Adler, let alone to evaluate his enormous output, was itself a sort of challenge. This particular study focuses on the composer's six (seven) symphonies, for they have the advantage of being major statements that range over his entire career to date: *Symphony No. 1* (1953), *Symphony No. 2* (1957), *Diptych, Symphony No. 3* (1960), *Symphony No. 4* (1967), *Symphony No. 5* (1975), the revised *Diptych* (1980), and *Symphony No. 6* (1985).[1] Consequently, they trenchantly summarize the composer's artistic growth and development. In the course of this survey, there also will be reason to consider a few of his many other accomplishments, as well as some pertinent biography.

Adler wrote his *First Symphony* in the summer of 1953. He recently had established himself in Dallas as music director of that city's largest synagogue, Temple Emanu-El. Twenty-five years old, he already had earned a bachelor's degree from Boston University and a master's degree from Harvard, and had served in the Army for two years as conductor and founder of the Seventh Army Symphony Orchestra. It was an Adler family tradition to work hard and fast, though this Adler's incredibly breathless pace might have been fueled additionally by the sense of doom that hung over his early years, of which more will be said later (it is probably no coincidence that Karl Kohn, a Harvard friend who also narrowly escaped the Nazis, was one of Adler's few contemporaries who could approach him in terms of sheer prodigiousness). Also characteristic was the ease with which this Jewish German-American acclimated himself to Dallas, as he would some years later to Rochester, New York. Uprooted at an early age, Adler felt at home most anywhere, in Florida and Wales, in West Virginia and Israel. At the same time, his upbringing in Mannheim seemed to predispose him to provincial centers like Dallas and Rochester; he regarded major artistic centers, like New York, with some wariness. This was in some contrast to Kohn, who grew up in Vienna, and who settled in equally cosmopolitan Los Angeles. In fact, Adler had limited sympathies with urbane Harvard friends like Kohn, Spies, and Boykan who worked out of Claremont, Princeton, and Brandeis, respectively, and who for a while stood at serious music's fashionable hub. And they, in turn, had limited interest in his work. This is said just by way of distinction, however, for ultimately their sense of solidarity prevailed over any rivalry or skepticism.

The *First Symphony* was composed for a contest sponsored by the University of Texas for a major new work to be performed by the Dallas Symphony.[2] The work won first prize and was premiered by Walter Hendl and the Dallas Symphony on December 12, 1953. Hendl gave other performances in Dallas, around the country, and, as guest conductor, in Europe and South America. Like many of Adler's works, the *First Symphony* won its occasional champion, some academic prestige, polite remarks in local newspapers, and a cordial public reception: Adler often pleased audiences without winning them over completely. To do so would require repeated performances, and as especially concerned his symphonies and his larger works in general, those were few and far between.

The most immediately appealing aspect of the *First Symphony,* as with Adler's orchestral music in general, was its orchestration. Bright, warm, and suave, Adler's orchestral writing was totally expert, as well as imaginative, sometimes highly so. In the *Symphony's* first few pages, for instance, the main theme (Ex. 62), originally scored for unison horns, violas, and cellos, with harp, oboe and pizzicato bass accompaniment, a lovely sound in itself, was elegantly rescored at measure twenty-two for violins richly supported by full strings, harp arpeggios, and muted brass. The *Symphony* contained other, more subtle touches, such as the countermelody at measure 101 in the slow middle movement, a melody that passed from English horn to muted trumpet to the clarinets to bass clarinet; and more brilliant ones, too, such as the brightly scored tutti passages in the finale. The general orchestral balance of clarity and depth was exemplary. Adler's skill as an orchestrator had roots in long years of study of violin, viola, and other instruments; his experience as a conductor of orchestras, including his Classical High School Orchestra in Worcester, Massachusetts; the Seventh Army Symphony Orchestra in Germany, and many professional opera and symphony orchestras; and his studies with Koussevitzky (conducting) and Piston (orchestration). Adler's knowledge of the orchestra, in fact, eventually led to a commission by Norton Press to write the successor to Piston's famed *Orchestration* (Adler, *The Study of Orchestration,* Norton, 1982).

Another appealing aspect of Adler's *First Symphony* was its contrapuntal liveliness. Outstanding in this regard was the opening of the *First Symphony's* slow movement, in which the music progressed with growing contrapuntal complexity from the brass to the winds and, finally, to the strings. In the first movement, the juxtaposition of two main themes at measure 122 likewise showed a special contrapuntal flair. Adler's penchant for canonic writing was noticeable in this and much of his work in general, even those later, more advanced ones, where the sudden appearance of a canon was hardly expected but not any the less welcome and charming for that. His great

Example 62. Samuel Adler, *Symphony No. 1*, I.

admiration for Piston and Hindemith was certainly a relevant factor here.

The *First Symphony* was less successful in matters of formal and rhythmic cohesion. Here Adler's fast pace apparently took its toll: passages wandered feverishly, and endings come at the least expected moments. In later works, such tendencies were skillfully put to delightful, poignant, and highly dramatic purposes, but in the *First Symphony,* they did not keep step with the work's rather academic correctness. In the first movement sonata, for instance, the development seemed discursive, and the too ample recapitulation labored. Similarly, the rondo finale, after a taut exposition, dissipated into somewhat loose ramblings. Best was the ABA slow movement; but even here, the middle interlude, with its simple waltz rhythms, stood at odd angles to the surrounding sections. These shortcomings notwithstanding, Adler's *First Symphony* proved a skilled, ambitious work, rich in details.

This achievement—a large symphony by age twenty-five—was the fruit of many years' study with a series of distinguished teachers: Herbert Fromm, privately (1941–1945); Hugo Norden at Boston University (1946–1948); Piston, Thompson, Hindemith, and Fine at Harvard (1948–1950); and Copland at Tanglewood (1949, 1950). All of these composer-teachers had a large impact on Adler's stylistic development, with the exception of Norden, whom Adler considered a negligible influence in that he encouraged his students to write in the style of Mendelssohn, and whose own music distastefully reminded Adler of Tchaikovsky. Norden's knowledge of counterpoint won him some respect, but he nonetheless remained for many years the butt of jokes between Adler and his best friend at Boston University, the future Haydn scholar, H. C. Robbins Landon. Both preferred Karl Geiringer's classes in music history. Adler decided to pursue his studies with Piston over Norden's objections.

While the influence of Piston and Hindemith would prove paramount, his other teachers left their marks as well. The influence of Thompson and Fromm, for instance, was felt in Adler's considerable body of choral music: the oratorio *Visions of Isaiah,* written as a master's thesis in 1950, and revised in 1962, showed close familiarity with Thompson's work, while his synagogal liturgical music in general continued along the lines of Fromm. Copland, whom Adler called "a fantastic teacher," suggested to him the orchestral potential gained from careful attention to register and spacing. And, in fact, there were some Coplandesque features in Adler's scoring of the *First Symphony.* Copland, as well as Fine, brought Adler closer to Debussy, Ravel, and Poulenc, an orientation, however, that did not really manifest itself until the 1960s. Throughout his career, Adler showed himself very open to all kinds of composers, especially those he knew personally. Consequently, his music acquired an extraordinary breadth of stylistic allusion. Quite the opposite of the rarified, alienated artist, he enthusiastically greeted a wide variety of musics, as his textbooks on orchestration and choral conducting demonstrated, and he expressed the occasional dislike with sympathy and humor rather than condescension or disgust.

If Adler's music, then, came to resemble an archaeological dig, then one would find, at one of the lowest strata, the firm bedrock of Piston and Hindemith. The young Adler shared some natural affinities with these two composers. He was principally a violist, for instance, as were Piston and Hindemith. Further, he grew up in Mannheim—near Hindemith's native Frankfurt, and Worcester—near Piston's Boston. In any case, Adler strongly gravitated toward their music. As a violinist and violist, he loved playing their chamber music. He learned the Hindemith quartets and sonatas that way, as well as Piston's *Flute Quintet, Piano Quintet,* and *Partita.* He found Hindemith's *Six Chansons* indescribably moving, and retained great affection for Piston's *Second Symphony,* which he conducted in Europe in the early 1950s at least twenty times. Perhaps even more influential was the opening of Piston's *Fourth Symphony,* which Adler read in manuscript on a visit to Piston's summer home in Woodstock, Vermont, and which "stuck in my mind and stayed with me." The technique it embodied—taking a gesture, repeating it, adding to it, and going on from there, as Adler described it—made a profound and lasting impression.

As teachers, Hindemith and Piston were altogether different. With the domineering and "effervescent" Hindemith,

> . . . there was no doubt about what style you should
> write in. He had the idea that the way to learn was to
> copy a master. He felt that he was a master to be copied,
> and that's what he expected from his students. Now it
> killed some, and others it made whole.

Piston, on the other hand, was cool, aloof, what in later years,
suggested Adler, might be called "laid back." Such evasive-
ness often puzzled and troubled Adler, as he illustrated by
way of the following anecdote. For one of Piston's composition seminars, he brought in a large set of variations for piano.
After he and Piston "hacked through" the work at the piano,
Piston said, "Gee, Adler, that's very good. It sounds like a
cross between Leroy Anderson and Morton Gould." Morti-
fied, Adler could not compose for some weeks. When he
explained his predicament, Piston laughed and said, "Well,
what's the matter with them? They're making lots of money."
Adler, now even more unsure, continued to brood over this
episode. Did Piston mean that his music was too simple? too
stock? too commercial? Later he came to believe that it was
Piston's way of encouraging him to search out other models
like Stravinsky, something that such classmates as Spies,
Boykan, and Kohn needed less coaxing to do. Perhaps Piston
only meant for the ever-hurrying Adler to reflect on his own
individuality a little more.

In any case, Adler's *First Symphony* clearly derived from
Hindemith and Piston. The entire first movement, with its
triple-meter first theme gently propelled by hemiolas (see Ex.
62), its dramatic bridge, its folksy second theme, and its
muted coda, stemmed directly from Piston's *Second Symphony*.
The *Symphony*'s finale was also very Pistonian. The melodic,
harmonic, and textural details, however, seemed closer to
Hindemith, for example, the flute melody in the first
movement at measure sixteen, with its Neapolitan cadence,
and the lovely theme in the slow movement beginning at
measure thirteen. Adler's rhythms, too, were often more like
Hindemith than Piston.[3]

The 1957 *Second Symphony*, premiered, once again, by
Hendl and the Dallas Symphony, was a more accomplished
work, not only in its tauter, more controlled forms, but in

its more individual voice. This individuality involved Adler's
dual identity as a German Jew and as an American in
the Southwest. Such influences were already detectable
in the *First Symphony,* especially in its second movement, which opened with a modal brass choir that pointed to
Adler's Jewish background, and which also contained a
middle section that had a Spanish-American lilt. But both
traditions were given more forceful scope in the *Second
Symphony.*

Adler dedicated the *Second Symphony* to "the blessed
memory of my beloved father," Hugo Chaim Adler. The
composer's father, born in Antwerp, Belgium in 1894, was an
exact contemporary of Hindemith and Piston and was also a
composer, mostly of sacred and liturgical works. He studied
for a time with Ernst Toch, and served as cantor for a
synagogue in Mannheim before immigrating to the United
States in 1939. Adler accepted the post of music director and
cantor for Temple Emanuel in Worcester, Massachusetts,
where he died in 1955.

Hugo Adler was associated with German Reform Judaism,
a movement that flourished in Germany from the early 1800s
until Hitler's rise to power in 1933.[4] In a short biography of
the composer, Rabbi Alexander Schindler noted that his
birthdate, January 17, coincided with the anniversary of the
death of Solomon Sulzer, the pioneer composer of Reform
Judaism.[5] Musically, this movement had two main directions.
The first was toward acculturation and modernization, which
meant especially the use of the organ, four-part chorus, texts
in the vernacular, and the adoption of Western art music
styles, especially German ones from Mendelssohn onward
(Hugo Adler was influenced by Brahms; Fromm and the
younger Adler proved closer to Hindemith). The second
trend involved the study and exploration of Hebrew prosody
as well as traditional Jewish melodies and modes, a great
landmark of which was the scholarship of Abraham Idelsohn.
The movement contrasted its dignity with the mystical
tradition of Chassidic Judaism and its vulgar off-shoots, and
its purity with the work of more assimilated Jews like Bloch
and Schoenberg. Emigrés from Nazi Germany like Hugo
Adler helped encourage and shape the movement's growth in
the United States and Israel.

As a choir director, composer, editor, arranger, and record producer, Sam Adler notably assisted its continuation into the late 20th century. One example was his 1972 compilation for the High Holiday evening service, *Yamim Noraim* (revised, 1990), which included works by his father, Fromm, and Isadore Freed, who was his favorite composer in this area. More than this, Adler's own compositions and arrangements went far toward fulfilling the ideals of the Jewish reformers of the Enlightenment. Vigorous, imaginative, and modern, they were more authentic than the sanctimonious clichés that typified even the best of 19th-century Reformed synagogal music. His sacred music, moreover, was more adventurous than his father's and more refined than Fromm's. And yet he easily maintained what Fromm once referred to as the proper "liturgical tone."[6] Indeed, it was possible that Adler served the limits of Fromm and his father all too well.

As trends in Jewish music Adler steadily had opposed and decried[7] began to gain greater acceptance, his own sacred music, having firmly established itself, began to fall somewhat out of favor. But his output was so vast, and the smaller works in particular so useful, that his place in Jewish music seemed assured. Surely, any composer in the 1990s aspiring to the ideals of Reform Judaism would find help and inspiration in Adler's sacred music.

Indeed, Adler's sacred music may have been his most important accomplishment, but it was also significant that he brought this tradition to bear on many secular concert works, including the *Second Symphony*. In this work, it was evident, above all, in the use of a cantillation written by his father, a chant that the older Adler "was particularly fond of and had used in his own composition."[8] Put forth by a solo cello, it appeared in the slow introduction to the first movement (Ex. 63). The melody, in the aeolian or "magen-avot" mode, contained characteristically Jewish sighing motives, and equally characteristic rocking back and forth between the tonic minor and minor subdominant. In addition, its syncopations and triplets suggested the cantor's kind of rhythmic flexibility. This chant colored much of the work's melodic material, especially the first movement's main theme (measure 49) and the finale's second theme (measure 52), both of which were likewise in the magen-avot mode. The middle

Example 63. Samuel Adler, *Symphony No. 2*, I.

section of the slow movement (mm. 33–72) was also
decidedly Judaic, with its exotic main theme for flute (m. 33)
later nostalgically transformed into a simple lullaby (m. 57).
(In the 1983 *Concerto for Piano and Orchestra,* Adler again used
a melody of his father's, one that his mother had sung to him
as a lullaby.) The *Symphony's* strong Jewish cast suggested
similarities with Bernstein, although Adler's German Reformed background clearly distinguished itself from Bernstein's more Eastern European roots.

The *Second Symphony* showed, too, the impact of the
American Southwest. Adler was impressed with the freedom
and openness of Texas and its people. Soon after assuming his
post at Temple Emanu-El, a Reformed Synagogue founded in
1872, Adler's involvement in the community began to widen:

he conducted the Dallas Lyric Theater for two years (1955–1957), organized the Dallas Chorale (1954–1956), and taught at Dallas's Hockaday School (1957–1966), as well as at North Texas State University (1958–1966). Adler also wrote the scores to a number of plays for the Dallas Theater Center, including Howard Fast's *The Crossing* and a production of Jewel Gibson's *Joshua Beane and God* with Burl Ives. These scores occasionally used authentic regional tunes, but more often original tunes in the regional idiom. There was concert music that reflected this interest too: *Five American Folk Songs* for chorus (1961), *Four Early American Folk Songs* for string orchestra (1962), and *Southwestern Sketches* for band (1961), which used some of the music from *Joshua Beane and God,* and which became one of the composer's most successful works. Above all, there was Adler's 1959 opera, *The Outcasts of Poker Flat,* based on a short story of the same name by Bret Harte.

The Southwestern character of the *Second Symphony* was most clearly suggested by the second theme group of the first movement (Ex. 64) and by the main theme of the finale. Somewhat reminiscent of Piston and Copland, these themes were more old-fashioned, more redolent of the Old West, with a touch, too, of the Ländler about them. As *Poker Flat* demonstrated, it was an idiom suitable to the picturesque charm and burlesque humor of Bret Harte, if not necessarily to Harte's kind of morbid intensity.[9]

The Southwestern and Jewish styles in the *Second Symphony* could be distinguished. The latter tended toward modal chromaticism, chantlike rhythm, the interval of the fourth, contrapuntal textures, and the use of English horn and cello, while the former leaned toward pentatonicism, rhythmic vitality, the interval of the third, homophonic textures, and the use of oboe, brass, and percussion. The combination of Jewish pathos and American vitality in this and other works made for a vivid, dramatic style whose poignancy was not so unlike Bernstein's after all.

Adler's *Third Symphony* (1960) was commissioned by Robert Boudreau and the American Wind Symphony Orchestra, who premiered the work in Pittsburgh on June 22, 1961. Adler intended it as a kind of experiment, and, indeed, unlike the first two symphonies, the work did not conform to the classical symphonic tradition: it was scored for wind orchestra; it had only two movements, both highly unusual in form; and it had an evocative title, *Diptych,* though the composer meant no pictorial or religious allusions by it.

Diptych was also stylistically adventurous. Its advanced chromaticism was especially noteworthy, as it contrasted so dramatically with Adler's earlier style. The melodies—some long, most little snippets—retained a tonal bearing of sorts, but the harmonic fabric was densely chromatic, and the firm tonal ending was somewhat surprising. While not a repudiation of Hindemith and Piston, the work expressed the composer's desire to go beyond them. Here Copland's encouragement to study Stravinsky finally took hold, and the work showed clear ties to the *Rite of Spring* and *Symphonies of Winds.* This was in part due to the fact that by the late 1950s Adler was conducting a good deal of Stravinsky, including *L'Histoire,* the *Octet,* and the *Symphony in C.* He even offered a course in Stravinsky during his year at work on the *Diptych.*

Adler found that Carter's *Etudes* and *Cello Sonata,* and Fine's *Partita,* were also helpful guides in branching out, and, indeed, the work's final fugato was somewhat Carteresque. The influence of Hindemith was still detectable, especially in the fugal and canonic passages of the second movement, and there were still also reminiscences of Adler's Jewish and Southwestern idioms, the former in the first movement's melancholy English horn solo, the latter in the same movement's raucous clarinet theme. But these were now secondary: the mood was introspective, severe, and abstract, and the brilliant and imaginative colors were very much the thing. The patchwork construction of the second movement eventually led Adler to remove the work from his catalog, and to write, after some attempt at revision, a totally new *Diptych* in 1980. But he admitted that the original *Diptych* was an important breakthrough.

The *Fourth Symphony* (1967) was written shortly after Adler moved to Rochester in 1966 to join the Eastman School, whose composition department he chaired continuously after 1973. Like the *Diptych,* the work was somewhat experimental in that it was the composer's first major work to use the 12-tone method. At the same time, it was the composer's only symphony in traditional four-movement form. The work was premiered by Donald Johannes and the

Dallas Symphony on March 15, 1970. The work's subtitle, "Geometrics," and subheadings for its four movements— "Squares," "Rectangles," "Triangles," and "Diamonds"— referred to geometric patterns derived from a particular "Babbitt square." Adler subsequently was to use some kind of "Babbitt square" for the rest of his career, especially for his more serious work, but his use of the 12-tone method, in this

Example 64. Samuel Adler, *Symphony No. 2,* I.

Symphony and in other works, was never very rigorous. Even in its most straightforward usage, as in the *Symphony*'s outer movements, the method's ultrachromaticism was offset by freely tonal countermelodies, or bass lines, or whole passages. "Unrelenting nontonality is devastating to the listener," Adler asserted, pointing especially to Schoenberg's *Wind Quintet*. He similarly expressed reservations about Webern:

> To me he is a skeleton without flesh and blood. You always feel he's just going to go someplace and then he stops. Of course, that's the aesthetic . . . I love everything up to the *Six Pieces* for orchestra. After that, there's such preciousness. I can't feel that each note is a jewel.

It was the combination of tonal and nontonal elements that most intrigued him, something that he likened to the modern equivalent of common practice modulation, and that warmed him a bit more to Berg. His own 12-tone works, such as the delightful *Sonata Breve* for piano (1963), the *Fifth Symphony* (1975), and even his most orthodox 12-tone work, the *Fifth String Quartet* (1969), used tonal materials. The row and its permutations were used primarily to shape fast passage work.

The *Fourth Symphony,* in addition, had a stark, austere quality related not only to Stravinsky, but more directly to medieval music, especially in the slow movement's two-part textures. Indeed, the keen interest in medieval music represented by this *Symphony* foreshadowed the more obvious medievalism of such pieces as *Nuptial Scene* for mezzo-soprano and eight instruments (1975), a work which actually used a medieval Catalonian wedding song; the *Sonatina* for piano (1979), whose slow movement had a modal two-part section that specified, "like a medieval chant"; *Joi, Amor, Cortezia* for chamber orchestra (1982), an arrangement of some medieval and Renaissance tunes; and the *Sonata* for two pianos (1983). Adler's medievalism allowed his interests in Jewish chant, black gospel singing, and Southwestern holy rollers to converge in a restrained yet daring way, while also accommodating his new search for a more abstract, mathematical technique.

A less enduring stylistic feature of the *Fourth Symphony,* and one that the composer admitted to be merely trendy, was the use of jazz for the scherzo's trio section. Its heavy-handedness contrasted with the Pistonian lightness of the scherzo proper, and was closer to the striptease music the young Adler conducted at Boston's Old Howard, a burlesque joint, than to real jazz. Adler actually disclaimed much affinity for jazz, saying, "much of it bores me." In Texas, he attended concerts by Stan Kenton and Woody Herman and listened to recordings by Miles Davis and Ornette Coleman. Prompted by his friend Gunther Schuller, he also investigated Charlie Parker. But Adler felt much closer to Gershwin, whose *Rhapsody in Blue* and *Concerto in F* he recorded with pianist Eugene List. And, indeed, one sometimes could detect a Gershwinesque sensibility in Adler's music (and long observed by Piston, it seems), a certain vitality that was at once endearing, exciting, and a bit showy.

If the trend in the 1960s was toward abstraction, as with *Diptych* and the *Fourth Symphony*, the trend in the 1970s was toward theater. Already in the late '60s there were two sacred oratorios, *The Binding* (1967), about Abraham and Isaac, and *From Out of Bondage* (1968), about the exodus from Egypt, which were particularly dramatic, especially the former. The ensuing decade witnessed *The Wrestler* (1971), a sacred opera about the reconciliation of Jacob and Esau; *The Lodge of Shadows* (1973), a music drama for baritone solo, dancers, and orchestra; *The Disappointment* (1974), a reconstruction of one of the first American ballad operas; and *The Waking* (1978), a celebration for dancers, chorus, and orchestra. This interest in theater and text spilled over into Adler's contemporaneous instrumental music, most notably in two works from 1975, the *Fifth Symphony*, "We Are the Echoes," for mezzo-soprano and orchestra, and the *Sixth String Quartet* for medium voice and string quartet to poetry by Walt Whitman. Pertinent to both was the fact that they were written in Vienna, a city associated for Adler with Gustav Mahler, his first wife's favorite composer. Adler, in fact, wryly called the *Fifth Symphony* his *"Leid" von der Erde*.

The *Fifth Symphony*, like *Das Lied von der Erde*, was an orchestral setting of five poems (one fewer than *Das Lied*). The work was commissioned by the Union of American Hebrew Congregations in celebration of the American Bicentennial, and its texts were selected in order "to convey the ideal of the Jewish experience brought to America." The first poem, a translation from the German of the poem, "We Go," by Karl Wolfskehl, discussed how Jews had been destined "to go on," spiritually as well as geographically. The second poem, Muriel Rukeyser's "Even During War," mused on the beauty of nature, transcendent of human disorder. The third poem, James Oppenheimer's "The Future," was a sardonic, Kafkaesque inquiry into life's ultimate purpose. The fourth poem, "We Are The Echoes," by the composer's wife, Carol, obliquely questioned the role of the modern Jew. And the title of the final poem, Abraham Heschel's "God Follows Me Everywhere" (translated from the original Yiddish), speaks for itself.

The *Fifth Symphony* thus addressed a moral concern that also informed Adler's dramatic works like *The Binding* and *The Wrestler,* namely, what it means to be a Jew. But this work proved particularly personal and intimate. It was colored, especially the first movement, by Adler's traumatic childhood in Nazi Germany, memories of which were stirred by this visit to Vienna. The Adlers had waited until 1939 to leave Mannheim, partly because visas were difficult to obtain, partly because Hugo Adler hated to desert his congregation. But then came the infamous "Kristallnacht" on November 9, 1938, the day before Hugo Adler's oratorio *Akedah* was to be premiered in Stuttgart. Adler remembered being awakened at 3:30 in the morning on November 10 to the sound of a huge explosion, and later that day walking to his all-Jewish school amid the broken glass, crystal, and china that littered the vandalized and terrorized Jewish neighborhood.[10] (Their own home was spared because the head of the SS in Mannheim lived next door.) Hugo eluded the Nazis and attempted an escape to Holland, but was caught at the border and sent, along with about 30,000 other German Jews, to a concentration camp, in his case, Dachau.[11] The Adlers anxiously left Germany as soon as they could after his release. The ominous knockings in "We Go" and "The Future," knockings that subtly unified the entire *Symphony,* reverberated with this chilling experience. Indeed, the beauty of nature ("Even During War") and nostalgic remembrance ("We Are The Echoes") provided small comfort; even the mystical presence of God was more agitating than soothing

("God Follows Me Everywhere"). This darkness, anxiety, and rebelliousness provided the background for the central conviction that the Jew is bound to act for the world's betterment.

Like Adler's theatrical works from the 1970s, the *Fifth Symphony* effectively used color and texture to impart much of its drama. This was accomplished for the most part with traditional orchestral techniques, but there were more novel devices too, most notably, aleatoric writing. Adler first employed aleatoric techniques in the cadenza to the *Fourth String Quartet* (1963) and continued to do so fairly regularly over the next twenty years. Such devices, however, were handled with considerable circumspection and judiciousness: the occasional aleatoric gesture always blended seamlessly into the larger fabric. Actually, the word "aleatoric" might overstate Adler's usage, which usually was limited either to a series of pitches to be repeated over and over as fast as possible (see the *Fifth Symphony*'s first movement, m. 100) or melodic lines that were not synchronized rhythmically (see the opening of the fourth movement[12]). The *Fifth Symphony* contained in addition a spooky, glissando passage for strings in which only approximate pitches and rhythms were notated (see the third movement, m. 31) and a passage in which the timpanist was asked to improvise with five pitches and the pianist was called on to "improvise inside the piano with the sostenuto pedal down" (see the fourth movement, m. 29).

The color ingenuity of the *Fifth Symphony* extended beyond these aleatoric devices to include the vocal and instrumental writing in general. The voice part was written specifically for Adler's colleague at the Eastman School, Jan DeGaetani, who premiered the work with the Fort Worth Symphony, the composer conducting, on November 9, 1975; many of its features—the wide leaps, grace notes, "Sprech-stimme," whispering, and humming—reflected her famous renditions of Schoenberg, Crumb, and others. As for the orchestra, the strings were asked to bow on the far side of the bridge; the winds and brass to blow into their instruments without their mouthpieces; and the pianist to play clusters both on the keys and on the strings. There was also, in the second movement, a dreamy wash of divisi strings involving mutes, harmonics, and a complicated, serialized rhythmic

scheme. Many of these devices related to the vogue for the
Polish composers Penderecki and Lutoslawski, both of whom
Adler met on a trip to Poland for the State Department
during the same year as the *Fifth Symphony*. They related, too,
although less directly, to electronic music. Indeed, by this
time Adler had taken some courses in electronic music, and
had considered using the medium for *The Wrestler*. Not liking
the sounds of electronic instruments that much, and preferring, moreover, the "fallibility" of traditional musicmaking,
he never did write electronic music. But the experience
inspired him to rethink his concept of sound. Said the
composer, "All my orchestration since my *Fifth Symphony* has
been influenced by electronic music," citing especially the
first movement of the *Flute Concerto* (1977).

The new *Symphony No. 3* or *Diptych* (1980), premiered by
Donald Hunsberger and the Eastman Wind Ensemble on
January 30, 1981, also manifested those electronic-like
features found in the *Flute Concerto:* long, sustained notes
gradually changing color; very high registers; washes of
sound; little repeated fragments; piles of major and minor
seconds; rhythmic fluidity; and a colorful percussion battery.
The work, on the other hand, used aleatoric techniques only
sparingly; indeed, such techniques were beginning to pass out
of the composer's vocabulary (the *Flute Concerto* made no use
of it at all). The *Symphony* seemed to attain a new stylistic
purity, as well as a special vibrancy and freshness that long had
been one of Adler's primary artistic aims.

This new *Diptych* also revealed a special closeness to
nature, most explicitly in the first movement passage in which
certain instruments were asked to play, at measure 40,
"chirpingly," an instruction, however, not found in the Peters
edition (Ex. 65). The melodies in the first movement, in
general, suggested birds: they utilized high registers, repeated
fragments of a small compass, grace notes, trills, and quiet
dynamics. Further, they were loosely coordinated rhythmically, or at least gave that impression, recalling the opening
section from the *Rite of Spring,* one of the great pinnacles of
musical landscape painting, according to Adler. The excitement and brilliance of *Diptych*'s second movement was
similarly comparable to one of the *Rite*'s fast dances, and
matched the composer's exuberance when he spoke of

nature's wildness. The sumptuousness of its nature painting, as opposed to Adler's earlier, more austere style, was related, possibly, to the lush, forested upstate New York region that was for many years now the composer's home.

The new *Diptych* also illustrated Adler's ever growing command of form. The first movement was in ternary form, and the second movement was in rondo form, but both so modified as to be strikingly personal. There were even antecedent-consequent constructions, and other symmetries too, but all subtly done to give a feeling of spontaneity and discovery. The work's basic logic resided in the use of three main ideas put forth in the first movement and subsequently transformed in the second: long-held notes (m. 1; later, repeated notes, m. 130); melodies shaped by the interval of the minor third (m. 2; later, m. 195); and sustained chords (as in Ex. 65), this last an elaboration of the other two. The melodies often were treated canonically, looking back to habits learned under Hindemith, while the sustained chords had an impressionistic richness that suggested a rapport with Adler's younger colleague on the Eastman faculty, Joseph Schwantner. There was also a Jewish quality about the melodies, especially in their use of the augmented second (sometimes disguised as a minor third), an interval that Adler associated with coarse Jewish clichés, but

Example 65. Samuel Adler, *Symphony No. 3* ("Diptych"), I (Henmar Press, 1985).

which nonetheless appeared in his own music with some prominence. The integration of all these elements was impressively taut and lucid.

Adler's integrative abilities continued into the 1980s with still greater flair and scope, especially in such major works as the 1983 *Piano Concerto,* the 1984 *Concerto for Saxophone Quartet and Orchestra,* and yet another symphony, the *Sixth,* commissioned by the Serge Koussevitzky Foundation and completed in March of 1985. This *Symphony,* even more than the revised *Diptych,* seemed to embrace the entire range of Adler's rich past: there were long swaying melodies like Piston and busy counterpoint like Hindemith; melodic fragments related to German-Jewish and Southwest-American idioms, and elegant harmonies close to Debussy, Stravinsky, and Copland; 12-tone-derived chromaticism, and textures like those of Penderecki and Schwantner; dense electronic-like sound webs, and delicate, chirping woodwind figuration. The outstanding new feature, perhaps, was the finale's ever-changing meters. Adler first exploited this resource in his 1974 Mass entitled *We Believe,* most notably in the "Sanctus," where its roots in Piston and Bernstein were clear enough. But it became a regular feature of his music only in the 1980s. Also new was the ease and straightforwardness with which this music was set forth.

These and other virtues earned Adler more commissions and performances than ever. As a symphonist, it is true, he was still a neglected figure. He regretted the missed opportunity of a champion like Koussevitzky; indeed, he missed the actual support provided by Hendl in the 1950s. No Adler symphony had been recorded yet professionally.[13] But Adler's other, smaller accomplishments—assorted chamber works, choral pieces, liturgical compositions, and so on— were known and admired among music lovers far and wide, so much so that his contribution to musical life in the 20th century seemed well-assured nonetheless.

Notes

1. Adler's first two symphonies were handled by Theodore Presser; the *Fourth* was published by Oxford University Press;

the *Fifth* by Boosey and Hawkes; and the new *Diptych* by C. F. Peters.

2. Adler, personal interview, August 23, 1983. Many of the quotes not footnoted are from this interview.

3. For an extended discussion of Hindemith's influence on Adler, see Joan Dawson Lucas, *The Operas of Samuel Adler* (PhD thesis, Louisiana State University, 1978), pp. 59–72.

4. Abraham Idelsohn, *Jewish Music in its Historical Development* (New York: Schocken, 1929), pp. 232–295.

5. Schindler, "The music of a father and his son," *American Conference on Cantors Bulletin* (June 1965), pp. 2–5.

6. Herbert Fromm, *On Jewish Music* (1978), p. 12. Scattered among the pages of this book are interesting references to the Adlers, father and son. Especially poignant is the portrait of Hugo Chaim and the young Hans, pp. 113–116 (Adler took the name Samuel, his middle name, after emigrating to the United States).

7. Adler, "An Urgent Need in Today's Synagogue Music," *Central Conference of American Rabbis Journal* Vol. 10, No. 4 (January 1963), pp. 27–30; and "Music in the American Synagogue," *American Choral Review* Vol. 6, No. 3 (April 1964), pp. 7–9; and Vol. 6, No. 4 (July 1964), pp. 3–6.

8. "Monday Symphony Has Soloist and Premieres," *Dallas Times Herald,* February 23, 1958.

9. Significantly, Adler and his librettist, Judah Stampfer, changed the story so that the young heroine, Piney, survives the blizzard, whereas in the original tale, she dies of cold and starvation.

10. Adler, program notes to *Stars in the Dust* (1988), an oratorio for soprano, tenor, baritone, narrators, chorus, and orchestra, premiered simultaneously in synagogues across the United States on November 9, 1988, in commemoration of the fiftieth anniversary of "Kristallnacht." Prior to this, Adler consistently turned down all requests for a work dealing directly with the Holocaust, preferring not to "name names." He feared, too, that such a work would not have the stirring universal import of Schoenberg's *Survivor from Warsaw,* but the more faddish quality of Bernstein's *Mass.* But in this work he addressed, with dignity and some irony, the prelude to the horror to come. The work, to a text by Samuel Rosenbaum, showed debts to Hindemith's *Mathis* and Copland's *Lincoln Portrait,* but had more the feel and pacing of a film documentary. The realism of its historical narrative was underscored by quotations of "Deutschland, Deutschland über alles" and the "Horst Wessell

Lied," along with a number of traditional Jewish chants, including "Eyn Keloheynu." In the process, the composer discovered that "Deutschland, Deutschland" and "Eyn Keloheynu" could be juxtaposed, noting that the counterpoint at first "seemed to work perfectly, but toward the end, as in reality, 'went sour.'"

11. Schindler. According to Schindler, more than 80,000 German Jews were sent to concentration camps following Kristallnacht, whereas historian Lucy S. Dawidowicz, *The War Against the Jews* (New York: Holt, Rinehart and Winston, 1975), p. 102, put the figure at about 30,000.

12. The chantlike melodies in this section are actual Jewish cantorials familiarly used in Torah and Haftorah readings, appropriately symbolizing the "echoes" of Carol Adler's poem.

13. There were two noncommercial recordings of Adler's symphonies. One was a private recording of the original, withdrawn *Diptych,* with the composer conducting the University of Houston Wind Ensemble; the other was a pirated recording of the *Fourth Symphony,* Aries Records, LP-1619. Although this last was released as being performed by the Aalborg Symphony Orchestra conducted by James Fredman, it was actually the premiere performance with the Dallas Symphony under Johannes. A superior example of Adler on disc was the recording of the *Flute Concerto* with flutist Bonita Boyd and the Rochester Philharmonic Orchestra under David Effron, Pantheon Records, PFN 2041.

14. "CARTER AND THE POSTWAR COMPOSERS" REVISITED: BILLY JIM LAYTON, YEHUDI WYNER, AND MARTIN BOYKAN

I N 1963, COMPOSER, TEACHER, AND CRITIC Martin Boykan wrote an article for *Perspectives of New Music* (and later anthologized in *Perspectives on American Composers*) entitled, "Elliott Carter and the Postwar Composers."[1] This four-page article discussed a few ways in which Carter expanded the limitations of earlier American music, thereby providing younger composers, especially those coming of age in the 1950s, with an exciting, liberating model. First, Carter's pathos, described by Boykan as haunted and tragic, psychological and dramatic, was more "truly American" than the "professional cheerfulness of much Americana" from the prewar years. Further, Carter rejected artificial restrictions made "out of an abstract loyalty to style." And, finally, Carter's harmonic texture was inflected rather than static.

While Boykan broadly asserted that "every young composer has been deeply involved with him [Carter]," he admitted that few showed "traces of his influence in their work," citing only Billy Jim Layton (b. 1924), Yehudi Wyner (b. 1929), and perhaps, by implication, himself (b. 1931). These three, significantly, were friends. Boykan also mentioned another friend, Seymour Shifrin (b. 1926), but qualified this inclusion, pointing to Shifrin's close ties with the tonal neoclassicism of a previous day (although in his hands, it acquired "an unexpected freshness"). Boykan might have noted, too, that whereas he, Layton, and Wyner had studied with Piston at Harvard, as had Carter himself, Shifrin had studied with Luening and Schuman at Columbia and Milhaud in Paris (though he might have thought this beside the point). In any event, this second look at Carter and the postwar composers limits itself to Layton, Wyner, and Boykan.

Billy Jim Layton, the oldest of the three, grew up in Corsicana, Texas, where he played the clarinet and saxophone in school bands.[2] He mainly was interested in jazz, admiring especially Benny Goodman, Artie Shaw, and above all, Duke Ellington, whom he considered the "greatest composer in that area." While in high school, he composed popular songs as well as a work for band inspired by Gershwin's *Rhapsody in Blue*. He spent most of his one year at Southern Methodist University (1941–1942) playing in dance bands and combos. Drafted at age eighteen into the Air Force, he served for a short time in military bands before being assigned to B-29 bomber crews in India, China, and the Pacific. During these three years of service (1942–1945), he decided to become a composer, and after his release, he earned a BM degree from the New England Conservatory (1945–1948), where he studied with Francis Judd Cooke, and wrote pieces in what he called a "mainstream American style, not too far from Piston and Copland," but also influenced by Bartók and Hindemith.

It was in the hopes of studying with Hindemith that Layton took an MM at Yale (1948–1950), but since Hindemith was on sabbatical, Layton studied instead with Quincy Porter. By the time Hindemith returned to Yale, Layton had "gone through a transformation" and had lost interest in studying with him. He remained at Yale as Porter's assistant so that his wife could complete her degree in music, and then went to Harvard to study musicology (1951–1959). His principal teachers there were Gombosi and Pirrotta (musicology) and Piston (composition). A winner of the Rome Prize, he interrupted his PhD program to spend three years (1954–1957) at the American Academy in Rome before returning to Harvard to complete his dissertation on medieval Italian settings of the Ordinary. He taught at Harvard for six years (1960–1966), and then founded and chaired the music department of the State University of New York at Stony

Brook, where he taught for over twenty years, making his home on a rustic peninsula in Setauket, Long Island.

Layton's catalog comprised only seven works, six of them written between 1952 and 1958: *Five Studies* for violin and piano, Op. 1 (1952); *An American Portrait* for orchestra, Op. 2 (1953); *3 Dylan Thomas Poems* for SATB chorus and brass sextet, Op. 3 (1956); *String Quartet in two movements,* Op. 4 (1956); *3 Studies* for piano, Op. 5 (1957); *Divertimento* for violin, clarinet, bassoon, cello, trombone, harpsichord, and percussion, Op. 6 (1958); and *Dance Fantasy* for orchestra, Op. 7 (1964). This small output won Layton important friends like Copland,[3] thanks in part to brilliant performances and recordings of the *Five Studies* by violinist Matthew Raimondi and pianist Yehudi Wyner; the *3 Studies* by Wyner; and the *String Quartet* by the Claremont Quartet. G. Schirmer intended to print it all, but in the end published only the *3 Studies,* the *Dylan Thomas Poems,* and the *Divertimento.*

The small size of Layton's oeuvre notwithstanding, his work very well may have come closer than most any other American composer to Carter's varied output. As with Carter, his more conservative works—*An American Portrait* and the *3 Dylan Thomas Poems*—won only respectful admiration, whereas the more daring efforts sparked real excitement. Unlike Carter, however, Layton's development did not progress slowly and linearly, but rather quickly and in a zigzag manner: the more conservative works were undertaken between the most experimental ones, namely, the *Five Studies* and *3 Studies.*

The composition of a conservative symphonic overture like *An American Portrait* on the heels of a strikingly experimental set of pieces for piano and violin like the *Five Studies* was inspired, in part, by Piston, who supervised the writing of both works. Not that Piston steered Layton in any particular direction; Layton noted that although *Five Studies* "was a type of composition which could be considered at the opposite extreme from Piston's own sane, moderate, richly traditional music . . . he never for a moment tried to turn me away from what I was doing, nor showed anything other than interest and friendly encouragement to me."[4] But Layton, an admirer of Piston's orchestral music especially, nonetheless found himself the following year "quite conscious of the attempt to reestablish contact with Piston and a whole school of practical, populist American composers." The resultant *American Portrait,* in fact, was intended as an homage to Piston, to whom it was dedicated, although it was not intended as a "portrait" of him per se.

Layton cast *An American Portrait* in a tight, inverted sonata form in which the second theme was recapitulated before the first theme. The form's cohesiveness, however, was obscured by big, sprawling gestures, ornate orchestral details, and an unusual tonal plan in which the principal tonalities of A and E were framed by a tonal center of D#. Its second theme was reminiscent of Piston in both melody and texture, but the work's prominent brass and percussion solos, and its dark, expressive tone brought it closer to younger composers like Carter and Schuman. The work was premiered in the Gardens of the Villa Aurelia by the Orchestra sinfonica di Roma under Bruno Maderna, but was never performed in America, or since, for that matter.

Layton's other relatively conservative work, the *3 Dylan Thomas Poems,* was more successful, winning a number of performances over the years. The middle poem, "O Make Me A Mask," was part of a 1954 commission of six Boston area composers for SATB and brass sextet settings of Thomas poems, ostensibly as some kind of memorial tribute. Later, in Rome, Layton added two shorter settings to form a triptych.

The work served Thomas's expressive, angry, and stylishly "beat" verse humbly and effectively. The music derived, above all, from Stravinsky's *Oedipus* and *Symphony of Psalms*— there were lively ostinati, elegant harmonic twists, long lines artfully dovetailed, bimodal clashes, and striking, idiomatic figures for the brass. (Not surprisingly, Layton cited Stravinsky as his favorite composer.) The work's dense harmonic spacing, however, had many distinctive features.

Performed more often than the *American Portrait* or the *3 Dylan Thomas Poems,* indeed, Layton's best-known work, *Five Studies* for violin and piano, was written more or less as a compositional exercise. Each Study, the preface states, "has a particular approach to rhythm, meter, harmony, melody, form, sonority, etc., as well as to style and expression." The first was a study in metrical organization: a steady violin pizzicato part in 4/2 and a syncopated piano part in changing

meters were juxtaposed (Ex. 66) until a hectic climax, after
which the roles were reversed. At the very end, in what would
become a characteristic gesture, the violin had a short, lyrical
tag. This first Study also flirted with the idea, not of a 12-tone
row, but of a 12-tone aggregate from which melodies and
harmonies were derived, an idea that Layton pursued and
systematized in later works. Layton feared that this particular
Study would prove too difficult to execute—a concern,
significantly, that Carter also had in regards to his contemporaneous *First String Quartet*—but the piece was shown to be
within the capabilities of musicians like Wyner and Raimondi.

The ensuing Studies were similarly adventurous, if not of
the same order of performance difficulty. The second Study,
based on a 9-note scale (C#-D-D#-E-F#-G-A-Bb-C), explored
a melismatic and rhythmically fluid lyricism within a strict
metrical framework. The third Study involved polyrhythms,
polytonality, and talea-like constructions in which a series of
notes were restated in ever-changing rhythmic configura-

Example 66. Billy Jim Layton, *Five Studies* for violin and piano, I.

tions. The fourth Study, highly constructivist, presented a
series of overlapping single notes of, for the most part, long
and varied durations, for which Layton created an unusual
rhythmic notation (Ex. 67). In this same Study, the pitches
formed an intricate intervallic pattern around a matrix of F#,
as well as a big, retrograde design. The last movement was
primarily a study in formal organization, in which measures
and, on a larger level, sections reappeared unchanged but in
different contexts, forming a rigid, undevelopmental discourse. Taken together, these *Five Studies* formed a surprisingly elegant and cohesive set, though it was its rich variety of
techniques and ideas that made it so memorably expressive.

Example 67. Billy Jim Layton, *Five Studies* for violin and piano, IV.

In his article on "Carter and the Postwar Composers,"
Boykan cited the *Five Studies* as having "all the devices which
were to become famous as Carter patents: independence of
the instrumental parts, rhythmic modulation, polyrhythms,
even the gigue-like motives of Carter's last movement."[5]
Boykan was referring here to Carter's *First Quartet,* the
centerpiece of his argument, a work whose importance to
American composers of the 1950s he compared to *The Rite*
forty years earlier. The implication, then, was that Layton's
Five Studies anticipated Carter's *Quartet,* which was impossi-
ble, since Carter's work was written the year before (this
confusion was said to have offended Carter). For his part,
Layton disclaimed any knowledge of Carter at this point, with
the exception of the *Piano Sonata,* which he heard played at

Yale, and possibly the *Cello Sonata,* which he might have heard over the radio. Further, he had not yet seen any Carter work in score. Of course, hearing the *Cello Sonata* (especially considering the first of the *Five Studies*), or even the *Piano Sonata,* would be relevant. But the *Five Studies* represented a more progressive stance, sooner resembling, in both technique and spirit, Carter's bold and experimental *8 Etudes and a Fantasy* (1950). Such resemblances might be ascribed more to a number of shared influences (including Stravinsky, Piston, Copland, jazz, 15th-century proportional notation, and Indian music) and to the temper of the times than to Layton's casual acquaintance with Carter's work. In this respect, it may be noted that Layton's kind of rhythmic adventurousness had certain features more reminiscent of, say, Messiaen than Carter. In any case, Layton's language, more restrained and lyrical than Carter's, was his own.

A similar confusion surrounded Layton's 1956 *String Quartet,* a work in which the experiments of the *Five Studies* were given large, commanding expression, and which almost surely seemed to be influenced by Carter's *First Quartet,* already five years old and a famous piece. According to Layton, however, he still had not heard the *Quartet,* though he had acquired, in the meantime, recordings of the *Piano Sonata* and the *Cello Sonata,* and he had heard enthusiastic reports about the *Quartet* from Yehudi Wyner. Did Wyner detail Carter's striking slow movement with its juxtaposition of sustained violins in their high register and growling declamations in the viola and cello? For there were similar passages in Layton's *Quartet*—and the composer had no knowledge of Ives's *Unanswered Question* at this point either! Further, Layton's busy, toccata-like string writing sounded remarkably Carteresque. But there was no reason to doubt Layton's word: the resemblances were perhaps fairly superficial after all. Carter's *Quartet* was stunningly new, rhythmically overwhelming, and texturally provocative, somewhat comparable to the abstract expressionist movement as represented by Franz Kline and Jackson Pollock. In contrast, Layton's *Quartet,* while fashionably strident, stood somewhat uneasily between the experimental daring of the *Five Studies* and the conservative restraint of the *Dylan Thomas Poems.*

This is not to deny the *Quartet*'s power and poignance,

which over the years recommended itself to many thoughtful
critics and listeners. Wilfred Mellers, in *Music in a New Found
Land,* devoted two pages to it, including two musical
examples. Mellers discussed the work in the context of
Carter, Ives, and at one point, Bartók, but noted, too, its
individuality, admiring the honesty of its "frail" and "forlorn"
conclusion.[6] The *Quartet* also won the admiration of Richard
F. French, who wrote:

> He [Layton] dares to use conventional formal ideas (the
> first movement is a balance of repeated sections, the
> second is a theme and variations) and shows that through
> familiarity with many other works based on these
> models he has come to understand their basic natures
> and potentialities—it is precisely this quality of under-
> standing that conveys itself in the free thrust and energy
> of the work. He asks the players to face and master
> unusual difficulties of technique, rhythm, and ensemble
> and provides them thereby with an invigorated musical
> language. His technical skill lies in an adroit correlation
> of melodic ideas with chordal organization and harmonic
> plan, and the technique thus produces a style capable of
> a flexibility and expressive range unhindered by eclecti-
> cism and unmindful of obscurity. . . . Here is a work of
> major importance to anyone interested in the continua-
> tion of our musical tradition.[7]

Amazingly, the *Quartet* was never published.

In his next work, the *3 Studies* for piano, Layton experimented more explicitly with the 12-tone method. Each Study
employed its own row in its own way. The three rows
(G#-A-F-F#-G-B-C-D#-E-D-Bb-Db; G#-A-F-F#-G-B-Bb-D-
Eb-E-C-C#; Ab-A-F-D-Eb-B-E-C-C#-Bb-F#-G) shared the
same opening three pitches, but deviated thereafter, the
second and third rows comprising the kind of row, favored by
Webern, in which the retrogrades and inversions were
identical. The first Study was the most straightforward in that
it used the row melodically, except for the soft trichords that
punctuated the form, and that looked ahead to the successive
studies. The highly virtuosic second Study also used the row
melodically, but often proceeded only through four or eight
notes of some row-form before going on to another. In the

third Study, Layton developed what he regarded as a very personal approach to the 12-tone method, in which the row was treated as a source for trichords, rather than melody. Further, the row was used cyclically, so that each row-form provided twelve trichords: 1-2-3, 4-5-6, 7-8-9, 10-11-12, 12-1-2, 3-4-5, 6-7-8, 9-10-11, 11-12-1, 2-3-4, 5-6-7, and 8-9-10. Layton recognized in this technique a debt to the later works of Schoenberg, but felt his contribution to 12-tone methodology to be, on the whole, distinctive. The actual choice of trichords resulted in harmonies different from Schoenberg as well as Carter, but the work taken as a whole revealed a profound kinship with the latter's *Piano Sonata;* consider, for example, the second Study's toccata-like piano writing, or the third Study's bold, declamatory opening (Ex. 68) and elaborate, fugal middle section.

Layton's harmonic approach to the 12-tone method was systematized and expanded in the *Divertimento* to permit four-, five- and six-note groupings. Each row-form, consequently, became the equivalent of a key area, with a full repertory of chords. And like key areas, the row-forms then could be placed in ordered degrees of closeness. The casual

Example 68. Billy Jim Layton, *3 Studies* for piano, III (G. Schirmer, 1966).

listener of the *Divertimento* would be struck less by such 12-tone ingenuities than by its striking closeness to jazz, including a drum solo with smashing cymbals. Also conspicuous was a quotation near the end of the work from Bach's D minor Fugue from *The Well-Tempered Clavier II*. One English reviewer thought the work's "fine architectural deployment of sonority, and the toughness, clarity and vigour of its emotional content are typical of what seems to us at any rate to be the ideal American music."[8]

According to the composer, his last work, the *Dance Fantasy* for orchestra, was his best work, but it hardly was known, receiving only a single perfunctory performance by the New Haven Symphony, which commissioned it. The work also explored, in part, a harmonic approach to the 12-tone technique, but it was principally an experiment in rhythm. Wrote Richmond Browne, "One best receives this *Dance Fantasy* . . . as a representation of the entire range of human experience with time."[9] This range included features derived from Tchaikovsky, Stravinsky, jazz, Cage, Stockhausen, Penderecki, and, above all, Carter.

The *Dance Fantasy* aimed toward the ideals put forth by the composer in an article written one year after, in 1965, entitled, "The New Liberalism."[10] This article took for its premise the assertion that the assassination of President Kennedy, "whose death caused a wrench of pain throughout the world such as had never been felt before . . . put an end to the power of extremism of whatever sort, whether of the Left or of the Right." According to Layton, the times now called for "a responsive and enlightened liberalism," open to the avant-garde, jazz, and music from around the world, but also in contact "with the great central tradition of humanism in the West." Layton's arguments resembled contemporaneous statements by Carter, and were similarly rife with the contradictions of an advanced artist who raises the issue of the artist's social responsibility in denunciation of those more avant-garde than himself. Carter, however, continued to compose; Layton, after the *Dance Fantasy,* produced no new work.

Layton found in Yehudi Wyner a superlative interpreter and loyal friend. They were similarly educated in later years, but their early backgrounds were quite different. Wyner, who changed the spelling of his last name to better suit English pronunciation, was the son of Lazar Weiner, a distinguished composer of Jewish liturgical music and Yiddish art song. Lazar was born in Kiev in 1897, and immigrated in 1914 to the United States, where he studied composition with Frederick Jacobi, Robert Russell Bennett, and Josef Schillinger. His music, profoundly marked by Eastern European Jewish folksong and chant, showed, too, the influences of Musorgsky and Debussy. Weiner was best known, perhaps, as the conductor of large Yiddish choruses and synagogal choirs, and as a teacher at the Hebrew Union College School of Sacred Music.[11]

Yehudi, born in Calgary, Canada, in 1929, was groomed to be a concert pianist, a training he remembered as "very painful."[12] As a child, he, along with a young friend, Charles Rosen, studied with Paul Boepple and Hedwig Kanner-Rosenthal; and at age fifteen, he entered Juilliard, where he joined the class of Lonny Epstein.[13] He temporarily renounced the piano in favor of a career in composition, and went to Yale to study with Hindemith, whose music he admired; but between the fact that Hindemith taught only graduate students, and that he was often away in Europe, Wyner earned both BA and BM (1946–1951) primarily under the guidance of Richard Donovan, a "matter-of-fact craftsman" who "demystified the whole notion of music making."

Still waiting for Hindemith to return from Zurich, Wyner spent one "very interesting and extremely demanding year" at Harvard (1951–1952). He studied medieval music with Davison, Handel with Thompson, counterpoint with Sapp, and, most disappointingly, analysis and composition with Piston: Although he understood that Piston's "forbearance" helped "protect his own inner life" and, moreover, showed respect for his students, Wyner recalled only dreary nit-picking in analysis, and the occasional "Bravo" during private lessons.

The following year Wyner returned to Yale to study finally with Hindemith, whose resourcefulness was more to his liking. After this, he spent three years at the American Academy in Rome (1953–1956), worked in New York City as a free-lance performer and teacher (1957–1962), and taught at Yale (1963–1978), the State University of New York at Purchase (1978–1988), and Brandeis (since 1988).

Wyner's early music developed largely under the influence of his father, Bloch, Donovan, and Hindemith. This included *Two Preludes on Southern Hymns* for organ (1950), a work dedicated to Donovan and written in a straightforward, modal style, full of canonic imitation. In 1951 he met Layton at Yale, and was struck by the emotional expressivity of an orchestral work Layton just had completed, an advanced piece of juvenalia never included in his catalog. The two men grew even closer during their year together at Harvard in 1952, and Wyner observed the composition of Layton's *Five Studies* with great interest. For his part, Layton followed the progress of Wyner's *Partita* for piano (Ex. 69) with equal interest, years later noting it to contain "neo-Bach mannerisms presented with a rhythmic verve that could only be produced by a jazz-indoctrinated American,"[14] a description that could serve some of his own work, not to mention some by Carter. Clearly, an "indocrination" in jazz was a strong, common bond between Wyner and Layton. For Wyner, this interest climaxed during his three years in Rome, during which time he befriended black novelist Ralph Ellison, and made some demonstration tapes of his own jazz, a solo piano style derived from the bebop of Charlie Parker and Dizzy Gillespie. Layton's significance for Wyner well may have been

Example 69. Yehudi Wyner, "Gigue," *Partita* for piano (Associated Music, 1976).

in suggesting ways of reconciling Hindemith and Parker; but if so, it was a model soon to be superseded by Carter.

Wyner first met Carter in Rome in 1953 and immediately came under his influence, writing a *Piano Sonata* (1954) in the spirit of the older composer's *Piano Sonata,* though one critic described it sooner as Stravinskian.[15] He subsequently heard a performance of Carter's *First String Quartet* at an ISCM concert in Rome, and enthusiastically recommended it to both Martin Boykan, then in Vienna, and Layton, soon to arrive in Rome himself. Wyner was most impressed with the way Carter "opened up an enormous number of possibilities" by writing a counterpoint full of contrast, but carefully controlled, "not meaningless like Ives, Honegger, and Harris." Like Layton, Wyner did not respond as enthusiastically to Carter's late music as he had to such early works as the *Piano Sonata* and *Cello Sonata;* but he deeply admired the *Concerto for Orchestra* as well as "View of the Capitol" and "O Breath" from *A Mirror On Which To Dwell,* which he heard his wife, Susan Davenny Wyner, sing numerous times.

Wyner's *Concert Duo* for violin and piano, begun in Rome in 1955, completed in 1956, and revised in 1957, was probably his first mature work, certainly his first real success. Richly expressive, finely crafted, the *Duo* was smartly attuned to new trends but very distinctive and personal at the same time. As with Layton's *Five Studies,* the impact of Carter was suggested especially by the work's very opening (Ex. 70). Throughout the work in general, the use of advanced tonality and metric modulation pointed to Carter, and, not surprisingly, it was cited by Boykan in his "Carter" article. On the other hand, Wyner's intriguing fusion of Baroque and jazz elements, while surely related to Carter, perhaps showed a greater closeness to Hindemith, especially considering the *Duo*'s relatively conservative second movement.

Wyner's *Duo* differed from both Carter and Hindemith, however, in some crucial ways. First, its melodies were deeply influenced by Jewish chant, as evident by their modal inflections, their falling seconds and thirds, their repeated-note recitations, and their cantorial rhythms and gestures (Ex. 71). The piano harmonies reflected this orientation as well, and the resultant mood was dark and restless, not least the work's concluding D minor harmony with its lingering E^b.

Example 70. Yehudi Wyner, *Concert Duo* for violin and piano, first three lines of the first movement. Copyright by Associated Music Publishers, Inc. All rights reserved. Used by permission.

Furthermore, the work's form was highly rhapsodic, full of
dramatic cadenzas and startling contrasts. In these respects,
the legacy of Ernst Bloch, especially as it pertained to Wyner,
was pertinent.

While perhaps not considered particularly fashionable in
the 1950s, the music of Ernst Bloch long had looked ahead to
just those features applauded by Boykan in "Elliott Carter
and the Postwar Composers"; consider the 1919 *Viola Suite,*
one of Bloch's first American compositions, with its explosive
tempo changes, irregular note values, polytonal textures, and
heightened expressivity. This was not mere coincidence: one
of Bloch's most devoted students was Roger Sessions, who in
turn exerted a large influence on Carter, not least in the fact
that he was the first composer, according to Boykan, to
employ metric modulation. Other Bloch students included

Example 71. Yehudi Wyner, *Concert Duo* for violin and piano, first two
lines of the second movement. Copyright by Associated Music Publishers,
Inc. All rights reserved. Used by permission.

Frederick Jacobi, one of Lazar Weiner's teachers; Quincy Porter, whom both Wyner and Layton knew at Yale; and Leon Kirchner, whose *Sonata Concertante* (1952) was an inspiration for Wyner's own *Concert Duo*. As one might expect from the son of a famous composer of Yiddish song, Wyner further shared Bloch's inclination toward Eastern European Jewish styles, at least in the *Concert Duo*. Profoundly Jewish and boldly rhapsodic, the *Concert Duo* was as much a successor to Bloch as it was to Hindemith or Carter.

In the 1958 *Serenade* for flute, horn, trumpet, trombone, viola, cello and piano, Wyner's Jewishness was elusively abstracted, but his rhapsodic impulse was given even greater scope. The work's large form was strikingly rich, comprising a slow "Nocturne"; a fast "Toccata"; a fast "Capriccio," in the midst of which appeared an "Aria" that was not quite a separate movement, but not quite a mere interlude; and a brief return of the "Nocturne." Some overall unity was achieved through Schoenbergian development of a leitmotif put forth by the trombone in the opening measures, but the music was, for all that, very episodic. The opening "Nocturne," for instance, was divided into four discrete sections, somewhat interrelated like variations, somewhat balanced symmetrically, but curiously disjointed, as epitomized by the double bar, drawn with dashes, that separated the first two sections. The composer's liner note to a recording of the work left no doubt that its formal subtleties were highly deliberate:

> Certain features were carried out with some consistency: exact sequences or imitations avoided; all recurrences varied; motivic, phrase and sectional lengths balanced in an asymmetrical way; no doubling of instruments (the surprising exceptions strengthen the rule); any material may appear in any movement, subject to affective transformation; prevailing instrumental timbre is contrast not blend, permitting clear separation of lines and independent plateaus of action. The listener is frequently offered a choice as to which material is principal, or secondary at any moment. The resultant web in which most parts may have equal weight banishes the idea of mere accompaniment. These ideas are common in dodecaphonic composition, less common outside that sphere.[16]

As this last comment suggested, the *Serenade* joined the Schoenbergian orbit without resort to the 12-tone method, a technique that held little personal interest for Wyner. Consequently, it was the atonal, predodecaphonic style of Schoenberg and Webern that truly enthralled him; the *Serenade*'s dark, bottom-heavy instrumentation in particular looked back to the expressionistic orchestral writing of Schoenberg and Webern, though here, instead of a chamber-like orchestral piece, there was, to much the same effect, an orchestral-like chamber work. Intended as a memorial tribute to a dying friend, the artist James Hoffman, the work had none of the traditionally amorous or lighthearted associations of the serenade, but was rather morbidly romantic, a mood Wyner often favored.

This expressionistic streak aside, Wyner's *Serenade* and Layton's *Divertimento,* both from 1958, had many similarities, and not just in title and instrumentation. For one, both showed a sensitivity to contemporary jazz currents. If Layton had something of the Modern Jazz Quartet's chic, Wyner had something of John Coltrane's daring. Second, both works displayed Baroque mannerisms, sometimes in neoclassical fashion, as in Layton's Stravinskian finale and Wyner's Hindemithian "Capriccio"; and sometimes in anticipation of the '60s fashion for quotation and pastiche, as in Layton's afore-mentioned quotation of a Bach fugue, and Wyner's veiled evocation of Bach in the "Aria" movement. Finally, both works had some connection to Schoenberg: Layton in his personalized use of the 12-tone method, Wyner more deeply in his choice of colors and textures. Wyner's admiration for Schoenberg only grew over time, and he came to regret he had studied with Hindemith and Piston rather than with him.

In the years after the *Serenade* and his return from Rome, Wyner's numerous activities, aside from teaching, included musical directorship of the Westchester Reform Temple, the Turnau Opera Association, and the New Haven Opera Society. He also led an active concert career, performing in a duo with violinist Matthew Raimondi, as keyboardist for the Bach Aria Group, and as partner with pianist Gilbert Kalish, and many singers including soprano Susan Davenny Wyner, his wife since 1967. The works written during these years often complemented these many activities. There were, for instance, practical liturgical works that used small ensembles and subtle harmonies to support their fluid, chantlike vocal lines, including the *Friday Evening Service* for cantor, choir, and organ (1963); the *Torah Service* for chorus, four brasses, and double bass (1966); *R'tzey* and *Kodosh Ato* for cantor, guitar, bongo, and recorder (1970); and *Memorial Music I* and *II* for soprano and three flutes (1971, 1973). There was also an instrumental sacred work, dedicated to his father, *Passover Offering* for flute, clarinet, trombone, and cello (1959), a kind of programmatic companion piece to the *Serenade*. And there were musical scores to productions of Robert Lowell's *Old Glory* and Isaac Bashevis Singer's *The Mirror*. Wyner also continued to write abstract instrumental works, many of which had titles that pointed to their quasi-improvisatory makeup: *3 Informal Pieces* for violin and piano (1961); *3 Short Fantasies* for piano (1963, 1966, 1971); and *Cadenza!* for clarinet and harpsichord or piano (1970).

In the early 1970s, Wyner became one of the first composers to be associated with the "new romanticism." His music, even from the 1950s, as we have seen, always had been highly charged; indeed, the tradition of Bloch long was predisposed to a certain romanticism, as opposed to Piston, who represented a more classic stance. Wyner's sympathies were clearly more in line with Bloch; of all Piston's students, Wyner probably was least susceptible to his influence. Reviewing Wyner's 1961 *3 Informal Pieces,* Everett Helm wrote that they "couldn't make up their mind between Romanticism and academic pointillism."[17] Very romantic indeed were the *Three Short Fantasies* for piano, with their dark moods (usually angry or sad) and their rhapsodic forms based on the alternation of a handful of shimmering chords subtly altered with each reappearance (shades of Schoenberg's Op. 16, No. 3). Even their occasional calm had a tortured immobility.

But beginning with *De Novo* for cello and ensemble (1971), which quickly made a friend of *The New York Times*'s arch-romanticist, Harold Schonberg,[18] Wyner favored more and more, and quite intentionally, the sentimental, the sensual, in short, the heart over the head. This new romanticism was propounded in the ensuing decade by such works as *Romances (Intermedio)* for soprano and strings (1974); *Fragments from Antiquity* for soprano and orchestra (1978), a work originally intended to be based on fragmentary remnants, "as when archeologists discover a pot shard in Greece and Syria and infer the rest," but ended up based on short texts from ancient China and Greece;[19] and the *Intermezzo* for piano quartet (1980).

In part, the *Romances,* with its sensuous vocalise for soprano accompanied by strings, followed in the tradition of the *Bachianas Brasileiras No. 5,* to which it seemed an intentional successor. There was also a connection to popular music: each of the work's three movements—entitled "Torch Song," "Up Tempo," and "Elegy"—alluded to "certain audible characteristics with the vernacular style of the 1930s."[20] This connection was discernable most clearly in "Torch Song," with its quartal harmonies, its blues motives, its pizzicato strings, and its "quasi improvvisato" indication (Ex. 72). But the work's sensibility was altogether different from both popular music and Villa-Lobos; there was nothing charming or breezy about it. Rather, it was, like Wyner's work in general, consistently ardent, with a red-hot intensity that, as one reporter noted, matched the "flaming red dress with décolletage" worn by Susan Wyner at the work's New York premiere.[21] Occasionally, the gestures and harmonies were even reminiscent of something deliciously "fin de siècle"; certainly, "Torch Song" was closer to Brangäne's torchlit nightwatch in *Tristan* than to anything by Jerome Kern or Harold Arlen. The work, in fact, suggested a kind of concert music parallel to Linda Ronstadt's 1983 renditions of the kind of torch songs Wyner more or less had in mind (*What's New*), renditions so steamy and romantic in their nostalgia that little room was left for the whimsical, the ironic, or the tender.

Even more earnest was the similarly titled *Intermezzo.* In this work, Brahms was occasionally evoked, but again, the style, fairly short on humor or calm, seemed closer yet to the hothouse romanticism of Scriabin or Griffes; if John Harbison's romanticism, as we shall see, derived from the 1930s, Wyner's seemed to spring from the first decade of the 20th century. And yet, the music, as always, was impressively stylish. One half expected it at certain moments to succumb to pastiche, but it refrained; one almost sensed it verging on the familiar, but it surprised. The marks of a sophisticated modernist were everywhere apparent; the music had only the

Example 72. Yehudi Wyner, "Torch Song," *Romances (Intermedio)*.

vaguest resemblance to the easier, more accessible styles of
Rochberg, Argento, and Del Tredici. Such virtues made it,
potentially, a model for scores of younger composers with
similar aims. On the face of it, these later works by Wyner
seemed an improbable offshoot of Carter, but not perhaps
when one considered Carter's admiration for Scriabin and
Griffes, and his own kind of ardor.

Martin Boykan met Wyner at Yale in 1952, where they
played Stravinsky's *Concerto* for two pianos together. Later,
Wyner introduced Boykan to Layton, and the three became
fast friends. Both Wyner and Layton were deeply impressed
with Boykan's dazzling musicianship, sharp mind, and high

ideals. For Wyner, he was the "most fluently brilliant musician I've ever known aside from Hindemith" and "one of the glories of our culture."

Boykan, like Wyner, had a particularly advantaged education. As a youth, in addition to schooling at the Ethical Culture School and Fieldston in New York, he studied piano with Abby Whiteside, Webster Aitken, and Edward Steuermann; theory and composition with Vivian Fine, Jerzy Fitelberg, and Nikolai Lopatnikoff; and harmony with George Szell. In 1947 he entered Harvard, graduating summa cum laude in 1951. In his freshman year he began to play Schoenberg at the piano, and wrote a *String Trio* inspired by him. He soon came under the influence of Piston's music, especially the *Second Quartet*, the *Third Symphony*, and the *Piano Quintet*, for which he played the piano part; his brilliant analyses of Piston's scores were to the advantage of classmate Sam Adler, who found his insights "illuminating." Aside from Piston, Boykan found the Harvard faculty, both in and outside music, disappointingly problematical,[22] the exact opposite of Wyner's experience there. More satisfying were friendships with fellow colleagues Fine (actually a junior faculty member by this time), Spies, and Des Marais, whose senior honors thesis, *Harmonic Technique in the Beethoven String Quartets* (1949), anticipated his own, *Rhetoric and Style in the Quartets of Beethoven's Middle Period* (1951).

Boykan's music from this period, later renounced as apprenticeship works, included a *String Quartet* (1949) and a *Flute Sonata* (1950), both strongly influenced by Piston. He continued along these lines during his two years with Hindemith at the University of Zurich and at Yale. Then, on a Fulbright Fellowship in Vienna (1953–1955), he suffered some uncertainties and stopped composing. It was also during this time that he heard enthusiastic reports from Wyner about Carter's *First Quartet*.

After his return, Boykan joined the faculty at Brandeis University, where he taught for more than twenty-five years. Further familiarity with Carter, as well as with Sessions, Imbrie, Shifrin, and others, helped him find his way. Ever the perfectionist (prior to 1975, his catalog contained only a handful of works), he finally wrote a work he considered mature, the 1967 *String Quartet No. 1*. The work subsequently won the Jeunesse Musical Prize and proved a suitable musical accompaniment to Montreal's modernistic Expo '67. The work also found favor with *Perspectives of New Music,* which reprinted it in its entirety, along with some remarks by John Harbison and Eleanor Cory.[23] Boykan's reputation as a composer for many years rested on this one intriguing work.

The *Quartet,* a large four-movement work, was ostensibly atonal, although some pitches, like C, seemed to carry more weight than others. The work's most careful observer, Eleanor Cory, while admitting the desirability of different analytical methods with regards to this work, found set-theory particularly helpful in analyzing it.[24] This seemed a valid approach, despite the fact that the work in question was not 12-tone. Boykan, after all, was an active contributor at the time to what had become the principal forum for set-theory, *Perspectives of New Music.* And while it is true that his reviews of Fine, Stravinsky, and Imbrie from the early '60s exhibited some wariness toward newfangled analytical methods and the 12-tone technique,[25] by 1967, the year of the *Quartet,* he showed, in discussions of Shifrin and Webern,[26] a clear assimilation of ideas derived from Babbitt. Eventually he wrote Babbitt a warm tribute;[27] he regretted not having known him or Sessions much earlier.[28]

Cory isolated two sets in the *Quartet,* both unordered: a chromatic hexachord (0,1,2,3,4,5) and a tetrachord (0,1, 5,6).[29] She further claimed that the hexachord, prominent in movements one and two, gave way to the tetrachord in movements three and four. Because three pitches from the tetrachord (0,1,5) were found also in the hexachord, it was difficult to distinguish one from the other. Notwithstanding a certain plausibility to Cory's claims, both sets seemed to coexist throughout the *Quartet,* sometimes in alternation, as in measures 7–8 of the scherzo, which moved from hexachord to tetrachord; or sometimes in combination, forming a seven-note set, as in measures 7–8 of the slow movement. A fairer distinction, perhaps, could be made between movements two and three, which tended to use the sets as harmonic blocks, or "fields," as Boykan's Brandeis colleague Arthur Berger would say; and movements one and four, which used the sets more contrapuntally. This latter usage was the more difficult to analyze, for the two sets, or different transpositions of the same set, could often be found simultaneously. In contrast, the more harmonic usage involved fairly discrete fields of about one measure's length, often initiated by the cello, and typically crossing the barline (Ex. 73).

Even here, however, an analysis based on these two sets posed problems and ambiguities, for example, the overlapping of two hexachords in measures 1–2; the fusion of two hexachords in measures 2–3; and the absence of a pitch, namely, G#, in measure six that would complete both the hexachord and the tetrachord. Consequently, while it appeared that the composer had "sets" of one sort or another in mind, the helpfulness of set-theory in analyzing this work was

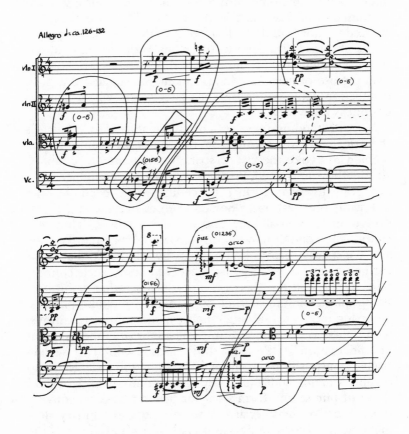

Example 73. Martin Boykan, *String Quartet No. 1*, II.

still questionable; perhaps other analyses along these lines would be more fruitful.

What was more readily apparent was the fact that Boykan broke up his sets into smaller bits to form principal motives and trichords. Hypothetically, these could have involved the intervals of the third and the fourth, but the composer clearly showed a preference for seconds and tritones, which consequently helped give the *Quartet* its rather cramped and craggy quality. The work's most prominent motive, the two-note semitone (0,1), was often found as a major seventh or minor ninth, as in the three lower strings at the very opening. In the slow movement, this motive was expanded into an oscillating figure whose melodic shape and harmonic setting were reminiscent of Stravinsky's *Agon* (Ex. 74). The *Quartet*'s favored trichord similarly derived from the first three pitches of the chromatic hexachord (0,1,2), as in the opening of the slow movement; the prominence of this particular trichord, as with the use of harmonic fields in general, suggested a close connection with Arthur Berger's later work, which Boykan doubtless knew well.

Notwithstanding these progressive features, the *Quartet*'s rhetoric, to borrow a word from the composer's senior thesis, seemed to evoke the classic string quartet literature, above all, Beethoven. Indeed, his thesis on Beethoven helped shed light on his own formal procedures, for example, the following observations: "Sonata themes are never able to evolve in a natural and undisturbed manner. They are continually coming into opposition with other motifs; they are constantly being bombarded by rhythmic halts, or harmonic shifts."[30] Cory also observed some such connection, noting that the *Quartet* "unfolds in a rather traditional string quartet idiom marked by extended melodic phrases, recurring motives, building climaxes, and subtle transitions, with non-arco devices used in the manner of embellishment or punctuation."[31] Perhaps the work's use of two sets in twelve transpositions was intended to function analogously to tonality's major and minor keys. But in any case, Boykan's sense of phrase and form went far beyond classical conventions. Most straightforward, it seemed, was the binary slow movement, whose compression Harbison admired,[32] and the finale, which comprised four contrasting sections marked off

Example 74. Martin Boykan, *String Quartet No. 1*, III.

by double bars, forming a sort of encapsulation of the entire work. The first movement seemed to suggest something of the dynamics of sonata form: first theme group (mm. 1–9), second theme group (mm. 10–18), development (mm. 19–37), and recapitulation (mm. 38–47). And the scherzo seemed to contain a quieter "trio" section. Harbison mentioned, too, the importance of the motive B-C in articulating form, while Cory pointed to the cadential function of certain trichords played "col legno battuto" in the scherzo.[33] One could certainly add to these the use of silence. But with these and like impressions, it was often hard to distinguish small caesuras from bigger endings, and, consequently, Boykan's forms remained highly elusive.

Boykan's *First Quartet* surely reflected close study of Carter's *First Quartet,* but for every similarity there was a distinction to be made. For example, the *Quartet's* opening page, with its soaring first violin, its middle voices in duet, and its rhapsodic cello, was texturally like Carter, but the melodic lines themselves were more spasmodic, less directed and defined than Carter's. Similarly, Boykan's organic approach to form echoed Carter, but whereas Carter's *Quartet* was rich in dramatic contrasts and gestures, Boykan's work was so intimate and personal that, in Harbison's words, "The Quartet asserts (almost aggressively, not with diffidence) the possibility of inwardness, of speaking one-to-one."[34]

Boykan's fluid, syncopated rhythms also derived from Carter, but had little to do with jazz, tending toward slow, steady beats intricately subdivided, rather than, as with Carter, quick beats energetically changing value. Overall, both quartets shared a darkly expressive intensity, but while Boykan tended to be unremittingly grim, Carter's range was broader, including moments of ironic wit and positive cheerfulness.

Boykan's *Second Quartet,* written in 1973, was even more brooding: according to the composer, it reflected his painful separation from his first wife, flutist Constance Boykan. It was a more accessible work than the *First Quartet,* however— less shrill and frenetic. Its dark, rich harmonies and intense melodies made for a powerfully personal statement, in some respects like Bartók. At the same time, its use of the 12-tone method reflected the composer's growing admiration for Babbitt.

Remarried to the artist, Susan Schwalb, Boykan aimed for greater calm in his *Third Quartet,* finally completed in 1984. In the end, the work turned out not too different from the earlier quartets: it was yet another impressive and expert effort in a highly serious and complex modernist style, this time combining something of the *First*'s anguish and the *Second*'s melancholy. Indeed, its steadfastness to the abstract expressionist ideals represented by the early Carter quartets stood out in a time marked by all kinds of revisionism.

In the context of Boykan's career, his article on "Elliott Carter and the Postwar Composers" consequently could be seen to be more personal tribute and artistic manifesto than historical account. The article's emphasis on the *First Quartet,* its omitted references to Carter's irony or relation to jazz, and its dismissal of an earlier generation of American composers said more about Boykan's own struggles and convictions than about Carter's place in American music. It was even somewhat distorted from the standpoint of such close friends as Layton and Wyner.

In 1963, the year of Boykan's article, Carter was at his height; like Beethoven, Carter was a composer whose middle-period works made the deepest impression in his own lifetime. After 1963, Layton, Wyner, and Boykan, whatever debt they owed Carter, pursued their own destinies. Layton, shocked by the political assassinations of the 1960s, was soon to give up composing altogether, putting his greatest hopes in the future of jazz. Wyner turned more and more to the ravishing surfaces of late Romanticism. And Boykan moved closer to Babbitt. All three retained enormous respect for one another and for Carter, who remained an ideal for artistic integrity, rhythmic vitality, and sonorous beauty. But in the end, their paths proved surprisingly distinct, and fairly solitary as well.

Notes

1. Martin Boykan, "Elliott Carter and the Postwar Composers," reprinted in *Perspectives on American Composers* (New York: W. W. Norton, 1971), pp. 213–216.
2. Layton, personal interview, September 28, 1984.
3. Copland, "1959: Postscript for the Generation of the Fifties," *Copland on Music* (New York: W. W. Norton, 1963), p. 178.
4. Layton, personal letter, October 8, 1977.
5. Boykan, p. 213.
6. Mellers, *Music in a New Found Land* (London: Barrie & Rockliff, 1964), pp. 230–231.
7. French, "Review of Records," *Musical Quarterly* 46 (1960), pp. 555–556.
8. Anthony Payne, "Modern Chamber Music," *Musical Times* 105 (November 1984), p. 836.
9. Browne, "Billy Jim Layton: Dance Fantasy," *Perspectives of New Music* 4 (Fall–Winter 1965), pp. 161–170.
10. Layton, "The New Liberalism," *Perspectives of New Music* 3 (Spring–Summer 1965), pp. 137–142.
11. A. W. Binder, *Studies in Jewish Music: Collected Writings of A. W. Binder,* edited by Irene Haskins (New York: Bloch, 1971).
12. Judith Hasan, "Dean of Music at State U. Describes His Role," *The New York Times,* August 2, 1981, WC5.
13. Wyner, personal interview, October 6, 1984.
14. Layton, "Yehudi Wyner," *Dictionary of Contemporary Music,* John Vinton, ed. (New York: E. P. Dutton, 1974), p. 824.
15. L. T., review in the *New York Herald Tribune,* January 20, 1958, reprinted in the *ACA Bulletin* 7 No. 3 (1958), p. 26.
16. Wyner, liner notes to a recording of the *Serenade,* CRI 141.
17. Helm, "ISCM Concert," *Musical America* 82 (May 1962), p. 40.

18. Schoenberg, "At Aldo Parisot's Cello Recital, 2 World Premieres," *The New York Times,* March 4, 1976, C30.

19. Hasan.

20. Wyner, liner notes to a recording of *Intermedio,* CRI 352.

21. Mark Blechner, "American Composers Alliance," *HiFi/Mus Am* 27 (June 1977), MA 28–29.

22. Martin Boykan, personal interview, February 10, 1984.

23. "Martin Boykan: *String Quartet* (1967) Two Views," *Perspectives of New Music* 11 (Spring–Summer 1973), pp. 204–248.

24. Cory, "Two Views," p. 205.

25. Boykan, "Current Chronicle," *Musical Quarterly* 48 (July 1962), pp. 385–387; " 'Neoclassicism' and Late Stravinsky," *Perspectives of New Music* 1 (Spring 1963), pp. 155–169; review of Imbrie's *Third Quartet, Perspectives of New Music* 3 (Fall–Winter 1964), pp. 139–146.

26. Boykan, review of Shifrin's *Satires of Circumstance, Perspectives of New Music* 5 (Fall-Winter 1966), pp. 163–169; "The Webern Concerto Revisited," *American Society of University Composers* (April 1968), pp. 74–85. This last was probably Boykan's most important piece of critical writing, as it took issue with a number of commonly held ideas about Webern.

27. Boykan, "For Milton," *Perspectives of New Music* 14–15 (1976), pp. 202–205.

28. Boykan, personal interview.

29. Cory, pp. 205–209; see also Cory, "Reviews of Records," *Musical Quarterly* 62 (October 1976), pp. 616–620.

30. Boykan, *Rhetoric and Style in the Quartets of Beethoven's Middle Period,* Senior Honors Thesis, Harvard Music Library.

31. Cory, "Reviews of Records," p. 616.

32. Harbison, "Two Views," p. 205.

33. Harbison, p. 205, and Cory, "Two Views," p. 208.

34. Harbison, p. 204.

15. MUSIC WITH NEW PERSPECTIVES: ROBERT MOEVS, KARL KOHN, CLAUDIO SPIES, PETER WESTERGAARD, AND JOHN MACIVOR PERKINS

THE MUSIC JOURNAL *PERSPECTIVES OF NEW MUSIC* was launched in 1962 primarily as a response to Boulez, Stockhausen, Babbitt, and others associated with the postwar avant-garde. *Modern Music,* which ended publication in 1946, was its forerunner, but *Perspectives* aimed for a more scientific and technical discourse. *Die Reihe* was its European counterpart, but *Perspectives* aspired to a greater scope and breadth. It quickly became the central forum for the discussion of new music in the United States.

Many of the early contributors to *Perspectives* had studied with Piston. Homage was paid: there was a 1964 article on his music by Clifford Taylor,[1] and a 1968 interview with Peter Westergaard.[2] Piston even served on the journal's editorial board. As for his former students associated with the early *Perspectives* in one capacity or another, they included Arthur Berger (one of the journal's founders), Robert Moevs, Karl Kohn, Claudio Spies, Peter Westergaard, John MacIvor Perkins, Billy Jim Layton, Martin Boykan, David Behrman, Frederic Rzewski, and John Harbison. This discussion singles out Moevs, Kohn, Spies, Westergaard, and Perkins, not that they formed any distinct group, but simply because the remaining composers are discussed in other contexts.

Robert Moevs was one of the first American composers to recognize the importance of Pierre Boulez, but throughout his career he remained most indebted to tastes learned in his native La Crosse, where he was born on December 2, 1920. Like many towns in Wisconsin, these tastes were established primarily by German immigrants, who long had dominated the state's cultural life. Moevs's piano teacher, the one-armed Don Jonson, was one such immigrant. A student of Sigismond Stojowski (who himself had studied with Liszt), Jonson "kept alive the romantic conception of music."[3] Moevs grew up, consequently, in a musical atmosphere dominated by Bach, Schumann, Chopin, and, above all, Liszt, but not Mozart, who was considered too trifling, nor Beethoven, who was considered too sublime for young students.[4] For Moevs, it was not unlike growing up in a small town in late-nineteenth-century Germany, the occasional piece by Nathaniel Dett or Leo Ornstein notwithstanding.[5] This orientation could always be gleaned in the romantic theatricality of his works, especially in the dazzling bravura of his piano writing.

At Harvard from 1938 to 1942, where his principal teachers were Hill (orchestration) and Piston (harmony, counterpoint, and fugue), Moevs thrilled to performances of Ravel by Koussevitzky, and learned to appreciate Beethoven, Hindemith, Stravinsky, and Piston. The only popular idioms that interested him were boogie-woogie and the blues, thanks to their opposition of a repetitive bass and improvised melody. He quietly discovered Varèse on his own, and found the repetition factor in Varèse's "concentrated insistence on a motive" similarly congenial, though in time, it became "a factor . . . to be combatted." His love for Bach, on the other hand, deepened, and became "the basis of my own style."[6]

In an interview for *Perspectives of New Music,* Moevs told James Boros that he liked Piston very much:

> He was patient and understanding of my excesses, such as some of the things I was writing which he thought were too extreme, untenable. (He was right, I'm sure!) Piston tried to help you do what you wanted to do, without trying to impose any style, showing how you could perhaps do something more effectively, which is the basic approach that I've taken ever since.[7]

The 1941 *Passacaglia* for orchestra testifies to the "close relationship" Moevs enjoyed with both Piston and Bach.

Piston introduced Moevs to Boulanger, with whom he later studied for a few years in Paris after serving as a pilot in the Air Force from 1942 to 1947, the last two years of which were spent in Rumania. With Boulanger's suggestions for more trenchant ways to state and develop material, Moevs "made tremendous advances in expressive power."[8]

In 1951 Moevs returned to Harvard to get a master's degree and then spent three years at the American Academy in Rome (1952–1955). In 1953 he married Maria Teresa Marabini, an Italian archaeologist. He taught at Harvard from 1955 to 1964, spending two of those years in Rome on a fellowship (1960–1961; 1963–1964). Randall Thompson helped him find a position at Rutgers University in 1964 after Harvard denied him tenure.

As a student of Boulanger's, Moevs wrote a set of variations on "Christ lag in Todesbanden" which eventually evolved into the 1947 *Piano Sonatina,* and a canon in sixteenth-notes, which became the 1949 *Piano Sonata*'s third-movement scherzo (Ex. 75). In this canon, Moevs first explored a compositional technique with which he eventually would identify himself, and which he called "systematic chromaticism," meaning the exhaustive, ultrachromatic manipulation of a single interval or tiny cell.[9] The idea of composing with a few chosen intervals was related to Boulanger's teachings, though in his mature view, Moevs saw it as principally derived from Debussy; discussing Debussy's *Cello Sonata* for *Perspectives,* Moevs wrote, "The interval has acquired a new self-sufficiency and independence as an entity in its own right. Isolation of the interval from a motivic or contrapuntal context permits its exploitation in more systematic fashion through symmetrical organization, planned alteration, and patterning."[10]

Moevs's *Piano Sonata* won the admiration and praise of Wilfred Mellers, whose description of the work as "Stravinskian" and "neoclassical,"[11] however, was somewhat misleading, as it overlooked the work's highly unique style, not to mention its basically romantic sensibility. Certainly Moevs was very different from contemporary admirers of Stravinsky like Berger, Fine, and Shapero. In fact, his contribution to

Example 75. Robert Moevs, "Canone," *Sonata* for piano (Max Eschig, 1950).

Perspectives' memorial issue on Stravinsky's death stood out in its somewhat disparaging tone.[12] The *Sonata's* toccata-like first movement was perhaps neoclassical in its debt to the modal-chromaticism of Piston and Hindemith, but it was closer yet to Debussy and Liszt. A connection with Liszt was also evident in the slow movement, with its tremendous contrasts, its dramatic flair, and even its Slavic-like exoticism, perhaps also related to the composer's two years in Rumania. The aforementioned canonic scherzo (see Ex. 75) had a coolness that suggested some tie to Carter and boogie-woogie, but, again, a Lisztian flavor came through strongly. The connection with Liszt was affirmed in the finale, a macabre dance, if not an actual "Totentanz," with flashy pyrotechnics and restless modulations climbing upwards by steps.

A similar blend of classical restraint and romantic exuberance was detected in Moevs's other works from the 1950s, such as the *Fantasia sopra un motivo* for piano (1951), the *Fourteen Variations* for orchestra (1952), the *String Quartet* (1957), and *Attis I* for tenor solo, chorus, percussion, and orchestra (1958). This restraint included a fairly conservative harmonic language, a preference for traditional ensembles, and a formal approach as epitomized by the concept of "systematic chromaticism," finally given full expression in the brilliant *String Quartet.* But as with the *Piano Sonata,* the romantic features—the tense chromatics, the instrumental virtuosity, the emotional outbursts abruptly articulated by silence—were at the fore. Such a blend presumably appealed to Leonard Bernstein, who had known Moevs at Harvard, and who gave memorable performances of the *Fourteen Variations.*

Even more memorable was the premiere of *Attis,* based on Catullus's poem about "a sensitive and civilized young man who succumbs to the savage barbarism that surrounds him."[13] Bruce Archibald wrote that its first performance by Richard Burgin and the Boston Symphony was "a particularly overwhelming musical event," one that was covered the following day "on the front page in some newspapers."[14] Another critic commented, "If the audience had been French and the year 1913, [the premiere] would have caused a greater scandal than that of Stravinsky's *Le sacre du printemps.*"[15] Thoughts of *The Rite* were not coincidental: *Attis* was clearly influenced by that work, and perhaps by *Oedipus* as well. A throwback to *The Rite* though it might have been, it was no mere copy; on the contrary, it was thrilling and vibrant on its own terms, and very possibly Moevs's masterpiece. The notoriety of the premiere never earned it the continued popularity it deserved, however; in fact, according to Moevs, it prejudiced a disapproving Harvard administration from awarding him tenure.

Moevs's kind of intellectualized romanticism drew him to Pierre Boulez early on. While in Paris, he obtained copies of the *Flute Sonatine* and the *First Piano Sonata,* and perused the score of the *Second Piano Sonata.* More importantly, he heard, on a program that included Bartók's *Concerto for Orchestra,* Boulez's *Le Soleil,* a work which made the Bartók seem as remote as Haydn. He was astonished at the dry, fragmented texture of the music, which he described as "match sticks" or "straws." These early Boulez works, with their kind of unremitting exploration of tiny cells, may have played a part in the development of Moevs's systematic chromaticism. But not until the 1960s did Moevs actually move into Boulez's orbit.

The first work to do so was the 1961 *Variazioni Sopra una Melodia* (Ex. 76). Its avant-garde features included the omission of barlines and meter signatures; complex beat divisions and fluctuating tempi; passages in which every note had its own dynamic marking; complicated variation form; and a fairly atonal texture, although the endings of each variation suggested some tonal repose. This bold advance surely received some impetus from Boulez's arrival at Harvard in 1960 to deliver the Norton Lectures, and the close friendship between the two composers that ensued; but it also reflected some personal crisis only vaguely alluded to by the composer.[16] Similar avant-garde features characterized the *Concerto Grosso* for piano, percussion and orchestra (1960, revised 1968), the *Musica da Camera* for chamber ensemble (1965), and a *Musica da Camera II* "on three notes by Steve Reich" (1972). The *Concerto Grosso,* in addition, made extensive use of aleatoric techniques, reaching almost complete disintegration by the work's end, save for the barely heard, periodic tolling of a bell every sixty beats, a gesture which was meant to suggest a faint but ineradicable, and, finally, victorious order amidst the surrounding chaos. The work won the 1978 Stockhausen Award.

For its part, the *Musica da Camera,* inspired by ominous passages in Rilke and Henry James,[17] experimented with a variant 12-tone procedure the composer labeled "anti-tonality"; each of its variations used a row of eleven or fewer pitches in which the missing pitch or pitches functioned as a ghostly tonal axis. Boulez himself performed this work in 1971, along with Steve Reich's *Four Organs,* which Moevs found annoyingly loud and redundant. In fact, the Reich work inspired a sequel, *Musica da Camera II,* in which the composer aimed to show what could be done with Reich's three pitches by subjecting them to "systematic chromaticism" and other modernist criteria. As Donal Henahan pointed out, however, the "neo-Webern" characteristics of works like the *Musica da Camera I* and *II* did not obscure the powerful, individual voice of their composer.[18]

An understanding of the power and individuality of these works ultimately would require some consideration of the many sacred works contemporary with them: *Et Nunc Regis*

Example 76. Robert Moevs, *Variazioni Sopra Una Melodia* for viola and cello (Piedmont Music, 1967).

for women's chorus, flute, clarinet, and bass clarinet (1963);
Et Occidentem Illustra for chorus and orchestra (1964); *Ave
Maria* for chorus (1966); and *A Brief Mass* for chorus, organ,
vibraphone, guitar, and double bass (1968). Like Liszt, Moevs
hoped to help rejuvenate the musical traditions of the
Catholic Church. *A Brief Mass,* a setting in English of the
Ordinary, in particular, was meant to demonstrate how the
"new international contemporary style" could serve "the current 'aggiornamento' of the Church,"[19] a subject the composer addressed at some length in an article for *Liturgical
Arts.*[20] He was little heeded; the aleatoric *Ave Maria* (Ex. 77),
dedicated to G. Wallace Woodworth, still awaited a first
performance in the 1990s.

In 1973 Moevs wrote an orchestral piece entitled *Main-
Travelled Roads* after Hamlin Garland's 1891 collection of
stories by the same name. Commissioned by the Wisconsin

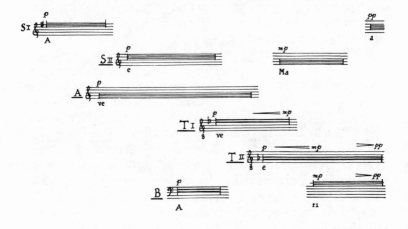

The decision to reproduce the present score as submitted by the composer was
occasioned by the notation: durations are for the most part represented spatially.

Example 77. Robert Moevs, *Ave Maria* (Harvard College, 1971).

American Bicentennial Commission for the Milwaukee Symphony, the work concerned itself less with the regionalism of Garland's stories, many of which were set near the composer's birthplace, than with the author's bleak, guilt-ridden portrayals of good farm people in hopelessly pathetic predicaments. Moevs's deep feelings for 19th-century farm life was evident not only in this work, but in his carefully preserved 19th-century farmhouse, with its dark, Victorian furnishings, in Blackwell's Mills, New Jersey.

As its title suggests, *Main-Travelled Roads* also was meant to reassert the composer's ties to the past, and, indeed, the work in some ways looked back to Moevs's work from the '50s. (Its subtitle, "Symphonic Piece No. 4," suggested, in particular, a continuity with his *Three Symphonic Pieces* from 1955.) Similarly, Moevs began to write piano works that had the Lisztian dazzle and bravura of the *Sonata* and the *Fantasia;* these included *Phoenix* (1971); *Ludi Praeteriti: Games of the Past* for two pianos (1976); and *Una collana musicale* (1977), a collection of thirteen small piano pieces. (The principal interpreter of these piano works was a pianist on the Rutgers faculty, Wanda Maximilien.)

While Moevs's career, consequently, took on the larger movement of adventure and return, so typical of composers born around 1920, this development need not be exaggerated. Moevs's evolution was gradual and personal. The works from the 1960s were not all that different from earlier works: the 1968 *Concerto Grosso,* for example, had much the power and élan of the 1958 *Attis I,* even though the style now included aleatoric and atonal elements. And the music of the 1970s could not be mistaken, very often, for works from the 1950s. This was clearly evident by comparing Moevs's 1974 *String Trio* with his 1957 *String Quartet.* Gone were the echoes of Beethoven and Bartók (as well as Piston: see the *Quartet's* scherzo movement); the music now moved in a rhythmic and harmonic flux, reminding one of Carter, though the content, as ever, was uniquely dramatic. Further, the *Quartet's* conventional four-movement scheme gave way to the *Trio's* large, one-movement design, ending poetically with a slow section. Similarly, Moevs's late piano music was texturally innovative, including some luminous sonorities produced by using the inside of the piano.

In short, throughout his career, Moevs was consistently daring, writing music of strong textural imagination, instrumental brilliance, and rhythmic power. Audiences readily appreciated this and responded well to his work. Indeed, he was one of the most accessible composers of his kind.

The brilliant imagination and soaring fantasy of Karl Kohn represented a high point in American music of the late 20th century. Indeed, his elegant, evocative handling of the most advanced musical styles, along with his stylish incorporation of more traditional idioms, suggested something of an American equivalent to his Italian contemporary, Luciano Berio (although Kohn's career did not include any dada-like phase). Like Berio, too, his music enjoyed expert performances by his wife, pianist Margaret Kohn, and the patronage of notable virtuosi, like French horn player, Barry Tuckwell. But his music was little known outside southern California, his home for most of his adult life, where he taught at Pomona College and directed Los Angeles's Monday Evening Concerts. Various factors conspired to create this regrettable situation: the spotty dissemination of his scores; the scarcity of recordings; the composer's penchant for unusual instrumental combinations; and the considerable difficulties of the music, as Pauline Oliveros emphasized in a sympathetic review of one such work,[21] difficulties which seemed to require Kohn's own talents as conductor and pianist. Consequently, while many works in his prolific catalog were worthy of detailed study, published material on the composer was particularly sketchy. This discussion only outlines the composer's career, paying special attention to his remarkable artistic development.

Kohn was born on August 1, 1926, in Vienna, and grew up in the small suburban community of St. Veit. For a while he attended school in nearby Hietzing, until the Anschluss forced the relocation of Jewish students into all-Jewish schools. Both his father, a textile salesman and a violinist, and his mother, a pianist, encouraged his piano lessons with Alice Löwinger-Feldstein, whom Kohn described as "strict, kind, loving but aloof, and awe-inspiring . . . my first and most important teacher."[22] He soon was able to play a Haydn piano concerto with an amateur orchestra comprised of Jewish war veterans (Jüdische Frontkämpfer), including his father. For this performance, he used the "sanitized" name, subsequently discarded, of Karl Georg (Georg being his middle name). Other memorable concerts of the Jüdische Frontkämpfer included guest appearances by the violinist Bronislaw Hubermann and the composer Jaromir Weinberger, who conducted his *Schvanda, the bagpiper.*

As the political situation grew more threatening, the Kohns made plans to leave, and received their American visas just prior to deportation to Poland. Their extended family on both sides was less fortunate: most were murdered by the Nazis. Löwinger-Feldstein, on the verge of getting to England, took her own life after war with Poland broke out and the British closed their borders. Kohn later reflected, "The most important influence on my early years was at the age of thirteen to survive imminent destruction in Nazi-occupied Vienna by being able to immigrate to the United States and be transplanted into the New World at the end of 1939."[23]

Kohn's family settled, symbolically enough, in Goshen, New York, and later in nearby Middletown. While still in high school (1940–1944), he attended the New York College of Music, where he studied piano with Carl V. Werschinger and conducting with Julius Prüwer. After one semester at Harvard (1944–1945), he served in the Army for two years as a bandmaster; by this time, he had achieved some skill playing percussion, oboe, bassoon, and French horn. Kohn returned to Harvard where he continued his studies with Piston, Fine, Thompson, and Ballantine, graduating with a BA, summa cum laude, in 1950. He subsequently taught at Pomona College and Claremont Graduate School in Claremont, California, with only a few years in absentia, including 1954–1955 at Harvard for the master's degree; 1955–1956 in Finland; 1961–1962 in Holland; and 1968–1969 in London.

Of his earliest music, Kohn commented, "The music I wrote before the middle 50's reflects my Harvard training and an orientation toward American neo-classicism."[24] This ostensibly included the composer's 1952 *Fanfare* for brass and percussion, his first published work, and certainly his 1955 *Five Pieces* for piano, one of his better-known early compositions. The influence of Piston in particular was felt in a passage like the following from the fifth Piece (Ex. 78), with

Example 78. Karl Kohn, *Five Pieces* for piano, V (Carl Fischer, 1965).

its sparse two-part writing, its imitative counterpoint, its melodic sweep, and its tonal fluctuations through E, E♭, and C#, full of subtle harmonic ambiguities. The shift to E♭ might recall Bernstein, too, and, indeed, Kohn's vague phrase, "American neoclassicism," nicely pointed to the fact that in these early works, there were resemblances to a number of composers who shared Kohn's "Harvard training," for example Berger, Fine, Binkerd, and Middleton. Even at this stage, Kohn's impulse was to accommodate a large variety of styles and sensibilities, rather than to choose among them.

This early orientation also was mentioned by the composer in program notes to his *Castles and Kings* (originally for four-hands, later orchestrated), written in 1958, that is, after the "the middle '50s," perhaps, but unmistakably in this same tradition of "American neoclassicism." Kohn remarked, in fact, that the work ". . . was motivated by my neo-classical training at Harvard where I studied with such men as Walter Piston, Irving Fine, and Randall Thompson."[25] The work's second movement, "Jugglers," in its bright textures and polytonal harmonies, was like the Piston of *The Incredible Flutist,* while the first movement, "The Knights and Ladies Enter," in its elegant diatonicism, was like the Fine of the *Partita.* Again, resemblances to early Bernstein were also detectable. As for Randall Thompson, his influence was felt more clearly in Kohn's choral music from this period, including *A Latin Fable* for men's voices (1956), *Three Descants from Ecclesiastes* for mixed voices and brass (1957), and *Three Goliard Songs* for men's voices a cappella (1958), this last also reminiscent, at times, of Piston's *Carnival Song.*

Kohn's kind of medievalism, in works like *Castles and Kings* and *Three Goliard Songs,* already posed a distinction from the earlier Harvard neoclassicists. The latter tended to use early music motifs in an abstract, modernized way, along the lines of, above all, Hindemith. Kohn's music was more visceral, picturesque and romantic.

Another difference was Kohn's assimilation of features from Bartók. Indeed, he had written, in 1950, his senior honors thesis on *Tonal Dodecaphony in Bartók: A Study of Five Concertos.* The very opening of the *Five Pieces* was highly Bartókian in its changing meters, its chromatic melody, and its triadic harmonies enriched with dissonances lurking in the bass (Ex. 79).

The combined influences of Piston and Bartók were typical enough for young Harvard composers of the early 1950s, as discussed in chapter 11. And the further nexus of Piston-Bartók-medievalism was also found in a few Harvard contemporaries, like Allen Sapp. Like all these composers, Kohn naturally gravitated toward the 12-tone method by the mid-'50s. But the manner in which this happened was atypical.

Kohn has written that it was while he was in Helsinki for

Example 79. Karl Kohn, *Five Pieces* for piano, I (Carl Fischer, 1965).

the academic year 1955–56 that the proximity of Vienna "aroused an intensive involvement with my at least geographically Viennese ancestry: atonality, twelve-tone procedures, and the current developments in multi-serialism evolved from that heritage."[26] It was this interest in "multi-serialism," meaning Boulez, Stockhausen, and others, that set Kohn apart from fellow Harvardians, who adopted the 12-tone method in more traditional ways (even Moevs, who came close to the European avant-garde, as we have seen, and who had some real affinities to Kohn, remained closer to the more conservative Boulez of the late '40s). The most dramatic result of all this was a work from 1959, *Two Short Pieces* for clarinet and piano, in which pitch, rhythm, duration, dynamics, and attack were all organized serially.

While in some respects this development proved ephemeral, it nonetheless had lasting consequences. Kohn's music after this time became highly elaborate rhythmically: syncopations, changing meters, irregular divisions of beats, independence of parts, and fluctuations in tempo were now—for the most part—the norm (see ahead to Ex. 81). The rhythmic complexities were perhaps not as formidable as Boulez, but not far behind, and certainly comparable to the Carter of the *Second Quartet*. Similarly, Kohn's melodic and harmonic writing, whether 12-tone or not, became richly chromatic. Most striking, perhaps, was the emergence of novel forms in which little bits of material created a whirl of brilliant colors; Kohn himself provided an apt metaphor for his forms by calling his 1964 string quartet *Kaleidoscope*. In time, other titles that pointed to such collage-like constructions included the 1966 *Episodes* for piano and orchestra, the 1973 *Bits and Pieces* for piano, and from the same year, *Centone* for orchestra, "centone" meaning "patchwork quilt" in Italian. In a review of the composer's 1961 *Serenade*, Lawrence Morton succinctly noted, "The principal formal device is not development but rather the juxtaposition of related musical ideas."[27] All this was related to new trends in European music.

Kohn, however, was not about to renounce the bigger performing and listening public to which his earlier works had been addressed, and in 1960 he imagined that he would solve this dilemma by continuing to write in both a neoclassical and a serial style, each one meeting different needs. An alternative presented itself in the same year with the composition of the *First Rhapsody* for piano, in which the composer used traditional patterns and figures within an athematic and ultrachromatic context. Looking back to this work in 1979, Kohn wrote, "This conscious but spontaneous attempt to integrate the past with the present proved to be a turning point and has played a dominant role in my compositional approach for nearly the last two decades."

At first, the balance was precarious, even somewhat contrived, as if the composer felt too keenly his historical mission as a serial classicist. In the *Serenade* for piano and wind quintet from 1961, Boulezian mannerisms rubbed shoulders with unisons, repeated notes, even triads. Similarly, triads rounded off Kohn's 1961 choral work, *Sensus spei,* which, for the most part, explored a new kind of choral style involving long-sustained sounds, somewhat like Ligeti, punctuated by single, isolated notes in the accompaniment. In yet another work from 1961, *5 Bagatelles* for piano, the result was closer to Schoenberg. The 1962 *Concerto mutabile* for piano and chamber ensemble, which made use of aleatoric techniques, represented a climax in Kohn's involvement with the international avant-garde, while in the 1963 *Little Suite* for woodwind quintet, which had moments reminiscent of Piston and Fine, neoclassical elements dominated. All these works were impressive and eloquent (they furthermore became Kohn's best known works), but the composer's really mature voice had yet to emerge.

This happened in the later '60s, with works like *Introductions and Parodies* for piano and chamber ensemble (1967) and *Impromptus* for eight winds (1969). The same historical mission—reconciling the old and the new—was strongly felt here, too, but it was carried off with greater ease, flexibility, and coherence. The general context of such works remained complex and daring, but the material itself had clearer, more traditional reverberations. This was accomplished in two principal ways: first, by using motives that were traditionally characteristic of the instruments at hand, for example, hunting calls for the French horns, glissandi for the trombones, chords for the harp, and so forth (this already was observed by Morton in a review of Kohn's 1962 *Capriccios* for flute, clarinet, cello, harp, and piano[28]); and second, by using familiar materials, such as tonal and modal bits, and triadic harmonies, in a more pervasive and integrated fashion. (Again, Ex. 81 provides an illustration of both these features.) Musicologist Gustave Reese's observation, "When, in his [Kohn's] music, he makes use of recent and experimental techniques, it nevertheless has logic and an inner quality that places it within the continuous flow of important music of the past,"[29] was particularly descriptive of those works written after 1965.

The use of familiar materials encouraged Kohn even to quote fragments from other composers: Mendelssohn in the *Introductions* and Stravinsky in the *Impromptus,* to be followed by Mahler and Berg in *Reflections* (1970); Liszt in the *Second Rhapsody* (1971); Tufts, Billings, Hopkinson, and the Stern-hold-Hopkins Psalter in *Innocent Psaltery* (1975); Schumann in *Prophet Bird I* (1976) and *II* (1980); and Giuliani, Carcassi, Ponce, and Villa-Lobos in *Recreations II* (1980). At the same time, he began to quote himself: *Episodes* in the *Introductions* and *Waldmusik* (1979); *Encounters II* and *III* and *Souvenirs* in the *Trio* for horn, violin, and piano (1972); *Encounters I* in *Paronym I* (1974); *Encounters V* in *Paronym II* (1978); and *Prophet Bird I* in *Prophet Bird II* (1980). Many other such quotations could likely be found within the dense fabric of Kohn's music. But in spite of the pervasiveness of such quotations, they were never particularly prominent (on the contrary, they were often subtly hidden); nor were they used for the purpose of pastiche: they bubbled up to the surface of the composer's music naturally, effortlessly, even ironically— somewhat analogous to quotation in James Joyce and T. S. Eliot.

In statements made in 1973, 1979, and 1980, Kohn made it clear that his interest in a wide array of past materials was motivated by the fact that the contemporary world was saturated with a vast store of musics, "both Western and global," thanks to the "massive publication of printed music," and even more decisively, to the "spectacular development of sound recordings and radio." At various times Kohn likened this "gluttonous exposure to music" to a warehouse, a botanical garden, a supermarket. While such developments could be praised "for making the cultural riches of the past and present accessible with a previously inconceivable boun-tifulness," they needed "to be recognized also for engendering different ways of perception and splintered attentiveness, and for upsetting the conventional, time-honored notions of tradition and heritage." The composer could not imagine the situation reversing itself ("except by cataclysmic changes perhaps too dreadful to contemplate") and concluded: "At least for the foreseeable future, therefore, the process of selective retrieval, recycling and reshaping of musical materials that come from an enormous and inexhaustive international reservoir, and its new implications for a music resonant with the spirit of our time, appears as the most natural and likely basis for our art."

Although Kohn regarded this situation as highly aberrant, he recognized that it was not altogether unique, citing Mendelssohn's preoccupation with Bach as an early precedent. Significantly, Kohn quoted Mendelssohn in the 1967 *Introductions,* and subsequently quoted Stravinsky's *Octet* (Ex. 80a), another predecessor of his kind of historical sensibility, in the 1969 *Impromptus* (Ex. 80b); this work was composed, furthermore, for the same combination of eight instruments. The connection to Stravinsky was felt in all of Kohn's works from the late '60s in general, including the 1968 *Recreations* for piano four-hands. Such connections were not limited to Stravinsky's "neoclassical" period. Like the opening pages of

Example 80a. Igor Stravinsky, *Octet,* I (Boosey & Hawkes, 1947).

Example 80b. Karl Kohn, *Impromptus* for eight winds (Carl Fischer, 1972).

The Rite, there were motives suggesting nature, especially bird and animal sounds; like the *Octet,* there were fragments reminiscent of the 18th century; and like *Agon,* there was material redolent of earlier, pre-18th-century music.

With the 1970 *Reflections* and the 1971 *Second Rhapsody,*

subtitled "Hungarian," in reference to Liszt (who was duly parodied), Kohn embarked on yet a new, more romantic phase. In addition to all the aforementioned features (from Piston and Bartók to medieval music to Boulez and Schoenberg to Stravinsky) that steadily were accumulating, there was now a lushness, sensuousness, and virtuosity related to the 19th century. This was true, too, of the 1972 *Trio* for horn, violin, and piano (one of the few outstanding examples for this ensemble since Brahms); the 1973 *Centone* for orchestra; the 1974 *Paronyms I* for flute and piano (in which the flutist was required to play piccolo and bass flute in addition to the standard flute); the 1976 *Prophet Bird* for flute, clarinet, bassoon, horn, bass trombone, percussion (vibraphone, marimba, and triangle), harp, violin, viola, and cello; and the 1977 *Piano Rhapsody No. 3.* Some works, like the delightful *Brass Quintet* from 1976, were more in the Stravinskian idiom of the late '60s, and one work, *Time Irretrievable,* an artistic exercise in nostalgia, even reverted to a more conservative style. But *Prophet Bird* was more emblematic of the mature Kohn, as evident from the continued production of such similar works as the 1980 *Prophet Bird II,* the 1983 *Capriccios II,* and the 1984 *San Gabriel Set.*

While this latest phase was surely related to the contemporary vogue for a "new romanticism," such a label could not account for the variety of Kohn's stylistic references, nor for the very content of his music. For Kohn avoided the rich, bold colors of romanticism for something cooler, more dissociated and detached, more full of nuance, shadings, mystery. Two works for two pianos, the 1981 *Shadow Play* and the 1983 *Dream Pieces,* suggested as much by their titles, as did the kind of art nouveau designs that his daughter Susanna created for their covers. Often, as in the following excerpt from *Prophet Bird* (Ex. 81), Kohn's exquisite, shimmering music reminded one, above all, of Debussy and the French symbolist poets. Indeed, the label symbolist seemed fairly appropriate; Kohn often had the subtlety and dreaminess of Baudelaire or Mallarmé. Such music—mythic, sensuous, alive to delicate fluctuations of sounds—was among the most poetic of its time.

While Moevs and Kohn stood somewhat peripheral to *Perspectives,* Claudio Spies and Peter Westergaard were

Example 81. Karl Kohn, *The Prophet Bird* for chamber ensemble, II.

central to it. Certainly Spies's articles on late Stravinsky,[30] and those by Westergaard on Webern,[31] helped set *Perspectives'* early tone. Significantly, both Westergaard and Spies eventually joined the music faculty at Princeton, which had close ties with the journal.

Spies was born on March 26, 1925, in Santiago, Chile, to German-Jewish parents. At age seventeen, he left for Boston. He studied with Boulanger and Shapero before entering Harvard, where he worked with Piston, Fine, and Hindemith (1947–1954). He remained at Harvard to teach there (1953–1957) and subsequently held positions at Vassar (1957–1958), Swarthmore (1958–1970), and finally Princeton (since 1970). The composer's Jewish, German, Spanish, and American backgrounds gave his music, and himself, a thoroughly cosmopolitan profile. Fluent in English, Spanish, German, and Italian, he set texts in all these languages, as well as in Hebrew and Latin.

Like Kohn's, Spies's early music, such as the *Three Intermezzi* for piano (1950–1954), was shaped, aside from the obvious influence of Brahms, by American neoclassicism. There was a closeness to Berger in its breezy allusions to popular music (Ex. 82), to Fine in its delicate harmonies, and to Shapero in its classical references. Immediately distinctive was the composer's ultrarefinement, honed down to the point of preciosity. There was also a personal, faintly Spanish flavor in the second "Intermezzo"'s lush harmonies and the third "Intermezzo"'s dancelike rhythms. Another work, *Il cantico di frate sole* (1959) to words by St. Francis, suggested, too, that Spies's Chilean background predisposed him more than the aforementioned composers to the devout Catholicism of Boulanger, and that of his close friend, Paul Des Marais.

Example 82. Claudio Spies, *Three Intermezzi*, I (Elkan-Vogel, 1966).

In the 1960s, Spies, again like Kohn, moved still closer to Stravinsky, but not to the spirit of the *Octet,* rather to the surface details of *Movements.* Unusual in his expert knowledge of Stravinsky's most recent scores, Spies was, not surprisingly, equally unusual in the extent to which late Stravinsky influenced his style. In the music for which he was best known—the 1962 *Tempi* for fourteen instruments, the 1963 *Impromptu* for piano, and the 1965 *Viopiacem* for viola and piano—one felt the impact of late Stravinsky in their subtly shifting meters of 6/8, 5/16, 4/8, and 9/16; their barlines between the staves; their crisp grace notes and staccatos; their elegant harmonies; and, quite generally, in their austere restraint. Even Spies's catalog resembled late Stravinsky: there were a series of canons (7 *Canons,* 1959; *Canon* for 4 flutes, 1960; *Canon* for violas, 1961); texted works often supported by intriguing chamber ensembles; and the occasional piece to honor a birthday or mourn a death.[32]

Also related to Stravinsky was Spies's unorthodox handling of the 12-tone method, first used in his 1959 5 *Psalms* for chorus. His use of the technique in *Tempi* and *Viopiacem* was examined in some detail by Paul Lansky.[33] The little *Impromptu* for piano (Ex. 83) provides a good introduction to such usage, for though it is only two pages long, it contains many of the features noted by Lansky in the larger works.

The *Impromptu*'s 12-tone row (D^b-B^b-E^b-C-$F^\#$-A-E-G-D-F-B-A^b) was stated fairly straightforwardly in the work's first measure (and last three measures), but for the most part, the use of the 12-tone method was considerably free. There were five principal liberties taken: notes were omitted from the row (see mm. 11–12, R^9); rows were elided (see m. 20, where D belongs to both P^2 and P^4); rows were reordered (see m. 16, where pitches 7 and 8 of I^2 are reversed); rows were sustained only in part (see mm. 2–4, P^0); and finally, rows were begun at internal points (see m. 18, which begins with pitch 5 of I^4). These liberties, especially the last, were complicated by the fact that the row itself generated three row-forms (R^7, I^6, and RI^2) that, starting from different internal points, comprised the same row.

More perceptible than these 12-tone details, however, was the work's rarified atmosphere, which was due, in part, to its delicate harmonic shadings. Just in the opening measure was

Example 83. Claudio Spies, *Impromptu* for piano (Elkan-Vogel, 1964). Used by permission.

found: pitches 1 and 2 suggesting a G♭ major triad; 3-4-5 outlining a diminished triad, with 5 affirming G♭ major, at least enharmonically; 6 turning major to minor; 7 and 8 filling out, again enharmonically, a dominant seventh chord; 9 and 10, ambiguous at first, with 11 and 12 confirming 10 as an anticipation of V⁷ in G♭, the apparent tonal center, after all. (The piece—subtitled "cradle music"—concluded with a variation of this dominant seventh harmony, suggesting, in the tradition of Schumann's *Kinderscenen,* the child falling asleep.) There was an exquisiteness in all these slippery turns, as well as a sort of Wagnerian yearning. The connection with Wagner was especially suggested by Spies's penchant for dominant chords with added ninths, elevenths, and thirteenths, for example: the C# dominant seventh at measure four (where placed over a tonic pedal as it is, it recalled the Rhinemaidens); more Debussian, the E^7 harmonies found in measures seven and eight; and another C# dominant seventh, with an added ninth, at measure ten, the melodic Bb functioning as a suspension. More Brahmsian than Wagnerian was the sequence of falling fifths outlined in measure eighteen's uppermost "voice" (D-G, C#-Gb), one of those moments referred to by Lansky in which the primary concern was registral voice-leading (for another example, see mm. 1–3, and the chromatic ascent in the soprano voice from Eb to G). The *Impromptu*'s refined harmonic palette reminded one, too, of Fine, who doubtless would have appreciated the notion of writing such highly sophisticated "cradle music."

In later years, Spies's work was mostly for voice. This included *Three Songs on Poems by May Swenson* for voice and piano (1969); *7 Enzensberger Lieder* for baritone, clarinet, horn cello, and percussion (1972); *Shirim Le Hathunatham* (texts by Yehuda Halevi) for soprano, flute, clarinet, violin, cello, and piano (1975); *Five Sonnet-Settings* (texts by Shakespeare) for vocal quartet and piano (1977); *Rilke: Rühmen* for soprano, clarinet, trumpet, and piano (1981); and *Tagyr* (texts by Gaspar Núñez de Arce and Robert Herrick) for baritone, flute, clarinet, bassoon, horn, and viola (1983).

The Swenson settings were in Spies's '60s-styled 12-tone idiom: refined, delicate, with considerable tonal inflection. As with the *Impromptu,* this work continued along the lines of Fine, here not only musically, but in its psychological and picturesque exploration of the animal world as suggested by its texts. The tradition of Fine was felt as late as the *Sonnet-Settings,* which the composer discussed in the context of Brahms, but which seemed related as well to the neo-Renaissance style of Fine's Ben Jonson settings. Certainly madrigal-like were the tortured dissonances of a line like, "Weary with toil, I haste me to my bed." Such dark and passionate reflections on these great poems were persuasive, making the *Sonnet-Settings* one of Spies's most compelling works.

By this time, Spies had begun to incorporate aspects from Babbitt as well. One can approximately date this development to the 1972 *Enzensberger-Lieder*, written shortly after Spies joined Babbitt on the Princeton faculty, and dedicated, in fact, to Babbitt and his wife. The work itself was somewhat conservative in tone, but its heightened romanticism looked ahead to the kind of Babbitt-like theatricality found in *Shirim Le Hathunatham*, the *Rilke: Rühmen*, and even the *Sonnet Settings*. Although *Shirim* was clearly related to *Pierrot* and *Marteau*, it had neither Schoenberg's irony nor Boulez's detachment: it was thoroughly impassioned, sometimes even melodramatic (Ex. 84). The jittery instrumental accompaniments of such works in particular owed some debt to Babbitt. This influence well may have been reciprocal: Babbitt's 1981 *The Head of the Bed* was written for an instrumental ensemble almost identical to that used in *Shirim*.

Concurrently, Spies came to repudiate Boulanger, Piston,

Example 84. Claudio Spies, *Shirim Le Hathunatham* for soprano and chamber ensemble.

and Copland for what he alleged was a condescending attitude toward Schoenberg motivated in part by anti-German and possibly anti-Semitic sentiment. He retained fond memories, however, of Fine and Shapero, whose *Symphony for Classical Orchestra* he considered to be even better than Stravinsky's *Symphony in C*.[34] His music, too, retained its highly polished elegance; one dream was to write an opera about that aristocratic anti-fascist, Raoul Wallenberg.

Peter Westergaard was born in Champaign, Illinois, on May 28, 1931. Soon after, his father accepted a position at Harvard's School of Engineering, and the family moved to Belmont, not far from Piston's home. As a boy, Peter studied flute and sang in the choir of Christ Church in Cambridge.[35] By age twelve he was composing music.[36]

Westergaard pursued his music studies at Harvard partly because of Piston's presence there. He performed and admired the *Flute Sonata,* which he had studied with its dedicatee, Boston Symphony flutist Georges Laurent. Laurent, who preferred Piston's *Sonata* to Hindemith's, taught him to appreciate the music's rhythmic sinuousness; the common notion of Piston's rhythms as inflexible or motoric consequently never took hold. Westergaard admitted that some works, such as the *Prelude and Allegro* for organ and strings, made stylish use of a more straightforward "back-to-Bach" idiom, but the 1946 *Divertimento* confirmed his preference for the more sinuous Piston.

As a teacher, Piston excelled at "imagining what the student was trying to get at," a trait Piston himself had admired in Boulanger, as Westergaard reported in his *Perspectives* interview. Questions like, "Do you really want to make that note that long?", helped Westergaard find the clear, crystalline textures characteristic of his mature style.

After graduating from Harvard in 1953, Westergaard spent time in Europe on a Paine Traveling Fellowship, studying with Milhaud and Messiaen. The former reaffirmed a Pistonian sense of clarity. During these years Westergaard wrote a *Symphonic Movement* for orchestra, an attractive work in the American neoclassical tradition, resembling, somewhat, the music of such Harvard contemporaries as Kohn and Spies. Other works reflected, too, Westergaard's admiration for

Arthur Berger, who, in his view, had brought Piston's elegance to a greater refinement.

After meeting Edward Cone in Salzburg, Westergaard decided that graduate work with Sessions and Babbitt at Princeton would be more intellectually stimulating than staying at Harvard. Harvard, he felt, suffered from the "Harvard gentleman problem," the attitude (derived, he believed, from English universities) that no gentleman should admit a serious interest in teaching or composition. Westergaard felt that Piston himself embodied a certain ambivalence in this regard; while undoubtedly a serious composer and musician, Piston seemed to take his teaching responsibilities rather lightly, for example, periodically canceling class because of "a half-inch of snow."

Piston, along with Allen Sapp and Otto Gombosi, supported Westergaard's decision to go to Princeton. Like Sapp, Piston thought Babbitt, "a very smart man." "His one worry," remembered Westergaard, "was that I might go the way of so many of Sessions' students." To help explain what he meant by this, Piston flipped through his own *Orchestration* drawings to the bass tuba and the smaller Wagner tuba looking, in Westergaard's words, "reverently upward." "You see," said Piston, pointing at the bass tuba, "there's Roger," and then pointing to the Wagner tuba, said, "and there's you. That's what I'd be worried about."

Unlike Spies, Boykan, and Harbison, who similarly left a Harvard orbit for a Princeton one, Westergaard did not cite Harvard's antipathy toward Schoenberg and Webern as a reason. In fact, as an undergraduate, he had written an honors thesis on Schoenberg and was delighted and surprised to discover that Piston was interested in and informed about the still little-known Webern. (Piston's interest in Webern actually dated back to the 1930s, and possibly earlier.) Furthermore, Westergaard detected in Piston's own work a debt to 12-tone music, not only in the 12-tone samplings of the early '40s, but quite generally, even in as early a work as the 1930 *Flute Sonata*. As he perceived it, Harvard's hostility toward Wagner, Bruckner, and Schoenberg emanated principally from A. Tillman Merritt and Randall Thompson.

Westergaard graduated with a Princeton MFA in 1956. As it turned out, Sessions proved disappointingly preoccupied, but Babbitt was a revelation. From 1956 to 1958 he studied abroad with Fortner. He subsequently taught at the Staatliche Hochshule, Freiburg (1957), Columbia (1958–1966), Amherst (1967–1968), and, finally Princeton (since 1968).

In his mature work, certainly by the time of the 1963 *Variations for Six Players,* admired by George Crumb in a review for *Perspectives,*[37] Westergaard was associated, above all, with Webern; indeed, he reflected the sort of direct response to Webern that Spies did to late Stravinsky. He appeared removed from the complexities of the intervening "neo-Webern" serialists, arguing, like his exact contemporary Martin Boykan, against any serial or protoserial interpretation of Webern's rhythms.[38] His closeness to Webern was unmistakable, as in the opening page of his chamber opera for two singers, *Mr. and Mrs. Discobbolos* (to a nonsense poem by Edward Lear), his best-known work (Ex. 85). At times, Westergaard also went beyond style to approximate Webern's kind of expressivity, as in the little piano piece, *Alonso's Grief,* written for Roger Sessions.[39]

Westergaard's use of the 12-tone method was at once so individual and so systematic as to practically constitute a new method. This method involved the free play of a limited number of hexachords rather than the use of a wide range of row transpositions and transformations. Consider, for example, the opening of *Mr. and Mrs. Discobbolos* (see Ex. 85). Measures 1–8 put forth the row, which happens to be combinatorial: F-G-$F^{\#}$-A-$G^{\#}$-$A^{\#}$-$C^{\#}$-B-$D^{\#}$-C-E-D. Very neatly, measures 1–4 comprise the first hexachord; 5–8 the second hexachord; 9–10 the retrograde of the first hexachord; and 11–12 the retrograde of the second hexachord. Similarly, the voice parts enter with the first hexachord ("Mr. and Mrs. Discobbolos"), followed by the second ("Climbed to the top of a wall"), accompanied all the while by combinatorial versions of the hexachords (P^7: 1–6, 7–12). Beginning with the next phrase, "And they sat to watch the sunset sky," the work continues to use the hexachords, but with utter freedom as to their ordering, sometimes even serving, apparently, tonal references and traditional harmonies, although the composer claimed to be an atonalist.[40] The fact that the hexachords were used so straightforwardly, and that, furthermore, each hexachord unfolded within its own narrow

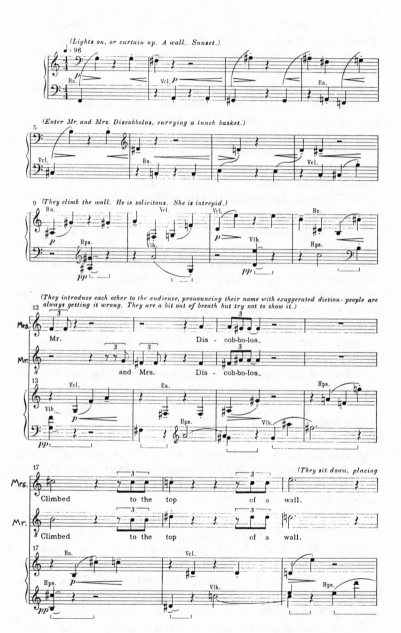

Example 85. Peter Westergaard, *Mr. and Mrs. Discobbolos* (Continuo Music, 1968).

range of the fourth, made Westergaard's procedures thoroughly perceptible. As George Crumb noted, "Structure in Westergaard's music is something aurally tangible rather than an abstraction whose relationships must be isolated by close analysis."[41]

The real novelty of *Mr. and Mrs. Discobbolos* was in using such Webernesque traits as the 12-tone method, unusual instrumental combinations, and widely-spaced vocal lines to create a little comic gem. The aforementioned passage, with its simple rhythms put forth by the voices in unison with bassoon and cello, established the basic mood: mock-innocence. Similarly ironic was the silly duet that Mr. and Mrs. Discobbolos sing at the end of Part I; here, the singsong repetitions and consonant intervals looked back to a sort of Irving Fine playfulness (indeed, the work was a successor to Fine's Lewis Carroll settings). But there were new sounds and textures too, even haunting ones to express the Discobbolos's fear of isolation and death. Such expressive flexibility turned Lear's nonsense poetry into a fashionable exploration of the absurd, and a poignant allegory with almost Beckett-like resonance.

Aside from *Mr. and Mrs. Discobbolos* (the score to which Westergaard sent Piston, who found it amusing), Westergaard was known principally as a teacher and as the author of a widely-used theory text (*An Introduction to Tonal Theory,* 1975, W. W. Norton) which combined Fuxian and Schenkerian features. His musical output was quite small; he told Margaret Fairbanks that compositions were like children, and that one should not have too many of either. He spent close to twenty years setting *The Tempest* to music, which was scheduled for a June, 1992 premiere by the Opera Festival of New Jersey.

Another composer associated with the early *Perspectives* was John MacIvor Perkins, who contributed to that journal an article about the limitations and potentialities of conventional rhythmic notation,[42] as well as discussions of Berger[43] and Dallapiccola,[44] both former teachers. Perkins, born on August 2, 1935, learned academic habits in St. Louis under John Kessler, and unlearned them at Harvard under Piston, Spies, and Des Marais.[45] His college works had a neoclassical cast;

this included a 1958 opera, *Divertimento* (libretto by Wayne Shirley), which reminded Neal Zaslaw, a classmate and future Mozart authority, of *Così fan tutte*. After graduating from Harvard in 1958, Perkins continued his studies abroad with Boulanger in Paris, Rubbra and Gerhard in London, and most importantly, as far as the composer was concerned, Dallapiccola in Rome. On returning to the States, he did graduate work at Brandeis, where he worked with Berger, Shapero, and Fine. By this time he had adapted the 12-tone method for his own purposes. The 1962 *Variations* for flute, clarinet, trumpet, piano, and percussion, for instance, made use of chromatic, unordered hexachords, according to Spies in a harsh review of his former student's work.[46] This usage naturally suggests a kinship with Westergaard.

Caprice for piano (1963) and *Music for Thirteen Players* (1964), both written at the University of Chicago where Perkins taught from 1962 to 1964, were probably the composer's best-known works. The youngest composer in this chapter, Perkins, like others closer in age, responded in such music more directly to the European avant-garde (about which many of the more senior musicians associated with the early *Perspectives* had ambivalent feelings, to say the least). *Caprice,* for instance, came remarkably close to Boulez's early works, and its fugal episode had some of the ingenuity of a comparable section found in the last movement of Boulez's *Second Sonata*. Indeed, admirers of early Boulez were likely to find *Caprice* altogether admirable. At the same time, the work's rhythmic vigor, bright textures, whimsical humor, and occasional harmonic stasis betokened an American identity and a continuity with the music of Carter and Berger, placing it, after all, in the tradition of American neoclassicism.

In *Music for 13 Instruments,* another respectable effort in the avant-garde idiom, the connection was perhaps more with Stockhausen, especially *Kontra-Punkte*. But again, the light, jazzy use of the percussion battery and the warm, nostalgic harmonies for the strings helped to distinguish it.

Perkins returned to Harvard to teach there from 1965 to 1970, after which he joined the faculty at Washington University in his native city. In a 1967 interview he expressed deep concern over the dwindling audience for new music, the contemporary obsession with originality, and the dizzying array of artistic alternatives.[47] One wonders what choices Perkins proceeded to make: his small output after 1967, including a 1980 stage work, *Andrea de Sarto*, was virtually unknown.

The composers discussed in this chapter all shared an interest in and sympathy for many of the new trends and styles that prompted the creation of *Perspectives of New Music* in 1962. They made important contributions to its early growth, and their own music was reviewed within its pages. They also shared a similar background in that their formative years at Harvard had nurtured a neoclassical sensibility under Piston's guidance. Consequently, connections with Stravinsky, Bartók, and older Americans like Berger, Fine, and even Piston himself, were present alongside ideas suggested by Webern, Boulez, and Babbitt. The resultant dialectic was rather characteristic of mainstream compositional trends in America of the 1960s. At the same time, it was worth noting the uniqueness of these five composers, and the shared experiences that contributed to their varied achievements.

Notes

1. Taylor, "Walter Piston for his Seventieth Birthday," *Perspectives of New Music* 2 (1964), pp. 102–114.
2. Westergaard, "Conversation with Walter Piston," *Perspectives of New Music* 7 (1968), pp. 3–17.
3. Moevs, personal letter, January 12, 1985.
4. Moevs, personal interview, January 5, 1985.
5. James Boros, "A Conversation with Robert Moevs," *Perspectives of New Music,* Vol. 28, No. 1 (Winter 1990), p. 325.
6. Boros, p. 326.
7. Boros, p. 326.
8. Boros, pp. 327–328.
9. For an extended discussion, see James Boros, "The Systematic Chromaticism of Robert Moevs," *Perspectives of New Music,* Vol. 28, No. 1 (Winter 1990), pp. 294–323. This article also contains a catalog and discography.
10. Moevs, "Intervallic Procedures in Debussy: Serenade from the Sonata for Cello and Piston, 1915," *Perspectives of New Music* 8/1 (1969), p. 82.

11. Mellers, *Music in a New Found Land*, p. 222. Other critics also referred to Moevs as "neoclassical," including Bruce Archibald, "Composers of Importance Today: Robert Moevs," *Musical Newsletter* 2/1 (April 1971), p. 21.
12. Moevs, "Mannerism and Stylistic Consistency in Stravinsky," *Perspectives of New Music* 9/2 (1971), pp. 92–103.
13. Moevs, Boston Symphony Program Notes, February 12, 1960.
14. Archibald, p. 20.
15. Harold Rogers, quoted in Ewen, *American Composers* (New York: G. P. Putnam's, 1982), p. 492.
16. Moevs, liner notes to a recording of the *Variazioni*, CRI 223.
17. The *Musica* was prefaced by the following quote from Rilke: ". . . das ungewisse Licht von Nachtmittagen in denen man sich fürchtete als Kind," though in conversation with Ewen, p. 463, as well as myself, Moevs mentioned in this regard a similarly ominous setting in James's *Turn of the Screw*.
18. Henahan, "Review of Records," *Musical Quarterly* 54 (1968), pp. 386–387.
19. Moevs, liner notes to a recording of *Brief Mass*, CRI 262.
20. Moevs, "Music and Liturgy," *Liturgical Arts* 38/1, pp. 4–9.
21. Oliveros, "Karl Kohn, *Concerto Mutabile*," *Perspectives of New Music* 22 (1964), p. 87.
22. Kohn, personal letter, June 1, 1985.
23. Ewen, p. 374.
24. Kohn, "Statement," 1960. This, and other unpublished "Statements" (1973, 1979, 1980), are courtesy of the composer.
25. Kohn, liner notes to *Castles and Kings*, Inter-American Musical Editions OAS-007.
26. Kohn, "Statement," 1979.
27. Morton, liner notes to *Serenade*, Desto DC-7166.
28. Morton, review of Kohn's *Capriccios, Musical Quarterly* 49 (April 1963), pp. 229–235.
29. Reese, quoted in a brochure on Kohn published by Carl Fischer.
30. Spies, "Notes on Stravinsky's *Abraham and Isaac*," *Perspectives of New Music* 3/2 (1965), pp. 105–126; "Notes on Stravinsky's *Variations*," *Perspectives of New Music* 4/1 (1965), pp. 62–74; "Some Notes on Stravinsky's Requiem Settings," *Perspectives of New Music* 5/2 (1967), pp. 98–123.
31. Westergaard, "Some Problems in Rhythmic Theory and Analysis," *Perspectives of New Music* 1/1 (1962), pp. 180–191; "Webern and 'Total Organization': An Analysis of the Second Movement of the Piano Variations, Op. 27," *Perspectives of New Music* 1/2 (1963), pp. 107–120; "Toward a Twelve-Tone Polyphony," *Perspectives of New Music* 4/2 (1966), pp. 90–112.

32. Spies, "A Between-Birthday Bagatelle (for Roger Sessions' 80th–81st)," *Perspectives of New Music* 16/2 (1978), pp. 150–153; "Verscheiden (A Lament for Seymour Shifrin)," *Perspectives of New Music* 17/2 (1979), pp. 1–8.

33. Lansky, "The Music of Claudio Spies," *Tempo* 103 (1972), pp. 38–44; see also Lansky, "Spies," *Vinton's Dictionary,* pp. 703–704.

34. Spies, personal interview, January 6, 1985.

35. Westergaard, personal interview, November 15, 1988.

36. Westergaard, interview with Margaret Fairbanks, April 28, 1967, Rodgers and Hammerstein Sound Archive, New York Public Library.

37. Crumb, "Peter Westergaard: *Variations for Six Players,*" *Perspectives of New Music* 3/2 (1965), pp. 152–159.

38. Westergaard, "Webern and 'Total Organization.' "

39. Westergaard, "Alonso's Grief," *Perspectives of New Music* 16/2 (1978), pp. 146–148.

40. Westergaard, interview.

41. Crumb, p. 159.

42. Perkins, "Note Values," *Perspectives of New Music* 3/2 (1962), pp. 47–57.

43. Perkins, "Arthur Berger: The Composer as Mannerist," *Perspectives of New Music* 5/1 (1966), pp. 75–92.

44. Perkins, "Dallapiccola's Art of Canon," *Perspectives of New Music* 1/2 (1963), pp. 95–106; "In Memoriam," *Perspectives of New Music* 13/1 (1974), pp. 242–244.

45. Perkins, interview with Margaret Fairbanks, c. 1967, Rodgers and Hammerstein Sound Archive, New York Public Library.

46. Spies, "John M. Perkins, *Quintet Variations,*" *Perspectives of New Music* 2/1 (1963), pp. 67–76.

47. Perkins, interview.

16. FOUR WOMEN: EUGENIA FROTHINGHAM, VICTORIA GLASER, BETSY WARREN, AND ROSAMOND BRENNER

WOMEN AS WELL AS MEN studied with Piston. If they pursued musical composition, however, they were likely to do so only fairly late in life, either because of prevailing attitudes toward women composers before 1970 or because of familial responsibilities, or both. An exception was Roslyn Brogue (1919–1981), who earned an MA (1943) and PhD (1947) at Harvard and who composed steadily and prolifically throughout her life. Her scores, some of which made use of the 12-tone method, and tapes were left to Tufts University, where she taught from 1962 to 1977. More typical were the experiences of the four composers discussed here, all of whom were active in the 1990s: Eugenia Frothingham, Victoria Glaser, Betsy Warren, and Rosamond Brenner.

Eugenia Frothingham, born on January 26, 1908, came from a distinguished family that had settled in Boston in 1627.[1] Her great-grandfather Nathaniel served the Adams family as Unitarian minister, and her father Langdon taught pathology at the Harvard Medical School. Her mother Olga was a skilled pianist who turned down an offer by Karl Muck to play a concerto with the Boston Symphony because she feared her own abilities. Nonetheless, there was no small concern when, in the late '20s, Eugenia decided to become a composer, something that Boston society regarded as highly dubitable even for men. She persisted in studying privately with Piston and Merritt. As it turned out, these studies proved disappointing; but Piston was encouraging, and she took his suggestion that she study with Boulanger, which she did at Fontainebleau during the summer of 1931. On her return, Frothingham enrolled in the New England Conservatory, where she was the only woman composer in the school. She worked especially hard to please her teachers Converse and McKinley, who were suspicious not only of her gender, but of her social background. Two college works—a *Scherzo* and an *Overture,* both from 1935, and both for chamber orchestra—helped dispel school gossip that she was a dabbling debutante; the *Scherzo*'s 5/4 meter was considered even rather daring and became the talk of the school.

In 1935 Frothingham graduated, and in 1937 she married and moved to Swarthmore, where her husband taught.[2] She continued to compose, and in 1951, she published a *Meditation and Fantasy* for piano.

In the late '50s, Frothingham studied violin along with her daughter and eventually gained enough proficiency to join the Arlington Philharmonic Orchestra. This new involvement inspired her to write some short pieces for violin as well as a few small works for orchestra. These included *Simplicity* for two violins and piano (1963), *Sunrise* for two violins (c. 1966), *Along the Way* for two violins (c. 1966), *Soliloquy* for English horn and orchestra (1973), *A Thought* for orchestra (1974), and *Idyll* for oboe and piano (1980). None of these or other works were published, but they were played by friends and community orchestras, especially the Arlington Philharmonic under John Bavicchi. All this music was highly consistent stylistically, and *Soliloquy,* which was actually the slow movement of an English horn concerto, was itself largely a rewriting of the earlier *Simplicity* for two violins and piano.

Frothingham's music seemed a quintessential New England product: its small dimensions contained something of Ruggles's ruggedness, and something of Hill's gentility. There were bold, raw sevenths and ninths that had no clear tonal references, and there were delicate, elegant whole-tone passages that served as transitions from one thematic area to another. From Piston, Boulanger, and perhaps others, she learned to think contrapuntally, so her harmonies, often piquantly touched by a tritone, ninth, or other added note, arose quite naturally out of individual melodic habits that usually involved slow, steady rhythms in 3/4 or 4/4. At climactic moments, some kind of embellished F major harmony would often appear regardless of the tonal context, like an idée fixe.

Frothingham's expressed ideal was music that was lucid and yet possessed "depth and immensity." It was Beethoven who set the highest standards for this ideal, she claimed, and Shostakovich who came closest to it in her own time. Familiar with over three generations of American composers, she found that nationally this ideal was met best in the work of Arthur Foote, Leonard Bernstein, and John Harbison.

She herself best expressed this ideal, perhaps, in *Simplicity* for two violins and piano. Its opening evoked a rich atmosphere with very economical means (Ex. 86). The modality precluded any sure tonal center; it could be C major or G mixolydian or F lydian. The harmonic changes were subtle, as at measure eight, though the music built assuredly to the inevitable F major climax (m. 13). Along the way, a C$^\sharp$ leading tone juts through the modal texture (m. 11) suggesting some classical intention. Leading tones also figured in mm. 29–30, where momentary use of traditional harmonic function provided a sort of clearing from the prevailing mistiness. As in other works, the modulations were smoothly handled, usually having some recourse to whole-tone inflections.

Despite the strengths of a work like *Simplicity,* there was something small about Frothingham's achievement, consisting as it did primarily of a handful of short works that seemed more like sketches than finished pieces. But the honesty and poise of such music were admirable. Rough, unpretentious, but not without a real charm and poignance, Frothingham perhaps deserved the attention of a Grandma Moses, a figure whom the composer matched in liveliness and compassion.

Victoria Glaser was born in Amherst, Massachusetts, in 1918; her German heritage could be detected, perhaps, in the Ländler-like movement that concluded her *Pluckers' Harvest* for two cellos (1981). Prior to college, she studied counterpoint with Dorothy Fay Little and harmony with Stephen Tuttle.[3] While at Radcliffe, she presided over the Choral Society (1939–1940) and took piano lessons with Margaret

Macdonald and Frederick Tillotson at the Longy School. She received an MA from Harvard in 1943.

At Harvard, her classes included choral conducting with Davison, whom she called a "crackerjack teacher"; 16th-century counterpoint and Fauré with Merritt; fugue and harmony with Piston; and orchestration with Hill. She also took a seminar with Boulanger. Glaser thought Hill's advice

Example 86. Eugenia Frothingham, *Simplicity* for two violins and piano.

regarding the distinct functions of the different orchestral choirs was based on a limited understanding of Mozart. In contrast, she very much liked Piston's course in fugue, which she took three times, the first time writing only an exposition, the second time writing episodes, and only by the third time writing an entire fugue. She also recalled with gratitude the fact that Piston could appreciate the musical qualities of a naive, rudimentary effort of hers, and at the same time "flatten a hot shot" with the remark, "very cleverly written, but it sounds awful." Glaser wrote a *Fugue in Memory of Walter Piston* in 1990.

It was at Harvard that Glaser became a great admirer of Hindemith, writing an honors thesis on the *Gebrauchsmusik of Hindemith* and composing a *Chorale Prelude* in his style. In 1985 Glaser still considered Hindemith an outstanding 20th-century composer, along with Ravel, Schoenberg, Webern, Berg, Chanler, Carter, Fine, and Piston, especially as represented by his *Incredible Flutist* and *Three New England Sketches*.

In the 1940s Glaser began a distinguished teaching career that took her from Wellesley and the Dana Hall School to twenty-five years at the New England Conservatory and, finally, to the Longy School. She also was known and respected for her choral arrangements of over one-hundred works ranging from Lassus to Gershwin. She composed little in the way of original music during these years, as she was very busy teaching, arranging, writing, and conducting; she also was demoralized by an unfinished PhD. (Glaser would have completed her PhD in the 1950s had her advisor, Otto Gombosi, not died: his successor, John Ward, insisted that she give up her teaching post at the New England Conservatory, a condition she could not meet.) But beginning with *3 Orchestral Pieces* of 1970, Glaser resumed a compositional career. Another orchestra piece, a *Birthday Fugue* on "Happy Birthday to You," was performed occasionally by Fiedler and the Boston Pops and became her best-known work; it could not be published, however, because of copyright problems concerning its famous fugue subject.

More characteristic were a series of short chamber works, including *Encounter with a Spirit* for piano, *Epithalamion* for violin and cello (1979), *On Seven Winds* for young voices,

piano, recorder, and small percussion instruments (1980), and
Pluckers' Harvest for two cellos (1981). They were not
necessarily intended for concert halls. *Epithalamion* celebrated the marriage of two friends. *On Seven Winds,* in which
the young singers, in the tradition of Orff, were asked to play
some of the percussion parts themselves, obviously was
well-suited to school use. Similarly, *Pluckers' Harvest,* which,
like *On Seven Winds,* consisted of seven short movements, was
intended primarily as a duet for teacher and student.

The relation between all these pieces and Glaser's orientation toward Hindemith and "Gebrauchsmusik" was clear
enough. Stylistically, however, Glaser showed more decisively the impact of American neoclassicism: there were
echoes of Fine, for instance, in the spiky diatonicism of
"Cherchons nous la paix" from *On Seven Winds* (Ex. 87); and
of Piston, in the chromatic modality of *Epithalamion* (Ex. 88).
Also reminiscent of Piston were the sicilianas from *Pluckers'*
Harvest and *On Seven Winds.*

At the same time, Glaser employed all sorts of modish

Example 87. Victoria Glaser, "Cherchons Nous La Paix," *On Seven Winds.*

Example 88. Victoria Glaser, *Epithalamion* for violin and cello.

ideas: 12-tone technique (*On Seven Winds*), aleatoric notation
("Mid-Night Mosquito Hunt" from *Pluckers' Harvest*), piano
strings (*Encounter with a Spirit*), new string techniques
("Outer Space," from *Pluckers' Harvest,* in which the quarter-
tone glissandi were meant to imitate the Doppler effect),
quotation (Brahms's lullaby in the "Mid-Night Mosquito
Hunt"), and even a bit of "performance art" (in "Mosquito
Hunt" the student was called on to slap a nearby chair at the
work's climax to suggest the killing blow). All these novelties
were so marked by classic restraint, and so enlivened by
humor, that the end result was very entertaining.

Perhaps the most provocative feature of Glaser's music was
its extreme brevity. The opening movement of *Pluckers'
Harvest* comprised sixteen measures, and the successive
movements were not much longer. The seven movements
from *On Seven Winds* were shorter still! Single-movement
works, like *Epithalamion* or *Encounter with a Spirit,* lasted but
a few minutes. Rarely was there time to modulate, though the
longer pieces like *Epithalamion* and the siciliana from *On
Seven Winds* did so, both to the supertonic, by the way.
Lacking a tautness like Webern's, these little pieces struck
one as little more than casual epigrams. (Significantly, her
work appeared most formally coherent in those rare in-

stances, like "Outer Space," where it was atonal.) The composer recognized this limitation in herself and in women's music in general, guessing that it had something to do with "left brain interference" caused by feelings of anger and inferiority. On the other hand, she thought that the music of Louise Talma and Nadia Boulanger possessed a "wonderful sense of structure," while there were pieces by men, including the "Humoresque" by Dvořák, and several works by Philip Glass, that she considered next to mindless.

Betsy Warren used three names: Mrs. Betsy Davis, her married and personal name; Betsy Frost, her stage name; and B. Warren, her maiden and pen name. She used the initial "B." in anticipation of bias against women composers.[4]

Born in Boston in 1921, Warren was raised in Maine, the daughter of theater-loving parents who coached her in Shirley Temple routines. After two years at the University of Maine, she attended Radcliffe and Harvard (1940–1944), earning both a bachelor's and master's degree. At Harvard she studied 16th-century counterpoint with Merritt, and fugue, harmony, and composition with Piston. She also studied with Boulanger but decided that "Piston had everything Boulanger had plus a sense of humor." She especially was moved by Piston's "complete integrity," by the way he made his students feel like "humble servants before the throne of Bach, Beethoven, and Brahms." Warren herself dedicated much of her music "to the glory of God."

After graduation, Warren formed a singing trio modeled on the Andrew Sisters, served shortly as a music critic for the *Christian Science Monitor,* taught at the New England Conservatory and at private schools, and sang with Goldovsky's Opera Company. Busy as teacher, singer, mother, and wife, with homes in Boston, London, and Bath, Maine, Warren found no time to compose. But starting in 1975 came a flood of compositions, mostly chamber works, but symphonies and operas also. And as she and her husband owned Wiscasset Music, she had a convenient means for publishing almost everything she wrote.

The modal-chromatic counterpoint at the heart of Warren's music, like Glaser's, derived from Piston and Hindemith. But in many works, for example, *Ride-A-Cock-Horse* for piano

(1975), the music's sparse textures, singsong rhythms, and spiky dissonance were peculiarly austere (Ex. 89). Likewise idiosyncratic were the meandering forms, the sudden tempo changes, and the enharmonic clashes. There were also references to popular styles, as in the second movement of the *Sonata No. 1* for violin and piano (1977); they seemed to retain more the preciousness of Shirley Temple than the irony of the Andrews Sisters.

More attractive, it seemed, was Warren's sacred music, like the *Mass in E,* with its fluid vocal writing and delicate modal hue. Perhaps better still were the collaborations with David McCord: *Five Songs in 5 Minutes* for chorus; *Balloons and Frog Music,* two ballets for five-piece chamber group; and a chamber opera after O. Henry's *The Gift of the Magi* (1985). In any case, sympathetic listeners probably could find in

Example 89. B. Warren, *Ride-A-Cock-Horse* (Wiscasset, 1981).

Warren's work an appeal not unlike Billings and Ives, a New England tradition to which she felt close.

Rosamond Brenner was born in Cambridge, Massachusetts, in 1931. She studied piano and organ, and wrote some chamber and piano pieces while in high school.[5] At Radcliffe and Harvard from 1949—1954 (BA, MA), she studied orchestration and 20th-century music with Piston, and organ privately with Melville Smith. During these years she learned an enduring love for Bach, Handel, and Debussy, as well as Stravinsky's *Orpheus* and Piston's symphonies; she also concluded that atonal and 12-tone music were too radical for her. Although Piston was encouraging, she gave up composition, considering it to be a man's perogative. She continued her musical studies in Europe, where she studied organ with Anton Heiler and Pierre Segond and harpsichord with Gustav Leonhardt, and at Brandeis, eventually earning a PhD in 1968.

It was not until Brenner joined the Bahá'í faith that she once again began to compose music. A resident of Glen Ellyn, Illinois, she started attending the world-famous Bahá'í House of Worship (designed by Louis Bourgeois) in Wilmette and found that music was needed for devotional services held on Sundays and on the first day of each month. Brenner subsequently helped meet this need with a series of songs and choral pieces; many of the songs she performed herself in her rich, contralto voice. One of her first contributions, a setting of *Psalm 30* for voice and tambourine (1971), reflected the "world-encompassing"[6] nature of the Bahá'í, but most later works took for their texts the writings of the religion's founder, Bahá'u'lláh (1817–1892), or those of his son, Abdu'l-Bahá. For the most part these were set in English translation, but some were in other languages, including Esperanto, reflecting yet another Bahá'í ideal, the creation of a universal auxiliary language. One such work in Esperanto was a setting of Bahá'u'lláh's "Unity Prayer," *Unueco* for unaccompanied voice (1984), a text Brenner earlier had set in Spanish (the 1981 *Unidad* for voice and piano). Brenner proved herself outstanding in this area: her setting of Bahá'u'lláh's "Darkness Hath Fallen Upon Every Land" from her choral cantata, *The Choice,* represented the United States in a large international publication, *The Bahá'í World.*[7]

Stylistically, such music was certainly related to Eastern, and in particular, Middle Eastern idioms, for example, the melodic turns and rhythmic syncopations found in "Darkness Hath Fallen Upon Every Land" or in *Love and Unity* (1973), also for chorus. But there was also a resemblance to American Christian music of the 1970s and '80s, which itself tended towards a merging of traditional hymnal styles with new popular ones, especially rock. One heard both these features in a work like *Be Not Grieved* (Ex. 90): hymns in their melodies, with their strong rhythms, two- and four-bar structures, diatonic content, and long notes at the ends of phrases; rock in their harmonies, with their modal inflections (often teetering between I and bVII), closely spaced triads in root position, root movement by descending step, and pervasive 4-3 suspensions.

This particular amalgam of Eastern, hymnal, and popular styles served America's and, perhaps, the world's Bahá'í community effectively. Certainly it represented yet another intriguing fusion of Eastern and Western traditions. In addition, Brenner's craftsmanship enabled some distinctive touches, including the kind of textural depth afforded by some use of modal ambiguity, untraditional harmonies, and imitative counterpoint. Such means helped the composer

Example 90. Rosamond Brenner, *Be Not Grieved* (Donna Kime and Rosamond Brenner, 1986).

toward those qualities of restraint and expressiveness, elegance and nobility that she prized in Piston's music.

Finally, unlike Piston, Brenner often engaged in certain untraditional freedoms, as when she called for an unspecified melody instrument in *Exaltation* for chorus (1980), or when she instructed the pianist to arpeggiate chords "up and down very rapidly" in *Healing* for voice and piano (1981). She herself sang and accompanied herself at the piano quite freely, sometimes substituting a harmony built of fourths for a notated triad. Among her more definitive projects was a collection of five choral pieces in *Inspirational Music* for solo voice and choir, published independently in 1987 in collaboration with another composer for the Bahá'í faith, Donna Kime. No matter how the composer herself might perform such works, here they were carefully scored for unaccompanied chorus, with special attention paid to dynamic nuance.

For all their differences, Frothingham, Glaser, Warren, and Brenner all shared gratifying memories of Walter Piston. His respect and encouragement stood in contrast to the contempt and indifference that women composers often encountered. Perhaps his wife, Kathryn Nason, a painter and feminist, as indicated by the fact that she retained her maiden name, helped make Piston more sensitive in this regard. In any case, Piston apparently enjoyed the modesty and good humor of many of his female students, qualities that they, in turn, admired in him. Their relationships bore less tension and rivalry than that between Piston and his male students; the women were likely to laugh at those typically hard-boiled remarks that could so devastate the men. And in their music—in its responsiveness to practical needs, in its uncompromising individuality, and in its calm—they also proved close to Piston in varied and special ways.

Notes

1. Frothingham, personal letter, April 22, 1984, and personal interview, January 6, 1985.
2. Frothingham's married name was Mrs. Lombard.
3. Glaser, personal interview, January 7, 1985.

4. Warren, personal interview, March 9, 1985.
5. Brenner, personal interview, November 6, 1984; and personal letter, October 24, 1984.
6. Shoghi Effendi, *The Faith of Bahá'u'lláh* (Wilmette: Bahá'í Publishing, 1959), p. 6.
7. Brenner, "Darkness Hath Fallen Upon Every Land," *The Bahá'í World*, Vol. 16 (Haifa: Bahá'í World Centre), pp. 704–723.

17. A NEW AGE AND A NEW LEFT: DAVID BEHRMAN AND FREDERIC RZEWSKI

J OHN ROCKWELL, IN HIS BOOK ON COMPOSITION in the late
twentieth century, *All American Music,* devoted separate
chapters to David Behrman and Frederic Rzewski.[1] There
was no obvious reason to compare these two figures, and
Rockwell understandably elected to discuss, rather, Charles
Dodge in the context of Behrman ("Electronic and Computer
Music and the Humanist Reaction") and Rochberg in the
context of Rzewski ("The Romantic Revival and the Dilemma
of the Political Composer"). But the nature of this study
encourages some consideration of the deep personal and
artistic ties that linked these two composers.

This friendship dated back to the early '50s, while both
were students at Phillips Academy Andover. Behrman, the
son of the distinguished playwright S. N. Behrman and Jascha
Heifetz's sister, was born in 1937 in Salzburg, where his
parents were vacationing; he grew up in New York City.
Rzewski, born one year later in 1938, was from Westfield,
Massachusetts. Both were pianists—Rzewski, the more accomplished—and both were writing music, too; Behrman's
work, mostly piano pieces, resembled Prokofiev, while
Rzewski's came under the influence of Shostakovich.[2] Both
detested McCarthyism, and Behrman took pride in the fact
that his father had written one of the first anti-fascist plays in
America.

Graduating in 1954, Rzewski went to Harvard, while
Behrman studied privately for one year with Wallingford
Riegger, "a wonderful man who introduced his students to

the work of Cowell, Varèse, Ives; and to radical left politics; and to species counterpoint and serialism, among other things."[3] Behrman subsequently enrolled at Harvard himself, graduating in 1959, one year after Rzewski.

At Harvard, Behrman and Rzewski studied counterpoint, orchestration, and composition with Piston, whom Behrman respected as "a skilled craftsman and as a creator of music with grace and a style that sprang from an intelligent, complex mind with a sharp, understated New England wit." They admired, too, his sympathetic kindness, and learned an abiding love of Bach. But Piston's music was not at the "burning focal point" of their interests, and in this respect, their associations with Claudio Spies and Christian Wolff proved more satisfying.

Spies, a former Piston student recently appointed to the Harvard faculty, encouraged Behrman and Rzewski to investigate the second Viennese school, as he himself was beginning to do. They needed little encouragement and very soon surpassed Spies in their excitement over serialism as represented, above all, by Boulez's *Le Marteau sans Maître* (1953) and Stockhausen's *Gesang der Jünglinge* (1956). Rzewski wrote a senior honors thesis that dealt largely with the philosophical implications of serialism from Schoenberg through Stockhausen ("The Reappearance of Isorhythm in Modern Music"), while Behrman wrote one which specifically detailed Boulez's innovations, and which, incidentally, cited Rzewski's thesis at one point ("Theory and Technique in the Work of Pierre Boulez").[4] Both theses shared an appreciation for the use of nondevelopmental forms and ritual as found in Boulez and Stockhausen.

Christian Wolff, another composer at Harvard, made a particularly decisive impression on Behrman and Rzewski. A PhD candidate in classics, he avoided Harvard's music department; indeed, he long had steered clear of any formal musical education. But as an already established avant-garde composer just a few years older than Behrman and Rzewski (he was born in 1934), they discovered one another to their mutual delight. Wolff, who along with Earle Browne and Morton Feldman had come under Cage's influence in New York in the early '50s, for some years now had been writing startlingly far-out pieces that exploited a large array of chance

techniques. Behrman and Rzewski were impressed. To-
gether, all three sponsored concerts more or less under Music
Department auspices that featured this kind of music,
including guest appearances by Morton Feldman and pianist
David Tudor. In the following decade, Rzewski was to
become almost as famous an interpreter of Cage, Wolff, and
Stockhausen as Tudor himself. In 1971, Wolff, Behrman, and
Rzewski reunited to record Wolff's *Burdocks.*

After graduation, Behrman spent one year (1959–1960) in
Europe on a Paine Fellowship studying with Stockhausen, as
well as with the Belgian composer, Henri Pousseur. He
returned to New York City and established a home base in
Greenwich Village. Rzewski, in the meantime, spent two
years with Sessions and Babbitt at Princeton (1958–1960),
two years in Rome on a Fulbright Fellowship (1960–1962),
and two years in Berlin on a Ford Foundation grant (1963–
1965). He subsequently settled in Rome but often traveled
abroad, especially to New York and London.

Little is known about their music before 1966. Behrman
seems not to have done much composing in the early '60s,
instead devoting his energies to investigating homemade
electronic devices, making contacts with other musicians in
the avant-garde, and establishing a career as a record producer
for Columbia Records (his 1967 production of Terry Riley's
In C initiated the minimalist movement). Rzewski became, as
mentioned, a well-known performer of avant-garde piano
works, especially in Europe, where his career was followed in
such journals as *La Rassegna Musicale* and *Ruch Muzyczny.*[5]
But he began to gain some notoriety for his own music, too.
One such work, the 1961 *Three Rhapsodies for Two Slide
Whistles,* exhibited a Cagean interest in toy instruments,
while another work of the same year, the *Octet,* explored,
according to Eric Salzman, "intricate cueing games similar to
those used by Christian Wolff."[6] His major work from these
years was *Nature Morte,* begun in Rome in 1963 and
completed in Berlin in 1965. In the tradition of Boulez, the
work's novel instrumentation included eight winds, violin,
cello, electric organ, piano, harp, and a vast percussion
battery, but more in the tradition of Cage, one also found the
piano to be elaborately prepared, the percussion battery to
include tin cans, baby rattle, and toy horn, and additional parts

for two transistor radios, phonograph (with three discs, including "a disc of orchestral music, heavily scratched"), and vacuum cleaner ("or other similar electric device"). Then in 1966 Behrman helped form the Sonic Arts Group (SAG) and Rzewski similarly helped found Musica Elettronica Viva (MEV), and both quickly came to the fore as composers in the avant-garde.

The proliferation of such new music ensembles as SAG and MEV in the late 1960s was one of that period's most distinctive features. In addition to SAG (a New York group comprised primarily of Behrman, Robert Ashley, Alvin Lucier, and Gordon Mumma) and MEV (a Rome group comprised mainly of Americans, including Rzewski, Alvin Curran, Jon Phetteplace, Allan Bryant, and Richard Teitelbaum), there was Ann Arbor's ONCE and Davis's NEM (New Music Ensemble), as well as ensembles organized by Steve Reich and Philip Glass. These groups formed an intricate artistic network (Ashley, for instance, was a member of both SAG and ONCE) with John Cage acknowledged as a sort of guru. Their ideals and activities were best recorded by *Source,* a periodical edited by NEM's Larry Austin and published during the heyday of such groups, that is from 1967 to 1974. These ideals tended toward the extremes of neoprimitivism and ultramodernism, sometimes in combination, sometimes not: one found simple noisemakers and electronic synthesizers, static drones and atonality, repetitive rhythms and nonpulsed flux (one European group of this ilk even called itself Fluxus). While improvisation was very much de rigueur (the popular slogan, after all, was "do your own thing"), one could distinguish, nonetheless, those groups like ONCE and MEV in which the artists aimed for extensive creative collaboration, and those like SAG and the Reich and Glass ensembles in which improvisation was more or less gauged by a particular composer.

It was as a member of SAG that Behrman earned the reputation as a composer of electronic music. His sympathy for electronic sounds, perhaps sparked by Varèse, already had been evident in his college thesis, in which he wrote:

> The young composers' exploration of electronic media was the result of two trends in their thought and idiom.

One was their growing tendency to create works of great
complexity, in which fine distinctions of rhythms and
dynamics played an integral role in musical structure.
The other was a distrust of the physical media inherited
from the past.[7]

In Europe he benefited from Stockhausen's and Pousseur's
expertise in this area. Back in New York, deprived of the
rare, expensive, and bulky apparatus that then constituted
electronic media, he devised his own homemade equipment
with the help of Mumma and Rzewski, who both shared such
interests. By the time SAG was formed, Behrman was
composing electronic pieces regularly, and no SAG concert
was quite complete without one such work on the program.
Only two of these works, however, were recorded: the 1966
Wave Train and the 1967 *Runthrough*. Record producer
though he was, Behrman seemed disinclined toward that kind
of self-promotion.

Wave Train, though electronic, used an acoustic sound
source, namely, certain strings of one or two grand pianos,
depending on the number of players. The options for players
ranged from two to five: at least one player was needed to
produce the sounds, and another to control the feedback
equipment.[8] Another work from 1966, *Players with Circuits,*
similarly called for four performers: two playing piano, guitar,
or zither, and two handling the oscillators that controlled the
ring modulator through which the acoustic sounds were fed.
As the decade progressed, Behrman made other electronic
music based on acoustic sounds, that is, a "musique concrète."
Questions from the Floor (1968) and *A New Team Takes Over*
(1969), for instance, both used recorded political speeches of
the time. *Runway,* from 1969, employed whistling, seagull
sounds, and Japanese folk music. An intriguing work not
included in Behrman's catalog, namely, *Intermission Collage,*
overdubbed a Japanese version of a Chopin tune popularized
by an American (presumably, "I'm Always Chasing Rainbows") with a Brazilian version of the same song that already
had been mixed with jungle bird sounds; the result, for
Behrman, gained "a greater poignancy and beauty than it ever
would have had again when played alone on the piano."[9]
At the same time, Behrman composed works like *Run-*

through that were totally electronic; that is, their basic sounds were produced by modulators and generators. *Runthrough* called for four players: two to turn dials on the generator to produce the sounds, and two to wave flashlights to control the sounds, which were photocell sensitive. Other purely electronic works included *Sinescreen* (1970), *Pools of Phase-Locked Loops* (1972), and *Home-Made Synthesizer Music with Sliding Pitches* (1973).

Whether the music was purely electronic or a kind of "musique concrète," it typically featured long, sustained sounds. In 1972 Behrman explained:

> Given a new instrument, one's first musicianly impulse is to make sounds which are natural to it. Continuously sustaining sounds is natural to electronic oscillators and sets them apart from acoustic instruments of the past. On the other hand, most musicians whom I admire tend away from building music to and from climaxes, in the old Western sense, whether they make electronic or acoustic sound. Electronics arrived on the scene at the same time as the return (in our culture) of the need for nonclimactic forms—music on a plateau, to oversimplify—and that's why there is a connection (though not an absolute one) between the two.[10]

In *Wave Train,* the sounds were sustained at a certain frequency from a few seconds to about a half-minute, often growing in amplitude, then dying out. The "wave" metaphor was certainly appropriate; Adrian Jack, in fact, evoked the sea in his review of Behrman's *Home-Made Synthesizer Music:* "It consists of chordal rainbows which bloom with colours that run a bit as they ripen, then fade, slowly and periodically one after the other, each erasing gently the memory of the former, like the continuously renewed edges of the sea."[11] The "train" metaphor seemed equally apt, if not more so, for *Wave Train*'s overlapping sounds created a rich texture reminiscent of the hum, rumble, and echo of the subways beneath Behrman's adopted Greenwich Village. (Sometimes, the sounds were also reminiscent of the static between radio stations, a sound, incidentally, that Rzewski called for in *Nature Morte.*) There were overlapping, sustained sounds in *Runthrough* as well, but they were more aggressive, more like the whirr of a helicopter, or the boing of toy ray guns, or, for Rockwell, "like some electronic washing machine churning through its cycles."[12] Further, the individual threads of sound did not begin slowly or languish away but rather started and stopped abruptly, creating an energetic, humorous mood. In both *Wave Train* and *Runthrough,* Behrman created interesting antiphonal textures that were idiomatically electronic.

How carefully planned were these works? In *Players with Circuits,* wrote Will Johnson, "Sound source players are presented with precise descriptions of what pitches they are to play; and performers of the electronic equipment are given precise instructions as to when and in what manner they are to make changes in amplitude, oscillator bandwidth, frequency, and tone control."[13] It seems that, at least, Behrman rounded out his work, for Tim Souster pointed to this feature,[14] and, indeed, the recorded version of *Runthrough* had a plopping noise heard only at the beginning and the end. How much of this sort of thing was written down or planned beforehand, however, was difficult to ascertain. The "score" to *Wave Train,* as published in *Source,* made no such provisions. What is certain is that considerable room was allowed for improvisation. Behrman, who had discussed the inadequacy of conventional notation in a 1965 article,[15] wrote about *Runthrough,* "Things are going well when all the players have the sensation they are riding a sound they like in harmony together, and when each is appreciative of what the other is doing."[16] Extensive, gamelike improvisations were an especially important element in Behrman's collaborations: these included the 1968 *Reunion* with Marcel Duchamp, Teeny Duchamp, Gordon Mumma, and David Tudor; and the 1970 *Communication in a Noisy Environment* with Anthony Braxton, Leroy Jenkins, Gordon Mumma, and Bob Watts. It was this emphasis on improvisation, as well as the use of small, homemade circuitry and overlapping waves of sustained sounds, that distinguished Behrman's work from the more mainstream electronic music produced at Columbia and Princeton.

Rzewski also became involved with electronic music during the 1960s; indeed, as mentioned, he helped Behrman devise homemade electronic instruments. His best-known electronic work was *Zoologischer Gärten,* created in Berlin in 1965.

Back in Rome, he helped found MEV specifically to promote live-electronic music, as the group's name indicated. But by the late 1960s, Rzewski and MEV were more associated with composing conceptual pieces and staging "happenings". In one case, remembered Rzewski:

> . . . we invited the audience to bring songs to a forum we called the sound pool. We'd invite people to bring sounds to the concert and throw them into the pool. Very often, there would be 300 or 400 people making these sounds, and we would try to guide it or steer it in some way.[17]

The aesthetic principles of the various MEV members were explored in a 1968 issue of *Source,* including the following contribution by Rzewski, entitled, "Commandments to Myself":

> Don't make images: create meaningful rituals.
> Don't construct time: interpret the moment.
> Don't command obedience: welcome the intruder.
> Don't occupy space: identify with it.
> Don't forge ecstasy: return to zero.
> Don't play possibilities: do the necessary.
> Don't wear masks: rejoice in nakedness.
> Don't practice magic: be automatic, be nothing.
> Make music with whatever means are available.[18]

Three of Rzewski's concept pieces from 1968—*Street Music, Symphony,* and *Plan for Spacecraft*—also were published by *Source.* In *Street Music* "for many performers, in the street or other public place, bearing portable sound sources (voice, objects, instruments, and battery-powered electronic devices)," each performer interacted with his portable sounds in specified ways. In *Symphony* "for several performers (sometimes stationary, sometimes in movement) in a space, singing" and "a few simple instruments (bells, drums, etc.) used sparsely," the performers were asked to produce two sounds: a low, continuous drone and a higher, ornamental melody.[19] And in *Plan for Spacecraft,* the composer instructed the participating performers to make "music in the way in which he knows how, with his own rhythms, his own choice of

materials, etc., without particular regard for the others, or for
setting up some kind of simple ensemble situation."[20] It was
hoped that, in this last work, the players quickly would merge
together as if transformed "through magic," though the
composer allowed for two other possibilities: first, that a
magical transformation might occur only after hard work and
careful listening to one another's rhythms; or second, that no
transformation would occur, in which case the performer
could either give "vent to violence" or drift "into nothingness."

In 1969 Rzewski wrote his first real success, *Les Moutons de
Panurge* (after Rabelais) "for any number of melody instruments plus any number of non-musicians playing anything."
The score consisted of a 65-note melody (Ex. 91) and instructions regarding its elaborate sequence (1, 1–2, 1–3 . . .
1–65, 2–65, 3–65 . . . 65). The players were to begin
together, but the composer expected them eventually to fall
out of unison and continue on in a sort of free canonic web. In
a recorded version by the Blackearth Percussion Group,
which Christopher Rouse thought "spellbinding,"[21] the
work's connection to Steve Reich was unmistakable. Ultimately, *Les Moutons* proved transitional. Elements like its
unspecified instrumentation, its aleatoric structure, and certainly its call for nonmusicians making loud noises (the
preface to the 1980 edition played down this feature) looked
back to the conceptual pieces and happenings of the preceding years. On the other hand, the moody minor-major
modality and the strong rhythmic energy (sometimes forming
little groups of five and seven eighths not so different from
Copland and Piston) looked ahead to future works, as did
some textural features (in this regard, see especially the 1972

Example 91. Frederic Rzewski, *Les Moutons de Panurge.* ©1980 Zen-On
Music Company, Ltd., Tokyo. All rights reserved. Used by permission of
European American Music Distributors Corporation, agent for Zen-On
Music Company, Ltd.

Coming Together and the 1977 *Song and Dance* for flute, clarinet, vibraphone, and piano). Moreover, whereas the conceptual works tended to begin chaotically and move, it was hoped, to some kind of transcendental unity, *Les Moutons* commenced in unison and broke down into greater and greater disorder. While on one level this was merely descriptive of Panurge's sheep, it also presaged Rzewski's overtly political works with their emphasis on the conflict and breakdown of capitalist society.

There always had been a strongly left-wing underpinning to the avant-garde musical groups of the late 1960s. Clearly, they paralleled the vogue for communal living, quasi-ritual marijuana smoking, "back-to-nature" sentiments, and other manifestations of the contemporary counterculture. Indeed, their heyday corresponded to that of the counterculture and to the disaffection incited by the Vietnam War in general. And as with the counterculture, the politics of these groups, as well as Cage, tended toward the anarchistic and pacifistic. In this sense, Rzewski's *Plan for Spacecraft* suited well the temper of the times, for one sensed in it the anarchist's optimism.

But unlike the majority of the American avant-garde, their sympathies with Mao Zedong notwithstanding, Rzewski was a committed and militant Marxist. His college thesis already had displayed a Marxist orientation (at one point associating tonality with the "bourgeois order") and had shown a profound, if somewhat critical, interest in Max Weber and Theodore Adorno.[22] In 1963 he married a young socialist, Nicole Abbelos. He was enthused by the worldwide student protests of 1968 (with their promise of "vast, sweeping changes"), as well as by a workers' demonstration in 1969, in which "over 100,000 metalworkers from all over Italy marched through Rome carrying bells and pipes and buckets and chains, cooking up an enormous racket."[23] About this same time he befriended Judith Malina and Julian Beck, then in Europe because of nonpayment of U.S. taxes, and approved of their Living Theater's controversial merging of theater and leftist propaganda. In a statement for the 1968 Festival Internationale de Teatro Universitario-Parma, Rzewski called attention to the over one-hundred-million people murdered in the preceding sixty years and spoke of

the composer's role as follows: "To create means to be here
and now: to be responsible to reality on the high-wire of the
present. To be responsible means to be able to communicate
the presence of dangers to others."[24] These aspirations
informed his music from the 1960s; *Street Music,* for instance,
surely hoped to duplicate the rowdy solidarity of the
metalworkers with their chains and buckets. Indeed,
Rzewski's interest in live-electronic music itself was inspired
in part by his aversion to the traditional role of the composer,
especially the European composer, whom he likened to a
headwaiter: "On one hand he mimics his social betters who
come to eat in the restaurant, but on the other hand he is not
one of them; he's just a slob like everyone else. He apes the
mannerisms of the ruling class without having the real
stuff."[25] But with the failed promises of 1968 and 1969 came,
it seems, a recognition on Rzewski's part of the incompatibil-
ity of the pacifistic '60s avant-garde with successful class
struggle.

Another friend, the English composer Cornelius Cardew,
shared these concerns. Two years older than Rzewski,
Cardew (b. 1936) similarly had come under the influence of
Stockhausen and then Cage. It was in this context that he
initially followed Rzewski's career with admiration. A committed Marxist himself, Cardew also wondered about the
possible failure and irrelevance of the '60s avant-garde, and
he shared Rzewski's distress when MEV, while on tour in
England, was "greeted with hurled hot dogs and Coke tins" by
a young audience.[26] How much Cardew and Rzewski shaped
one another's reassessment of the '60s avant-garde in their
private discussions of the matter is hard to say, but by the time
Cardew gave such reassessment formal utterance, namely in
the 1974 *Stockhausen Serves Imperialism and Other Articles,*[27]
he could point to Rzewski's *Coming Together* and *Attica* as
exemplary alternatives to the '60s avant-garde.

Both written in 1972, *Coming Together* and *Attica* were
inspired by the 1971 riot at New York's Attica Prison in
which thirty-one prisoners and nine guards were killed in a
military attack ordered by Governor Nelson Rockefeller.
Probably no other contemporary event so well encapsulated
the Marxist perspective: here was the combined power of
capitalism and government in the figure of a Rockefeller

responsible for the deaths of prisoners and their guards alike. *Coming Together* took its text from a letter by one of the uprising's leaders, Sam Melville, a political prisoner killed in the onslaught. *Attica*'s text, in contrast, consisted of but a single line spoken by another leader, Richard X. Clark, upon his release from prison: "Attica is in front of me."

Both works reasserted, with greater finesse and control, the renewed interest in pulse and tonality represented by *Les Moutons*. In *Coming Together,* for speaker, vibraphone, synthesizer, alto sax, viola, trombone, piano, and bass, the piano played the pivotal role of establishing the mostly melodic-minor modality and the sometimes nervously shifting pulse; the other instruments decorated this bedrock of activity with sustained and detached notes, forming alluring textures. In addition, little instrumental fragments repeated themselves, matching the use of the text as a source for short phrases to be repeated in varied permutations; this feature strongly suggested the influence of Steve Reich's similarly titled *Come Out.* In contrast to the "incessant noise" and "hysterical ravings" so incisively depicted in *Coming Together, Attica,* for a similar ensemble, was much calmer, with its slow, marchlike pulse and its major mode with parallel sixths in the piano. Despite innovative textural subtleties derived, perhaps, from a close knowledge of Boulez and Stockhausen, the style bore resemblance to Copland, and, in general, to leftist styles from the 1930s.

A similar musical language to that of *Coming Together* and *Attica* subsequently was used for a number of effective vocal works on political themes, including three from 1974: *Struggle,* a cantata for baritone and ensemble; "Lullaby: God to a Hungry Child" (text by Langston Hughes) for baritone, vibraphone, and clarinet; and "Apolitical Intellectuals" (text by Otto Rene Castille) for baritone and piano. But Rzewski became best known in the 1970s for a series of big, virtuosic piano works, some of which he performed and recorded himself: *Variations on 'No Place To Go But Around'* (1973), *The People United Will Never Be Defeated!* (1975), *Four Pieces* (1977), and *American Ballads* (1978).

The *Variations on 'No Place To Go But Around'* was inspired by a play by Beck and Malina called *The Tower of Money,* described by the composer as "a grand theatrical presentation of the Anarchist view of society and its transformation by spontaneous and non-violent means."[28] Some of its material, in fact, originally was intended as incidental music. The theme and variations proper comprised roughly half the work and were meant to symbolize the various classes of capitalist society: lumpen, industrial workers, petty bourgeoisie, clerical-military, and big bourgeoisie. Following this was a large improvisatory section corresponding to "the middle of the play in which situations of social conflict are enacted." The work closed with a return of the theme, but not the victorious conclusion one might expect, rather, as often with Rzewski's mature work, a quiet whimper suggestive of a sort of despair.

The theme itself well matched its title, "No Place To Go But Around," in that it had a drudging, cyclical quality, in large part due to its sequential chromatic descent of minor harmonies. One detected the influence of Hans Eisler, whom Rzewski had come to regard as his principal forbear, and perhaps also to Wagner; a similar harmonic progression significantly characterized the composer's setting of the apocalyptic Castille text, "Apolitical Intellectuals" (Rzewski deeply admired Wagner, and perhaps saw in Wagner's response to 1848 some precedence for his own experiences in 1968). The theme itself, however, was classically shaped, with strong internal cadences and hierarchical units of two, four, and eight measures; and although the subsequent variations grew more and more daring, both harmonically and pianistically, the thematic framework remained firmly perceptible. It even could be heard in the very attenuated introduction and coda, in which individual notes were isolated in the extreme ranges of the piano: this was variation form breaking new barriers.

The middle, improvisatory section warrants special consideration. As played by Rzewski on a recording for Finnadar, it represented a stunning feat of technical virtuosity and musical ingenuity. The composer subjected bits from the preceding variations to erratic tonal and rhythmic twists with demonic, Lisztian flair. Periodically, in utter contrast, fragments and echoes of the socialist anthem, "Bandiera Rossa," were heard in noble, Schubertian fashion, often modulating by a third. In Rzewski's other piano works, similar allowance was made for improvisation, perhaps not quite on this scale, but of considerable weight nonetheless. Here the avant-garde and neoclassical met on equal footing: such improvisations reflected the composer's Cagean orientation, but at the same time, they looked back to improvisatory traditions represented by Mozart and Chopin. In later works, these improvisations were often optional, but to omit them, as Paul Jacobs and Ursula Oppens did in otherwise brilliant performances, or even to minimize them, did a disservice to their work's dramatic wholeness.

The People United Will Never Be Defeated! similarly comprised variations on a theme in the minor mode. The theme, however, was not an original one, but rather a Chilean song that had become a familiar leftist chant around the world, "El Pueblo Unido Jamás Será Vencido" by Sergio Ortega and Quilapayun. This 1975 work well may have been intended as an ironic commentary on the American bicentennial, for the song was associated, above all, with the Chilean leftist regime that the United States assisted in deposing. An hour-long set of thirty-six variations, *The People United* stood out in terms of its sheer enormity, and quickly established itself as Rzewski's best-known work and one of the most imposing piano works of its time. In fact, its lofty architecture and stylistic diversity readily suggested comparisons with Bach's *Goldberg Variations* and Beethoven's *Diabelli Variations.*[29]

In liner notes to a recording of the work by Ursula Oppens, Christian Wolff summarized the complex form of *The People United* as follows:

> The variations are grouped in six sets of six. The sixth variation of a set, itself in six parts, consists of a summing up of the previous five variations of the set, with a final sixth part of new or transitional material. . . . Finally, the sixth set of variations (31 through 36) becomes a gathering together of elements of all the preceding thirty variations. In this sixth set, the first variation draws together, in units of four bars each, elements of the first variation of the first set, the first of the second set, the first of the third, and so on. The second to fifth variations of this last set proceed similarly. In the sixth variation of the set, the 36th and last of the entire piece, the preceding five variations are summed up, even as they had been a summation of the

preceding thirty variations. Elements of each variation
are now compressed into a fraction of a bar.[30]

Wolff sensed, as many listeners no doubt would, that "the
music has a kind of program, not literalistic, but suggestive."
This partly was due to the strong programmatic implications
of the theme itself; partly due to the additional use of the
Eisler-Brecht "Solidarity Song," and, once again, "Bandiera
Rossa"; partly from knowing, as Wolff mentions, such playing
directions in the score as "with foreboding," "relentless,
uncompromising," and so on; and partly from the music itself,
which in Wolff's words, evokes "some of the anguish of
struggle and moments of defeat."

One, however, would be hard pressed to attach specific
meanings to any one particular variation, let alone their
summations. The music was too abstract for that, and many
variations had no suggestive playing directions. Further, the
ornate form had none of the dialectical sweep found in *No
Place To Go But Around.* Nonetheless, each of the work's six
"sets" (each set consisting of six variations) tended toward
some general characteristic. The first set proceeded through
a cycle of fifths from D to $C^{\#}$ (D-A-E-B-$F^{\#}$-$C^{\#}$), and
remained particularly close to the theme. Many of these initial
variations mentioned "determination" and "firmness." The
second set, which continued the cycle from $G^{\#}$ to G
($G^{\#}$-$D^{\#}$-B^{b}-F-C-G), was more tense, and more stylistically
daring, Var. 10 being a kind of Boulezian adventure, Var. 11
being indebted to Cage in its use of whistles, cries, and
slammed keyboard lid. Here "impatiently" and "recklessly"
seemed key words. The third set, centered back in D,
introduced the Eisler song and "Bandiera Rossa." It also was
characterized by more improvisatory-like rhythms, including
irregular subdivisions of the beat, changes in tempo, freely
notated durations, and jazzy syncopations. The fourth set,
also rooted in D, was, in contrast, rhythmically crisp and
direct, climaxing on a ffff tremolo, "like an alarm." The fifth
set, as Wolff pointed out, was the most complex: it deviated
most freely from the theme, often suggesting despondent,
angry meditations. In its own way, it recapitulated the tonal
motion of set one, from D to $C^{\#}$. And like set two, set six
completed the motion from $G^{\#}$ to G-D, this time with

appropriate key signatures (for the minor mode, which dominated this work). This last set's summation was hardly conclusive, but rather full of conflict and tension; here, in what had to be one of the most Dostoievskian moments in American music, the composer seemed poised at the edge of madness. After an optional cadenza, however, the work concluded with a reprise of the main theme, more vigorous than ever. In its entirety, then, the work suggested the movement from determination, to mobilization, to exaltation, to struggle, to defeat, to madness, and again to determination. But this was only a rough interpretation of a work full of subtle, contradictory meanings.

Although *The People United* had its debts to Boulez and Cage, as we have noted, the work's style overall was relatively traditional, indeed, it was exceptionally rich in its historical allusions. The theme itself (Ex. 92) bore resemblance, both melodically and harmonically, to Paganini's famous "Caprice," so it was not surprising that the work often echoed variations of that famous melody by Liszt, Brahms, and Rachmaninov. The initial arrangement of the theme, and much of the work's general thrust, seemed related to Schubert. There were a number of other associations—the octave displacements of Copland in Var. 1 (Ex. 92a); the modern jazz styles in Var. 13 (Ex. 92b); the drive of

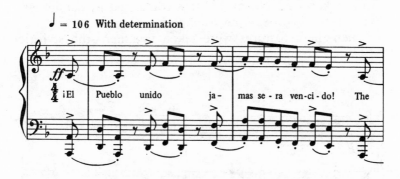

Example 92. Frederic Rzewski, *The People United Will Never Be Defeated!*
©1979 by Zen-On Music Co., Ltd. All rights reserved. Used by permission of European American Music Distributors Corporation, agent for Zen-On Music Company, Ltd.

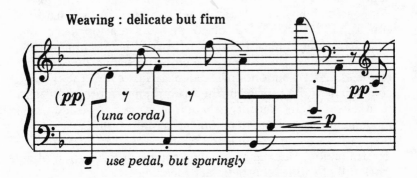

Example 92a. Variation 1.

Beethoven in Var. 21 (Ex. 92c); Wagner in Var. 25 (Ex. 92d); and Philip Glass in Var. 27 (Ex. 92e). But these varying styles were more integrated than these observations suggest. There was, for example, the prominent flavor of both jazz and Chilean popular music. But, above all, one felt the commanding presence of Bach, not only in the evocation of the first Prelude from the first book of *The Well-Tempered Clavier* at the end of Var. 28, but more generally in the skilled, florid counterpoint, often two- or three-voiced in texture. Unity was also achieved by means of some pervasive variation techniques, for instance, the use of the theme's perfect fifths as the takeoff for chains of fifths connected by semitones. Example 93 provides a few examples.

When these features were taken together—the stylistic

Example 92b. Variation 13.

Example 92c. Variation 21.

Example 92d. Variation 25.

Example 92e. Variation 27.

breadth, the incorporation of jazz elements, the indebtedness to Bach, the chromatic sequencing of a small motive—a connection with Piston emerged. It might not have been a paramount connection, nor one that was as pertinent to all the variations as to some. But it was worth noting, not least for the light it shed on something like the opening of Piston's *Flute Sonata* (see Ex. 1). On the other hand, something like the *Flute Sonata*'s rollicking finale was fairly remote from Rzewski. Rzewski's kind of pessimistic despair preferred a texture saturated with minor triads and keys; even his occasional hopefulness had a grim coloring.

One encountered more major triads, however, in Rzewski's next two works: *Four Pieces* and *American Ballads,*

Example 93a. Frederic Rzewski, "Variation 3," *The People United Will Never Be Defeated!* (Zen-On, 1979).

both for piano. Both works also showed a more Debussian interest in the sheer sound potential of the piano. *Four Pieces* had no program; indeed, it fitted very well the tradition of the four-movement piano sonata. It, nonetheless, contained deep ties with Rzewski's overtly leftist works, and it doubtless represented an attempt to give nonprogrammatic expression to his political feelings. Each of the four *American Ballads,* in contrast, used a tune familiar to native labor and peace movements, and further created a resonant dialectic by contrasting harmonious, diatonic settings of these tunes with dissonant, polytonal juxtapositions of tune fragments (Ex. 94). One naturally thought of Ives. Rzewski returned to American folksong for his 1980 piano concerto, *Long Time Man,* which used a song that had been discovered and recorded by Pete Seeger, "It Makes a Long Time Man Feel Bad." Christian Wolff wrote of this concerto that despite its "experimental features," it recalled "American music of the 1930s, say Copland."[31] Under the influence of Rzewski, Wolff had come to use leftist materials in his own work by this time.

Example 93b. Variation 8.

Example 93c. Variation 19.

In considerable contrast, Rzewski's *To The Earth* for speaking percussionist, a short work from 1984, returned to a '60s sensibility in its use of a speaker-musician as well as in its unusual scoring for four flower pots (each to a designated pitch) and knitting needles. The text was a Homeric hymn to Mother Nature, translated into English. Consequently, the marvelously gentle sound of knitting needles struck against flower pots was symbolically appropriate. In view of the work's limited, modal pitch material, it revealed continued

Example 94. Frederic Rzewski, "Down By the Riverside," *Four American Ballads* (Zen-On, 1982). (Rzewski Down by the Riverside from North American Ballads) ©1982 by Zen-On Music Co., Ltd. All rights reserved. Used by permission of European American Music Distributors Corporation, agent for Zen-On Music Company, Ltd.

links with Riley, Reich, and Behrman. But it had its own political resonance, representing, as it did, a transition from the left-wing's anti-war, pro-labor agenda of the 1960s to the ecological "green" movements of the 1980s.

Behrman also had some left-wing affiliations. In 1959 he took part in a concert arranged by Pousseur and sponsored by the Belgian Communist Party; and in the '60s, he participated in a festival held by Artists Against the War in Vietnam. Groups like SAG were, as mentioned, implicitly left-wing, and Behrman even wrote two works for SAG that were overtly political: *Questions from the Floor* and *A New Team Takes Over.* But this was exceptional; Behrman's interests lay primarily in the abstract world of electronic, aleatoric music, and remained so in the 1970s and '80s. In his mature view, he subscribed to a notion that had been denounced by Rzewski, that of art as a "form of protest in itself."[32]

Behrman's post-1970 work witnessed significant changes, however. Rather than purely electronic music, or acoustical sound altered by electronic means, Behrman began to favor traditional instruments in dialog with electronic ones. This development was explored initially in the 1974 *Voice with Trumpet and Melody-Driven Electronics,* and two works form 1975: *Cello with Melody-Driven Electronics* and *Voice with Melody-Driven Electronics.* In these works, musicians and machines could interact directly, without recourse to any intermediary. The computer, which Behrman first used in 1977 with *Figure in a Clearing* for cello with microcomputer and electronics, and *On the Other Ocean* for various instruments with microcomputer, pitch-sensors and electronics, offered even greater potential for such interaction. In *Figure in a Clearing,* the computer chose among various chords and tunings, as well as among accelerating or decelerating rhythms "modelled after the velocity of a satellite in falling elliptical orbit about a planet," while the cellist responsively improvised using six prescribed pitches.[33] In *On the Other Ocean,* the interaction was more complex, as the computer could respond—thanks to a pitch-sensing device—to the musicians, who again were restricted to six pitches. Behrman's work from the 1980s—including *6-Circle* for two trumpets and computer system (1984) and *Interspecies Small-talk* for violinist, electric keyboard player, and computer music system (1984)—was even more technologically sophisticated, involving the occasional use of computer graphics. There was a portentous, philosophical aspect to all this intimate rhapsodizing between man and machine, as well as something quite playful and not dissimilar to the contemporary vogue for computer games.

The very content of Behrman's work changed dramatically, too. Whereas the electronic music of the 1960s consisted primarily of simple sine waves, the electronic sounds of his post-1970 music came closer to real pitch, beginning with the use of triangle-wave generators in *Pools of Phase Locked Loops* (1972) and *Home-Made Synthesizer Music with Sliding Pitches* (1973). Behrman further enhanced the purity of the triangle wave (which resembles an organ tone, but is lighter, due to missing partials) by tuning his frequencies to just temperament. The electronic parts to these later works often provided a sustained background of drones, perfect intervals, or plain chords, with fancier figuration for *Interspecies Smalltalk*. The instrumental parts, in contrast, were more melodic, with their melodies, as mentioned, derived from a limited number of pitches. These pitch sources often suggested the dorian or mixolydian mode, which gave the music a certain exotic and ancient air. Both the electronic and instrumental parts further tended toward tonal stasis, and one jazz critic called *On the Other Ocean,* "a kind of slow motion electronic analogy of Coltrane's delving into the implications of a single chord/mode."[34]

Rhythmically, these works unfolded in a kind of nonpulsed flux. This was related, at least in part, to Behrman's long association with the Merce Cunningham Dance Company, for whom many of his works were intended, including *For Nearly An Hour* (1968, for the dance, *Walkaround Time*); *Voice with Melody-Driven Electronics* (1975, for *Rebus*); and *Interspecies Smalltalk* (1984, for *Pictures*). Since Cunningham never coordinated music and dance, but rather had musicians improvise on the spot, it was obviously advantageous to have music that was rhythmically fluid and unpulsed, so as to not overpower the dancers' own rhythms.

The combination of triangle waves, just temperament, drones, perfect intervals, modal melodies, tonal stasis, and rhythmic flux gave Behrman's mature work a quality that

could be described as peaceful, ethereal, and meditative,[35] a
quality in keeping with their pastoral and galactic titles. Such
work could even be classified as "new-age music," a contemporary trend described by H. Wiley Hitchcock as "improvisatory, modal or microtonal, open-ended, tensionless, climax-
less, trance-like, essentially amorphous music that was
strangely becalming" (though Hitchcock himself placed
Behrman in the context of "Timbral, Tonal, Temperamental,
and Technological Outreach," no doubt thinking in particular
of Behrman's earlier music).[36] Behrman could not be confused with new-age jazz artists like George Winston, or
rock-flavored orientalists like Steven Halpern, let alone
Vangelis Papathanassiou's 1982 soundtrack to *Chariots of
Fire,* in which a Hollywoodized version of the idiom could be
used with slow-motion footage to suggest the transcendental
euphoria of track runners. But there was a kinship of sorts,
and in relation to Brian Eno's "ambient music," as represented by his 1978 *Music for Airports,* the kinship was
profound indeed: one similarly found modal melodies against
a wash of nonpulsed, electronic sounds, essentially static,
though inflected by subtle, slow-moving harmonic change.
There was no break with Cage here.

Differences with Eno were as instructive as similarities,
however. Eno's electronic sounds were richer, deeper, more
like a brass choir, whereas Behrman's, as explained, were
lighter, more like a chorus of recorders, or the brighter stops
of an organ. Behrman's fusion of live and electronic sounds
was also more blended. Furthermore, Eno used triads and
harmonic function to create patches of tension and resolution,
sometimes even reminiscent of older, romantic styles, like
Barber; Behrman's scale was more spacious, and his textures
were more intricate, creating an endless contrapuntal web of
sustained electronic sounds that suggested some connection
with Bach. And finally, Eno's music admittedly was meant as
background music, Muzak, in his own words, intended not to
stimulate, but "to induce calm and a space to think."[37]
Behrman's music was never very far from the extraordinary
choreography of Merce Cunningham.

There were also distinctions to be made among different
works by Behrman. For instance, while Behrman often wrote
for solo instruments and electronic media, the use of two

instruments—flute and bassoon—for the Lovely Music recording of *On the Other Ocean* created an even more elaborate contrapuntal fabric than usual. The work was also more pastoral in its mood, and matched Hitchcock's "new-age" definition better than some other of his works. *Figure in a Clearing,* which gradually progressed from dark, fuzzy beginnings to a bright, radiant conclusion, was more like James Tenney, and closer to the composer's roots in the '60s avant-garde. For its part, the whimsically titled *Interspecies Smalltalk* contained relatively ornate figuration (computer-generated), and had more of an Eastern, perhaps Indian, flavor, like classical sitar music. Somewhat distinctive, too, was its dip into a lengthy stretch on bVII before returning to the tonic. It seemed, in fact, that Behrman set different problems for himself with each new composition.

By 1985 Behrman seemed on the brink of yet new changes. He had begun to feel the limitations of music without some pulse,[38] and had made some tentative steps in that direction with *Interspecies Smalltalk.* He also expressed concern over an ever-changing technology, in that it exacted too much of a composer's time and money, and, moreover, prevented the establishment of a stable repertory. In 1984 he wrote his first non-electronic work in many years, the *Orchestral Construction Set* for orchestra. But his electronic music, even that from the 1960s, continued to sound fresh, no doubt because of its personal and imaginative relation to the technology being used.

By the year John Rockwell wrote his book on American music—1983—Behrman and Rzewski seemed, indeed, were poles apart. Behrman had established a reputation primarily for nonpulsed, abstract works for computer and instrumentalists (often performed in conjunction with the Merce Cunningham Dance Company), Rzewski for virtuoso piano works that used leftist chants and folksongs. When one considered, too, the careers of John Harbison, a "neoromantic," and the somewhat younger John Adams, a "minimalist," it could be argued that the Harvard graduates of their generation provided a microcosm of the often mentioned "pluralism" of American "postmodernism."

But ties between these two friends, both so shaped by shared formative experiences, remained. The contrapuntal concerns of their mature work, for instance, showed a respect and under-standing of Bach, nurtured under Piston's guidance. There was also a connection with American modernism itself, above all the Copland of *Appalachian Spring:* for Behrman, this included the work's serenity, as in its glowing opening pages, and its relation to Martha Graham, Merce Cunningham's mentor; for Rzewski, this connection resided principally in the left-wing sensibilities that informed Copland's use of American folk styles. Finally, both men retained the ideals of improvisation, spontaneity, and social change that characterized their involve-ments in the counterculture of the 1960s. The end results were, to be sure, different, but aligned; as with progressive journals and cooperatives of the 1980s, Eastern-styled spiritualism and Marxist political action somehow were understood to reflect some common worldview.

In a way, the careers of Behrman and Rzewski seemed to reenact a conflict found in two earlier Harvard composers—Carter and Bernstein—and endemic to many left-wing artists of the 20th century: whether, like Behrman, to create new sounds in order to transform the human community, or whether, like Rzewski, to use traditional means in order to foster class consciousness. Here, the responses seemed even more antithetical than with Carter and Bernstein, Behrman providing an altogether transcendental and utopian ritual, Rzewski an unremittingly grim look at contemporary society. As with Carter and Bernstein, there was often the question of how art could really serve to change or restructure life: Behrman was accused, like Carter, of being self-indulgent and hermetic;[39] and Rzewski, like Bernstein, of being self-righteous, facile, eclectic, even reactionary.[40] But their luminous scores, so full of new, provocative kinds of artistic expression and communal interaction, won enough friends like John Rockwell to ensure lively interest in their work for many years to come.

Notes

1. Rockwell, *All American Music* (New York: Alfred A. Knopf, 1983).
2. Behrman, personal interview, September 4, 1985.

3. Behrman, personal letter, April 24, 1985.
4. Rzewski, "The Reappearance of Isorhythm in Modern Music"; Behrman, "Theory and Technique in the Work of Pierre Boulez," Senior Honors Thesis, Harvard Music Library.
5. See especially Roman Vlad, "Le niove vie della giovanne musica," *La Rassegna Musicale* 31 (1961), p. 349; and Mirosaw Kondracki, "A Na 'Jesievi' Wiosennie," *Ruch Muzyczny* 16 No. 24 (1972), pp. 5–10.
6. Salzman, "The Avant-Garde," *Stereo Review* 32 (June 1974), p. 116.
7. Behrman, "Theory and Technique," p. 50.
8. Behrman, "Wave Train," *Source,* Vol. 2 No. 1 (January 1968), pp. 28–32.
9. Jay Huff, "An Interview with David Behrman," *Composer* 4 No. 1 (1972), p. 29.
10. Huff, p. 32.
11. Jack, "Sonic Arts," *Music and Musicians* 22 (February 1974), pp. 51–52.
12. Rockwell, p. 139.
13. Johnson, "First Festival of Live-Electronic Music 1967," *Source* Vol. 2 No. 1 (January 1968), p. 51.
14. Souster, "Three 'Music Now' programmes," *Tempo* 89 (Summer, 1969), pp. 23–24.
15. Behrman, "What Indeterminate Notation Determines," *Perspectives of New Music* (Spring-Summer 1965), pp. 58–73.
16. Behrman, liner notes to a recording of *Runthrough,* Mainstream MS 5010.
17. Ken Terry, "Frederic Rzewski and the Improvising Avant Garde," *Down Beat* 46 (January 11, 1979), p. 21.
18. Rzewski, "Words," *Source* Vol. 2 No. 1 (January, 1968), p. 25.
19. Rzewski, *Street Music* and *Symphony, Source* Vol. 3, No. 2 (July 1969), p. 41.
20. Rzewski, *Plan for Spacecraft, Source* Vol. 2 No. 1 (January 1968), pp. 67–68.
21. Rouse, "New American Music in Cross Section," *Stereo Review* 37 (September 1976), pp. 126–127.
22. Rzewski, "The Reappearance," p. 119, pp. 122ff.
23. Terry, pp. 20–21.
24. Rzewski, "Statement," *Source* Vol. 3 No. 2 (July 1969), p. 90.
25. Rzewski, "Is the Composer Anonymous," *Source* Vol. 1 No. 2 (July 1967), p. 1.
26. Cardew, "A Note on Frederic Rzewski," *Musical Times* 117 (January 1976), p. 32.
27. Cardew, *Stockhausen Serves Imperialism* (London: Latimer, 1974).

28. Rzewski, liner notes to a recording of the *Variations,* Finnadar SR 9011.
29. Eric Salzman, "The Young Pianist," *Stereo Review* 38 (June 1977), p. 136.
30. Wolff, liner notes to a recording of *The People United,* Vanguard VSD 71248.
31. Wolff, review of *Long Time Man, Hi Fi/Mus Am* 30 (June 1980), MA 19–20.
32. Terry, "Rzewski," p. 20; Behrman, interview.
33. Behrman, liner notes to a recording of *Figure in a Clearing,* Lovely Music LML 1041.
34. Jon Balleras, review of *On the Other Ocean, Down Beat* 46 (May 17, 1979), p. 26.
35. Joan La Barbara, "New Music," *Hi Fi/Mus Am* 27 (June 1977), MA 14–15: Rockwell, p. 141.
36. Hitchcock, *Music in the United States,* third edition (Englewood Cliffs: Prentice Hall, 1988), pp. 318–319, 335.
37. Eno, liner notes to a recording of *Ambient #1. Music for Airports,* Editions EGS 201.
38. Behrman, interview.
39. Sarah Thomas, "The Sonic Arts on Tour," *American Musical Digest* 1 (November 1969), pp. 5–6; Adrian Jack, "Sonic Arts," *Music and Musicians* 22 (February 1974), p. 52.
40. Ainslee Cox, "New York," *Music Journal* 30 (May, 1971), p. 50; Paul Driver, review of *The People United, Tempo* 136 (March 1981), p. 27.

18. THE ELUSIVE BALANCE: JOHN HARBISON

I F Behrman and Rzewski seemed to replay the conflicts and
ideals of Carter and Bernstein, John Harbison emerged as
an heir to Irving Fine. Harbison suggested Fine in
numerous ways: in his straddling the classicisms of Piston and
Sessions; in his attraction to the Metaphysical poets; in his
interest in writing popular songs and in using popular
elements in concert works; and in his association with a "new
romanticism." More than this, Harbison stylistically incorporated, either directly or via Stravinsky, aspects of Fine
and his closest associates. Consequently, there was in Harbison a clear continuity with Piston's students from an earlier
time.

John Harbison was born on December 20, 1938, in
Orange, New Jersey. A classmate of Behrman's and
Rzewski's at Harvard, he spent 1960–1961 in Berlin (like
Behrman) and pursued graduate work with Sessions at
Princeton (like Rzewski). But in contrast to them, Harbison
never participated in that side of the '60s avant-garde
associated with the counterculture or the international
student-worker movement, but, rather, addressed an audience more conservative in its values. His work, in fact, often
confronted metaphysical questions that were traditional in
scope.

Harbison's interest in metaphysics was inherited from his
father, Princeton historian E. Harris Harbison, whose well-
known essays on *The Christian Scholar in the Age of the
Reformation*[1] were written while John was in high school. In
his many text settings, the composer, it is true, only rarely
chose sacred texts, but he clearly favored writers who sought

to renew in poetic terms the essence of the New Testament, a parallel to his father's interest in Reformationist churchmen and scholars who sought to do this in scholarly or doctrinal terms. Harbison's constant search "for some kind of summation, epiphany or grace," his fascination with "the ritual element," and his "faith in the organizing force of harmony,"[2] bespoke a deeply ingrained religious sensibility.

Harbison also learned, both from his father, who composed popular and serious music in his spare time, and his mother, a writer, pianist, and singer, a love for music, especially the songs from American musical comedies. By his teens he could play over three-hundred such tunes at the piano, without knowing their original contexts, or even their authors; instinctively he gravitated toward Gershwin, Rodgers, Warren, and, above all, Kern, whom he called "the most European of our popular song composers."[3] He played such songs in a jazz style, and performed them more or less professionally, as a soloist and in combos, throughout the '50s and '60s. After 1970 he rarely did so publicly, an exception being a lecture on Kern at Cornell in 1985, at which he played six Kern songs, calling his renditions "more meditations than actual pieces." The very idea of meditating on popular theater songs seemed itself a sort of Reformationist ideal, and suggested the strong confluence of the spiritual and secular in his makeup. In any case, Harbison argued that such songs profoundly shaped his musical development, at least on a subconscious level.

One fully conscious use of such material was to be found in the composer's setting of Michael Fried's "Depths" from a 1976 work for baritone and chorus, *The Flower-Fed Buffaloes*. This movement began with a pastiche of some early 20th-century popular songs that shared the same three-note incipit, including Kern's "They Didn't Believe Me," Friml's "Indian Love Song," Warren's "I Only Have Eyes For You," and Berlin's "Always" (Ex. 95). Each of these related melodies were staggered repeatedly in separate voices to create a kind of collage, an effect reminiscent of the composer's 1971 setting of Blake's "Hear the Voice of the Bard" from *Five Songs of Experience* (Ex. 96). In both cases, these collages were meant to represent paradise lost, a dream world at odds with painful reality. Fried's poem, in fact, recalled Blake, especially the latter's "London," one of the

Example 95. John Harbison, "Depths," *The Flower-Fed Buffaloes*.

Songs of Experience that Harbison did not set. Again, the unity of the spiritual and the secular suggested by this comparison seemed indicative of the composer's strong metaphysical bent.

The overt use of popular idioms in *Flower-Fed Buffaloes*, however, was unusual in the broader context of the composer's career, and could be explained by the fact that the work was a reflection on the American bicentennial. Aside from a jazz atmosphere often found in Harbison's music, connections with the popular songs the composer loved were oblique. He never aspired to write a musical comedy, nor did

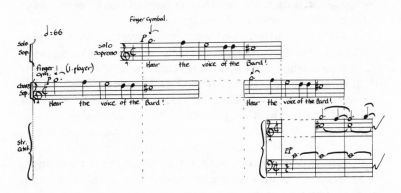

Example 96. John Harbison, "Hear the Voice of the Bard," *Five Songs of Experience* (Associated Music, 1975).

his melodies reveal the easygoing tunefulness of Tin Pan Alley. Perhaps there was something of "Indian Love Song" in the fluttertongue second theme in the finale to the *Wind Quintet;* perhaps a touch of Kern's "All the Things You Are" in the *First Symphony's* "hammer theme," especially as Harbison played the tune. Many listeners noted resemblances between Harbison's one-act opera, *Full Moon in March* (1977), and the musicals of Stephen Sondheim, especially *Pacific Overtures* (1976) and *Sweeney Todd* (1979). Sondheim, in fact, was a contemporary who had studied music at Princeton at about the same time as Harbison. It was not a comparison to intrigue Harbison, who had little interest in the American musical written after 1960. He was glad to think that the influence of popular music was restricted to the likes of Kern and Berlin, and, furthermore, had remained largely subliminal.

Harbison's formal musical education began at an early age, and by the time he graduated Princeton High School, he was fairly proficient at the piano, violin, viola, and tuba. His most important early teachers were violist Nicholas Harsanyi and pianist Mathilde McKinney, who encouraged him to compose. In 1954 he won a BMI award for a *Capriccio* for trumpet and piano. Meanwhile, he studied voice with Princeton High's Thomas Hilbish, who offered him the opportunity to both conduct and compose for the school choir. This proved the beginning of an eminent career in choral conducting, above all, with Boston's Cantata Singers, which he led from 1969 to 1973, and again from 1980 to 1982.

Feeling that Princeton was "too socially conformist," Harbison decided to go to Harvard so that he could live in Cambridge, where "no one cared what anyone else did." He liked especially the nonconformity of Cambridge's "West Coast-style beatniks, with their greasy leather jackets."[4] He attended Harvard from 1956 to 1960, studying harmony, composition, and 20th-century music with Piston, Spies, and Layton, and earning a number of awards: the Chorus Pro Musica Composition Prize, the Bohemian Prize, the Knight Prize, and a Paine Traveling Fellowship. Already familiar with the music of Stravinsky, Schoenberg, Bartók, Hindemith, and Sessions from high school, his overall preference for Stravinsky was reaffirmed at Harvard. There he also learned to admire Shapero, Fine, and Carter, less so Piston, whose *Sinfonietta,* which he conducted, he found cold and distant.[5]

Harbison's conservatism vis-à-vis Behrman and Rzewski was already evident at Harvard. Whereas their senior honors theses concerned Boulez, Harbison's was on *Mozart's music for 'Thamos, König in Aegypten.'*[6] Harbison gladly submitted to Harvard's "thorough pounding of early music," and he eventually became well-known for his performances of Bach and Schütz with the Cantata Singers. This interest in early music was related to the composer's involvement with classic poetry. A poet of some accomplishment himself (he won the Academy of American Poets Prize and the Hatch Prize while in college), Harbison went on to write an instrumental work after Donne's *Devotions,* and to set words from the Old Testament, Shakespeare, Blake, and Goethe, in addition to various 19th- and 20th-century poets.[7]

The influence of early music on his own music was, as with popular music, fairly subtle, but evident enough in, for instance, the fact that he composed a series of cantatas— *Cantatas Nos. 1* and *2* for soprano and orchestra (1965, 1967), and *Cantata No. 3* for soprano and string quartet (1968)—as well as a motet cycle, the *Mottetti di Montale* for mezzo-soprano and piano. Further, many of the vocal works quite generally featured florid solo numbers and chamber-sized instrumental accompaniments in ways that recalled earlier, especially Baroque practices. And as there was a jazz ambiance to much of Harbison's work, so, too, there was often an intimate, delicate, mystical quality seemingly related to early music.

Upon graduation from Harvard, Harbison was awarded a Paine Fellowship to study in Europe. Roger Sessions (whose son John was a longtime friend of Harbison's) discouraged him from working with Boulanger, suggesting either Blacher or Dallapiccola instead. Harbison chose Blacher, spending the year 1960–1961 in Berlin. His weekly lessons with Blacher were "often useful," even though only five minutes long; he remembered, in particular, a lesson in which Blacher represented the young American's counterpoint by holding out four fingers, and then entwined them, saying, "It should go like this."[8] Perhaps Harbison's dramatic part-crossings,

such as that huge X in the fifth page of the *Piano Concerto,*
owed something to this advice. One sensed, too, the influence
of Blacher's rhythmical style in the rapidly shifting 2/8, 5/16,
3/8, 4/8, and 5/8 meters in the "Fanfare" that opened *Full
Moon in March.* Harbison, however, disclaimed much interest
in Blacher's music, or in the music he then heard for the first
time from Darmstadt.

On returning to the States, Harbison spent two years
(1961–1963) at Princeton studying with Sessions and Earl
Kim. He remembered Sessions as "a great enabler, someone
who could help people go ahead and write. He was interested
in the long line and in our getting work under our belt[9]. . . .
Kim, on the other hand, would give advice and criticism about
details, and it was very helpful to have someone who would
take the trouble with, for example, the structure of a
particular chord."[10] Whereas modern music at Harvard
primarily meant Stravinsky, Bartók, and older French composers, the new music holding sway in the halls and
classrooms of Princeton seemed to Harbison less restrictive,
encompassing Webern's *Three Songs,* Op. 25, Schoenberg's
Trio, Boulez's *Mallarmé,* Stravinsky's *Huxley Variations,*
Carter's *Second Quartet,* and Babbitt's *Philomel.*[11] Furthermore, Sessions's belief in "suspending taste" encouraged him
to express unreservedly his admiration for Tchaikovsky,
Rachmaninov, Prokofiev, and Irving Berlin.[12] It was also at
Princeton that Harbison met his future wife Rosemary, a
brilliant violinist who was to premiere and perform many of
his works, including the solo parts for the *Sinfonia* for violin
and double orchestra (1963) and the *Violin Concerto* (1980).

After Princeton, Harbison spent five years (1963–1968) at
Cambridge on a fellowship from Harvard's Society of Fel-
lows, which allowed him ample time to compose. After this,
he taught for one year at Reed College, and then returned to
Cambridge to accept a position at MIT. In the 1970s, his
reputation grew, and he won some prestigious awards,
including Brandeis's Creative Arts Award (1971), an American Academy of Arts and Letters Award (1973), and a
Guggenheim Fellowship (1977). In the 1980s he served as
composer-in-residence for the Santa Fe Music Festival (1981)
and the Pittsburgh Symphony Orchestra (1982–1984). His

summers usually were spent at his in-laws' farm in Token Creek, Wisconsin.

Harbison's development as a composer was gradual, consistent, and subject to careful self-examination. Most of his music prior to 1966 was never seriously put forth, or else later withdrawn. This included works from the late '50s written at Harvard, which the composer compared to early Sessions, and music written in the period 1960 to 1966, much of which was 12-tone. One of these 12-tone works retained in his catalog was the 1965 *Confinement* for flute, oboe/English horn, clarinet/bass clarinet, alto saxophone, trumpet, trombone, violin, viola, cello, double bass, piano, and percussion. It was Harbison's first work to win national attention, thanks to a recording by Arthur Weisberg and the Contemporary Chamber Ensemble, and it provides a good introduction to the composer's music.

Somewhat like contemporaneous works by John Perkins, *Confinement* struck a fine balance between the international serialist avant-garde and certain national traditions. The impact of the avant-garde, especially Boulez, was evident in the work's novel colors, for instance, its opening for brass and bongos; in its nervous repetitions and gigantic leaps; in its avoidance of strong downbeats; and in certain harmonies. Less obvious, perhaps, but no less profound, was the work's indebtedness to the native traditions of Piston, Copland, Sessions, and their successors, a tradition evident in the work's jazzy pairing of muted trumpet and cymbals; in its vigorous rhythms; in its clear, restrained textures, including unisons and two-part writing; and in its freewheeling energy. In this and in later Harbison works, there was also, like the older American modernists, a special connection to Stravinsky, a connection the composer hoped was not too mannered.

Aside from this intriguing if not thoroughly digested synthesis of the serialist avant-garde and American modernism, what characterized *Confinement* as the composer's own? First, as one critic wrote of the 1980 *Violin Concerto,* there was "a broad expressive range,"[13] a range that seemed to alternate three primary moods: dark wit, nostalgic sorrow, and quiet meditation. The first such emotion colored the rhythmically snazzy section near the beginning; the second, the string duet near the end; and the third, the shimmering textures just after that. Later works like *Full Moon in March,* the *Piano Concerto,* and the *Piano Quintet* confirmed the primacy of these moods. These emotions were communicated not only by traditional associations, but by a sensitive and keen ear for all sorts of new colors, textures, and harmonies.

Confinement's sectional form also proved characteristic of its composer. Cast in one large movement, the work's sections originally had subtitles "associated with lines on the subject of illness drawn from John Donne's *Devotions.*"[14] Consequently, the work perhaps was best understood as a sort of tone poem with Donne as protagonist. *Parody-Fantasia* for piano, written three years after (1968), was similarly a one-movement work divided into sections with the following subheadings: "Preamble," "Take-offs," "Flights," "Arrivals," "Games," and "Post-Mortem." A still later work, the *Piano Concerto,* had a finale comprised of three large sections: "Alla marcia," "Alla canzona," and "Alla danza." These sectional forms tended to be blocklike, and to progress without any "apparent logic," or so thought William Flanagan in a review of *Confinement.*[15] There was, in addition, a lack of formal urgency within the sections themselves, with the dramatic opposition of contrasting ideas often taking the place of motivic development. In *Confinement,* for instance, shrill, declamatory chords regularly cut off fledgling melodic phrases, which were forced to begin again and again. Similar procedures were used in critical portions of the first movements of the *Wind Quintet,* the *Piano Concerto,* and the *First Symphony.* The resultant formal looseness was not necessarily compensated by the large archlike designs favored by the composer. As for the long, soaring melodies characteristic of his vocal music, they often began strongly enough, but tended, according to some critics, to fizzle out or go round in circles, without cohesive shape or clear goals. Stephanie Van Buchau, reviewing *The Winter's Tale,* noted that the vocal lines "though lyrical . . . never get anywhere" and "evaporate just when they should come to a climax."[16] Piston may have had some such deficiency in mind when he told Harbison that "concert music was not for him,"[17] and suggested, rather, that he consider a career in popular music (something Harbison would do from time to time). Harbison's vocal works probably showed him to best advantage in this respect; certainly, few of his instrumental works moved with the conviction and brilliant pacing of *Full Moon in March*. But even the instrumental works found such discerning admirers as Gunther Schuller and Ellen Pfeifer, who wrote that the *Violin Concerto* moved "with a sure sense of momentum and accumulating intensity."[18]

While in matters of content and form Harbison showed considerable constancy, in matters of style and technique there were striking changes and developments. *Confinement* actually proved to be one of Harbison's last 12-tone works, a fact that gave its title a metaphorical resonance that was purely technical. Like Crumb, Rochberg, Druckman, and other slightly older composers, Harbison gave up the 12-tone method in the mid-'60s for a more freely chromatic style. And like these older composers, he made some use of parody, notably in a series of works—*Four Preludes* for 3 treble instruments (1967), *Parody-Fantasia* for piano (1968), and *The Bermuda Triangle* for amplified cello, tenor saxophone, and electric organ (1970)—collectively known as *December Music:* these works used, as a cantus firmus, the Christmas chant, "Veni Emmanuel." In *Four Preludes,* the aeolian melody was found in the middle voice, its identity obscured, however, by fragmentation, attenuation, abbreviation, and perhaps, above all, by the surrounding chromatic parts that clearly betokened the composer's earlier 12-tone orientation (Ex. 97). The resultant texture was colorfully dissonant and yet anchored in an elusive and static tonality.

Harbison used parody only intermittently after this, for the *Flower-Fed Buffaloes,* as mentioned, and the *Mottetti,* which quoted Delibes, Ravel, and Schoenberg. Its usefulness was ultimately incidental: it may have helped wean the composer from the 12-tone technique, but it did not provide the basis for a new style, as with, say, Karl Kohn. Music like *Four Preludes,* with its special kind of extended tonality, could be effected without any quotation. The composer, indeed, accomplished this in two principal ways. The first way was to use a tonal or modal melody in counterpoint with some other line, or lines, that had some other center, or no center at all, a technique that could be considered a kind of polytonality, though perhaps deserving its own term. The second way

Example 97. Five measures from page 2 of John Harbison's *Four Preludes,* a publication of McGinnis & Marx. Copyright 1973 by Josef Marx. Used by permission of McGinnis & Marx Music Publishers.

involved the use of traditional harmonies—open fifths, triads (especially the diminished triad because it featured Harbison's favorite interval, the tritone) and seventh chords—but only fleetingly, without recourse to common function. Both techniques presumably derived, at least to some extent, from Carter.

Carteresque works like *Four Preludes* and the *Parody-Fantasia,* however, proved to be another transitional step in Harbison's development. He sought, above all, greater accessibility. In the 1970 *Bermuda Triangle,* the composer experimented with a "third stream" style by incorporating a fairly authentic jazz saxophone part within the context of a more purely modernist idiom. He later regarded such attempts as poorly integrated and symptomatic of inner contradictions.[19] In the early '70s, he even composed popular songs, hoping that one might be taken up by someone like

Helen Reddy, Carly Simon, or James Taylor. And his motivations for this were not entirely pecuniary, though he was impressed with the fact that a friend had made thousands of dollars with one such song. None of his ever sold, however.[20]

Harbison's first real successes were to be found, rather, in a series of serious texted works written in the course of the 1970s: *Five Songs of Experience* for chorus, strings, and percussion (1971); *The Winter's Tale* (1974); *The Flower-Fed Buffaloes* for chorus, baritone, and ensemble (1976); and *Full Moon in March* (1977).

The *Five Songs* contained many hallmarks of Harbison's mature style, and rightly can be considered among his first mature works. Its opening phrase, "Hear the voice of the bard" (see Ex. 96), was itself emblematic, for Harbison's mature melodic style typically was composed of such drooping scalar figures, often outlining the tritone, as here, or else a major or minor third. This included the four-note sighing figure that opened the 1981 *Piano Quintet*. Such drooping phrases often were treated canonically, as at the very start of the *Five Songs* and *Piano Quintet;* othertimes, they were developed sequentially, characteristically rising upward by seconds or thirds: see, for example, the phrases, "Doubt is fled, and clouds of reason, Dark disputes and artful teasing," from the fourth of the *Five Songs*. These restless, Wagnerian-like sequences became more prominent in later works, and helped give such works a surging, romantic quality.

The harmonic language of *Five Songs* similarly foreshadowed the composer's mature style. It was a simpler, more traditional, and more euphonious language than that cultivated by Harbison in the 1960s. This new reserve was epitomized by the second song, "Earth's Answer," for which all of the harmonies were inversions and transpositions of the opening chord, C-D♭-G♭-G (Ex. 98). *Five Songs* was still highly chromatic, but the dissonances were more clearly subsumed by traditional triads, or by suggestions of traditional triads, so that the most dissonant note often could be heard as a nonchordal tone of one kind or another.

A particularly distinctive feature of *Five Songs* was the extent of its musical symbolism; words and phrases like "seeking," "fallen," "raised up," "weeping," "tangled roots," "endless maze," and "fiery forge" received highly ornate musical depictions. The instrumental parts were no less symbolic; consider, for example, the lengthy ascent by the strings at the end of "Ah! Sunflower" to suggest the heavenly flight of souls, or the rattling percussion in "The Voice of the Ancient Bard" to represent the "bones of the dead." Such symbolism undoubtedly was related to the composer's love and familiarity with Baroque choral music, a connection especially noticeable here because of Blake's language. Such symbolism spilled over to his mature work in general, if, considering *Confinement,* it had ever been absent.

Finally, the use of rhythmic and tonal ostinati in the last song, "A Divine Image," to produce a kind of concluding immobility also proved characteristic. Similar endings were found in *Flower-Fed Buffaloes* and *Full Moon in March.* In the instrumental works, this impulse often took the form of long codas in the tonic key coming in the wake of extensive tonal ambiguity, as in the *Piano Concerto.* The specific instance of "Divine Image" was problematic in that Blake intended the poem as an afterthought (the cycle really ends with "The Voice of the Ancient Bard"), and it consequently made for a somewhat abrupt and disjointed finale. The endings to *Buffaloes* and *Full Moon* worked more successfully, thanks to

Example 98. John Harbison, "Earth's Answer," *Five Songs of Experience* (Associated Music, 1975).

the symmetrical ordering of poems in the former, and the organic cohesiveness of the latter. Andrew Porter admired the ending of *Flower-Fed Buffaloes,* writing "Harbison's affirmations—and his final C pedal—are not glib but are achieved after delicate, even painful pondering, reflected in the rhythmic and harmonic tension of the score."[21] These epilogues owed much to Stravinsky, and perhaps something to the minimalist vogue as well, but taken into consideration with other characteristic features, they were yet another touchstone of the composer's individuality.

Harbison's two operas, *The Winter's Tale* and *Full Moon in March,* created a stir in the opera world by their both receiving productions in 1979. Reviewers, however, tended to complain that the words were often inaudible, blaming this on the elaborate vocal parts and the overly rich instrumental writing.[22] These flaws seemed the more damaging in *Winter's Tale,* for the composer's condensation of Shakespeare's sprawling play was so compressed as to leave the uninitiated audience, according to Stephanie Van Buchau, "hopelessly confused."[23]

Full Moon in March, which only slightly revised the Yeats original, was a greater success, perhaps because its plot had a mythic directness: a swineherd woos a cold virgin queen, who after having him decapitated, dances around the severed head. This sort of vehicle, resembling as it does *Salome* and *Turandot,* has proven congenial to opera, and, indeed, Harbison's work had an effective, fin de siècle theatricality. But the success of *Full Moon* resided more specifically in the opportune match of poet and musician: Yeats's mordant wit, exotic passion, stylized ritual, and metaphysical undercurrent fitted Harbison's gifts very nicely. That the composer was particularly inspired was suggested by the opera's tremendous drive, by the absence of the sort of digression or slack that sometimes impeded his work. In a *New Yorker* column devoted entirely to the opera, Porter commended Harbison's "natural command of dramatic music (that is, of pacing, gesture, 'color,' and above all communicative melody)."[24] The work reminded Porter alternately of Stravinsky, Britten, Szymanowski, and Rimsky-Korsakov. The comparison with Britten seemed most telling, both in terms of the opera's Noh-like features, and in a more general stylistic sense—in

Harbison's extension of Stravinskian modernism in a romantic and relatively conservative direction. Not surprisingly, Harbison expressed special admiration for Britten, as well as for Tippett and Davies.[25]

In the late '70s, Harbison began to apply his new conservative style to purely instrumental contexts. The result was a string of works whose popularity often exceeded the earlier texted pieces. These included the 1978 *Wind Quintet,* the 1980 *Piano Concerto,* the 1980 *Violin Concerto,* the 1981 *Piano Quintet,* the 1981 *First Symphony,* and the 1985 *String Quartet.* The warm accessibility, the traditional instrumental combinations, the solid craftsmanship, and the romantic élan of these works were such that critics agreed that they stood a good chance of entering the standard concert repertory.[26]

Like the operas, such works strongly echoed a variety of styles. As with some other composers of highly allusive music, one naturally could argue whether or not such eclecticism came at too great a cost to individuality and daring. But it was hard to deny the expertise of the composer's craft or the breadth of his sympathies. This breadth included Shostakovich in the first movement of the *Symphony.* But of special interest to this study was the way Harbison evoked at various times Piston, Carter, Bernstein, Berger, Shapero, and Fine. There was, for instance, something of Berger's crispness in the last movement of the *Woodwind Quintet,* something of Shapero's athleticism in the opening movement of the *Piano Quintet* (Ex. 99), and something of Bernstein's sassiness in the finale to the *Symphony.* Considering Harbison's ability to give sense and direction to textures both rhythmically and harmonically complex, his greatest affinity may well have been to Carter. But he seemed closest of all to Fine. The Harbison *Symphony* in particular was very much like Fine's *Symphony,* not only in its general stylistic language, but in its emotional preoccupations (only Harbison's proceeded in an opposite direction, starting from an almost immobile, dirgelike helplessness rather than ending that way). Indeed, the climate that awarded Harbison the Pulitzer Prize in 1987, was well-prepared to rediscover in Fine's 1962 work an outstanding precursor of well-favored contemporary trends.

There were also certain technical features, especially in the

Example 99. John Harbison, "Overtura," *Piano Quintet.*

concertos, that were reminiscent of Piston: a counterpoint that had three distinct levels of rhythmic activity; an orchestral texture in which a high, sustained melody was supported by a lively middle voice, and a slow, chromatic bass; a broad 4/4 enlivened by syncopations and triplets; a fast alternation of 5/8 and 6/8 meters; and allusions to jazz and folk idioms. Similarly, the 1985 *String Quartet* seemed a successor to the Piston quartets, above all, in the realm of texture. Such affinities were surprising considering the coolness with which these two composers apparently regarded each other. Perhaps they saw in one another some resemblance they preferred not to acknowledge; Allen Sapp suggested that Harbison "represents the inner side of Piston, that part which Walter Piston could never allow to escape."[27]

It must be noted too, however, that the differences between Harbison and Piston were significant. Harbison's dramatic unisons, rich doublings, romantic harmonies, surging sequences, fluctuating pulse, and blocklike forms, in short, much of the essence of his musical style was aesthetically at some distance from Piston's. There was a bit of late Ravel in Harbison's work, for instance, the oboe melody surrounded by piano filigree in the slow movement of the *Piano Concerto,* but little of the French-related modernist ideals with which Piston was so affiliated.

Indeed, Harbison showed, rather, a strong inclination toward German Romanticism. The very opening of the *Quintet,* with its French horn, in its high register, accompanied by tremolo winds, was a sort of "Waldmusik." And the ensuing second movement (with its sweet waltzlike melody) and scherzo (with its burlesque octave leaps) similarly suggested German Romantic antecedents. Most romantic were the slow movements of the *Piano Quintet* and the *First Symphony,* lush, moody landscapes whose sentimentality and dramatic restlessness reminded some listeners of Wagnerian movie music, and whose evocation of bird calls strongly recalled Mahler. In this context, it was worth noting, too, that Harbison wrote works inspired by Goethe and Hölderlin.[28]

Harbison's vocal works, however, continued to reveal the composer at his most intimate and inimitable. *The Natural World* (1984–1986), a setting for voice and five instruments of three rather melancholy poems by Robert Bly, Wallace

Stevens, and James Wright, even contained something of the anguished severity of his 12-tone music composed in the 1960s, before he had become well known. The arresting harmonies and emotional climaxes recalled, for example, *Confinement*. The scoring for the five accompanying instruments—the same as for *Pierrot Lunaire*—showed, too, a daring economy of means, with incisive use of unison and two-part textures. Some knowledge of these songs would place in perspective a view of the composer based on the more lush and accessible instrumental music of the 1980s.

The Flight Into Egypt (1986) similarly aimed to "bring renewed attention to . . . the darker side of Christmas, and the realities of urban life that we are too eager to overlook."[29] In depicting the Biblical story of Mary and Joseph's flight into Egypt, the composer intended, ostensibly, to draw an analogy between their hardship and the plight of the homeless in contemporary America. Such social concerns also harkened back to Harbison's work of the late 1960s and early 1970s.

This "sacred ricercar" also evoked the Baroque cantata ideal that had long informed some of the composer's best music. The scoring for soprano, baritone, chorus, and small chamber ensemble was similar to that of any number of Baroque cantatas; the instrumentation for two oboes, English horn, bassoon, three trombones, chamber organ, and strings was, although novel, antique in flavor. Harbison set the text (Matthew 2:13–23) in one large movement: as the baritone unfolded the narration, the soprano assumed the part of the angel, and the chorus depicted the words of Jeremy and Joseph.

The choral writing, which featured expert contrapuntal writing, seemed especially felicitous. The final chorus, "He shall be called a Nazarene," captured the kind of mystical urgency heard only intermittently since the composer's Blake settings. Wrote Richard Dyer, "The end is full of mingled anger, heartbreak, compassion, and promise."[30]

The Flight Into Egypt also exhibited Harbison's text painting abilities in their full maturity; the music illuminated the story clearly and poignantly. The effective scoring and instrumentation even suggested some vague connection to the Biblical film epics of Harbison's youth: the reeds for the travels of Joseph and Mary; the brass for the violence of

Herod and Archelaus; and the strings for the sadness of
Rachel. At the music's end, the brass motive returned,
ominously.

Although the score suggested most immediately similar
works by Stravinsky and Britten, some of its most personal
features revealed the composer's American background and
training. The basic sound—if not sentiment—of the work had
an important precedent in Piston's *Psalm and Prayer of David*.
The work also reminded one of Daniel Pinkham; in many
ways, Harbison seemed the natural—if more brooding—
successor to this older Bostonian.

When *The Flight Into Egypt* earned Harbison the Pulitzer
prize in 1987, it became the first sacred choral work so
honored. If Rzewski and Behrman persuasively championed
Marxist and Asian philosophical thought, respectively, Harbison showed that Christianity could still inspire music that was
thoughtful, sensitive, and modern. Such an accomplishment
possibly represented Harbison's greatest contribution to
American music. In any case, one looked forward to more
choral works.

The romantic bent, if not essence, of Harbison's music
tended to distract listeners from connections with the
baroque, with American neoclassicism, with political activ-
ism, and with Christianity; rather, the music could be made to
fit the popular catch-all of the 1980s, the "new romanticism."
Harbison himself had no problem with the term, which for
him simply betokened an accepted modification of the
hermetic and off-beat trends of the 1960s. He understood his
music to establish its closest ties not with 19th-century music,
but with the earlier 20th-century, especially the 1930s,
another decade that in its time was considered "neoromantic." Indeed, Harbison's basic orientation was toward composers and trends that today would be considered neoclassical.

In short, Harbison demonstrated the limitations of any
simplistic classic-romantic dialectic. His music could be
morose, but the more romantic extremes of hysteria and
anarchy played little part in his work. He even proved
different from the elegant, almost hedonistic romanticism of
another Carter enthusiast, Yehudi Wyner, who tended to
regard the 20th century, except for perhaps Schoenberg, as

quite askew, and who insisted on a return to 19th-century ideals. In more the Harvard tradition, Harbison found room for both Schoenberg and Stravinsky; he strove not to favor the heart over the head, like Wyner, but to balance the two. It was a balance that differed from composer to composer. But Harbison was characteristic in trying to achieve it.

Notes

1. E. Harris Harbison, *The Christian Scholar* (New York: Scribner's, 1956).
2. Ellen Pfeifer, "John Harbison," *Hi Fi/Mus Am* 32 (March 1982), MA 7.
3. Harbison, "Jerome Kern," lecture at Cornell University, April 11, 1985.
4. Pfeifer, p. 7.
5. Harbison, personal interview, April 10, 1985.
6. Harbison, *Mozart's music*, 1960, senior honors thesis, Harvard Music Library.
7. Harbison's songs included settings of Dickinson, Baudelaire, and Rilke (*Autumnal*, 1964); more Dickinson (the *Cantatas*, and *Elegiac Songs*, 1974); Shakespeare (*Shakespeare Series*, 1965), Goethe (*Book of Hours and Seasons*, 1975); Hardy (*Moments of Vision*, 1975); Gary Snyder, Michael Fried, and Ian Hamilton (*3 Harp Songs*, 1975); the *Old Testament* (*Samuel Chapter*, 1978); and Eugenio Montale (*Mottetti di Montale*, 1980). His choruses included settings of Shelley (*Music When Soft Voices Die*, 1966); Blake (*Five Songs of Experience*, 1971); more Snyder and Fried, as well as Vachel Lindsay and Hart Crane (*The Flower-Fed Buffaloes*, 1976); and the *New Testament* (*Nunc dimittis*, 1979). There were operas after Shakespeare's *Winter's Tale* and Yeats's *Full Moon in March* (1974, 1977), and incidental music to Shakespeare's *The Merchant of Venice*. The instrumental works inspired by texts included *Confinement* for 12 instruments (1965) after Donne's *Devotions*, and *Die Kürze* for chamber ensemble (1970) and *Diotima* for orchestra, both after Hölderlin. There was also a set of variations for oboe on the song *Amazing Grace* (1972).
8. Pfeifer, p. 7.
9. Pfeifer, p. 8.
10. David Ewen, *American Composers* (New York: Putnam's, 1982), p. 9.

11. Harbison, interview.
12. Harbison, talk with Cornell composers, April 11, 1985.
13. Ellen Pfeifer, "Debuts and Reappearances," *Hi Fi/Mus Am* 31 (June 1981), MA 24.
14. Eric Salzman, liner notes to a recording of *Confinement*, Nonesuch H-71221.
15. Flanagan, "Nonesuch's 'Spectrum: New American Music,'" *Stereo Review* 23 (August 1969), p. 95.
16. Van Buchau, "San Francisco," *Opera News* 44 (December 1979), p. 51; *Opera* 30 (December 1979), p. 1185.
17. Pfeifer, "Interview," p. 7.
18. Pfeifer, "Debuts."
19. Harbison, "Kern."
20. Harbison, interview.
21. Porter, *Music of Three More Seasons 1977–1980* (New York: Alfred A. Knopf, 1981), p. 161.
22. Van Buchau, *Opera;* Marilyn Tucker, "San Francisco," *Hi Fi/Mus Am* 29 (December 1979), MA 20; Andrew Porter, p. 377.
23. Van Buchau, *Opera.*
24. Porter, p. 374.
25. Harbison, interview.
26. Joan La Barbara, "New Music—Running the Gamut," *Hi Fi/Mus Am* 30 (September 1980), MA 14; Pfeifer, "Debuts."
27. Sapp, personal letter, August 1, 1984.
28. See n7.
29. Richard Dyer, "Boston," *American Choral Review*, 30 (Winter 1988), p. 18.
30. Dyer, p. 20.

CONCLUSION: WALTER PISTON AND HIS STUDENTS IN WIDENING CONTEXTS

NADIA BOULANGER ONCE REMARKED in conversation, "A man isn't made of one image but of a multitude. It is the composition of images that make up the man."[1] Boulanger was referring specifically to Stravinsky, but her observation could apply to Piston or anyone else. In fact, she offered one such image of Piston, but more on that later.

At about the same time as these Boulanger conversations were published (1985), two other writings came out containing reminiscences of Piston that exemplified Boulanger's observation: Clarissa Lorenz's 1983 memoirs, *Lorelei Two*,[2] and Erich Segal's 1985 novel, *The Class*.[3] The former recounted Lorenz's ten tempestuous years (1926–1936) as lover and second of three wives to Piston's friend, poet Conrad Aiken. Piston makes the occasional appearance: visiting their Boston "love-nest" in 1927 and '28 to have a game of chess with Aiken and play the beat-up, beer-hall upright "with fine abandon . . . growing more antic and witty with each drink" (pp. 46, 62); and visiting the married couple in Sussex, England, in 1931 and 1935 for more chess, witty banter, and now, Ping-Pong. Lorenz appreciated the fact that Piston, unlike so many of Aiken's old friends, did not snub her because of her naiveté, or because of some moralistic loyalty to Aiken's first wife; in fact, he encouraged her to pursue her musical studies. She also appreciated Piston's way of calming her moody, often suicidal husband, and experienced no little relief when Aiken left his revolver with Piston prior to a trip to England. But when their marriage began to fall apart in 1933, Lorenz began to associate Piston with Aiken's darker side, accusing her husband of attending "wild parties" at Piston's Belmont studio, with "couples swapping partners and vanishing into darkened bedrooms, ex-lovers trying to recapture their mistresses, a nymphomaniac stalking you, and all the rest of it" (p. 179).

Piston also makes a cameo appearance in *The Class,* Segal's novel about the Harvard Class of 1958. Himself a member of this class, Segal never studied with Piston, but as an aspiring musician of sorts, encountered him occasionally in the corridors of Paine Hall. In the novel, Piston figures in the life of one of the main characters, Danny Rossi, who "from the time he entered high school . . . had his heart set on going to Harvard where he could study composition with Randall Thompson, choral master, and Walter Piston, virtuoso symphonist" (p. 11). Piston refuses the freshman, however, a place in his Composition Seminar, saying, "But if I take you now, you might be in the paradoxical position of—how can I put it?—being able to sprint and not to walk. If it's any consolation, when Leonard Bernstein was here we forced him to do his basic music 'calisthenics' just like you" (p. 39). (And it seems that the character of Rossi was modeled, at least in part, after Bernstein; he goes on to become a renowned pianist, conductor, and composer of classical scores and a Broadway hit.) When Rossi finally takes the seminar in his junior year, he is disappointed, finding the assignments "limiting" (p. 102). And when Piston counsels him to continue his studies with Boulanger, saying that his music lacks "sufficient discipline," Rossi thinks, "What good did Boulanger do *you?* Your symphonies aren't *that* great. And when's the last time that an orchestra asked you to be their soloist? No, Walter, I think you're just a little jealous. I'm going to give the Boulangerie a miss" (p. 185).

These two portrayals of Piston as genial, tactful, encouraging, and, ultimately, remote, had their similarities. But there was quite a difference between the man who played the beer-hall upright with abandon and hosted wild parties in Belmont as depicted by Lorenz, and the upholder of academic traditions and the Boulangerie as described by Segal. Of course, one would expect Lorenz, the wife of an intimate, to have a different perspective of Piston than Segal, an awed undergraduate. But the differences also pointed to distinctions of time and age: Lorenz depicted a man in his thirties against the background of the late '20s and early '30s, whereas Segal portrayed a man in his sixties in the late '50s. This age factor similarly had to figure into any discussion of Piston and his students: Lorenz, after all, was about the same age as Vincent, Carter, and Anderson; Segal was a contemporary of Rzewski, Behrman, and Harbison. A chronological approach to the subject of Piston and his students is consequently in order.

Piston's 1925 *Three Pieces* for flute, clarinet, and bassoon, his first published work, exhibited a brilliant technique and a modern sensibility; and like many of the composer's works to come, it quickly entered the standard repertory. Piston was not the only significant American composer to emerge in the 1920s—there was Copland, Thomson, Sessions, Harris, Chanler, Porter, Hanson, Thompson, Antheil, Cowell, and others. Their diverse achievements were anticipated by a slightly older generation of composers that included Griffes, Ives, Carpenter, Converse, Farwell, Gilbert, Taylor, and Mason. But the young composers of the 1920s worked their way into the larger fabric of American, and even world, musical culture in a more successful way than had these older composers, either because the older composers lacked the requisite craft, or daring, or vision, or whatever (Griffes and Carpenter to some extent proved exceptions, as, of course, did Ives; but none of this music had much importance to the young composers of 1940). The special importance of the generation of the 1920s to American music was perhaps best compared not to contemporary literary or artistic figures, who after all worked in mediums with well-established traditions, but to developments in popular music with Gershwin, Porter, Kern, and Berlin, and in jazz with Armstrong, Ellington, "Jelly Roll" Morton, and Bessie Smith. This was no mere coincidence: these repertories had varying degrees of closeness to each other and to common origins. They reflected, in any case, a new national identity that was progressive, vibrant, and sophisticated.

Boulanger's contention, stated in the '20s, that American music was about to take off as Russian music had in the mid-19th century, consequently proved nothing less than prophetic. Indeed, American music of the 1920s and '30s claimed the sort of importance that Russian music of the

1860s and '70s had: it provided a cornerstone, a reference, a "golden age," as Thomson called it, for subsequent national developments. It is, therefore, helpful to give this legacy some consideration.

The spirit of the '20s really was hatched in the last years of the First World War. Works which have come to be recognized as emblematic of the postwar era—Stravinsky's *L'Histoire* and *Ragtime*, Bartók's *Miraculous Mandarin*, Satie's *Parade*, Ravel's *Tombeau de Couperin*, Prokofiev's *Classical Symphony*, Berg's *Wozzeck*—were actually written or begun in 1917 and 1918. Schoenberg's 12-tone method also must be considered a product of these years, at least to some extent. The values represented by these works differed from composer to composer, but one noted such trends as a revival of the ideals of craft, structure, polyphony; a rejection of emotional bombast, sentimentality, or any bohemian exaltation of the artist; a cool, skeptical tone; an ironic humor; and a steadfastness before violence, horror, machinery, in short, the modern world. The clean, clear surfaces only made the prevailing anger at the War more penetrating, and the prevailing sorrow, and perhaps guilt, for surviving the War more poignant. One tried hard to laugh it off like Charlie Chaplin, the period's central persona.

The American generation of the '20s reflected these trends in varying ways and with varying success. Copland's own taste singled out Piston, Sessions, Thomson, Harris, and himself for a series of one-man concerts in 1935 at the New School, and later for a book on 20th-century music; called by Thomson, in a typical bit of '20s humor, American music's "commando unit," they proved to be among the most enduring composers of their generation. Again, to place Piston in perspective, it was necessary to consider these five composers, even if but briefly, so as to establish the larger context for his particular achievement.

Piston (b. 1894) was the oldest of the generation of the '20s, and, indeed, its members thought of him as such, even more than his few years seniority might suggest. This was perhaps due to his quiet, detached manner, as well as to his highly controlled and elegant music, which exhibited a more profound relation to the classic tradition of Bach, Mozart, Chopin, and Brahms than was characteristic of his generation.

At the same time, his music was forward-looking in its harmonic, rhythmic, and textural vocabulary.

Sessions (b. 1896) stood somewhat apart in that he seemed in direct lineage to, from the '20s perspective, the dreaded Wagner. His instrumental works, far from being fashionably cool and ironic, were like condensed Wagner operas full of heated passion, but at the same time recognizably American. In time an opera about *Montezuma* would prove an appropriate vehicle. Significantly, Sessions initially showed less interest in the 12-tone method (a '20s innovation, after all) than Piston or Copland, and yet became one of the few composers of his generation to embrace atonality (a prewar Viennese development). Significant, too, was the fact that he was the only member of the "commando unit" who did not study with Boulanger but rather with Bloch, who seemed to reaffirm his prophetic notion of the artist and, in general, his post-Wagnerian orientation.

Thomson (b. 1896) was the freshest and sharpest voice of his generation. As close to a Mark Twain as American music has produced yet, he lived up to the reputation of Missourians as the world's greatest skeptics. His musical language was at once so simple and so sophisticated as to pose a unique kind of challenge, a challenge not unlike Satie, with whom Thomson sometimes identified. Like Satie, Thomson proved a favorite with iconoclasts of many varieties.

Harris (b. 1898) was arguably the most striking and original composer of this group; or at least that was the prevailing sentiment in the 1930s. Certainly his music had only indirect connections with the day's most famous styles, and yet it was gripping and, in its own way, quite chic. Its spiritual intensity, which brought Harris close to early European musics, derived, in part, from his teacher Arthur Farwell. The prophetic posture was somewhat like Sessions; the iconoclastic appeal was more like Thomson, but for the opposite reasons, not for any ironic simplicity, but rather for its imposing loftiness. Many admirers of Harris in the '30s were happy to rediscover Ives in the '50s: both composers had a kind of earnestness that thrived on both social idealism and personal egotism.

Finally, there was Copland (b. 1900), who sounded what became the most clearly American note. This was intentional,

as intentional as Gershwin, who shared similar aims, and in
whom Copland perhaps saw a distorted image of himself.
Under Boulanger's guidance, Copland's music moved more
ambitiously to establish some contact with modern international trends. At the same time it aimed to promote a
progressive political ideal. Copland's stance made him a
natural spokesman for American music, and he successfully
promoted a wide variety of musics as he hoped to unite a wide
variety of citizens.

These five composers constituted a broad spectrum: a
Yankee classicist (Piston), a Catholic romanticist (Sessions), a
skeptical Midwesterner (Thomson), a Western mystic (Harris), and a Jewish populist (Copland). Few composers born
after 1900 were untouched by at least one of these major
composers: directly for composers born between 1900 and
1930, at least indirectly for composers born after that. To use
Boulanger's analogy once more, in a certain sense one defined
oneself as an American composer vis-à-vis these five as a late
19th- and 20th-century Russian composer defined himself by
relation to Tchaikovsky, Musorgsky, Borodin, Rimsky-
Korsakov, and Balakirev. This was certainly true for most
younger composers trained at Harvard.

These students might be said to comprise five waves: the
students of the late '20s, the '30s, the War years, the postwar
years, and the late '50s.

Elliott Carter and Leroy Anderson figured among the first
group. Such early students from the late '20s simply stumbled
across Piston, as yet little-known. The *Three Pieces* was a
brand-new piece, and it and the works to follow "dazzled"
Carter and his colleagues, presumably Anderson also, "by
their remarkable command." In the 1946 article from which
this last quote was taken, Carter summarized Piston's
accomplishment by observing the composer's "native musical
gifts, his love of métier, his openness to new developments,
and his continuous devotion to the high principles of purely
instrumental music." He also noted the distinctly American
quality of the composer's textures, sonorities, and rhythms.
Above all, Piston's "unique contribution is to have done this
particular work with outstanding excellence in a country
where few have ever made a name for themselves as
thoroughly craftsman-like artists." Carter's biographer reaf-

firmed the importance of *Three Pieces* in persuading the young composer of the strengths of the new '20s classicism, and, in fact, Carter requested that this work be played at a seventieth birthday celebration in his honor.

Piston was not only progressive as a composer, but as a theorist and teacher as well. Harvard had had an esteemed reputation for its music instruction, and the courses in counterpoint, orchestration, and harmony given by Davison, Hill, and Spalding, respectively, had assisted to varying degrees in the education of Sessions, Thomson and Piston themselves. But Piston much more than they recognized how counterpoint, orchestration, and harmony as practiced by the great masters were all interrelated, and related moreover to form and rhythm; and how they served individual expressive needs as well. Carter and Anderson regarded Piston's fresh approach to musical analysis highly.

In teaching composition, Piston emphasized stylistic consistency and artistic variety, as well as the need to be objective. Anderson stated, "Piston always advised us to listen to our compositions as though someone else had written them." As a composer, a theorist, and a teacher Piston adapted principles learned from Dukas and Boulanger to his own sensibility.

Carter and Anderson were probably rare among Piston's students, taken as a whole, in knowing his 1929 *Suite* for orchestra, a work that soon would be almost wholly forgotten, but outstanding in its time for its direct use of jazz idioms, a work comparable in the Piston catalog to Copland's *Piano Concerto*. Carter and Anderson were responsive, and for all their differences, a direct incorporation of jazz elements remained a shared aspect of their work. It might be noted also that in Carter's senior year, 1930, Piston composed his rather jazzy *Flute Sonata;* Carter himself wrote a *Flute Sonata* in 1934, one of his many early works later withdrawn that, if known, would probably give further evidence of Piston's influence.

By 1933 Piston was no longer an obscure instructor on the Harvard faculty, but an assistant professor of considerable repute. His major achievements of that year—the *Concerto for Orchestra,* the *First String Quartet,* and his first theoretical work, the *Principles of Harmonic Analysis*—were making themselves known, as would his article on "Roy Harris" in *Modern Music* the following year. Significantly, many of his students in the '30s, having done their undergraduate work elsewhere, came to Harvard as graduate students specifically to work with him: this list included Vincent, Berger, Helm, Kubik, and Kohs. Piston's presence at Harvard may have affected the decision of Fine, Bernstein, Glaser, Braithwaite, Shapero, Moevs, and others to do their undergraduate work there as well, though this was less likely and, in any case, of no particular importance in and of itself.

Notwithstanding its individual profile, Piston's work from the '30s had, in its own way, an impressively wide stylistic range. And perhaps this was particularly well-illustrated in the way such work established contact with his students from that decade. Consider the three-movement *Concerto for Orchestra*. Its first movement had the sort of ironic, acerbic classicism that influenced Berger, Kubik, and Fine. The second movement had an amiable, breezy jazziness that was echoed by Shapero and Bernstein, as well as by Anderson (who, though graduated, stayed on to direct the Harvard Band, teach at Radcliffe, and study Scandinavian languages), and to a lesser extent, Kubik and Vincent. The last movement had the kind of detached "neue Sachlichkeit" that informed the work of Helm, Kohs, Glaser, and Moevs.

These three aspects of Piston related, respectively, to Stravinsky, Copland, and Hindemith, composers, significantly, well-touted at Harvard. Piston and his colleagues invited Copland to replace him in 1934 (and later in 1944 and 1951 as well), an invitation, incidentally, that possibly had a decisive impact on Copland's career.[4] Stravinsky gave the 1939 Norton Lectures, and over the next few years held periodic guest seminars at Harvard as well. Hindemith eventually lectured at Harvard in 1949, but there was no doubt as to his importance among young Harvard composers of the 1930s. Piston, Copland, Stravinsky, Hindemith: this was the four-man orbit around which Piston's second wave of students principally circled. Fine's honors thesis discussed Stravinsky, Bernstein's discussed Copland, and Glaser's discussed Hindemith. Harris also made some impression on these students, but knowing Piston's critique, as they presumably did, they were perhaps more sensitive to Harris's shortcomings than was characteristic of some reviewers (while made, at the same time, aware of his virtues).

Nearly all of these composers gave testimony, often unsolicited, to Piston's importance. Vincent wrote in the preface of his major study, *Diatonic Modes,* Piston's "penetrating criticism did much to ensure the validity of my ideas during the development stage." Berger devoted a 1935 article on Piston for *Trend,* writing, "I feel he is one of the most important composers writing today and . . . I think the measure of his fame—relative, to be sure, to that of other moderns—is scarcely proportionate to the degree of his significance."[5] Berger, like Fine and Carter, owned and knew nearly every Piston score from the 1930s, a not inconsiderable volume of work. Of this corpus, both Fine and Shapero shared a special fondness for the 1939 *Violin Concerto.* Fine went on to admire the "clarity and nobility" of Piston's 1943 *Prelude and Allegro,* claiming it superior to similar works by Sowerby, Hanson, Porter, Poulenc, and others, an assessment almost identical to one made years later by a younger student, Daniel Pinkham (who well may have known Fine's review). Kohs was attracted to Piston's music because it was "very sane and well-organized, sprightly, healthy, and at the same time not without melodic interest." Bernstein loved Piston's music, noting it to offer "the highest standards of craftsmanship and clarity of sonic intention." Bernstein also admired Piston's "non-pedantic approach to such academic subjects as fugue"; his subsequent books and television shows, in fact, could be seen as a successful popularization of Piston's pedagogy. *The Incredible Flutist* was a favorite for Helm, Bernstein, and Glaser, who also singled out the later *Three New England Sketches.*

Much as Piston's 1929 *Suite* represented something special to his students from the '20s, so his 1938 *Incredible Flutist* and *Carnival Song* had distinctive meanings for his students from the '30s. The former was written for the Boston Pops, the latter for the Harvard Glee Club, "Gebrauchsmusik" of the most sophisticated kind, Piston, certainly, at his most determinedly accessible. This temper was also reflected by his students, and remained some part of their basic outlook: the late '30s witnessed Anderson's first pieces for the Boston Pops (Fiedler recorded *The Incredible Flutist* and Anderson's

Jazz Pizzicato at the same recording session in 1939); Carter's 1938 *Tarantella* for the Harvard Glee Club, and his hope that the Boston Pops might play something of his own; Kubik's 1938 *In Praise of Johnny Appleseed;* and Bernstein's 1939 music for a Classical Club production of *The Birds* (with Ellis Kohs in the pit), and his own production at Harvard of Blitzstein's *The Cradle Will Rock.* As with the 1929 *Suite,* Piston's work from the late '30s did not initiate a trend, hardly so, but rather gave such trends—in this case, populism— classically elegant and highly personal expression.

Whereas Piston's students tended to lag behind a bit through the '20s and '30s, as Piston himself once noted, by the third and certainly by the fourth wave of students, they were quicker than he to ferret out new ideas, often suggesting directions for the older man. As Piston remarked to Eric Salzman upon his retirement from Harvard in 1960: "You know these boys were never yes-men; we had some pretty hot sessions. Sometimes I had the impression that they wound up doing the teaching and I was the student."[6]

This third wave of students, including Middleton, Sapp, Van Slyck, Pinkham, Brogue, Lee, and Warren, arrived at Harvard during the Second World War, at a time when Piston was at the height of his reputation with younger American composers. In 1940 Carter wrote his "Walter Piston piece," the *Pastoral,* and in 1941 both Kubik and Shapero dedicated works to Piston. 1941 also saw the publication of *Harmony,* which made the teaching of *Principles* known to thousands of music students who may not have heard any of Piston's music.

This third wave of students knew Piston's music, and knew it well. Sapp loved the *Concerto for Orchestra* and the *Concertino* especially. Pinkham, an organist, paid special attention to the *Prelude and Allegro;* his 1946 ballet, *Narragansett Bay* (later withdrawn), reminded Fine of *The Incredible Flutist* (as well as *Billy the Kid*).[7] Similarly, Middleton and Lee regarded Piston's music as among the most important of its time.

It was Piston's 1940 *Chromatic Study* and 1944 *Partita* that seemed the emblematic works for this wave of composers, not that they admired these works in particular, but because these works presaged one of the dominant concerns of this group of composers, namely, the reconciliation of the 12-tone technique with neoclassical traits and aspirations.

How much their own 12-tone adventures owed to these 12-tone works (actually, only a movement of the *Partita* is 12-tone) written during their Harvard years is undocumented, but their mature concerns and ideals seem to echo forth from them.

This wave of students was the first to speak of Piston's coolness. Pinkham disliked Piston initially, finding him aloof, deciding, after some years, that it was really a kind of shyness, but for all that never warming up to him enough to call him by his first name, even when he taught one year at Harvard (1957–1958). Lee, disappointed with Piston's laissez faire, turned to Fine for support. Middleton, who had the feeling that Piston was hiding something, dropped out of Harvard, reconciling himself to Piston somewhat only after the War. Sapp thought Piston's shyness almost pathological and once referred to him as "curiously absent and opaque."[8]

What caused this dramatic change in only a few years? One answer is that as his students began to take the offensive, so to speak, as they arrived at Harvard more sophisticated and savvy, Piston backed away. But related to this, and of deeper resonance, was the influence of the War itself. This third wave of students arrived at Harvard between 1939 and 1942. Piston was strongly affected by the War, writing to Berger, "As a composer, I had a slump for the first year of the war, feeling that writing music was about the most futile occupation,"[9] strong words from a man who chose his words cautiously (he went on, however, to state that he had now "completely recovered a sense that it is important"). Did his sense of futility extend to his teaching? Was he too preoccupied to concern himself with his students? The answers are far from clear, but there seems little doubt that this third wave marked a changed response in Piston's relations with his students, that the change was connected to the War, and that the change was fairly irreversible.

For a number of other reasons, however, this third wave belonged more properly with the preceding waves in distinction to the following ones. First, they still held Stravinsky, Hindemith, Copland, and Piston as the day's seminal composers. Second, many of these composers, including Middleton, Sapp, Pinkham, and Lee, turned to Boulanger for further guidance, as had Carter, Frothingham, Vincent, Berger,

Kubik, Fine, Glaser, Shapero, and Moevs before them (Anderson had hoped to; Bernstein, for his part, established a warm friendship). And third, they served in the Second World War in some capacity or another, as did most of these composers from Piston (who was an air warden) on down. Consequently, the third wave was a transitional one, and, indeed, most of these students participated in the transition by returning to Harvard after the War.

The postwar scene at Harvard was lively, rich in contradictions, and prescient with change. Piston, now the author of another famous text, *Counterpoint,* and a Pulitzer-Prize-winning *Third Symphony* (both from 1947), attracted more students than ever. In the period 1946–1954, Brogue, Glaser, Middleton, Sapp, Lee, and Van Slyck continued their studies, while Binkerd, Bavicchi, Layton, Spies, Kohn, Adler, Wyner, Brenner, Boykan, Westergaard, and others arrived for the first time. Randall Thompson joined the faculty in 1948, but like E. B. Hill in the 1930s, he was a secondary figure for most of these students, if they studied with him at all (there were, however, notable exceptions, such as Kohn and Adler). Fine, now on the faculty as well, was to make a deeper impression.

Piston's music from this period itself revealed changes: it was less taut and mannered, more relaxed and varied in its textures, more genial and warm in its expressive content, in strange contrast to the personal impression he then was making. Far from the *Three Pieces,* with their kind of bold austerity, there was a series of rather grand symphonies, symphonies loved by Binkerd, Bavicchi, Kohn, Adler, Brenner, Boykan, and others. Adler performed the *Second Symphony* (1943) over twenty times in Europe, while the opening of the *Fourth Symphony* (1950), seen in manuscript, became a wellspring for his own technique. Binkerd wrote three symphonies in the 1950s, the third of which (1959) was dedicated to Piston. Layton aimed to establish some kind of contact with the Piston symphonies in his 1952 *American Portrait* (not a portrait of Piston per se, but dedicated to him nonetheless) as did Westergaard in his 1954 *Symphonic Movement.* Bavicchi and Brenner saw the Piston symphonies as outstanding among the wide range of 20th-century musics. Boykan carefully studied the *Third Symphony,* which along with the *Fourth* well might be said to be the archetypal Piston works for this group (in some contrast to the part played by the *Three Pieces* and *Suite* for the first wave, the *Concerto for Orchestra* and *The Incredible Flutist* for the second wave, and the *Chromatic Study* and *Partita* for the third wave). Spies and Kohn, to round out our picture, also showed close ties to Piston, but perhaps via Berger and Fine. Wyner, at Harvard for one year, established an ephemeral link with his 1952 *Partita*.

At the same time, there lurked an atmosphere of rebellion. Few of these postwar students studied with Boulanger (Spies had studied with her before the War). Indeed, these composers were content to complete their formal education with Piston, itself a striking development, as some postgraduate study in Europe was a long-established tradition. Another change, related to the dramatic loss of interest in Boulanger, was the new and intense interest in Bartók and Schoenberg: Kohn and his colleague Howard Meyer Brown wrote honors theses on Bartók in 1950 and 1951, respectively, and Westergaard and his contemporary Frona Brooks wrote honors theses on Schoenberg in 1953 and 1954, respectively. This change was most striking as concerned Schoenberg, who far from being the outdated expressionist he was before the War, was now very much in vogue. Schoenberg's presence at Harvard in 1947 for the premiere of his *Trio* left a profound impression, as did the piece itself, the basis for Berger's and many others' reevaluation of the composer. Piston, who copied out the parts for this performance, indulged in some humor at Schoenberg's expense, which had long been his way, but which now began to sit uneasily with some of his students, including Middleton and Spies. Piston's relation to Schoenberg was certainly intricate and ambiguous—there was a serious regard for Schoenberg's theoretical writings, and an application of the 12-tone technique as early as 1940, indirectly, as early as at least 1930. On differing occasions before the War, Berger and Krenek[10] recognized connections between the two in both theoretical and artistic contexts, as did Westergaard later on. But now some students regarded Piston's feelings about Schoenberg as problematic, an attitude that would intensify with the fifth wave of students, and play some part in the decision of Rzewski and Harbison to do their graduate work with Sessions at Princeton. (Westergaard had preceded them in this, but his decision to study at Princeton had less to do with Schoenberg's status at Harvard than with certain genteel aspects of its academic life that he identified as "Harvard's gentleman problem.")

A related development, in the opinion of some, was Fine's exclusion in 1948 from membership in the Harvard Musical Association out of anti-Semitic sentiment, and his denial of tenure in 1950; in any case, it cast Harvard in an unsavory light for many postwar students, most of whom had studied with Fine and were extremely fond of him.

Such changes soon reflected on the music of Piston's students, past and present. Shapero's 1948 *Piano Sonata* was hissed at its New York premiere, suggesting that neoclassicism had had its day. Carter's 1948 *Cello Sonata* and 1951 *String Quartet,* in contrast, were immediately hailed as masterpieces, and, moreover, as models for a new American music. Kohs's 1946 *Passacaglia,* Sapp's 1949 *Piano Trio,* and Fine's 1951 *Quartet* ushered in a rather comprehensive assimilation of the 12-tone method among Piston's students. The expressionistic and classical mingled evocatively: Layton wrote the wild, experimental *Five Studies* in 1951, and the relatively tame and conservative *American Portrait* the following year.

By the late 1950s, Piston's position, if not exactly denigrated, was subject to major revision. The author of the 1955 *Orchestration* text, and the 1956 *Sixth Symphony* and *Wind Quintet,* now was regarded principally as an authority on instruments. Whereas Fine spoke in 1948 of Piston's slow movements of "longing tenderness" and finales "that bubble and bounce along with sparkling gaiety," in 1957 he criticized Piston's slow movements for seeming "too long and stretched out," and the finales for seeming "too short and almost perfunctory." While extolling Piston's "wit and elegance" in 1948 in comparison with Sessions ("unrelievedly pessimistic," Fine wrote of Sessions as late as 1952[11]), Fine now saw Sessions, along with Copland, as the most significant forces in American music, recommending even Barber's newest work over Piston's, which "no longer offers us any surprises." Fine might have underestimated Piston's surviving legacy to the late 1950s: certainly in the context of the composer's 1944

Partita, 1945 *Sonatina,* 1946 *Divertimento,* 1956 *Serenata,* 1958 *Psalm and Prayer of David,* and his postwar string quartets and symphonies, that is, the bulk of his opus 1944–1958, it is worth noting the partitas by Pinkham (1958) and Shapero (1960); the sonatinas by Sapp (1956) and Lee (1959); the divertimentos by Kubik (1957), Layton (1958), Kohn (1959), and an opera so-called by Perkins (1958); the serenades by Bernstein (1954), Fine (actually entitled *Romanza,* 1958), and Wyner (1958); the psalm settings by Kohs (1958), Boykan (1958), Des Marais (1959), and Spies (1959); the string quartets by Moevs (1957), Berger (1958), and Carter (1959); and the symphonies by Vincent (1954), Adler (1957), and Binkerd (1957, 1959). It even might be argued that the late '50s witnessed a high tide in the expansion and individuation of Piston's influence. At the same time, the content of much of this music tended toward the expressionistic, the shrill, the morbid, in short, toward modes of expression at some odds with Piston's basic sensibility.

The situation was somewhat different for Piston's last wave of students, including Perkins, Behrman, Rzewski, and Harbison. Having never really come under Piston's influence in the first place, there was little to expand, or adapt, or even repudiate. They knew the music nonetheless. Harbison conducted Piston's *Sinfonietta,* which he found unpleasantly cold. Rzewski and Behrman admired Piston's craftsmanship and wit, but devoted little time to the music itself. More interested in Pierre Boulez, who figured prominently in their honors theses of 1958 and 1959, respectively, they invited David Tudor to come to Harvard to play Cage and Wolff. Piston wrote "More Views on Serialism" in 1958, as he had written "Roy Harris" in 1934, to provide a balanced and thoughtful appraisal of contemporary trends;[12] but the young were not listening now: tonality, and even traditional instruments themselves, were, for the moment at any rate, part of an old, oppressive order. The history of Piston's students had come full circle, from students in the late '20s who accidentally discovered him and found him a revelation, to students in the late '50s who knew him as a legend and found him somewhat irrelevant to their concerns. Breaking an established pattern, hardly any prominent composers stayed on or came for graduate work with Piston after 1955.

The above history suggests an epochal turning point in American music during the 1950s: the importance of Piston and Harvard, which had been *the* educational training ground for young composers since at least the 1890s, was usurped, in this regard, by Sessions and Princeton and Juilliard. This paralleled a major shift in taste and sensibility, from, if you will, classicism to romanticism, and, to some degree, from French models to German ones. Harvard's heroes—Bach, Mozart, Chopin, Brahms, Fauré, Ravel, Bartók, the Stravinsky of the *Octet,* Hindemith, Shostakovich, and Nadia Boulanger—were being supplanted by Beethoven, Wagner, Mahler, Debussy, the second Viennese school, the Stravinsky of the *Rite,* Dallapiccola, and Heinrich Schenker. Similarly, the cognoscenti now touted Ives over Copland or Harris or Thomson.

This change did not merely represent, as is occasionally implied, some victory for the 12-tone method, a method, after all, which Piston and Copland (not to mention Stravinsky) made use of without any rejection of earlier ideals. (It appeared that, in fact, the going preference was for Schoenberg's so-called freely atonal works, not for those smart and brittle 12-tone pieces from the 1920s.) Rather, it meant a victory for romanticism, so that when the 12-tone method was overhauled in the 1960s in favor of collage and quotation, and when collage gave way in the 1970s and '80s to the "new romanticism," a similarly romantic tone usually remained in place. And not surprisingly, in the forefront of all these developments, typically, were many of Sessions' students, among them, Milton Babbitt, Ross Lee Finney, Andrew Imbrie, Leon Kirchner, Donald Martino, Earl Kim, David Del Tredici, Hugo Weisgall, and Ellen Taaffe Zwilich, as well as former Harvardians Rzewski and Harbison. Indeed, the fact that Kirchner replaced Piston at Harvard in 1960 signaled Harvard's acknowledgment of such trends. (One notes a concurrent development in popular music, surely not coincidental, as the jazz era, in the 1950s, starts to rock; how relevant this is to the subject at hand is hard to say, though rock undeniably represented a romantic movement of sorts.) This trend continued as, in 1967, Kim joined Kirchner on the Harvard faculty, and in 1968, Sessions delivered that year's Norton Lectures.

All of Piston's students, and Piston himself, remained responsive and attuned to these trends, though to varying degrees and in varying ways. On the one hand, composers as different as Carter, Fine, Boykan, Spies, and Harbison welcomed such developments and even helped to forge them; while on the other, Kubik, Binkerd, Shapero, Pinkham, and others were rather appalled. Most steered some middle course. None, however, was untouched by some nostalgia for the '20s or '30s or '40s, for some work by Copland or Piston *back then;* and none could be said to be totally representative of the post-'60 era. In fact, the fairly dismal history of Piston and his students after 1960, as follows, suggests that the times, when compared to the glory days of the late '40s and early '50s, were hardly congenial.

Piston retired from teaching in 1960, glad to devote more time to composition, and probably relieved to give up his role as a walking monument to past greatness. With his retirement, Piston's hegemony, or what was left of it, came to a dramatic end. The 1960 *Seventh Symphony,* which earned him a second Pulitzer Prize, was his last big success. There was, too, a certain symbolism in the fact that Bernstein conducted Piston's *Second Violin Concerto,* also from 1960, at his farewell concert at Carnegie Hall, dedicating the concert to his "beloved teacher." True, Robert Middleton dedicated his *Quattro Duetti* to Piston in 1962, the *Fifth Quartet* won the New York Music Critics Award in 1964, a Walter Piston day was proclaimed by the State of Maine in 1965, and so on. But the years between 1960 and his death in 1976 generally were marked by obscurity and rejection. The numerous works written during this time met with considerable apathy: Shapero, more sympathetic than most, called the 1965 *Eighth Symphony,* "a dreary mess."[13] Bernstein gave a few performances of the 1967 *Ricercare,* a favorite of Gunther Schuller's, but of no particular importance to the general public.[14] Some works, like his 1967 *Souvenirs* (dedicated to Boulanger), languished in manuscript, which was really remarkable for a composer whose every work since 1929 but for a minor commission, the 1944 *Fugue on a Victory Tune,* had been published. And similarly, whereas most of his works had been recorded at least once, only two late works—the 1962 *Fifth Quartet* and the 1965 *Eighth Symphony*—were recorded during the composer's lifetime, and by small companies with limited distribution. Doriot Dwyer, dedicatee of the 1971 *Flute Concerto,* requested that the composer rewrite the finale, which he did.[15] Many followers of Heinrich Schenker, representing the new academic mainstream, repudiated Piston's texts, ignoring his sort of attention to contrapuntal and rhythmic nuance in favor of large-scale abstractions. Mark DeVoto, a former student of the fifth wave who collaborated with Piston on a fourth edition of *Harmony,* completed the venture after Piston's death, making many changes he assumed Piston would hate.[16]

1960 proved a watershed for Piston's students as well. Many of them tended not to fare too well afterwards either; indeed, they were lucky to fare as well as their teacher. Fine's death and the launching of *Perspectives of New Music,* both in 1962, again seemed symbolic of change. The number of composers to fade from the new music scene was significant. Shapero virtually gave up composition after 1960, creating mostly electronic "Hausmusik" for himself and his daughter. Similarly, Sapp pretty much stopped composing from 1960 to 1978. Anderson's essentially last efforts were undertaken in 1962. Layton's final work was the 1964 *Dance Fantasy.* Des Marais devoted himself to the study of underwater mammals and plant life. Vincent, Helm, Kubik, and Kohs composed relatively little after 1960, their later work attaining only a fraction of the kind of interest elicited in the '40s and '50s. Similarly, Carter and Bernstein met with the sort of success that was unsatisfactory in light of earlier years. After the 1961 *Double Concerto,* called a "masterpiece" by Stravinsky, Carter's work seemed to snare listeners in a web of complexities, climaxing with the 1971 *Third String Quartet,* whose Pulitzer Prize did not suffice to win it the kind of audience attracted by its two predecessors. Bernstein's 1963 *Kaddish Symphony* and 1971 *Mass* were faulted as tasteless and contrived, and his 1976 *1600 Pennsylvania Avenue* was a flop. Piston's reputation was not the only casualty of the 1960s.

Some other Piston alumni, especially younger ones, appeared to adjust to the changing climate with greater ease. This included a number of composers associated with *Perspectives of New Music,* Berger, Moevs, Spies, Westergaard, Perkins, and Harbison among them, who used the 12-tone method, already in vogue in the 1950s, to plunge into atonal or virtually atonal textures and complex variations forms: Moevs wrote a 1961 *Variazioni,* Perkins a 1962 *Variations,* and Westergaard a 1963 *Variations.* (Piston surely had these trends in mind when he composed his 1966 12-tone *Variations* for cello and orchestra, which he discussed at some length in an interview with Westergaard for *Perspectives.*) Wyner and Boykan, like Carter before them, cultivated a similar style without actual recourse to the 12-tone method. Also on the cutting edge were the colorful collages of Karl Kohn and the aleatoric works of Robert Middleton.

A more conservative spectrum of former Piston students, including Binkerd, Bavicchi, Van Slyck, Pinkham, Lee, and Adler, continued to produce works more varied in their uses, and not disdainful of tonality, though not unadventurous either. Some belonged to the third wave of Piston's students, others to the fourth wave who had sought out Piston for graduate work. They were young enough to face the '60s with vigor, and old enough to retain some classic poise. Piston, who never renounced tonality, nor lost his elegant clarity either, had connections to this category of composers as well.

Meanwhile, former students like Frothingham, Glaser, Warren, and Brenner, to varying degrees spurred by society's changing attitudes toward women composers, resumed writing music that typically answered highly practical needs. At the same time, the counterculture found representation in the electronic works and concept pieces of Behrman and Rzewski. Their challenging voices set the decade's tone and found reverberations in composers as different as Shapero, Middleton, and Pinkham.

From the perspective of Piston and his students, the '60s, overall, was a time of decline and fragmentation, but not without its achievements. In some respects, as Piston himself noted, the decade resembled the 1920s, and there similarly followed a period—the '70s and '80s—where the concern was largely in reestablishing some contact with a large audience. But notwithstanding the fact that Rzewski and Harbison turned specifically to the 1930s for some guidance, the period ultimately proved distinctively somber and romantic, with little of the 1930s' kind of arch humor or social ideals. Wyner helped initiate the period with the 1971 *De Novo* for cello and ensemble, and an ensuing series of lush works that intentionally favored the heart over the head. Fantasies, caprices, and especially nocturnes became plentiful: Sapp resumed composition with his 1978 *Nocturne*, Middleton returned to conventional notation with his 1979 *Four Nocturnes*, Carter wrote his 1980 *Night Fantasies*, and Bernstein composed a 1981 *Nocturne*. Ties with the 19th century in general were affirmed: Binkerd's 1974 *Fantasies*, Lee's 1975 *Caprices*, Kohn's 1976 *Prophet Bird*, and Harbison's 1981 *Piano Quintet* all shared a close relationship to Schumann and Brahms. Piston, ever attuned, contributed his 1970 *Fantasia* for violin and orchestra. Berger, who like Moevs, made a more conscious return to styles from the '40s and '50s, began to teach Piston's *Passacaglia* in his classes at Brandeis, and was encouraged by its enthusiastic reception.[17] Meanwhile, minimalism, the time's most fashionable trend, had some impact on many of these composers, including Sapp, Kohn, Behrman, and Rzewksi.

This chronology gives some idea as to the dynamics of Piston's influence—from crucial in the '20s and '30s, to important in the '40s and '50s, to remote in the '60s and '70s. Were there any general or lasting features? Some areas of agreement among the students themselves included Piston's high standard of craftsmanship (Carter, Bernstein, Binkerd), his economy and clarity (Kubik, Fine, Bernstein, Sapp, Bavicchi), his lyrical vitality (Berger, Pinkham, Adler), his expert knowledge of instruments (Bavicchi, Behrman), his objectivity and rationality (Carter, Anderson, Kohs, Layton), his wit (Fine, Bernstein, Shapero, Glaser, Warren, Pinkham, Adler, Behrman), and his respect for his students' individuality (Vincent, Glaser, Kohs, Layton, Moevs).

This respect for individuality naturally precluded much in the way of some expected conformity. Edgar Driscoll, in fact, reported that Piston's students "say his greatness in teaching was that he did not impose himself on his students. He forced them to think for themselves. No teacher can do more."[18] Piston told Eric Salzman, "I am very proud of the fact that none of my students writes music like any other, and none writes music like me, grazia a Dio."[19] Piston's students came to Harvard as young adults, with individual temperaments and sensibilities. These were not squashed: Vincent's interest in Southern folklore; Carter's youthful friendship with Ives; Kubik's experience touring the Midwest; Berger's enthusiasm for motion pictures; Bernstein's summer camp theatrical productions; Pinkham's "conversion" at a Trapp Family concert; Fine's lessons with Frances Grover, Moevs's lessons with Don Jonson, and Kohn's lessons with Alice Löwinger-Feldstein; Layton's dance-band gigs; Warren's Shirley Temple routines; Adler's and Wyner's closeness to the Hebrew melodies and Yiddish songs composed by their fathers, respectively; Behrman's decisive year with Riegger; and Harbison's attraction to popular song, all helped to provide distinctive backgrounds that were allowed to color, shape, and inform whatever was learned at Harvard. Indeed, Piston argued with Copland on just this point: Americans were so diverse in their backgrounds that it was essentially self-defeating to work toward the establishment of a national school of composition on the order of the French, or Italians, or Germans, or English, as Copland hoped to do.[20] If Piston looked for particular backgrounds (and, in fact, he had a large say especially in the selection of graduate students), it was, as described by Elliot Forbes, "qualities not only of musicianship but also of breadth of humanistic interest and knowledge."[21] Richard French, another colleague, spoke of Piston's concern that his students fulfill their human and thinking potential.[22]

The individuality of these students reflected itself also in their choices for subsequent teachers. Those attracted to French music might study with Boulanger, Milhaud, Honegger; those more attracted to German music might seek out Hindemith, Fortner, Blacher; some went to Italy to study with Malipiero or Dallapiccola; others studied with Copland or Sessions. The varied directions and teachers pursued upon graduation from Piston's classes was itself somewhat remarkable in its catholicity.

At the same time, Piston imbued his students with a belief in the continued relevance of the classical tradition, especially as represented by Bach and Mozart. This emerged as an appreciation and concern for clear, subtle textures; contrapuntal sophistication; expert knowledge of instruments; and formal finesse. But it also involved the very essence of such music—its message, or what Piston might have preferred to call its communication. Piston admitted that this side of music was "elusive," something that ultimately was a private matter between the composer and the listener. Yet one surely sensed that Piston appreciated the tone of such music: frank, honest, ironic, compassionate, humble. Certainly, Piston aimed for a similar tone, both in his teaching and his music.

And then there was a widely shared sympathy for various popular idioms (especially jazz), a sympathy in itself related to a particular understanding of 18th-century music (for but one example, see Bernstein's comparison of the Mozart "Singspiel" with the Broadway musical). In Piston's case, this use of popular material involved primarily New England and Italian folk styles, but also urban American and Latin-American songs and dances—not surprising, for an Italian-American from Maine living in Boston! If Piston was not commonly thought of as "earthy" in the sense that Harris, Thomson, and Copland were, this was partly because the popular styles close to him were more European in complexion, but mostly because these popular styles were more thoroughly subsumed and controlled by both classical models and individual sensibilities—another perceived legacy of Bach and Mozart. For all his admiration for Schoenberg and Webern, Piston probably felt that the absence, or at least obscurity, of such connections resulted in an exploration of one's own psyche that, while fascinating perhaps, fell short of the 18th century's sense of community. There is some evidence that Piston similarly had some objection to abstract art, not a wholesale rejection, but a feeling that, say, Kandinsky, like Schoenberg, did not represent the real continuance of the European humanism that he found in Modigliani.

On the other hand, folkloric styles, whether proud or quaint, also fell short of this ideal. For Piston, this kind of self-consciousness was yet another distortion of 18th-century classicism, transmitted by 19th-century nationalism. It seemed to distance him from Copland, and, perhaps, from Bartók as well, although he admired both men's music very much. He made it known, in any case, that he disapproved of quoting popular melody (though he himself did so briefly and subtly in *New England Sketches*). He similarly found Stravinsky's occasional appropriations problematic, distinguishing between the Stravinsky that was "real"—like *The Rite of*

Spring and *Symphony of Psalms*—and the Stravinsky that ostensibly was not (*Pulcinella? The Fairy's Kiss?*). Where Stravinsky rated particularly high, for Piston, was in the matter of technical accomplishment and finish. And in the *Octet*, there was, too, the fuller achievement of a classically humanistic statement. It appeared, however, that of all his contemporaries, Piston most admired Hindemith, and, perhaps, Shostakovich. His own blend of national, classical, and modernist elements came even closer to his Czech contemporary, Martinů, whose humanism must have been to his liking as well.

What, specifically, did this humanist tradition mean for Piston? His few programmatic works reflected on the tenderness of love, the beauty of nature, the humor of human frailty, and the sadness of loss. Often one heard the voice of a small community—revelers at a carnival, shoppers in a store, attendants at a state fair, worshippers in a sanctuary—a community that could never represent a nation, but in its own way could stand for all humanity. The community, indeed, was understood to be a collection of individuals, and the interaction of individuals within the community was of interest and concern.

To these bare clues might be added some biographical details, for instance, Piston's commitment to republican virtues—to independence, freedom, and civic responsibility. He saw such ideals threatened left and right by the growing encroachment of big business and big government, by the decimation of the small farmer, by the exploitation of the land, by the population explosion, and by human selfishness and apathy. His financial support of the Audubon Society, Planned Parenthood, Help the People of Florence, the Boston Public Library, the North Universalist Chapel Association, and other groups suggested many deeply-felt values.

The core of Piston's humanism, I think, was just this: that he recognized that while the integration of one's intellectual and emotional life always had posed a challenge to mankind, this challenge had become, perhaps, more acute in the twentieth century. Men and artists alike tended toward the extremes of total rationality, with its inhuman subjugation of feeling, and total irrationality, with its unthinking, uncritical mysticism and overindulgence. He looked back to the achievement of Bach and Mozart, to the Bible and Renaissance poetry, to the ancient Greeks and Chinese, as guideposts, as landmarks of the kind of humanist integration he sought in life and in art. He only vaguely alluded to the political and social implications of non-integration, but no doubt gave this subject serious thought, perhaps seeing in Soviet Communism and German Nazism just those kind of imbalances that worried him. His own achievement was to understand, intellectually and objectively, the art of counterpoint, harmony, and instrumentation, while at the same time personalizing and expanding such resources in his own music.

In short, Piston taught that a crucial artistic goal was in finding the "perfect balance" between instinct, individuality, emotion ("the heart") and intellect, tradition, craft ("the head"). Piston shared such concerns with many contemporary figures, especially those whose sensibilities were formed in the wrenching upheaval caused by the First World War. As seen in chapter 1, this was a paramount, perhaps *the* paramount concern in the novels of James Gould Cozzens. But it possibly was voiced most trenchantly by Piston's exact contemporary, Aldous Huxley, at the philosophical climax of a 1928 novel that in many ways spoke for that whole generation, *Point Counter Point;* here, the painter Mark Rampion argues to his friends:

> A man's a creature on a tightrope, walking delicated, equilibrated, with mind and consciousness and spirit at one end of his balancing pole and body and instinct and all that's unconscious and earthy and mysterious at the other. Balanced. Which is damnably difficult. And the only absolute he can ever really know is the absolute of perfect balance. The absoluteness of perfect relativity. Which is a paradox and nonsense intellectually. But so is all real, genuine, living truth—just nonsense according to logic. And logic is just nonsense in the light of living truth. You can choose which you like, logic or life. It's a matter of taste. Some people prefer being dead.[23]

Confronted with the logic of assorted 20th-century "isms"—both in and out of music—Piston was similarly wary and skeptical to an extraordinary degree. There were no aesthetic pronouncements, no political agendum, no religious pieties, no theoretical claims—only a weighted consideration of varied viewpoints scrupulously pondered in private. In this sense, the Pistons portrayed by Lorenz and Segal always coexisted: he was always part rebel, part traditionalist. It was a paradoxical legacy that critics of "relativism" could cite as a moral failure (and there seemed to be something world-weary about it), but that to friends often had the stuff of courage and integrity.

His students, one after the other, reflected Piston's paradoxical legacy when they, as they did so often, respected the classics while asserting their individuality; juggled the demands of idealism and practicality; adopted the 12-tone technique, but in highly instinctive ways; and acknowledged the competing demands of popular styles and the avant-garde, the great masses and the intellectual elite. So, if the students of Piston as a whole, like Piston himself, seemed to comprise the conservative progressives of their time (and no label, even a paradoxical one, could do justice to the balance that Piston advocated based on his understanding of Bach and Mozart), then this paradoxical inheritance in part must be ascribed to tensions represented by Piston himself.

Whatever the exact nature of Piston's feelings, they were strong, as epitomized by the four-page *Passacaglia* for piano (1943), with its dramatic changes of feeling, climaxing at the end with a searing expression of anger, perhaps even rage. Or the even shorter *Improvisation* for piano (1945), with its more resigned conclusion comprised of quartal and quintal harmonies in some haunting E modality (Ex. 100). In such works, each and every note was fraught with meaning and sincerity.

Example 100. Walter Piston, *Improvisation* for piano (Leeds Music, 1946).

For many, if not all of Piston's students, the composer's humanism, such as it might have been understood, was limited. Moreover, as seen in the aforementioned discussion of student "waves," the trends tended to move farther and farther from Piston's ideals. Even with the first and second waves, the New Deal (suspect to Piston) and the Allied struggle (which Piston conscientiously but sadly supported), inspired different ideals, ideals that were more populist, and very often Marxist. With the widespread disillusionment of the postwar years, the third and fourth waves emerged with an interest in expressionistic, more alienated art as represented first by Bartók, then by Schoenberg and sometimes Webern. And, finally, amid the chaos and disintegration of the 1960s, came the fifth wave's call for magic and ritual, and the subsequent fascination for Eastern and medieval musics, chance concepts, and parody. Each wave, like Piston himself, adapted to these changing trends, as many continued to adapt to the romanticism of the 1970s and '80s; but each wave tended to remain fairly constant to its original, youthful ideals.

Concurrently, though each wave seemed to share an abiding love for Bach, such orientations took on different manifestations. With Piston, as with Hindemith, it was the modernist's love, which expressed itself in the more austere aspects of Bach—motor rhythms, linear counterpoint, and textural clarity. The first wave, represented by Carter and Anderson, quickly veered off to "Empfindsamer" and the "Galanter," respectively. The second wave, profoundly influenced by Haydn and Beethoven, regarded Bach with a more classical sensibility, while the third wave, often Schumann enthusiasts, reinterpreted the Baroque as romantic, ornate, and lush. The fourth wave, like Brahms and Wagner, brought a more Gothic, medieval sensibility to bear, while the fifth, like Mahler, alternately could make the most subtle connections, and those that were blatantly nostalgic or parodistic. In other words, in the mere fifty years from 1925 to 1975, a full cycle somewhat like that of Bach to Mahler transpired.

But perhaps the more important point is that the love of Bach did take hold, and that this happened not only because of Piston's inspired teaching of Bach, but because in many instances these Harvard composers understood, in Piston's own music, Bach's relevance to a vital and modern sensibility. In fact, unlike many other listeners, the Harvard composers tended not to speak of Piston's classicism or academicism, but of his expressivity and subtlety. Carter, for instance, wrote, "a flexibility of motion and feeling is the distinguishing mark of Piston's music";[24] Berger noted, "The music is always significant, meaningful";[25] Fine, as mentioned, spoke of Piston's "longing tenderness" and "sparkling gaiety"; and Sapp, after discussing Piston's preoccupation with craft and structure, commented, "Yet, as we all know, his music is passionate, lyrical, full of sensuous expressive modes."[26] How large was Sapp's "we all"? This was certainly open to question, considering the number of persons who thought of Piston's music as, in fact, rather unsensuous, let alone those who paid it no attention whatsoever. But by "we all," Sapp, in any case, probably had Piston's students specifically in mind, for this was the context in which his remark was made.

Why this special sensitivity to Piston's music among his students? First, they knew the music particularly well. They heard it at the Boston Symphony conducted by Koussevitzky and Munch; they studied it in score; many of them performed it themselves. But their familiarity with the man himself also assisted such understanding; the two seemed to go together so neatly, as was often observed. And what about the man himself? For all their qualifications, Lorenz and Segal similarly portrayed a man whose kindness, tact, and wit were memorable. Indeed, it was little wonder that Segal chose to depict Piston from among all the professors he knew at Harvard, even though he knew him only from afar. Boulanger similarly recalled, in the aforementioned conversations, that Piston

> . . . was gifted with an extraordinary delicacy, over and above his talent. One day I received a letter from him: "As you perhaps realize, I left Paris owing you a hundred dollars"—I had no idea he owed me anything whatsoever. "I am sending them to you with my apologies for being so slow. I know that I cannot offer you the interest, you would not accept it, but I am enclosing an additional sum which you can give to a pupil who needs it." That was marvelous. Others never even think of bringing you a violet; not that they aren't nice, it just doesn't occur to them.[27]

Those students who recognized Piston's nobility, wit, and
delicacy in a quiet remark were perhaps better prepared to
perceive it in some melody played softly by the cello or flute.
Analyzing the *Fourth Symphony,* William Austin, himself a
former student, wrote of its opening theme as follows:

> Listening I sense just behind this theme his cool voice,
> rather low but not quite level, and the sharp, dark eyes
> glancing out of the large, relaxed face, taking in at a
> glance more detail than an ordinary man sees in a staring
> gaze, or expressing with a glance some precise grading
> of values that would need many vehement gestures for
> another conductor to communicate. He is a man nothing
> can surprise, nothing can hurry, and in the long run
> nothing can distract or obstruct; yet anything can touch
> him and whatever is beautiful in anything he recognizes.
> He seeks no shelter from the difficulties of the modern
> world, but faces them with patient skill, and economizes
> his energies for the next encounter.[28]

For all his obvious displeasure in being placed on a pedestal,
Piston often was perceived by his students—at least early
on—as a sort of quiet, almost saintly hero.

Piston's students were not the only composers touched by
the man and his music, however. There was David Diamond
(b. 1915), Robert Palmer (b. 1915), and Lukas Foss (b. 1922),
to name three. Indeed, any thorough study of these composers would need to take some account of their relation to
Piston. Diamond's work from the 1940s, such as the *First
Violin Sonata* (1946), came particularly close to Piston, both
in terms of its long, poised melodies and its choice of textures
and harmonies (Diamond went on to dedicate his 1964
Seventh String Quartet to Piston in honor of his seventieth
birthday). But for our purposes, distinctions are in order.
Diamond's enthusiasm for English composers like Vaughan
Williams and Bax, and for German composers like Schreker
and Stefan, enthusiasms taken up while at study with Rogers
at Eastman, was reflected in his music's distinctive blend of
stately dignity and romantic flamboyance, the latter further
fostered by studies with Sessions; unlike those Boulanger
students initially taught by Piston, Diamond's experience
with Boulanger was problematic. (Piston's tutelage tended to

predispose his students favorably toward Boulanger.) Palmer, another student of Rogers's, cultivated a heightened intensity like his other teacher, Harris, and of a similarly impressive order of originality. Foss, one of the most persuasive and enduring classicists of his generation, remained primarily indebted to Hindemith, his principal teacher. This hardly means that Piston had any less appreciation for these composers, or vice versa. It only suggests that an apprenticeship with Piston was often telling, though involving subtle matters of tone, taste, and ideals.

If we can speak of a Piston school, however, it is not only because of Piston's particular input, but because the idea of an academy, in the Socratic sense, was intentionally cultivated. While Piston did meet with composers individually, such sessions primarily were given over to questions of orchestration. More characteristic were his composition seminars, described by Charles Shackford, who attended one in 1946–1947, as follows:

> Piston was given more to asking questions than to making statements. Each utterance was well thought out; there were no wasted words. He encouraged students to comment on each other's work. The atmosphere he engendered was gentle, quiet and thoughtful. He had a keen gift for recognizing creative ability and knew how to encourage it. In the presence of pretension he could be scathing.[29]

Binkerd similarly remarked, "Pressures came from fellow members of the class. At least, that was my experience. Not from him." Most students, looking for direction, were disconcerted, if not actually discontented, by such instruction; few possessed the equanimity of Shackford's account. But what these sessions, and what Piston in general nurtured, aside from the lonely pursuit of truth, was an atmosphere congenial to sharing and dialog. Certainly many profound friendships and associations emerged. In the 1930s, for instance, Fine, Berger, Shapero, and Bernstein formed a close-knit group, lasting at least through the '50s, when all four taught at Brandeis. Shapero dedicated his 1941 *4-Hands Sonata* to Bernstein, and Bernstein premiered Shapero's

Symphony in 1948. Bernstein also championed Moevs, another classmate. Kohs, in the meantime, responded to Bernstein's aspirations.

The friendships in the second and third waves of students proved equally strong. Des Marais, Middleton, Sapp, Bavicchi, Van Slyck, and Spies joined forces in varied permutations throughout the '50s and early '60s to launch new music concerts in the Boston area. Van Slyck dedicated his *First Piano Sonata* to Lee in 1947 and his *Third Sonata* to Bavicchi in 1952, the year Brogue dedicated her *Duo Lirico* to the Pinkham-Brink Duo, who would, in turn, perform Bavicchi's *Short Sonata*. Layton, Wyner, and Boykan formed an especially intimate subgroup, supporting one another in numerous ways. Sapp and Westergaard shared helpful ideas on Schoenberg, Spies and Des Marais on Stravinsky. Binkerd dedicated a little piano piece to Adler's oldest daughter, Deborah.

As for the last wave, outstanding was the continuing friendship of Behrman and Rzewski.

Associations also cut across generational lines, in good measure because so many of Piston's students stayed on at Harvard or Radcliffe as faculty members; this included Anderson, Fine, Middleton, Sapp, Spies, Des Marais, Moevs, Pinkham, and Layton (in addition, Perkins and Berger taught at Harvard after Piston's retirement). Most composers of the third and fourth waves studied harmony with Fine, and often aided him in some capacity or another (Sapp helped complete the *Wonderland* score, Binkerd assisted his classes, and Kohn premiered *Music for Piano*). Some, like Wyner, studied with Sapp. Still younger composers, like Brenner and Perkins, studied with Fine, Berger, and Shapero at Brandeis. Spies, himself a student of Fine and Shapero, had some importance as a teacher for Behrman, Rzewski, and Harbison.

Then there were ties of a more strictly artistic order. This principally involved Carter and Fine. The former was a seminal figure for Glaser, Layton, Adler, Wyner, Boykan, Harbison, and surely others. Meanwhile, these same composers, along with Sapp, Lee, Spies, and others, were also admirers of Irving Fine, who proved of enduring importance to those close to him. There were many other such connections: Sapp, for instance, admired Moevs; Spies, Shapero;

Adler, Bernstein; Westergaard and Perkins, Berger. And Frothingham saw in such younger figures as Bernstein and Harbison the best American composers of her time.

Finally, it is important to note that this survey is not comprehensive: how, for instance, did Josef Alexander, Joseph Goodman, Yorgos Sicilianos, Russell Woollen, and Mark DeVoto contribute to the larger picture?

Most of Piston's students became teachers themselves and led distinguished careers in major colleges, universities, and conservatories across the country. Others became prominent as performers, conductors, and writers. By the 1990s, Piston's influence was so widely disseminated as to be virtually incalculable. The nature of this legacy was equally elusive. Each former student, trained to "think for himself," performed as he or she best saw fit. There were distortions, adaptations, repudiations, and extensions of whatever it was that was learned from Piston. The variety itself was a legacy of sorts. If Piston was, as described by Carter, a "ray of light," then his students formed a complex prism, refracting the light into a multitude of varied colors.

Notes

1. Bruno Monsaingeon, *Mademoiselle* (Great Britain: Carcanet, 1985), p. 86.
2. Lorenz, *Lorelei Two. My Life with Conrad Aiken* (Athens, Georgia: University of Georgia Press, 1983).
3. Segal, *The Class* (New York: Bantam, 1985).
4. Neely Bruce, review of *Copland: 1900 through 1942, American Music* Vol. 4, No. 1 (Spring 1986), p. 102. Bruce writes, "One can only speculate, of course, but if he had not been invited to teach at Harvard when he was, perhaps his radicalization would have been consummated."
5. Berger, "Walter Piston," *Trend* (January–February 1935), p. 210.
6. Salzman, "Piston: Ex-Teacher," *New York Herald Tribune,* March 31, 1961.
7. Fine, "English in Boston," *Modern Music* 23 (1946), p. 211.
8. Sapp, personal letter, September 23, 1977.

9. Piston, quoted in *Letters of Composers. An Anthology 1603–1945,* Norman Gertrude and Miriam Lubell, eds. (New York: Alfred Knopf, 1946), p. 367.

10. Berger, "Walter Piston," p. 211, and "Why Not Write a Book?" *Modern Music* 21 (1943–1944), p. 62; Pollack, *Walter Piston* (Ann Arbor: UMI, 1981), p. 72.

11. Fine, "Reviews of Records," *Musical Quarterly* 38 (1952), p. 481. Fine also spoke of Sessions' "gray" piano writing and "serpentine" chromaticism.

12. Piston, "More Views on Serialism," *The Score* 23 (July 1958), pp. 46–49.

13. Shapero, personal interview, December 1, 1978.

14. Schuller, quoted by Michael Steinberg, "Happy 80th Birthday, Walter Piston," *Boston Globe,* January 20, 1974.

15. Pollack, pp. 158–159.

16. DeVoto, personal letter, July 24, 1980.

17. Berger, personal letter, February 11, 1984.

18. Driscoll, "Walter Piston, composer and Harvard Professor," *Boston Globe,* November 13, 1976.

19. Salzman.

20. Pollack, p. 174.

21. Forbes, personal letter, July 12, 1986.

22. French, personal interview, January 4, 1978.

23. Huxley, *Point Counter Point* (New York: Harper & Row, 1928), pp. 410–411.

24. Carter, "Walter Piston," *Musical Quarterly* 32 (1946), p. 361.

25. Berger, "Walter Piston," p. 211.

26. Sapp, personal letter.

27. Boulanger, quoted by Monsaingeon, p. 73.

28. Austin, "Piston's Fourth Symphony. An Analysis," *Music Review* 16 (1955), p. 121.

29. Shackford, personal letter, October 30, 1977.

INDEX

Note: Boldface page numbers indicate musical examples.

Abbelos, Nicole 379
Adams, John xv, 393
Adams, John Quincy 357
Addinsell, Richard 29
Adler, Carol 294
Adler, Deborah 446
Adler, Hugo 280, 288, 293
Adler, Samuel (b. 1928) xv, xvii–
    xviii, 228, 273–294, 315,
    428, 431, 435–37, 446–47
  works:
    The Binding 287–88
    Concerto for Saxophone Quartet
      292
    The Crossing (incidental mu-
      sic) 283
    Diptych (see Symphony No. 3)
    Five American Folk Songs 283
    Flute Concerto 290, 294
    Four Early American Folk
      Songs 283
    From Out of Bondage 287
    Joi, Amor, Cortezia 286
    Joshua Beane and God (inci-
      dental music) 283
    The Lodge of Shadows 287
    Nuptial Scene 286
    The Outcasts of Poker Flat 283
    Piano Concerto 282, 292
    Piano Sonatina 286
    Sonata Breve 286
    Sonata for Two Pianos 286
    Southwestern Sketches 283

    Stars in the Dust 293
    String Quartet No. 4 289
    String Quartet No. 5 286
    String Quartet No. 6 287
    Symphony No. 1 273–75, **276,**
      277–80
    Symphony No. 2 273, 279–81,
      282, 283, **285,** 431
    Symphony No. 3 (Diptych,
      1960) 273, 283–84, 287,
      294
    Symphony No. 3, revised
      (*Diptych,* 1980) 273, 290,
      291, 292
    Symphony No. 4 ("Geomet-
      rics") 273, 284–87, 294
    Symphony No. 5 ("We Are the
      Echoes") 273, 286–90
    Symphony No. 6 273, 292
    Visions of Isaiah 277
    The Waking 287
    We Believe 292
    The Wrestler 287–88, 290
    Yamim Noraim 281
  writings:
    The Study of Orchestration
      275
Adorno, Theodore 379
Aeschylus 128
Aiken, Conrad 9, 128, 417, 447
Aitken, Webster 315
alcohol 15, 189, 206
Aldrich, Putnam 192

aleatoric music 12, 96, 124–25,
    189, 198, 202–3, 205,
    216–19, 250, 289, 290,
    328, 330–31, 337, 363,
    371–2, 378, 390, 435, 442
Alexander, Josef xiv, 447
Allanbrook, Douglas xv
Ameche, Don 32
American Academy of Arts and
    Letters Award 402
American Indian 111, 255, 257
  Ponca Indian Reservation 255
  Rosebud Sioux Reservation
    255
Anderson, Eleanor xvii, 20, 39
Anderson, Kurt xvii, 39
Anderson, Leroy (1908–1975)
    xiii–xv, 20–40, 62, 279,
    419, 422–25, 428, 434,
    436, 442, 446
  works:
    Arietta 32, 35
    Balladette 32, 35
    Belle of the Ball 27, 29, 34–
        35
    Birthday Party 33
    Blue Tango 20, 27–29, 34
    A Bugler's Holiday 31, 34
    The Captains and the Kings
        32, 34
    Chicken Reel 27, 34
    China Doll 27
    Clarinet Candy 32
    Concerto in C 29–**30**
    Fiddle-Faddle 27, 34
    The First Day of Spring 31,
        34
    Forgotten Dreams 29, 31, 35
    The Girl in Satin 29, 34
    The Golden Years 32
    Goldilocks 20, 31–**33**, 39–40
    Governor Bradford March 27,
        34
    Harvard Fantasy 23–24, 33
    A Harvard Festival 33
    Home Stretch 32
    Horse and Buggy 27, 34–35
    Jazz Legato 24, 34
    Jazz Pizzicato 24–25, 34, 426

    Lullaby of the Drums 33
    March of the Two Left Feet 33
    Menuet 21
    The Penny-Whistle Song 27,
        33
    The Phantom Regiment 27
    Plink, Plank, Plunk 27, 34
    Promenade 25–26, 34
    Rondo 21–22, 37
    The Sandpaper Ballet 31, 34,
        38
    Saraband 27, **28**, 34
    Serenata 27, 29, 34, 39
    Sleigh Ride 20, 27, 29, 34–35,
        36–7, 38
    Song of the Bells 29
    Suites of Carols 26
    Summer Skies 29, 34–5
    The Syncopated Clock 20, 25–
        29, 34, 40
    A Trumpeter's Lullaby 27, 34–
        35
    The Typewriter 27, 35, 38
    Waltz Around the Scale 33
    The Waltzing Cat 27, 29, 34
  writings:
    "Music, Romanticism, and
        Rousseau" 21
Andrews Sisters 365
Antheil, George 97, 419
anti-Semitism (*see also* Harvard)
    xiii, 17, 294, 348
Anton, Brewer 20
Apel, Willi xi, 70, 228
Archibald, Bruce 327
Argento, Dominick 314
Arlen, Harold 313
Armstrong, Louis 419
Ashbery, John 126, 128
Ashley, Robert 373
Asia and Asian music
  China 296, 313
    Nanking 245
  India 111, 296, 301, 393
  Japan 374
    Tokyo 236
  Korea 130, 236
  Middle East 367
  Okinawa 236

atonality 4, 132, 216, 220, 250,
    311, 316, 328, 331, 336,
    350, 364, 366, 373, 421,
    432, 435
Auden, W.H. 109, 128
Audubon, John 50
Auric, Georges 146
Austen, Jane 10
Austin, Larry 373
Austin, William xvii–xviii, 18, 444
Austria
    Hietzing 332
    Salzburg 349, 370
    St. Veit 332

Babbitt, Milton 65, 80, 151, 184,
    285, 316, 320–21, 323,
    347, 350, 354, 372, 402,
    432
Bach, C.P.E. 169
Bach, J.C. 146
Bach, J.S.
    Bavicchi 237, 239, 252
    Behrman 371, 392, 394
    Binkerd 256, 260
    Brenner 366
    Fine 132
    Harbison 401–2
    Harvard composers 432, 442
    Kohn 339
    Kohs 69, 71
    Layton 304, 311
    Middleton 212–13
    Moevs 324–25
    Pinkham 191, 199–200
    Piston 2, 10–11, 348, 364, 420,
        437–38, 440–41
    Rzewski 371, 383, 386–87, 394
    Shapero 171, 176
    Van Slyck 243, 252
    Wyner 311
Bacon, Peggy 137
Balakirev, Mily 422
Balanchine, George 112, 128,
    147, 181, 187
Baldwin, James 249
Ballantine, Edward 21, 160, 333
ballet (*see also* dances, modern
    dance) 5, 24, 42, 64, 108,

    128, 174, 187, 194, 241,
        365, 426
Barber, Samuel 29, 46, 58, 65, 71,
    80, 107, 110, 131, 180,
    194–95, 219, 224, 392,
    430
barcarolle 212, 219
Barkin, Elaine 82, 97
Barlow, Howard 187
Baroque
    Anderson 25
    Binkerd 257, 260–61, 268
    Carter 307
    Fine 132, 146
    Harbison 401, 408, 413–14
    Harvard composers 442
    Helm 62
    Kohs 71
    Layton 311
    Pinkham 192, 199, 204
    Piston 2
    Sapp 221
    Shapero 171, 175, 183–4, 185
    Van Slyck 243
    Wyner 307, 311
Bartók, Béla xii, 420
    Bavicchi 232–33, 236–39, 246,
        248, 251–52
    Binkerd 224, 262, 265
    Boykan 320
    Harbison 400
    Harvard composers 231, 252,
        354, 402, 429, 432, 442
    Helm 63
    Kohn 335, 341
    Kohs 70–71, 74
    Layton 296, 302
    Lee 245–48, 251–52
    Middleton 224
    Moevs 328, 331
    Piston 438
    Sapp 224
    Shapero 184
    Van Slyck 240–42, 244, 246,
        251–52
Bassett, Gordon 9
Baudelaire, Charles 249, 341, 415
Bauhaus (*see also* neue Sachlich-
    keit) 194

Baumgarten, Bernice 9
Bavicchi, John (b. 1922) xv, xvii,
    231–241, 245–48, 251–
    52, 358, 428, 435–36, 446
  works:
    Cello Sonata No. 2, Op. 25
      237
    Clarinet Concerto 238
    Clarinet Sonata No. 1, Op. 20
      (unaccompanied) 232–33,
      238, 247
    Clarinet Sonata, Op. 57 239
    Divertimento, Op. 1 237
    *Fantasia on Korean Folk
      Tunes,* Op. 53 236
    Festival Symphony, Op. 51
      239
    Oboe Sonatina, Op. 30 238
    Short Sonata 446
    Six Duets, Op. 27 238
    Six Korean Folk Songs, Op. 35
      236
    Trio, Op. 4 (for viola, clarinet
      and piano) 232–33
    Trio, Op. 13 238
    Trio No. 4, Op. 33/33a (for
      violin, clarinet, and piano/
      harp) 234, 235, 236–38
    Violin Sonata No. 4 238
Bax, Sir Arnold 141, 444
Beck, Julian 379
Beckett, Samuel 110
Beddoes, Thomas 271
Beebe, Lucius 9
Beethoven, Ludwig van
  Anderson 38
  Bavicchi 236–37
  Boulanger 169
  Boykan 315, 318
  Carter 116, 320
  Des Marais 315
  Fine 140, 149, 156
  Frothingham 359
  Harvard composers 442
  Kohs 70, 76
  Middleton 209
  Moevs 324, 331
  Piston 10, 364
  Princeton 432

Rzewski 383, 386
Shapero 169–71, 173–74,
    176–78, 181–83, 186,
    188, 260
  Symphony No. 3 178
Behrman, David (b. 1937) xiii, xv,
    xvii, 323, 397, 401, 414,
    419, 431, 435–37, 446
  works:
    *Cello with Melody-Driven Elec-
      tronics* 390
    *Communication in a Noisy En-
      vironment* 376
    Figure in a Clearing 390,
      393
    For Nearly An Hour (for
      Walkaround Time) 391
    *Home-Made Synthesizer Music
      with Sliding Pitches* 375,
      391
    Intermission Collage 374
    Interspecies Smalltalk (for *Pic-
      tures*) 390–91, 393
    A New Team Takes Over 374,
      390
    On the Other Ocean 390–91,
      393
    Orchestral Construction Set
      393
    Players with Circuits 374, 376
    Pools of Phase-Locked Loops
      375, 391
    Questions from the Floor 374,
      390
    Reunion 376
    Runthrough 374–76
    Runway 374
    Sinescreen 375
    6-Circle 390
    *Voice with Melody-Driven Elec-
      tronics* (for *Rebus*) 390–91
    *Voice with Trumpet and Mel-
      ody-Driven Electronics* 390
    Wave Train 374–76
  writings:
    "Theory and Technique in
      the Work of Pierre
      Boulez" 371
Behrman, S.N. 370

Bélamich, André 249
Belgium
  Antwerp 280
Bellow, Saul 99
Benét, Stephen Vincent 50
Bennett, Robert Russell 305
Béranger, Alphonse 271
Berg, Alban 147, 151, 237, 286,
  338, 361, 420
Berger, Arthur (b. 1912) xiv–xv,
  xvii, 78–103, 161, 437,
  446
  Anderson 25
  Bernstein 445
  Boulanger 427
  Boykan 318
  Brenner 446
  Fine 131, 146–47, 153, 445
  Harbison 410
  harmonic fields 316
  Kohn 334, 429
  Perkins 352–53, 446–47
  Perspectives 323, 354
  Piston 424–25, 427, 431, 434,
    436, 443
  Schoenberg 429
  Shapero 181, 186, 445
  Spies 343, 429
  Stravinsky 169
  "Stravinsky school" 109, 141–
    42, 325, 445
  Westergaard, 348–49
  works:
    Capriccio 80
    Chamber Music for 13 Players
      79, 82
    Duo for Cello and Piano 80
    Five Pieces for Piano 81–82,
      86–88, 93–95
    Ideas of Order 80–81, 95
    Partita 95, 102
    Polyphony 95
    Septet 98, 102
    Serenade Concertante 95, 108
    String Quartet 79, 95, 102,
      431
    Three Bagatelles 82, **83–85,**
      89–95
    Three Pieces for Two Pianos 82

    *Trio for Guitar, Violin, and
      Piano* 82
    Two Episodes 79
    Woodwind Quartet 82, 95,
      169
  writings:
    Aaron Copland 78
    "Copland and Hollywood"
      97
    "Form is Feeling" 96
    "The Postwar Generation in
      Arts and Letters" 78
    "Stravinsky and the Younger
      American Composers" 78
Berio, Luciano 332
Berlin, Irving 33, 121, 398, 400,
  402, 419
Berlioz, Hector 42–43
Bernstein, Leonard (1918–1990)
  xiii–xv, 104, 112, 118–31,
  160–1, 434, 436–37
  Adler 282, 292–93, 447
  Anderson 25, 31
  Berger 445
  Binkerd 262–63
  Boulanger 428
  Copland 424
  Fine 131, 135, 143–44, 153,
    159–60, 445
  Frothingham 359, 447
  Harbison 410
  Helm 64
  Kohn 334
  Kohs 71, 426, 446
  Moevs 327, 446
  Mozart 438
  Pinkham 197
  Piston 418, 424–26, 431, 433,
    436
  Rzewski 394, 397
  Segal 418
  Shapero 167–68, 177, 181,
    183, 186, 445
  works:
    Candide 111, 118, 120–22,
      127, 129–30
    Clarinet Sonata 106, **107,**
      127, 168
    Divertimento 126

Facsimile 110
Fancy Free 108–12, 128
Flute Sonata 127
I Hate Music! 109
The Lark (incidental music)
    111
Mass 110, 125–26, 293, 434
Nocturne 436
On the Town 112, 118–20,
    122
On the Waterfront (film score)
    58, 120
Prelude, Fugue, and Riffs 124
Serenade 110, 431
1600 Pennsylvania Avenue
    434
String Quartet 127
Symphony No. 1 ("Jeremiah")
    107–11
Symphony No. 2 ("Age of
    Anxiety") 110, 112
Symphony No. 3 ("Kaddish")
    126–27, 263, 434
Trouble in Tahiti 118, **119**,
    120, **121**, 122, **123**, 125,
    153
West Side Story 104, 118–20,
    122–24, 135, 144, 168
Wonderful Town 118
writings:
    "The Absorption of Race Ele-
        ments into American Mu-
        sic" xiii, 108
    "American Musical Comedy"
        126
    The Unanswered Question
        128–29
Berrigan, Father Phillip 125, 130
Berry, Wallace xvi
Bible 50, 110, 158, 199, 204,
    248, 287, 335, 413, 440
Apocryphal New Testament 200
New Testament 199, 398, 415
Old Testament 199, 401, 415
Psalms 74, 128, 184, 199, 344,
    366, 414, 431
Biggs, E. Power 190
Billings, William 50, 198, 338,
    366

Binkerd, Gordon (b. 1916) xiv–
    xvii, 211, 224–26, 228,
    254–72, 334, 428, 431,
    433, 435–36, 445–46
works:
    Cello Sonata 254, 258, **259**,
        260
    Entertainment for Piano 265
    Essays 266, **267**
    An Evening Falls 266
    Flute Sonatina 257, 260
    Four Songs for High Soprano
        268
    In a Whispering Gallery 269,
        270
    Jesus Weeping 269
    The Lamb 268
    Movement for Orchestra 267
    O Sweet Jesu 268
    Piano Miscellany 265
    Piano Sonata No. 1 254, 261,
        268
    Piano Sonata No. 2 254
    Piano Sonata No. 3 254, 268
    Piano Sonata No. 4 254, 268
    Poem after Thomas Wolfe 257
    The Recommendation 269
    Shut Out That Moon 268
    String Quartet No. 1 254, 265
    String Quartet No. 2 254,
        264–65
    Suite for Piano 266–67
    Sun Singer 257–58
    symphonies 254
    Symphony No. 1 254–55,
        261–63, 428
    Symphony No. 2 254, 261,
        262, 263, 428, 431
    Symphony No. 3 263, 428,
        431
    Symphony No. 4 267
    Violin Sonata 268
    and viva sweet love 268
    The Young Pianist 265–66
writings:
    "Contemporary Music" 271
    "The Professional Music The-
        orist" 271
Bishop, Elizabeth 125, 128

Blacher, Boris 245, 401–2, 437
Black Panthers 130
Blackearth Percussion Group 378
Blainville, Charles Henry de 42
Blake, William 61, 157, 268, 271,
        398, 401, 408, 413
Blitzstein, Marc 15, 153–54, 426
Bloch, Ernst 280, 306, 309–10,
        312, 421
Blum, Etta 255
Bly, Robert 412
Boepple, Paul 305
Bogart, Humphrey 57
Boretz, Benjamin 82
Borodin, Alexander 43, 422
Boston, Massachusetts (*see also*
        Cambridge, symphony or-
        chestras, Universities) xi–
        xiii, 21, 27, 32, 133, 192,
        208, 220, 231, 239, 245,
        278, 287, 298, 343, 357,
        364, 400, 417, 438, 446
    Cantata Singers 400–1
    Creative Concerts Guild 220
    King's Chapel 189–90, 198
    Musical Association 12
    Nova Art Gallery and Concerts
        239
    Old Howard 287
    Public Library 439
    Ritz Carlton 24
    South End Music Center 240
Boudreau, Robert 283
Boulanger, Ernest 42
Boulanger, Nadia xi, 432
    American music 419, 422
    Anderson 22, 428
    Beethoven 169
    Berger 79, 96, 427
    Bernstein 428
    Carter 127, 427
    Diamond 444
    Fine 133, 145, 428
    Frothingham 358, 427
    Glaser 360, 428
    Harbison 401
    Harvard composers 427–29,
        432, 437, 444–445
    Haydn 169

Kubik 51–53, 428
Lee 245, 427
Middleton 209, 427
Moevs 325, 428
Mozart 169
Perkins 353
Pinkham 194, 427
Piston 1, 13, 16, 348, 417–18,
        423, 433, 443
Sapp 221, 427
Sessions 401, 421
Shapero 168–69, 428
Spies 343, 347–48, 429
Vincent 42, 427
Warren 364
Boulez, Pierre xiii, 93, 113, 118,
        147, 250, 323–24, 328–
        29, 336–37, 341, 347,
        353–54, 371–72, 381,
        384–85, 401–3, 431
Bourgeois, Louis 366
Bowles, Paul 56, 78
Boyd, Bonita 294
Boykan, Constance 320
Boykan, Martin (b. 1931) xv, xvii,
        58, 274, 279, 295–96,
        307, 309, 314–22, 323,
        349–50, 428, 431, 433,
        435, 446
    works:
        Flute Sonata (withdrawn) 315
        Psalm (1958) 431
        String Quartet (withdrawn)
            315
        String Quartet No. 1 315–16,
            317, 318, **319**, 320
        String Quartet No. 2 320
        String Quartet No. 3 320
        String Trio 315
    writings:
        "Elliott Carter and the Post-
            war Composers" 295, 300,
            309, 320
        *Rhetoric and Style in the Quar-
            tets of Beethoven's Middle
            Period* 315
Bradley, Scott 56–57
Bradstreet, Anne 128
Brahms, Johannes **267**, 436

Adler, Hugo 280
Anderson 38
Binkerd 228, 257, 260, 266–
    68, 270
Carter 116
Fine 138, 147
Glaser 363
Harvard composers 432, 442
Kohn 341
Kubik 56
Middleton 209
Pinkham 192
Piston 3, 10, 25, 364, 420
Rzewski 385
Sapp 223
Spies 343, 346
Vincent 43
Wyner 313
Braithwaite, Coleridge xiii–xiv,
    xvi, 24
Brant, Henry 204
Braxton, Anthony 376
Brazil 63, 374
Brenner, Rosamond (b. 1931) xv,
    xvii, 357, 366–69, 428,
    435, 446
    works:
        Be Not Grieved 367
        The Choice 366
        Exaltation 368
        Healing 368
        Inspirational Music 368
        Love and Unity 367
        Psalm 30 366
        Unidad 366
        Unueco 366
Bricken, Carl 69
Briggs, George Wright, Jr. 31
Brink, Robert 192, 205, 446
Britten, Benjamin xiii, 153, 409–
    10, 414
Broadway musicals (*see* musicals)
Brodky, Erwin 152
Brogue, Roslyn xiv, 357, 426,
    428, 446
Brooks, Frona 429
Brown, Howard Mayer 429
Browne, Earle 371
Browne, Richmond 304

Browning, Elizabeth 271
Bruckner, Anton 43, 147, 228,
    349
Bryant, Allan 373
Burchfield, Charles 270
Burgin, Richard 327
Burgos, José 128
Burns, John Horne 132
Burns, Robert 271
Busoni, Ferruccio 242
Byrd, William 198

Cage, John xiii, 65, 82, 93, 185,
    217–18, 304, 371–73,
    379–80, 383–85, 392,
    431
Caldwell, Sarah xii
Cambridge, Massachusetts 20–1,
    216, 239, 366, 400, 402
    Christ Church 348
    High and Latin School 21
    New School of Music 240
Campion, Thomas 271
Canada 192
    Calgary 305
    Montreal 316
Carcassi, Matteo 338
Cardew, Cornelius xiii, 380
Carmichael, Hoagy 29
Carnegie Hall 433
Carpenter, John Alden 97, 105,
    137, 419
Carroll, Lewis 135–39, 157, 352
Carter, Elliott (b. 1908) xiii–xv,
    62, 104–118, 124–130,
    186, 430, 434, 436
    Adler 284, 446
    Bartók 252
    Bavicchi 238
    Behrman 394, 397
    Berger 80
    Binkerd 260–61, 265
    Bloch 309
    Boston Pops 24
    Boulanger 427
    Boykan 295–96, 300, 307, 309,
        315, 319–21, 435, 446
    Fine 157
    Glaser 361, 446

Harbison 401, 406, 410, 414, 446
Helm 64, 69
Ives 437
jazz 423
Kohn 336
Kubik 58
Layton 295–304, 307, 320–21, 446
Moevs 327, 331
Perkins 353
Pinkham 197
Piston 419, 422–23, 425–26, 431, 436, 442–43, 447
Princeton 402
Sessions 309
Shapero 186
Wyner 295–96, 306–7, 309–10, 314–15, 320–21, 414, 435, 446
works:
Cello Sonata 110, 112, 284, 301, 307, 430
Concerto for Orchestra 110, 125, 307
Double Concerto 110, 115, 129, 434
8 Etudes and a Fantasy 112, 113, 114–116, 238, 284, 301
Eight Pieces 112
Flute Sonata (withdrawn) 127, 423
"Harvest Home" 109
Holiday Overture 109–11, 116
The Minotaur 128
A Mirror on Which to Dwell 307
Night Fantasies 110, 436
Pastoral 105, **106**, 108, 426
Piano Concerto 110, 126
Piano Sonata 58, 108, 112, 300–1, 303, 307
Pocahontas 108, 111, 128
Sonata for Flute, Oboe, Cello, and Harpsichord 115–16
String Quartet (withdrawn) 127

String Quartet No. 1 104, 110, 115–6, 118, 299–301, 307, 315, 319–20, 430
String Quartet No. 2 110, 115, 117–18, 124, 336, 402, 431
String Quartet No. 3 116, 434
Symphony for Three Orchestras 110, 116, 126
Symphony No. 1 107–8, 110
Syringa 116, 126
"Tell Me Where Is Fancy Bred" 111
"To Music" 111
Variations for Orchestra 110, 115–16, 157
Violin Sonata 132
writings:
"Expressionism and American Music" 126
cartoons 35, 56, 58
Casella, Alfredo 24
Castille, Otto Rene 381–82
Cather, Willa 258
Catullus 327
Cazden, Norman xiv
Cetina, Gutierre de 271
Cézanne, Paul 270
chaconne (see forms: passacaglia)
Chadwick, George 21, 41, 46, 205
chance music (see aleatoric music)
Chanler, Theodore 8, 361, 419
Chaplin, Charlie 31, 420
Chapman, John Jay 50
Chase, Gilbert 20, 71, 74, 265
Chávez, Carlos 15
Chesterton, Gilbert 271
Chiasson, Jean Claude 192
Chile 343, 383, 386
Santiago 343
Chopin, Frédéric 324, 374, 383, 420, 432
Christ, William xvi
Citkowitz, Israel 78
Civil War 201
Claremont Quartet 297
Clark, Richard X. 381

Clarke, Henry Leland xiv, xvi
classicism 62, 66, 76, 231, 354,
    424, 430, 432, 437–38,
    442
  Anderson 37
  Bavicchi 234, 252
  Berger 78–79, 96
  Binkerd 254, 257, 260, 262–
    63, 270
  Carter 118, 127, 423
  cartoons 56
  Cozzens 5, 9–13
  Fine 145–46, 151
  Foss 445
  Glaser 362
  Harbison 397, 414
  Helm 65
  Kohn 333–36, 339–40
  Kohs 71, 75
  Layton 311
  Lee 248, 252
  Middleton 210
  Moevs 325–26
  Pinkham 189, 195, 352–53
  Piston 2–3, 9–13, 70, 168, 420,
    439, 443
  Rzewski 383
  Sapp 221
  Shapero 145, 168–70, 174,
    181, 183, 186
  Shifrin 295
  Spies 343
  "Stravinsky school" 141–42
  Thomson 3, 64
  Van Slyck 242, 252
  Vincent 43
  Westergaard 348
  Wyner 311
Clementi, Muzio 106
Cocteau, Jean 78
Cohen, David 263, 265
Cohn, Arthur 161, 163
Coleman, Ornette 287
Collaer, Paul 78
collage technique 96, 99, 336,
    398, 432, 435
Collins, Anthony 141
Coltrane, John 311, 391
Comden, Betty 118, 128

computer music 185, 370, 390–
  91, 393
Cone, Edward 349
Confrey, Zez 25
Contemporary Chamber Ensem-
  ble 403
Converse, Frederick 41, 205, 358,
  419
Cooke, Francis Judd 236, 296
Copland, Aaron xi–xii, 419–22,
    424, 427, 432–33, 437–38
  Adler 277–78, 283–84, 292–
    93
  Anderson 20, 29
  Berger 78, 96–97, 102
  Bernstein 104–7, 111, 122,
    126
  Carter 104–5, 107, 126, 301
  Fine 131, 138–41, 151–53,
    157, 430
  Harbison 403
  Helm 64–65, 69
  Kohs 71, 73
  Kubik 55, 59
  Layton 296–97, 301
  Lee 245–46, 249
  Pinkham 194
  Piston 13, 15
  Rzewski 378, 381, 385, 388
  Sapp 221, 224, 226
  Shapero 166–67, 169, 171,
    181–83
  Spies 348
  "Stravinsky school" 109
  works:
    Appalachian Spring 20, 127,
      140, 394
    Billy the Kid 128, 426
    Danzón cubano 140
    Emily Dickinson Songs 141,
      161
    Fanfare for the Common Man
      144
    Lincoln Portrait 293
    Music for the Theatre 59
    Old American Songs (arrang. I.
      Fine) 138
    Piano Concerto 423
    Piano Quartet 150

Index **459**

Piano Variations 96
El Salón México 128
The Tender Land 127, 154
Corelli, Arcangelo 243
Corley, John 240
Corso, Giuseppe 128
Cory, Eleanor 316, 318–19
Couperin, François 195, 200,
    227, 420
Cowell, Henry 81, 101, 184,
    204–5, 371, 419
Cowper, William 271
Cozzens, James Gould (1903–
    1978) xvi, 5–7, 8–19, 440
  writings:
    Ask Me Tomorrow 11, 18
    By Love Possessed 5, 7, 9, 17
    Castaway 7, 10–11
    Children and Others 14
    Cock Pit 15
    Confusion 12, 15
    Guard of Honor 5, 9
    The Last Adam 7, 9, 14–15
    Men and Brethren 15
    Michael Scarlett 10
    Morning Noon and Night 14
    S.S. San Pedro 5–7, 9, 15
Craft, Robert 182, 188
Crane, Hart 109–10, 128, 415
Crane, Stephen 139, 154
Crapsey, Adelaide 272
Crashaw, Richard 269
Creely, Robert 203
Crumb, George 250, 289, 350,
    352, 405
Cuba 14
cummings, e.e. 268, 272
Cunningham, Merce 147, 391–
    92, 394
Curran, Alvin 373

Dahl, Ingolf 56, 58, 141–42
Dallapiccola, Luigi 209–10, 220,
    352–53, 401, 432, 437
Danburg, Russell 255
dances (*see also* ballet, modern
    dance)
  beguine 34
  Charleston 159

fox-trot 34
gallop 46
gigue 74, 146, 232
march 4, 14, 27, 33–34, 135–
    36, 144, 158–59, 232,
    238, 240, 242, 247, 381
polka 4, 34, 135
polonaise 34
reel 27, 34
sarabande 27, 34, 73
siciliana 246, 362–63
tango 4, 20, 27–29, 34, 121,
    184
waltz 27, 29, 33–4, 38, 46, 51,
    168, 232, 238, 268–77,
    412
D'Annunzio, Gabriele 63
Darwin, Charles 190
Davies, Sir Peter Maxwell 410
Davis, Betsy (*see* Betsy Warren)
Davis, Miles 287
Davison, Archibald xi, xv, 131,
    228, 237, 256, 305, 360,
    423
Debussy, Claude 3, 13, 43, 94,
    110, 126, 132, 137, 146,
    209, 213, 224, 227–28,
    245, 261, 265, 270, 278,
    292, 305, 325–26, 341,
    366, 432
Defoe, Daniel 10
DeGaetani, Jan 289
Del Tredici, David 314, 432
Delibes, Clément 405
Delius, Frederick 97
Depression (Great) 49, 255
Des Marais, Paul xiv, 220, 315,
    343, 352, 431, 434, 446
Descartes, René 42, 47–48
Deutsch, Babette 272
DeVoto, Bernard 8
DeVoto, Mark xv, 434, 447
Diamond, David 19, 107, 110,
    444
Dickinson, Emily 128, 141, 272,
    415
Disney, Walt 57
Dodge, Charles 370
Donne, John 401, 404

Donovan, Richard 305–6
Douglass, Frederick 190
Dr. Seuss (Geisel, Theodor Seuss)
    57
Driscoll, Edgar 436
Dryden, John 272
Duchamp, Marcel 376
Dufay, Guillaume 191
Dufresne, Gaston 21
Dukas, Paul 1, 13, 46, 423
Duke, Vernon 134
Duns Scotas, John 59
Durant, Will 47
Dutilleux, Henri 157
Dvořák, Antonín 43, 364
Dwyer, Doriot 434
Dyer, Richard 413

Eddy, Nelson 120, 129
Edson, Lewis 198
Effron, David 294
Einstein, Alfred 63
Eisenhower, Dwight D. 14
Eisenstein, Sergei 109
Eisler, Hans 382, 384
electronic music (*see also* instru-
        ments: electronic) 185–86,
        189, 191, 198, 203–5,
        290, 292, 370, 372–77,
        380, 390–93, 434
Elgar, Edward 68
Eliot, George 10
Eliot, T.S. 99, 338
Elizabeth I, 213
Elizabethan (*see* Renaissance)
Ellington, Duke 29, 296, 419
Ellison, Ralph 306
Elwell, Herbert 261
Emerson, Ralph Waldo 10, 270
Enescu, Georges 21–22
Engel, Lehman 32
England 27, 333, 417
    London 245, 333, 353, 364,
        372
Eno, Brian 392
Epstein, Lonny 305
Estes, Lydia (*see* Lydia Pinkham)
ethnomusicology 41
Evans, Bill 187

Evans, Mark 56
Evett, Robert 151
Ewen, David xvii
Expo '67 316
expressionism 7, 125–26, 130,
        146, 151, 261, 311, 429–
        31, 442
    abstract 125, 130, 301, 320

Falstaff, Jake 137
Farber, Norma 197, 199, 203
Farwell, Arthur 419, 421
Fast, Howard 283
Faulkner, William 10, 13
Fauré, Gabriel 10, 13, 26, 42–43,
        141, 195, 197, 212, 360,
        432
Felciano, Richard 203
Feldman, Morton 371–72
feminism 200, 206, 368, 425
Ferlinghetti, Lawrence 126, 128
Fiedler, Arthur xi, 23–27, 361,
        425
film music (*see* motion pictures)
Fine, Audrey 139
Fine, Charlotte 139
Fine, George 139
Fine, Irving (1914–1962) xiv–xvi,
        62, 131–165, 354, 428,
        430, 433–34, 437
    Adler 277–78, 284
    Berger 80, 97, 161, 445
    Bernstein 161, 445
    Binkerd 256, 262, 269
    Boykan 315–16
    Glaser 361–62
    Harbison 397, 401, 410
    Helm 62
    Kohn 333–34, 337, 429
    Kohs 71
    Lee 245, 427
    Middleton 210–11, 213
    Moevs 325
    Pinkham 194, 197, 426
    Piston 424–25, 436, 443
    Sapp 221, 226, 229
    Schoenberg 162
    Shapero 161, 181, 184, 186,
        445

Spies 343, 346, 348, 429
Stravinsky 161
"Stravinsky school" 109
as teacher 446
Westergaard 352–53
works:
  Alice in Wonderland (inciden-
    tal music) 135, 136, 137,
    139, 144, 150, 157, 446
  "Blue-White" 154
  Blue Towers 154, 158
  *Childhood Fables for Grown-
    ups* 137, 142–44, 152,
    154, 161
  Choral New Yorker 137, 139
  *Christmas Sparrow or Double
    or Nothin'* 132
  Diversions for Orchestra 137,
    159
  Doña Rosita, the Spinster (in-
    cidental music) 135
  Fantasia 131, 136, 149, 156
  Homage à Mozart 137, 158
  The Hour-Glass Suite 151,
    197
  "Hymn for Brandeis" 154
  "In Grato Jubilo" 158
  "Interlude" 134
  "It's Funny Honey" 134
  "It's the Navy" 133, 135
  "A Kiss from Mister Liszt"
    134
  "A Letter from Paris" 134
  Lullaby for a Baby Panda 136,
    158
  Maggie 139, 154, 155
  McCord's Menagerie 137
  Music for Piano 143, 145,
    146, 159, 446
  Mutability 139, 149, 156
  "My Name Is Mussolini" 133
  Notturno 136, 147, 148, 149,
    151, 156
  "An Old Song" 139, 158
  One, Two, Buckle My Shoe 137
  Partita 131, 143, 145–47,
    156, 284, 334
  Partita on an Israeli Theme
    158

  Passacaglia 132
  Pastorale 132
  Preludium and Fuga 132
  Romanza 156, 431
  Serious Song 137, 154
  "A Short Alleluia" 158
  "Springtime" 134
  String Quartet 149–51, 156,
    162, 430
  Suite 132
  Symphony 149–51, 156–58,
    410
  "There'll Come a Day" 134
  Thing 132
  "This is Heaven" 134
  Toccata Concertante 133, 143,
    146, 156–57, 162
  Victory March of the Elephants
    136, 158
  Violin Sonata 132, 143, 146,
    159
  "What Is This Warm Feeling"
    134
  "When Men of War Roll
    Ashore in Cambridge
    Town" 133
writings:
  "Composers in France"
    147
Fine, Verna xvii, 131, 133–34,
    156
Fine, Vivian 78, 315
Finland 333
  Helsinki 335
Finney, Ross Lee 70
Fitelberg, Jerzy 315
Fitts, Dudley 9
Fitzgerald, F. Scott 15
Flaherty, Robert 61
Flanagan, William 195, 261, 404
Flaubert, Gustave 10, 12
Fluxus 373
folk music (*see also* Asia and Asian
    music, barcarolle, Jewish
    music, lullaby, popular mu-
    sic) 4, 41–43, 46, 50–51,
    60, 68, 125, 135, 138, 181,
    184, 194, 209, 231, 236,
    238, 252, 279, 283, 305,

374, 388, 393–94, 412, 437–38

Foote, Arthur 205, 359
Forbes, Elliot 437
Ford, Joan 31
forms
  canon 54, 68, 122, 213, 243, 260, 275, 284, 291, 306, 325, 327, 344, 378, 407
  fugue 21, 29, 46–47, 105, 113, 124, 132, 146, 156, 172– 73, 180, 192, 200, 209, 212, 220, 237, 243, 246, 256, 284, 303–4, 311, 324, 353, 360–61, 364, 425, 433
  inventions 71–72, 200, 211, 213, 218, 243–44
  passacaglia 71, 73, 102, 132, 184, 325
  rondo 21–22, 37, 200, 260, 277, 291
  suite 1–2, 13, 24, 26, 50, 132, 197, 211, 221, 222–23, 226, 232, 243, 266–67, 309, 337, 423, 425–26
  variations 49, 52, 58, 71, 79, 82, 89, 92, 96, 110, 115, 149, 156–57, 170, 174– 76, 178–79, 182–83, 209, 211, 216, 219, 223, 225– 26, 243, 246–48, 258, 266, 279, 302, 310, 325, 327–29, 350, 381–87, 402, 415, 435
Fortner, Wolfgang 350, 437
Foss, Lukas 65, 141–42, 147, 161, 224, 227, 444–45
Foster, Stephen 23, 50, 64
Fox, Charles Warren 81
France (*see also* French music and art) 50, 141, 209, 249
  Fontainebleau 358
  Paris 9, 13, 42, 99, 109, 133, 147, 231, 245–46, 296, 325, 328, 353, 443
Franck, César 43
Franklin, Benjamin 46
Fredman, James 294

Freed, Isadore 281
French, Richard F. 302, 437
French music and art 10, 13–14, 16, 25, 35, 51, 137, 141, 146–47, 157, 195, 219, 227, 250–51, 341, 402, 412, 432, 437
Frescobaldi, Girolamo 260
Freud, Sigmund 17, 99
Frey, Nathaniel 32
Fried, Michael 398
Friedhofer, Hugo 97
Friedland, Sherman 239
Friml, Rudolf 398
Fromm, Herbert 277–78, 280– 81
Frost, Betsy (*see* Betsy Warren)
Frost, Robert 128
Frothingham, Eugenia (b. 1908) xv, xvii, 357–59, 368–9, 427, 435, 447
  works:
    Along the Way 358
    Idyll 358
    Meditation and Fantasy 358
    Overture 358
    Scherzo 358
    Simplicity 358–59, **360**
    Soliloquy 358
    Sunrise 358
    A Thought 358
Frothingham, Langdon 357
Frothingham, Nathaniel 357
Frothingham, Olga 357
Fulbright Fellowship 147, 315, 372

Gabrieli, Andrea and Giovanni 198
Garcia-Renart, Luis 218–19
Garland, Hamlin 330–31
Garrigue, Jean 272
Garrison, William Lloyd 190
Gay, John 109, 128
Gazzara, Ben 32
Gebrauchsmusik (*see also* Paul Hindemith) 194, 206, 361, 362, 425
Geiringer, Karl 277

Geller, Esther 183
Gerhard, Roberto 353
German music 7, 13, 38, 68, 104,
    124, 146, 267, 280, 412,
    432, 437, 444
Germany (*see also* German music)
    142, 275, 280, 288, 324
    Berlin 372, 376, 397, 401
    Darmstadt 402
    Frankfurt 278
    Mannheim 274, 278, 280, 288
Gershwin George 10, 20–21, 23,
    26, 29, 43, 65, 120, 124,
    168, 287, 296, 361, 398,
    419, 422
Gesualdo, Carlo 42–43
Gibbon, Perceval 10
Gibson, Jewel 283
Gide, André 12
Gideon, Henry 21
Gilbert, Henry 419
Gilbert, W.S. (and Arthur Sulli-
    van) 120
Gillespie, Dizzy 306
Giuffre, Jimmy 184
Giuliani, Mauro 338
Glanville-Hicks, Peggy 81
Glaser, Victoria (b. 1918) xiv–xv,
    xvii, 357–64, 368–69,
    424–25, 428, 435–36,
    446
  works:
    Birthday Fugue 361
    Chorale Prelude 361
    Encounter with a Spirit 361,
      363
    Epithalamion 361–62, **363**
    *Fugue in Memory of Walter
      Piston* 361
    On Seven Winds 361, **362**, 363
    Pluckers' Harvest 359, 362–63
    3 Orchestral Pieces 361
  writings:
    Gebrauchsmusik of Hindemith
      361
Glass, Phillip 227, 373, 386
Glazer, Frank 58
Glazunov, Alexander 43, 141
Glenn, John 157

Glinka, Michail 43
Goethe, Johann Wolfgang von
    401, 412, 415
Goldberg, L. (Leah) 184
Goldman, Richard Franko xvi
Gombosi, Otto 228, 231, 296,
    305, 349, 361
Goodman, Benny 108, 296
Goodman, Joseph xiv, 447
Goodman, Paul 98
Gould, Morton 279
Gounod, Charles 42
Graham, Martha 394
Grandma Moses 359
Greece xiii, 42, 313, 440
Green, Adolph 118, 128
Green, Johnny 26–27
Green Shoe Manufacturing Com-
    pany 137, 154
Gregorian chant 48, 205, 286,
    296, 330, 405
Gretchaninov, Alexander 141
Greville, Fulke 7
Grieg, Edvard 43, 265
Griffes, Charles Tomlinson 204,
    249, 313–14, 419
Griffith, D.W. 31
Grover, Frances 131, 437
Gruenberg, Louis 97
Guggenheim Fellowship 402

Hagan, Dorothy 254
Haieff, Alexei 141–42, 161, 163
Halevi, Yehuda 184, 346
Halpern, Steven 392
Hamilton, Ian 415
Hamilton, Margaret 32
Hamm, Charles 20
Handel, George Frideric 199,
    243, 305, 366
Hanson, Howard 140, 187, 193,
    257–58, 419, 425
Hanson, Pauline 272
Harbison, E. Harris 397
Harbison, John (b. 1938) xiii, xv,
    xvii, 313, 316, 318–19,
    323, 349, 359, 393, 397–
    416, 419, 429, 431–37,
    446–47

works:
Amazing Grace (variations for oboe) 415
Bermuda Triangle 405–6
Book of Hours and Seasons 415
Cantatas 401, 415
Capriccio 400
Confinement 401, 403–5, 408, 413, 415
December Music 405
Diotima 415
Elegiac Songs 415
Five Songs of Experience 398, **399, 407, 408,** 415
The Flight Into Egypt 413–14
The Flower-Fed Buffaloes 398, **399,** 405, 407–9, 415
Four Preludes 405, **406**
Full Moon in March 400, 402, 404–5, 407–9, 415
Die Kürze 415
The Merchant of Venice (incidental music) 415
Moments of Vision 415
Mottetti di Montale 401, 405, 415
Music When Soft Voices Die 415
The Natural World 412
Nunc dimittis 415
Parody-Fantasia 404–6
Piano Concerto 402, 404, 408, 410–12
Piano Quintet 404, 407, 410, **411,** 412, 436
Samuel Chapter 415
Shakespeare Series 415
Sinfonia 402
Songs of Experience 399, 407, 415
String Quartet 410, 412
Symphony No. 1 400, 404, 410, 412
3 Harp Songs 415
Violin Concerto 402–5, 410–12
The Winter's Tale 404, 407, 409, 415

Woodwind Quintet 400, 404, 410, 412
writings:
Mozart's Music for Thamos, König in Aegypten 401
Harbison, Rosemary 402
Harder, Paul xvi
Hardy, Thomas 263, 269–70, 272, 415
harmony (*see also* atonality, modality, ostinato)
harmonic fields 93–94, 316–18
heterophony 148, 157
polytonal 3–4, 138, 247, 299, 309, 334, 388, 405
polytriadic 52–53
quartal 167, 221, 257, 313, 441
"referential" 263
Harris, Roy xii, 13, 15, 17, 42, 46–47, 64–65, 105, 107, 110–11, 127, 152, 167, 193, 224, 257, 263, 419–21, 424, 431–32, 438, 445
Harrison, Lou 75, 80, 204–5
Harsanyi, Nicholas 400
Harte, Bret 154, 283
Hartmann, Karl 237
Harvard xi, xiii–xv, 13, 152, 349, 354, 393, 402, 422–24, 426–32, 436–37, 442–43, 446
Adler 274, 277
Anderson 21–23, 26
anti-Semitism xiii, 140, 160–61, 430
Bartók 231, 252
Bavicchi 232
Behrman 371, 394
Berger 79, 96, 98–99
Bernstein 104–5, 108–9, 327, 426
Binkerd 224, 256–58
Bohemian Club 132
Boulez 328
Boykan 296, 315
Brenner 366
Brogue 357
Busch-Reisinger Museum 190

Carter 104–5, 109
Choral Society 360
Classical Club xi, 71, 426
Copland 161, 194, 447
Cozzens 9
Dramatic Club 135
Fine 131–33, 135, 137, 140, 152–53, 157
Frothingham 357
Glaser 360–61
Glee Club xi, 132–33, 135, 161, 425–26
Harbison 397, 400–3, 415
Harvard Club 157, 161
Hasty Pudding Club xi, 23
Helm 62–65, 76
Hindemith 231
Kohn 70–71, 333–36
Kohs 106
Layton 296, 306
Lee 245
Medical School 357
Middleton 208–9, 211, 218, 220, 224
Moevs 324–25, 327–28
Motherwell 99
Musical Association 140
Norton Lectures 128, 140, 169, 328, 424, 432
Paine Hall 21, 418
Paine Traveling Fellowship 22, 62, 348, 372, 400–1
Perkins 352–53
Pinkham 190, 192–93
Piston 1, 9
Princeton 80, 185, 274, 343, 347, 349–50, 372, 376, 397, 400, 402, 430, 432
Radcliffe College xiii, xv, 23, 133, 360, 364, 366, 424, 446
Rzewski 370–71, 394
Sapp 135, 208, 220–21, 224, 228–29
Sapp, Norma 221
School of Engineering 348
Schwartz 98–99
Segal 418
Shapero 166, 168, 186–87

Spies 343
Stravinsky 169
University Band 21
Van Slyck 240, 243
Vincent 41
Vincent Club 23
Warren 364
Westergaard 348–49
Wolff 371
Wyner 296, 305–6
Hawkins, Coleman 108
Hawthorne, Nathaniel 10
Haydn, Franz Joseph 80, 106, 145, 169–70, 181, 209, 237, 277, 328, 332, 442
Hayward, Susan 59
Hazlitt, William 10
Heifetz, Jascha 370
Heiler, Anton 366
Heilman, William 21
Hellman, Lillian 128
Helm, Everett (b. 1913) xiv–xv, 62–69, 76, 312, 424–25, 434
works:
Comments on Two Spirituals 69
Flute Sonata 65–66, **67**, 68
New Horizons 66–67
Piano Concerto No. 1 65–66, 68
Piano Concerto No. 2 65–66, 68–69
Requiem-1942 65
The Siege of Tottenburg 65
Sinfonia da Camera 65, 68
Sonata Brevis 65, **66**, 67, 69
Woodwind Quartet 68
writings:
"American Music" 64
The Beginnings of the Italian Madrigal and the Works of Arcadelt 63
Composer Performer Public. A Study in Communication 63
Music 63
Music and Tomorrow's Public 63

Hemingway, Ernest 7, 10, 13, 15
Henahan, Donal 79, 329
Hendl, Walter 274, 279, 292
Henry, O. (Porter, W.S.) 365
Henry, Pierre 147, 153
Herman, Woody 287
Herrick, Robert 109, 128, 228, 270, 272, 346
Herrmann, Bernard 97
Heschel, Abraham 288
Hilbish, Thomas 400
Hill, Edward Burlingame 13, 131, 137, 146, 157, 324, 358, 360, 423, 428
Hillyer, Robert 197
Hindemith, Paul (*see also* Gebrauchsmusik) xi–xii, xvi, 126, 424
  Adler, Hugo 280
  Adler, Samuel 228, 277–80, 284, 291–93
  Bavicchi 232–33, 237, 246
  Berger 78, 80
  Bernstein 104–5, 127
  Binkerd 264–65
  Boykan 315
  Carter 104–5
  Fine 132, 141
  Foss 445
  Fromm 280
  Glaser 361–62
  Harbison 400
  Harvard composers 231, 335, 427, 432, 437
  Helm 63, 67
  Kohn 335
  Kohs 71–72, 74, 76
  Layton 296
  Middleton 209, 213
  Moevs 324, 326
  Pinkham 193–94, 205, 228
  Piston 3, 167–68, 439, 442
  Shapero 167–70
  Spies 343
  Vincent 43
  Warren 364
  Westergaard 348
  Wyner 305, 307, 310–11

Hines, Earl 108
Hitchcock, H. Wiley xii, 20, 392
Hoffman, James 311
Holden, Oliver 198
Hölderlin, Friedrich 412
Holland 288, 333
Hollywood (*see* motion pictures)
Holst, Gustav 13
Holtzman, Howard 197, 203
Homer 128, 389
homosexuality 18, 132
Honegger, Arthur 194–95, 205, 307, 437
Hopkinson, Francis 61, 338
Hovhaness, Alan 204–5
Hubermann, Bronislaw 333
Hughes, Langston 128, 381
Hunsberger, Donald 290
Huxley, Aldous 440

Ibsen, Henrik 17
Iceland 25
Idelsohn, Abraham 280
Imbrie, Andrew 151, 220, 315–16, 432
Ingalls, Jeremiah 198
instruments
  electronic
    amplified cello 405
    electric guitar 203
    electric organ 405
    synthesizer 185, 203, 373, 381
    tape 199, 203, 204
  general
    bells 37–38, 191, 205, 328, 377
    bongos 119, 403
    carillon 191
    celesta 157, 191, 202–3
    clavichord 191–92
    cymbals 191, 242, 251, 304, 403
    English horn 203, 275, 283–84, 358, 403, 413
    glockenspiel 52, 157, 191
    guitar 82, 191, 203, 249–50, 312, 330, 374
    harp 16, 147–48, 157, 191,

195, 200, 234, 237–38,
275, 337, 341, 372, 415
harpsichord 25, 115–16,
129, 189, 191–93, 200–1,
203–5, 214–15, 228, 243,
246, 248, 250, 297, 312,
366
marimba 341
Orff instruments 207
organ 49, 59, 71, 140, 190,
193, 199, 202–4, 211,
215, 243, 260, 280, 306,
312, 330, 348, 392, 413
recorder 191, 200, 312,
362
saxophone 75, 220, 292,
381, 403, 405
tambourine 366
temple blocks 36
timpani 47, 112, 203, 289
triangle 341
vibraphone 191, 330, 341,
379, 381
viola da gamba 191
whip 36, 38
wood block 38
xylophone 52, 251
non-traditional
baby rattle 372
clock 34
flower pots 389
keyboard lid 384
knitting needles 389
phonograph 373
police whistle 119
sandpaper 31
slide whistles 372
snapping fingers 119
tin cans 372
toy horn 372
transistor radio 373
typewriter 27, 34
vacuum cleaner 373
piano
piano four-hands 208–9,
221, 241–42, 334, 339
piano strings 363, 374
prepared piano 82, 154, 250,
372

two pianos 59, 82, 199, 208,
241, 244, 286, 314, 331,
341
Ireland, John 141
ISCM 307
Israel 274, 280
Italy 69, 209, 379, 437
Rome 223, 296, 298, 305–7,
311, 325, 353, 372–73,
377, 379
Tremezzo 209
Ives, Burl 283
Ives, Charles 64–65, 78, 97, 104,
118, 126, 130, 249, 270,
301–2, 307, 366, 371,
388, 419, 421, 432, 437

Jack, Adrian 375
Jackson, Roland 52
Jacobi, Frederick 305, 310
Jacobs, Paul 383
James, Henry 10, 171, 328
Janáček, Leoš 229
jazz (see also popular music) xii,
108–9, 419, 424, 432
Adler 287
Anderson 27, 423
Bavicchi 238
bebop 113, 306
Behrman 392
Berger 82
Bernstein 71, 108–9, 124, 126,
186
blues 18, 43, 51, 108, 125, 134,
137, 168, 172, 184, 197,
266, 313, 324
boogie-woogie 58, 108, 134,
226, 266, 324, 327
Carter 108–9, 113, 117–18,
126, 301, 307, 423
Cozzens 15
Harbison 398–99, 401, 403,
406, 412
Harvard composers 438
Helm 65
Kohs 71
Kubik 51
Layton 296, 301, 304, 306,
311, 321

Perkins 353
Pinkham 194, 198
Piston 4, 15, 167, 412, 423
Rzewski 384–87
Shapero 167–68, 171–72, 177,
    181, 184, 186
swing 36, 108, 119
Vincent 43
Wyner 306–7, 311
Jenkins, Leroy 376
Jewish music (*see also* religions)
    281–84, 291–92, 310
folk 184, 280, 305
liturgical 73–74, 111, 281, 286,
    294, 305, 307
Yiddish 288, 305, 310, 437
Johannes, Donald 284, 294
Johnson, Anna 20
Johnson, Hunter 128
Johnson, Marlowe 197
Johnson, Will 376
Jones, Vincent 97
Jonson, Ben 151, 195, 346
Jonson, Don 324, 437
Jordan, June 128
Joyce, James 110, 118, 128, 338
Judd, George 23
Jugendstil 258

Kacinkas, Jeronimas 238–39
Kafka, Franz 74, 99, 118, 288
Kalish, Gilbert 311
Kandinsky, Wassily 239, 438
Kanner-Rosenthal, Hedwig 305
Kaplan, Maynard 134
Kazan, Elia 119
Kennedy, John F. 14, 201, 304
Kenton, Stan 287
Kern, Jerome 23, 32, 132, 313,
    398, 400, 419
Kerr, Jean 31
Kerr, Walter 31
Kessler, John 352
Kim, Earl 402, 432
Kime, Donna 368
King, Martin Luther 130
Kinkeldey, Otto 256
Kipling, Rudyard 32, 272
Kirchner, Leon 151, 310, 432

Kirstein, Lincoln 109, 181
Kline, Franz 301
Kohn, Karl (b. 1926) xv, xvii, 228,
    262, 265, 274, 279, 323,
    332–343, 348, 354–55,
    405, 428–29, 431, 435–
    37, 446
works:
    Bits and Pieces 336
    Brass Quintet 341
    Capriccios 337, 341
    Castles and Kings 334–35
    Centone 336, 341
    Concerto mutabile 337
    Divertimento 431
    Dream Pieces 341
    Encounters 338
    Episodes 336, 338
    Fanfare 333
    5 Bagatelles 337
    Five Pieces 333, **334–35**
    Horn Trio 338, 341
    Impromptus 337–39, **340**
    Innocent Psaltery 338
    Introductions and Parodies
        337–39
    Kaleidoscope 336
    A Latin Fable 335
    Little Suite 337
    Paronyms 338, 341
    Prophet Bird 338, 341, **342,**
        436
    Recreations II 338–39
    Reflections 338, 340
    Rhapsodies 337–38, 340–41
    San Gabriel Set 341
    Sensus spei 337
    Serenade 336–37
    Shadow Play 341
    Souvenirs 338
    *Three Descants from Ecclesias-
        tes* 335
    Three Goliard Songs 335
    Time Irretrievable 341
    Two Short Pieces 336
    Waldmusik 338
writings:
    Tonal Dodecaphony in Bartók
    335

Kohn, Margaret 332
Kohn, Susanna 341
Kohs, Ellis (b. 1916) xiv–xv, xvii,
    69–77, 210, 252, 424–26,
    430–31, 434, 436, 446
  works:
    Amerika 74
    The Automatic Pistol 70
    Bassoon Sonatina 71, 73
    Chamber Concerto 71, 73–74
    Clarinet Sonata 71
    Concerto for Orchestra 70
    Concerto for Percussion Quartet
        74–75
    Etude in Memory of Bartók 71,
        73
    Legend 71, 73
    Life with Uncle Sam 70
    Lord of the Ascendant 74
    Men 74
    Passacaglia 71, 430
    Piano Variations 71
    Psalm 23 74, 431
    Scherzo 71, 73
    A Short Concert (String Quar-
        tet No. 2) 71, 73–74, **75**
    String Quartet No. 1 70
    Symphony No. 1 71, 73
    10 2-Voice Inventions 71, **72**
    *Three Choral Variations on
        Hebrew Hymns* 71, 73
    3 Greek Choruses 74
    3 Medieval Latin Student Songs
        74
    3 Songs from the Navajo 74
    Variations on l'homme armé
        71
    Violin Concerto 75
    Violin Sonatina 71, 73
  writings:
    *An Aural Approach to Orches-
        tration* 69
    Music Theory 69–70
    Musical Composition 69, 74
    Musical Form 69
Korean War 29
Koussevitzky, Natalie 111
Koussevitzky, Serge xi, 133, 141,
    156, 224, 275, 292, 324,
    443
Koussevitzky Foundation 170,
    292
Kreisler, Fritz 25
Krenek, Ernst 166, 429
Kubik, Gail (1914–1984) xiv–xv,
    49–62, 69, 97–98, 240,
    242, 255, 257, 424, 428,
    431, 433–34, 436–37
  works:
    Boston Baked Beans 58
    C-Man (film score) 58
    Celebrations and Epilogue 50,
        54
    The Desperate Hours (film
        score) 57–58
    Divertimento I 50, 54, 58, 431
    Divertimento II 58–59, 431
    Earthquakers (film score) 55
    Five Theatrical Sketches
        (Divertimento No. 3) 59
    Folk Song Suite 50
    Gerald McBoing-Boing (film
        score) 51, 56–57
    I Thank a Fool (film score) 57,
        59
    In Praise of Johnny Appleseed
        49–50, 426
    Memphis Belle (film score)
        55–56, 58
    *Memphis Belle: A War Time
        Episode* 58
    Men and Ships (film score) 55
    Miles Standish 50
    The Miner's Daughter (film
        score) 58
    Mirror for the Sky 50
    Paratroops (film score) 55
    Piano Sonata 58
    Piano Sonatina 52, 53–54,
        55, 58
    Pioneer Woman 50
    Prayer and Toccata 59
    A Record of Our Time 50, 59
    Scenario for Orchestra 58
    Scholastics: A Medieval Set 52,
        59

Symphony Concertante 51–52,
    56, 58
Symphony for Two Pianos 59
Symphony No. 1 51, 54, 58–
    59
Symphony No. 2 51, 54, 58
Symphony No. 3 51, 54, 58
Theodore Roosevelt 50
Thunderbolt (film score) 55,
    58
Thunderbolt Overture 58
Twenty-One Miles (film score)
    55
Two Gals and a Guy (film
    score) 57
*Variations on a 13th-Century
    Troubadour Song* 49, 52
Violin Concerto 52
Woodrow Wilson 50
The World at War (film score)
    55–56

Landau, Max 255
Landon, H.C. Robbins 277
Landowska, Wanda 192, 205
Lang, Paul Henry 118
Lang, Philip 31
Lansky, Paul 344, 346
Larkin, Peter 32
Lasker, Henry xiv
Lassus, Roland de 361
LaTouche, John 128
Laurent, Georges 41, 348, 359
Layton, Billy Jim (b. 1924) xv,
    xvii, 64, 295–304, 306–7,
    314, 320–21, 323, 400,
    428, 430–31, 434, 436–
    37, 446
    works:
    An American Portrait, Op. 2
        297–98, 428, 430
    Dance Fantasy, Op. 7 297,
        304, 434
    Divertimento, Op. 6 297,
        303–4, 311, 431
    Five Studies, Op. 1 297–98,
        299–300, 301, 306–7, 430
    String Quartet, Op. 4 297,
        301–2

Three Dylan Thomas Poems,
    Op. 3 297–98, 301
Three Studies, Op. 5 297, 302,
    303
    writings:
    "The New Liberalism" 304
Lazar, Joel xv
Le Roux, Maurice 147
Lear, Edward 350, 352
Lee, Noël (b. 1924) xv, 69, 231,
    241, 245–53, 426–28,
    431–32, 435–36, 446
    works:
    *Caprices on the Name of
        Schönberg* 250–51, 436
    Chroniques 250, **251**
    *Commentaries on a theme from
        Aaron Copland* 248–49
    Convergences 248, 250
    Deux Mouvements 247–48
    Devouring Time 248
    Dialogues 248, **249**
    *Five Songs on Poetry by Federico
        García Lorca* 249–50
    Four Ballades 249
    Four Etudes 248–50
    "On a rhythm by Béla Bar-
        tók" 246
    On Chords from Charles Ives
        249
    Paraboles 249
    Piano Sonata 249
    Quatre Chants sur Baudelaire
        249
    Rhapsodies 248
    Sonatine 247–48, 431
    Three Intimate Songs 248
    Variations **246,** 247
LeGallienne, Eva 135
Lehár, Franz 120
Leibowitz, René 147
Leichtentritt, Hugo 41, 70, 152
Leonhardt, Gustav 366
Lerner, Alan Jay 128
Lesueur, Jean François 42
Lewis, Sinclair 13, 15
Lewis, Ted 18
Library of Congress xvii, 41, 132
Ligeti, György 337

Lindsay, Vachel 49–50, 415
List, Eugene 29, 287
Liszt, Franz 1, 63, 110, 134, 212, 218, 324, 326–27, 330–31, 338, 341, 382, 385
Lithuania 238
Little, Dorothy Fay 359
Loeffler, Charles Martin 249
Lombard, Eugenia (*see* Frothingham, Eugenia)
Longfellow, Henry Wadsworth 10, 241
Longy, George 13
Lopatnikoff, Nikolai 315
Lorca, Federico García 135, 249–50
Lorenz, Clarissa 417–19, 441, 443
Lowell, Robert 125–26, 130, 312
Lowenberg, Carlton 272
Löwinger-Feldstein, Alice 332–33, 437
Loy, Myrna 97
Lucier, Alvin 373
Lucretius 110, 116
Luening, Otto 296
lullaby 27, 33–35, 56, 135–37, 144, 282, 363, 381
Lutoslawski, Witold 218, 290
Lyon, James 198

MacDonald, Jeanette 120, 129
Macdonald, Margaret 359
MacDowell, Edward 65, 243, 265
MacDowell Club 12
MacDowell Colony 255
MacMeekin, Isabel 137
Maderna, Bruno 298
Mahler, Gustav 126, 147, 149, 176, 287, 338, 412, 432, 442
Mailer, Norman 181, 186
Makanowitzky, Paul 248
Malina, Judith 379
Malipiero, Gian Francesco 43, 62–63, 66, 68, 76, 437
Mallarmé, Stéphane 110, 341, 402
Mann, Thomas 110

Mao Zedong 379
Marabini, Maria 325
March, Frederic 57
Marinet, Jean-Louis 147
Martin, Frank 244
Martino, Donald 432
Martinu, Bohuslav 141, 439
Marx Brothers 31
Maslow, Abe 152
Mason, Daniel Gregory 419
Matthiessen, F.O. xi
Maugham, Somerset 13
Maximilien, Wanda 331
McCallum, John 18
McCarthy, Eugene 130
McCarthy, Joseph 152, 157, 370
McCord, David 137, 201, 365
McKinley, Carl 236, 358
McKinney, Mathilde 400
medieval music 42, 52, 60, 198, 200, 202, 205, 223, 227–28, 286, 296, 305, 335, 341, 442
Mehmet III 213
Mellers, Wilfred 20, 151, 182, 186, 202, 204–5, 302, 325
melody (*see also* atonality, ostinato, rhythm)
    Klangfarbenmelodie 148
    microtonal 392
    pentatonic 46, 72, 111, 283
    Sprechstimme 289
    whole-tone 94, 150, 238, 358, 359
Melville, Herman 10
Melville, Sam 381
Mendelssohn-Bartholdy, Felix 137, 183, 277, 280, 338–39
Menotti, Gian Carlo 65
Meredith, George 17
Merrick, David 31
Merritt, Arthur Tillman xi, xv, 131, 160, 237, 349, 357, 360, 364
Messiaen, Olivier 147, 213, 229, 250, 301, 348
MEV (Musica Electronica Viva) 373, 377, 380

Michelangelo 239
Middleton, Polly 208
Middleton, Robert (b. 1920) xiv–
    xv, xvii, 208–20, 223,
    229–30, 243, 250, 334,
    426–29, 433, 435–36, 446
  works:
    Approximations 216, **217**
    Command Performance 213–
    16
    Concerto di Quattro Duetti
    216, 219, 433
    Elizabethan Song Book 216
    Four Nocturnes 219
    Four Organ Preludes 211
    Inventions on the Twelve Notes
    211, **212**, 213, 215, 218,
    223, 244
    Keyboards and Crowns 215
    Life Goes to a Party 213
    The Nightingale is Guilty 213
    Nocturne 436
    Notebooks of Designs 216–17
    *Overture to "The Charterhouse
    of Parma"* 219
    Piano Sonata 211
    String Quartet 209, **210**, 212,
    219
    Two Duologues 216, 218
    Variations 216, 219
    vARIAzioni-variAZIONI 216
    *Vier Trio-Sätze in romantis-
    cher Manier* 216–19
    Violin Concerto 219
Milhaud, Darius 63, 65, 67–68,
    70, 146–47, 162, 296,
    348, 437
military service (*see also* Korean
    War, Vietnam War, World
    War I, World War II) xi,
    25, 55, 70, 133, 209, 225,
    236, 256, 296
Milland, Ray 50
Millay, Edna St. Vincent 128
Miller, Robert 95
Milles, Carl 258
Mingus, Charles 184
minimalism 112, 243, 372, 393,
    409, 436

Mitchell, Donald 52
Mitchell, Margaret 32
modality
    Adler 280, 283, 286
    Bartók 233, 247
    Bavicchi 232–33, 236
    Behrman 391–92
    Berger 89, 91–92, 169
    Bernstein 106
    Binkerd 257, 261, 269
    Brenner 367
    Carter 106
    Coltrane 391
    Eno 392
    Fine 158, 269
    Frothingham 359
    Glaser 362
    Harbison 405
    Hindemith 364
    Kohn 338
    Kohs 72
    Lee 247
    Moevs 326
    Pinkham 193–94, 205
    Piston 169, 193, 362, 364, 441
    polymodality 47, 55, 238, 247,
    298
    Rzewski 389
    Sapp 221–22, 228
    Shapero 169, 172
    Vincent 41–44, 47, 49, 59–60
    Warren 364–65
    Wyner 306–7
modern dance (*see also* ballet,
    dances) 105, 187
Modern Jazz Quartet 311
Modigliani, Amedeo 438
Moevs, Robert (b. 1920) xiv–xv,
    xvii, 29, 323–332, 341,
    354–55, 424, 428, 431,
    434–37, 446–47
  systematic chromaticism 325,
    327–29, 350
  works:
    Attis I 327, 331
    Ave Maria **330**
    A Brief Mass 330
    Concerto Grosso 328, 331
    Et Nunc Regis 329

Et Occidentem Illustra
330
Fantasia sopra un motivo 327,
331
Fourteen Variations 327
Ludi Praeteriti 331
Main-Travelled Roads (Symphonic Piece No. 4) 330–31
Musica da Camera 328–29
Passacaglia 325
Phoenix 331
Piano Sonata 325, **326**, 327,
331
Piano Sonatina 325
String Quartet 327, 331, 431
String Trio 331
Three Symphonic Pieces 331
Una collana musicale 331
Variations on "Christ lag in Todesbanden" 325
Variazioni Sopra una Melodia
328, **329**, 435
Moncion, Francisco 174, 187
Monk, Thelonious 82
Montale, Eugenio 415
Monteux, Pierre 13
Monteverdi, Claudio 42–43, 184
Moore, Thomas 272
Moravia, Alberto 10
Moross, Jerome 97
Morton, Ferdinand "Jelly Roll"
419
Morton, Lawrence 69, 336–37
Motherwell, Robert 99
motion pictures (*see also* Leonard Bernstein, Gail Kubik) 15,
26, 29, 48–50, 55–60, 73,
97–99, 120, 154, 200,
240, 251, 273, 392, 413,
437
Chariots of Fire 392
Mr. Roberts 26
Mozart, Wolfgang Amadeus 2, 3,
10, 98, 106, 124, 132, 137,
140, 169–70, 178, 209,
215, 237, 324, 353, 361,
383, 401, 420, 432, 437–38, 440–41

Così fan tutte 140, 353
Divertimento in Bb, K. 289 169
The Magic Flute 124
Thamos, König in Aegypten 401
Muck, Karl 357
Muir, Edwin 272
Mumma, Gordon 373–74, 376
Munch, Charles 156, 443
Murray, David 132
Murray, Ed xvii
musicals 10, 20, 26, 31–32, 65,
99, 112, 118, 120, 122,
124, 126, 132, 137, 153–54, 398, 400, 418, 438
musique concrète 147, 191, 374–75
Musorgsky, Modest 42–43, 305,
422
Muzak 28, 32, 392

Nash, Ogden 32
Nason, Kathryn 16, 368
Naval Training School Glee Club
133
NEM (New Music Ensemble) 373
Nemiah, John 152
neobaroque (*see* Baroque)
neoclassicism (*see* classicism)
neo-Elizabethan (*see* Renaissance)
neoromantic (*see* Romanticism)
neue Sachlichkeit (*see also*
Bauhaus) 62, 194, 239,
424
New York Music Critics Award
118, 433
Newlin, Dika 152
Newman, Ernest 38
Newman, Ruby 23
Newsong Fabrics 134
Nielsen, Carl 229
Nigg, Serge 147
nocturne 66, 110, 136, 147–49,
151, 156, 219, 228, 310,
436
Norden, Hugo 277
Norman, Gertrude 154
Norris, R.C. 199
Norway
Oslo 25

Núñez de Arce, Gaspar 346
Nype, Russell 32

O'Casey, Sean 272
O'Connor, Edwin 10
O'Hara, Frank 126, 128
O'Hara, John 15
Oliveros, Pauline 332
ONCE 373
opera xii, 98
  Adler 275, 283, 287
  Bavicchi 237
  Bernstein 118, 124
  Binkerd 265
  Cozzens 10, 14, 18
  Fine 152, 154
  Foss 142
  Goldovsky Opera Company
    364
  Harbison 400, 409–10, 415
  Helm 65
  Kohs 74
  Kubik 50
  Middleton 213–16, 219
  New York City Opera 216
  Perkins 353
  Pinkham 195
  Piston 4, 14
  Sessions 421
  Spies 348
  Turnau Opera Association 311
  Warren 364–65
  Westergaard 350–52
  Wyner 311
Oppenheimer, James 288
Oppens, Ursula 383
Orff, Carl 207, 362
Orgel, Irene 152
Ormandy, Eugene 42, 47
Ornstein, Leo 324
Ortega, Sergio 383
ostinato 51, 53–54, 56, 59, 225–
  26, 243
Ovid 128

Pachelbel, Johann 260
Paganini, Niccolò 385
Paine, John Knowles xii, 205
Palestrina, Giovanni 66, 198

Palmer, Robert 444–45
Papathanassiou, Vangelis 392
Parish, Mitchell 29
Parker, Charlie 113, 287, 306–7
Parker, Dorothy 128
Parker, Horatio 205
Payot, Jules 12
Penderecki, Kryzsztof 218, 290,
  292, 304
Perkins, John MacIvor (b. 1935)
  xiii, xv, 81, 323, 352–54,
  356, 403, 431, 434–35,
  446–47
  works:
    Andrea de Sarto 354
    Caprice 353
    Divertimento 353, 431
    Music for Thirteen Players 353
    Variations 353, 435
Perle, George 81
Perse, St. John 110, 125
Perspectives of New Music 78, 186,
  265, 295, 316, 324, 354,
  434, 437
Pfatteicher, Carl 190
Pfeifer, Ellen 405
Phetteplace, Jon 373
Philips, Ambrose 272
Picasso, Pablo 56, 267
Pinkham, Charles 190
Pinkham, Daniel 190
Pinkham, Daniel R. (b. 1923) xv,
  xvii, 189–207, 228, 243,
  414, 425–27, 431, 433,
  435–37, 446
  works:
    Agnus Dei 198
    Aspects of the Apocalypse 204
    Brass Quintet 204
    Cantilena and Capriccio 193,
     203, 205
    The Christmas Cantata ("Sin-
     fonia Sacra") 198
    Concertante 203
    Concertante No. 1 202
    *Concerto for Harpsichord and
     Celesta* 191, 193, 202,
     205
    Daniel in the Lion's Den 199

The Descent Into Hell 190,
  199–200
Dithyramb 191
Divertimento 205
Duo 194
Easter Cantata 191
Eclogue 205
For evening draws on 203–4
The Garden of Artemis 195,
  197
Glory Be to God 198
Homage to Wanda Landowska
  192
Jonah 198–99
Lessons 201
Liturgies 203–4
"Love Came Down at Christ-
  mas" 197
Masks 204
*Mourn for the eclipse of his
  light* 203
Narragansett Bay 194, 426
Nebulae 204
Organ Sonata 190, 193–94
*The Other Voices of the Trum-
  pet* 203
Partita 194, 200, **201**, 431
Passion of Judas 199–200
Prelude and Chaconne 202
Serenades 204
Shepherd's Symphony 191,
  203–4
Signs of the Zodiac 201–2
"Slow, slow fresh fount" 195,
  196, 197
A Song for the Bells 191
St. Mark Passion 191, 199
Symphony No. 1 191, 201–2
Symphony No. 2 201–2
To Troubled Friends 203
Toccata for the Vault of Heaven
  203–4
Transitions 197
*Two Poems of Howard
  Holtzman* 203
Witching Hour 190, 203
Pinkham, Isaac, 190
Pinkham, Captain Joseph 190
Pinkham, Lydia 189

Pinkham, William 190
Pirrotta, Nito 296
Piston, Walter (1894–1976) xi–
  xvi, 1–5, 8–19, 417–447
Adler 275, 277–79, 283–84,
  287, 292, 315, 428, 431,
  435–36
Anderson 21–2, 25, 37, 419,
  422–26, 436, 442
Bavicchi 232–33, 236–38, 252,
  428, 435–36
Behrman 371, 387, 394, 419,
  431, 436–37
Berger 79, 96, 102, 349, 424–
  25, 427, 429, 431, 436,
  443
Bernstein 104–7, 122, 126,
  418, 424–26, 431, 433,
  436, 438
Binkerd 254–58, 260, 262–65,
  269, 428, 431, 435–36, 445
Boulanger 1
Boykan 296, 315, 428, 431
Brenner 366, 368, 428
Carter 104–7, 111, 113, 116–
  17, 126–27, 301, 419,
  422–23, 425–26, 431,
  436–37, 442–43, 447
Copland 437
Dukas 1
Fine 131–33, 139–41, 144,
  146, 150–151, 154, 157,
  424–25, 430–31, 436–37,
  443
Frothingham 357–58, 368
Glaser 360–62, 368, 424–25,
  428, 436
Harbison 400–1, 403–4, 410,
  412, 414, 419, 429, 431,
  437
Helm 62, 64–66, 68, 424–25
Hindemith 3, 167, 278–79,
  305, 348
humanism 437–443
humor 167–68, 185, 192, 220,
  237, 279, 349, 361, 364,
  371, 417, 429, 436
Kohn 333–35, 337, 341, 354,
  428–29, 431, 437

Kohs 62, 70–73, 75, 424–26, 431, 436
Kubik 52, 55, 424, 426, 431, 436–37
Layton 296–98, 301, 428, 431, 436–37
Lee 231, 245–46, 252, 426–28, 431, 435
Middleton 209–11, 220, 229, 426–29, 433
Moevs 208–11, 216, 220, 229, 324–26, 331, 354, 424, 431, 435–37
Perkins 352, 354, 431, 435
Pinkham 192–95, 198, 202, 205, 425–27, 431, 435–36
politics 14–15, 19, 108–9, 439–41
Rzewski 371, 378, 387, 394, 419, 429, 431
Sapp 208, 220–22, 224, 226–27, 229, 243, 335, 426–28, 431, 436, 443
Schoenberg 4
Sessions 349
Shapero 166–69, 171, 180, 182, 185–87, 260, 424–26, 431, 433, 436
songwriting 195
Spies 343, 347–48, 354, 428–29, 431
Stravinsky 1
as teacher xii–xiv, 1, 22, 70, 76, 105, 127, 166–67, 171, 192, 220, 237, 245, 256–57, 279, 297, 324, 348, 358, 361, 364, 366, 371, 404, 418, 423, 425–27, 436–38, 445, 447
as theorist xii, xvi, 11–12, 43–44, 70, 423, 434
Van Slyck 231, 240, 242–43, 252, 424–426, 428, 435
Vincent 41, 43–44, 47, 419, 424–25, 431, 436–37
Warren, 364, 368, 426, 436–37
Westergaard 323, 348–49, 352, 354

Wyner 296, 305, 311–12, 428–29, 431
works:
   Carnival Song 11, 198, 335, 425
   Chromatic Study 71, 258, 426, 429
   Clarinet Concerto 117
   Concerto for Orchestra 32, 220, 262, 423–24, 426, 429
   Divertimento 348, 431
   Fantasia 436
   Flute Concerto 434
   Flute Quintet 246, 278
   Flute Sonata 1, 2, 3–4, 5, 9, 166–67, 348–49, 387, 423
   Fugue on a Victory Tune 433
   Improvisation 441
   The Incredible Flutist 1, 5, 9, 24, 64, 73, 113, 122, 127, 194, 246, 334, 361, 425–26, 429
   Minuetto in Stile Vecchio 10
   Oboe Suite 13, 232
   Partita 278, 426–27, 429, 431
   Passacaglia 102, 220, 436, 441
   Piano Concertino 68, 167, 220, 426
   Piano Quintet 278, 315
   Piano Sonata 1
   Piano Trio 66
   Pine Tree Fantasy 4, 14
   Prelude and Allegro 140, 193, 348, 425–26
   Prelude and Fugue 11
   Psalm and Prayer of David 414, 431
   Ricercare 433
   Serenata 431
   Sinfonietta 169, 401, 431
   Sonatina for violin and harpsichord 193, 269, 431
   Souvenirs 16, 433
   String Quartet No. 1 8, 423
   String Quartet No. 2 315
   String Quartet No. 5 433
   string quartets 10, 73, 167, 412, 431

Suite for Orchestra 1, 2, 423, 425–26, 429
symphonies 366, 418, 428, 431
Symphony No. 1 102
Symphony No. 2 64, 144, 279, 428
Symphony No. 3 9, 315, 428
Symphony No. 4 14, 64, 278, 428–29, 444
Symphony No. 6 430
Symphony No. 7 9, 64, 433
Symphony No. 8 433
Three New England Sketches 4, 14, 127, 361, 425, 438
Three Pieces 16, 113, 117, 419, 422–23, 428–29
Tunbridge Fair 129
Variations (cello and orchestra) 435
Violin Concerto No. 1 269, 425
Violin Concerto No. 2 433
Wind Quintet 430
writings:
Counterpoint 428
Harmony 426, 434
"More Views on Serialism" 431
Orchestration 275, 349, 430
Principles of Harmonic Analysis xvi, 16, 43, 423, 426
"Roy Harris" 424, 431
Piutti, Karl 44
Pizzetti, Ildebrando 43
Plato 110, 128
Pleasants, Henry 185
Poe, Edgar Allan 128
pointillism 312
Poland 290, 333
politics
Fascism, 56, 104, 274, 280, 288, 333, 440
green movements 390
left-wing xiii, 109, 130, 262, 371, 379, 381, 383, 388, 390, 393–94
liberalism 108

Marxism 379–80, 390, 394, 414, 440, 442
McCarthyism 152, 157
New Deal 442
populism 50, 240, 246, 298, 422, 426, 442
socialism 379, 382
Pollock, Jackson 301
Ponce, Manuel 338
pop art 125
Pope, Alexander 110
popular music (*see also* dances, folk music, jazz, musicals) 24–25, 104, 419, 432
Anderson 21, 28, 35
Bavicchi 239
Berger 90, 343
Bernstein 112, 124
Binkerd 268
Brenner 267
chanteys 14
cowboy songs 50–51
Cozzens 10
Fine 132, 134–35, 397
gospel 286
Harbison 397–401, 406–7, 437
Harvard composers 438, 441
hymns 14, 50–51, 58, 60, 71, 110, 183, 198, 205, 223–24, 239, 268, 306, 367, 389
"Aeterne Rerum Conditor" 48
"Amazing Grace" 415
"The Battle Hymn of the Republic" 133
Kubik 58
Layton 296
Moevs 324
Pinkham 194
Piston 4
rock 125, 367, 392, 432
Rzewski 386
Shapero 168, 172, 181, 183–84
song 51
Spies 343
spirituals 50, 69
vaudeville 51, 120
Warren 365

Wyner 313
Porter, Andrew 409
Porter, Cole 21, 23, 120, 140
Porter, Quincy 193, 296, 310,
    419, 425
Poulenc, Francis 140, 146, 154,
    278, 425
Pound, Ezra 228, 272
Pousseur, Henri 372, 374, 390
Powell, John 41
Powell, Mel 51
Prall, D.W. xi, 96, 98–99
Prendergast, Roy 56
Previn, André 183
Prix de Rome 167, 187
Pro Arte Quartet 70
Prokofiev, Sergei 38, 53, 71, 89,
    141, 181, 241–42, 244,
    246, 370, 402, 420
Proust, Marcel 118
Prout, Ebenezer 38
Prüwer, Julius 333
Pryor, Arthur 25
Puccini, Giacomo 409
Pulitzer Prize 9, 52, 61, 118, 410,
    414, 428, 433–34

Quilapayun 383
quotation 56, 134, 250, 293, 304,
    311, 338–39, 341, 363,
    405, 432, 438

Rabaud, Henri 13
Rabelais, François 128, 378
Rachmaninov, Sergei 105, 141,
    242, 265, 385, 402
racism xiii, 17, 123
radio 23, 28, 120, 338, 375
Raimondi, Matthew 218–19, 297,
    299, 311
Raksin, David 97
Rampion, Mark 440
Ravel, Maurice 13, 43, 131, 137,
    146, 209, 211, 227, 242,
    245, 249, 278, 324, 361,
    405, 412, 420; 432
Reddy, Helen 407
Redford, John 260

Reese, Gustav 338
Reich, Steve 227, 328–29, 373,
    378, 381, 390
religions
    Baha'i Church 366–68
    Catholicism 26, 48, 330, 343,
        422
    Christianity 198, 206, 367, 414
    Episcopalian 13
    holy rollers 286
    Judaism (see also Israel, Jewish
        music, World War II) xi,
        xiii, 26, 158, 160, 184,
        274, 280–81, 288–89,
        332, 343, 422
    Lutheran 257
    Mormon 187
    Protestantism 198, 228
    Quaker Church 189
    Swedenborgianism 189
    Unitarianism-Universalism xi,
        14, 190, 439
    Zen Buddhism 185
Renaissance 11, 62, 111, 184,
    191, 197–98, 202, 215,
    228, 237, 269, 286, 346,
    440
    Elizabethan 49, 191, 195, 197
Respighi, Ottorino 43
Revolutionary War 190
rhythm (see also dances, ostinato)
    changing meters 55, 57, 73,
        202, 257, 269, 292, 299,
        335–36, 344, 402, 412
    irregular meters 193, 336
    metric modulation 111, 307,
        309
    polyrhythms 130, 157, 299–
        300
    serialized 289, 336, 350, 371
Riegger, Wallingford 64–65, 370,
    437
Riemann, Hugo 44
Riley, Terry 372, 390
Rilke, Rainer Maria 128, 272,
    328, 346–47, 355, 415
Rimsky-Korsakov, Nikolai 409,
    422
Robbins, Jerome 112

Rochberg, George 182, 314, 370, 405

Rockefeller, Nelson 380

Rockwell, John 370, 376, 393

Rockwell, Norman 35

Rodgers, Richard (and Oscar Hammerstein) 21, 23, 65, 127, 134–35, 184, 191, 215, 398

Rogell, Irma 243

Rogers, Bernard 52, 255, 257, 444–45

Rogers, Daniel 190

Rogers, Nathaniel 190

Romanticism 21, 49, 104–5, 112, 312, 321, 370, 412

Romberg, Siegmund 23

Ronstadt, Linda 313

Roosevelt, Franklin D. 14

Rorem, Ned 149, 195, 249

Rosen, Charles 305

Rosenbaum, Samuel 293

Rosenfeld, Paul 109

Ross, Walter 432

Rossetti, Christina 197, 268, 272

Rossini, Gioachino 178

Rouse, Christopher 378

Rousseau, Jean-Jacques 21, 35

Roussel, Albert 13, 46, 157

Roy, Klaus George xv

Rubbra, Edmund 353

Rudnick, Verna (*see* Verna Fine)

Ruggles, Carl 64–65, 358

Rukeyser, Muriel 288

Russia 142, 419, 422

Rzewski, Frederic (b. 1938) xiii, xv, xvii, 323, 370–83, 387–90, 393–95, 397, 401, 414, 419, 429, 431–32, 435–36, 446
works:
"Apolitical Intellectuals" 381–82
Attica 380–81
Coming Together 379–81
Four American Ballads 381, 387–88, **389**
Four Pieces 381, 387–88
Long Time Man 388

"Lullaby: God to a Hungry Child" 381

Les Moutons de Panurge 378, 379, 381

Nature Morte 372, 375

The People United Will Never Be Defeated! 381, 383, **385–89**

Plan for Spacecraft 377, 379

Song and Dance 379

Street Music 377, 380

Struggle 381

Symphony 377

Three Rhapsodies for Two Slide Whistles 372

To the Earth 389

Variations on "No Place to Go But Around" 381, 384

Zoologischer Gärten 376
writings:
"Commandments to Myself" 377
"The Reappearance of Isorhythm in Modern Music" 371

SAG (Sonic Arts Groups) 373–74, 390

Saint Francis of Assisi 343

Saint-Saëns, Camille 43

Salomon, Trudi (*see* Trudi Van Slyck)

Salzman, Eric 372, 426, 436

Sandoz, Marie 255

Santayana, George 17

Sapp, Allen (b. 1922) xv–xvii, 135, 150, 208–9, 211, 219–30, 239–40, 243, 258, 305, 335, 349, 412, 426–28, 430–31, 434, 436, 443, 446–47
works:
Colloquies III 221
Crennelations 228–29
Double Image 223–24, 227
Eight Songs of Robert Herrick 228
Four Dialogues 208
Imaginary Creatures 228–29

The Lady and the Lute 228
A Maiden's Complaint in Spring-Time 227–28
"Marvoil" 228
Nocturne 228, 436
Piano Sonata No. 1 221–23
Piano Sonata No. 2 223
Piano Sonata No. 3 223–26
Piano Sonata No. 4 223–24, **225**, 226
piano sonatas 211, 221, 227, 229
piano sonatas for four hands 221
piano sonatinas 221, 431
Piano Trio 226, 430
Septagon 227
songs 221
Suite for Piano 221, **222–23**, 226
Taylor's Nine 227, 229
violin sonatas 221, 229
Sapp, Norma 208, 221
Sappho 128
Satie, Erik 13, 27, 126, 137, 146, 420–21
Sauguet, Henri 146, 162
Sayers, Dorothy 227
Scanlon, Roger 269
Scarlatti, Domenico 69, 145, 169, 243, 268
Schaeffer, Pierre 147, 153
Schapiro, Meyer 98–99
Schenker, Heinrich 352, 432, 434
Schillinger, Josef 305
Schindler, Rabbi Alexander 280
Schnabel, Artur 208
Schoenberg, Arnold xii, xvi, 162, 280, 420, 432
    Adler 286, 289, 293
    Bavicchi 237
    Berger 78–80, 82, 97, 99
    Binkerd 258–59
    Boulez 348
    Boykan 315
    Carter 104
    Copland 348
    Fine 141, 147, 151
    Glaser 361

Harbison 400, 405, 415, 429
Harvard composers 442
Kohn 337, 341
Kohs 70
Layton 303
Lee 250–51
Merritt 349
Middleton 212
Piston 3–4, 11, 348–49, 429, 438
Princeton 402, 430, 432
Rzewski 371, 429
Sapp 224–26, 258
Shapero 170
Spies 347–48
Vincent 42–43
Westergaard 226, 349, 430
Wyner 311–12, 414
works:
    Erwartung 97, 237
    Die Glückliche Hand 79
    Ode 162
    Orchestra Pieces, Op. 16 251, 312
    Piano Pieces, Op. 11 80
    Pierrot Lunaire 237, 347, 413
    String Quartet No. 2 162
    String Quartet No. 3 225–26, 237, 258
    String Quartet No. 4 70, 237
    String Trio 402, 429
    Survivor from Warsaw 293
    Variations 258
    Wind Quintet 258, 286
Schonberg, Harold 312
schools and academies
    Beaver Country Day School 360
    Cambridge High and Latin School 21, 359
    Dana Hall School 361
    Ecole Normale 42
    Erskine School 135
    Ethical Culture School 315
    Fieldston 315
    Harvard Grammar School 21
    Hockaday School 283
    James Madison High School (Brooklyn) 69

Phillips Andover Academy
190–92, 194, 370
Princeton High School 400
Schreker, Franz 444
Schubert, Franz 38, 174, 182–83,
245, 382, 385
Schuller, Gunther 65, 184, 287,
405, 433
Schuman, William 65, 105, 263,
296, 298
Schumann, Robert 126, 183, 211,
218, 237, 250, 252, 324,
338, 345, 436, 442
Schumann-Heink, Ernestine 49
Schütz, Heinrich 401
Schwalb, Susan 320
Schwantner, Joseph 291–92
Schwartz, Delmore 98–99
Schwarz, Stephen 128
Scriabin, Alexander 105, 126,
132, 313–14
Seeger, Pete 388
Segal, Erich 417–19, 441, 443
Segond, Pierre 366
Selznick, David 32
serialism (*see also* total organiza-
tion, twelve-tone method),
185, 336, 371, 431
Sessions, John 401
Sessions, Roger xvi, 13, 15, 17,
63–65, 70, 80, 129, 151,
157, 182, 309, 315, 349–
50, 372, 397, 400–3, 419–
23, 430, 432, 437, 444
set theory 316–17
Shackelford, Rudy 254–55, 263,
270
Shackford, Charles xiv, 445
Shakespeare, William 10, 128,
248, 346, 401, 409, 415
Shalom, Shin 184
Shapero, Hannah 185
Shapero, Harold (b. 1920) xv, 62,
108, 166–188, 424, 430,
433–35
Anderson 25
Berger 97–98, 445
Bernstein 445
Binkerd 254, 262

Brenner 446
Boulanger 428
Fine 142–43, 145–46, 153, 445
Harbison 401, 410
Helm 64
Kohs 70, 74
Kubik 58
Middleton 210
Moevs 325
Perkins 353, 446
Piston 262, 424–26, 433, 436
Spies 343, 348, 446
"Stravinsky school" 141–42
works:
A.B. 65 186
America Variations 183
Concerto for Orchestra (*see also
Credo*) 183
Credo 183–84
Four Pieces in Bb 185
Hebrew Cantata 184
9-Minute Overture 167, 168
On Green Mountains 184, 186
*Partita for Solo Piano and Or-
chestra* 184, 186, 431
Piano Variations 182–83
Sinfonia in C minor 183
Sonata for Piano Four-Hands
168, 445
Sonata in F Minor for Piano
172, 174, 183, 188, 430
Song Without Words 179
String Quartet 167, 187–88
*Symphony for Classical Orches-
tra* 108, 146, 166, 169–172,
173–75, 176, 177–80,
181–83, 186–88, 348, 446
Three Improvisations in B 185
Three Piano Sonatas 169, 186
3 Pieces for 3 Pieces 166
Three Studies in C# 185
The Travelers Overture (*see Sin-
fonia in C minor*)
Trumpet Sonata 166–68
Two Hebrew Songs 184
Two Psalms 184
Violin Sonata 169
writings:
"The Musical Mind" 169

Shaw, Artie 296
Shelley, Percy 415
Shifrin, Seymour 295–96, 315–
16
Shirley, Wayne 353
Shostakovich, Dmitri 112, 141,
167, 269, 359, 370, 410,
432, 439
Sibelius, Jean 70, 265
Sicilianos, Yorgos xiii, xv–xvi,
447
Simon, Carly 407
Singer, Isaac Bashevis 312
Singspiel 124, 438
Slonimsky, Nicolas 166
Slosberg, Sam 154
Smith, Bessie 419
Smith, Harold Wendell 213–14
Smith, Melville 366
Smith, Warren Story 195, 197, 205
Smither, Howard 264
Snyder, Gary 415
Soler, Antonio 190
Sondheim, Stephen 124, 128, 400
Sontag, Susan 122
Souster, Tim 376
South America 274
Sowerby, Leo 52, 140, 187, 425
Spain (see also Spanish music) 15,
214
Spalding, Walter 21, 423
Spanish music 14, 250, 280, 343
Spies, Claudio (b. 1925) xv, xvii,
220, 229, 274, 279, 315,
323, 343–48, 356, 371,
400, 428–29, 431, 433–
34, 446–47
  works:
    Canon (flutes) 344
    Canon (violas) 344
    Il cantico di frate sole 343
    5 Psalms 344, 431
    Five Sonnet-Settings 346–47
    Impromptu 344, 345, 346
    Rilke: Rühmen 346–47
    7 Canons 344
    7 Enzensberger Lieder 346–47
    Shirim Le Hathunatham 346,
347

Tagyr 346
Tempi 344
Three Intermezzi 343
*Three Songs on Poems by May
Swenson* 346
Viopiacem 344
Stampfer, Judah 293
Stanley, Pat 32
Steele, Wilbur 10
Stefan, Paul 444
Stein, Gertrude 74, 128
Steinbeck, John 10, 13
Stendhal, Henri 214, 219
Stephens, James 266, 272
Sternfeld, Frederick 51
Sternhold-Hopkins Psalter 338
Steuermann, Edward 52–53, 315
Stevens, Wallace 413
Stevenson, Robert 198, 205
Stock, David 98
Stock, Frederick 256
Stockhausen, Karlheinz xiii, 63,
371–72, 374, 380
Stoessel, Albert 187
Stojowski, Sigismond 324
Stowe, Harriet Beecher 133
Strauss, Johann 25, 38, 120
Strauss, Richard 43, 97, 110, 194,
215, 237
Stravinsky, Igor xi–xii, 98, 127,
129, 420
  Adler 279, 284, 286, 292
  Anderson 38
  Beethoven 188
  Berger 70, 79–80, 82, 96, 99,
169
  Bernstein 71, 104–5, 111, 123,
126
  Binkerd 261, 263, 267
  Boulanger 169, 194, 417
  Boykan 279, 314, 316, 318
  Brenner 366
  Carter 104–5, 126, 301, 434
  Copland 284
  Des Marais 446
  Fine 70, 132–33, 139–41, 146–
47, 149–50, 157, 397, 424
  Harbison 397, 400–3, 409,
414–15

Harvard composers 231, 354, 402, 424, 432
Kohn 228, 279, 338–41, 344
Kohs 71–72, 74
Layton 298, 301, 304, 311
Lee 245–47
Middleton 214
Moevs 324–25, 327
Motherwell 99
Pinkham 194, 202, 205
Piston 1, 3, 169, 279, 427, 438–39
Princeton 432
Shapero 70, 169, 181–83, 185, 188
Spies 279, 343–44, 348, 350, 446
"Stravinsky school" 78, 109, 141–44, 325
Vincent 43–44
works:
Agon 185, 318, 340
Apollo 147
The Fairy's Kiss 439
Firebird 127
L'Histoire du soldat 194, 284, 420
Huxley Variations 402
Movements 344
"Musick to Heare" 79
Les Noces 127, 153
Octet 80, 123, 124, 194, 284, 339, 340, 344, 372, 432, 439
Oedipus 298, 327
Orpheus 147, 366
Piano Sonata 261
Pulcinella 439
Ragtime 420
The Rake's Progress 214
The Rite of Spring 70, 263, 284, 290, 300, 327, 340, 432, 438–39
Symphonies of Winds 284
Symphony in C 169, 183, 284, 348
Symphony of Psalms 140, 298, 439
Two Piano Concerto 314

writings:
Poétique musicale 140
Wyner 307, 314
Stritch, Elaine 32
Styne, Julie 31
Sullivan, Barry 32
Sulzer, Solomon 280
Swados, Henry 50
Sweden 20
Christianstad 20
Stockholm 20, 25
Swenson, May 346
Swift, Jonathan 10
Swingle Singers 184
Switzerland
Zurich 305
symphony orchestras
Aalborg Symphony 294
American Wind Symphony Orchestra 283
Arlington Philharmonic 358
Boston Pops xi, 23–28, 240, 361, 425–26
Boston Symphony xi, 13, 21, 23, 27, 137, 141, 156, 181, 192, 236, 239, 327, 348, 357, 443
Buffalo Philharmonic 224
Chicago Summer Symphony 29
Chicago Symphony Orchestra 256
Classical High School Orchestra (Worcester, MA) 275
Columbia Symphony Orchestra 181
Dallas Symphony 274, 279, 284, 294
Fort Worth Symphony 289
Kingsway Orchestra 27
Milwaukee Symphony 331
New Haven Symphony 304
New York Philharmonic 181
Orchestra sinfonica di Roma 298
Philadelphia Orchestra 42
Pittsburgh Symphony Orchestra 402
Rochester Philharmonic 294

Seventh Army Symphony Orchestra 274–75
Syria 313
Szell, George 315
Szymanowski, Karol 409

Tallis, Thomas 198
Talma, Louise 141–42, 161, 364
Tanglewood xii, xiv, 140, 154, 158, 168, 194–95, 213, 277
Tate, Allen 128
Taylor, Brooke 227
Taylor, Clifford 323
Taylor, Edward 272
Taylor, James 407
Taylor, Joseph Deems 419
Tchaikovsky, Peter Ilyich 34, 97, 182, 187, 277, 304, 402, 422
Teitelbaum, Richard 373
television 28, 97, 137, 200, 425
  Ed Sullivan Show 28
  The Late Show 28
  "A Layman's Guide to Contemporary Art" 200
Temple, Shirley 364–65, 437
Tenney, James 393
Tennyson, Alfred 272
Theophrastus 110
Thomas, Dylan 297–98
Thompson, David xvi
Thompson, Randall 269, 277, 305, 325, 333–34, 418, 428
Thomson, Virgil 3, 13, 15, 17, 44–46, 55, 63–65, 128, 146, 183, 419–23, 432, 438
Thoreau, Henry David 10
Tillotson, Frederick 359
Tippett, Sir Michael 410
Toch, Ernst 280
total organization (see also serialism) 96, 113, 116
Trapp Family Singers 191, 193, 205, 437
Trash, Spencer 272
Trotsky, Leon 99
Tuckwell, Barry 332

Tudor, David 372, 376, 431
Turkey 213–14
Turner, Joseph 239
Tuttle, Stephen 359
Twain, Mark 421
twelve-tone method (see also serialism, total organization) 116, 432
  Adler 284–86, 292
  Bavicchi 239
  Berger 79, 93, 186
  Bernstein, 120, 263
  Binkerd 225, 258–63
  Boykan 316, 435
  Brenner 366
  Brogue 357
  Carter 113, 435
  Copland 150, 421, 432
  Crumb 405
  Druckman 405
  Fine 139, 149–51, 154, 156, 158, 186, 262, 430
  Glaser 363
  Harbison 403, 405, 413
  Harvard composers 427, 430, 434–35, 441
  Helm 67
  Kohn 335–36
  Kohs 71–72
  Layton 299, 302–4, 311
  Lee 250
  Middleton 210–12, 225
  Moevs 328, 435
  Perkins 353, 435
  Pinkham 189, 199, 202, 205
  Piston 4, 71, 150, 258, 349, 421, 426, 429, 432, 435
  Rochberg 406
  Sapp 150, 222, 225–27, 258
  Schoenberg 258, 420
  Sessions 421
  Shapero 166, 184, 186
  Spies 344–46
  Stravinsky 149, 344, 432
  Van Slyck 242
  Westergaard 349–52, 435
  Wyner 435
Tyler, Mary 190

Ukraine
  Kiev 305
UNESCO 63, 118
Union of American Hebrew Con-
  gregations 287
United States (*see also* Boston,
  Cambridge)
  Alabama
    Birmingham 41
  Arizona
    Phoenix 49
  California 63, 332
    Claremont 50, 333
    Davis 373
    Los Angeles 47, 60, 274, 332
    San Francisco 69
    Santa Monica 42
  Connecticut 20, 33
    New Haven 311
    Woodbury 26
  Florida 14, 274
  Illinois 254
    Champaign 254, 348
    Chicago 69, 256
    Glen Ellyn 366
    Monticello 258
    Wilmette 366
  Indiana
    Franklin 255
    Indianapolis 57
    Lafayette 245
  Kansas 49–50
    Garden City 255
    Manhattan 50
  Maine 4, 14, 349, 364, 433,
    438
    Bath 364
  Massachusetts 190
    Amherst 359
    Andover 190–91
    Belmont 348, 418
    Brookline 239
    Dedham 236
    Lynn 189
    Milton 22–23
    Salem 190
    Westfield 370
    Worcester 275, 280
  Michigan

    Ann Arbor 373
  Midwest 41, 49, 52, 60, 257,
    270, 422, 437
  Minnesota
    Minneapolis 62
  Missouri 421
    St. Louis 352
  Nebraska 255, 257
    Lynch 255
    Sandhills of 255
  New Hampshire 209
  New Jersey 352
    Blackwell's Mills 331
    Newark 236
    Orange 397
  New Mexico
    Santa Fe 402
  New York 15, 291, 380
    Attica Prison 380
    Goshen 333
    Greenwich Village 372
    Middletown 333
    New York City 14, 26–27,
      32, 69, 78, 97, 99, 118–20,
      183, 192, 218, 231, 274,
      305, 315, 370–74, 430
    Rochester 274
    Setauket 297
  Ohio
    Cincinnati 229
    Columbus 208
    Diamond 208
    Oxford 63
    Youngstown 208
  Oklahoma
    Coffeyville 49
  Pennsylvania
    Philadelphia 32, 219, 240
    Pittsburgh 283
  South 41, 46, 49, 60, 437
  South Dakota
    Black Hills 255
    Gregory 255
  Southwest 280, 282–84,
    292
  Tennessee
    Nashville 41
  Texas 282, 287
    Corsicana 296

Dallas 274
  Chorale 283
  Lyric Theater 283
  Temple Emanu-El 274
  Theater Center 283
Vermont 15
  Woodstock 278, 439
West Virginia 274
Wisconsin 330
  La Crosse 324
  Token Creek 403
Universities, Colleges, and Conservatories (*see also* Harvard, schools and academies)
American Academy in Rome 296, 305, 325
Amherst College 350
Berklee School of Music 239
Boston University xiv, 274
Brandeis University 79, 102, 147, 152–54, 184, 274, 305, 315–16, 353, 366, 402, 436, 445–46
Brown University 192
Cambridge New School of Music 240
Carleton College 62
Chicago, University of 353
Cincinnati, University of 229
City College of New York 79
Claremont 274, 333
Columbia University 296, 350, 376
Cornell University 42, 236, 245, 398
Eastman School of Music 255, 257, 284, 289, 291, 444
Florida State University at Tallahassee 229
Franklin College 255
George Peabody College 41
Hebrew Union College School of Sacred Music 305
Houston, University of 294
Illinois University 254, 257
Juilliard 70, 305
Kansas State University 50

Longy School 169, 190, 209, 240, 359, 361
Maine, University of 364
MIT 236, 240, 402
New England Conservatory xiv, 41, 189, 203, 209, 236, 240, 296, 358, 361
New School (Boston) 240
New School (New York) 420
New York College of Music 333
New York Institute of Musical Art 69
New York University 79, 97, 98
North Texas State University 283
Ohio State University 208
Pomona College 332–33
Princeton University 17, 80, 185, 274, 343, 347, 349–50, 372, 376, 397, 400, 402, 430, 432
Reed College 402
Rutgers University 325, 331
San Francisco Conservatory 69
Scripps College 50
South Dakota Wesleyan University 255
Southern California, University of 69
Southern Methodist University 296
Staatliche Hochschule (Freiburg) 350
State University of New York at Buffalo 229
State University of New York at Purchase 305
State University of New York at Stony Brook 296
Swarthmore College 343
Texas, University of 271, 274
Tufts University 357
Vassar 208–9, 216, 343
Washington University 353
Wellesley 361
West Virginia Wesleyan College 200

Western College 63
Yale University xiv, 22, 38,
  296, 301, 305–6, 310,
  314–15
Zurich 315

Valen, Fartein 162
Valéry, Paul 96, 249
Van Buchau, Stephanie 404,
  409
Van Doren, Carl 128
Van Gogh, Vincent 270
Van Slyck, Nicholas (1922–1983)
  xv, 231, 240–46, 251–52,
  426, 428, 435, 446
  works:
    Capriccio No. 3 242
    Diferencias 243
    Encore March 240
    Finger Paints 240, **241**, 242
    Fugue Cycle 243
    Gardens of the West 243
    Judgement in Salem 241
    The Legend of Sleepy Hollow
      241
    Nine Inventions 243
    Pantomime 242
    Piano Concerto No. 1 244
    Piano Concerto No. 2 244
    Piano Partners **244**
    Piano Sonata No. 1 241, 446
    Piano Sonata No. 3 241, 446
    Prelude and Fugue 243
    Sea Drift 241
    Seven Short Mysteries 243
    Six Sonatinas for Piano 240
    suites for harpsichord 243
    La Tomba di Scarlatti 243
    *12 Cadenzas: Preludes in all
      Keys in a Brilliant Style*
      242–43
Van Slyck, Trudi xvii, 241–44
Vanzetti, Bartolomeo 50
Varèse, Edgard 113, 151, 204–
  05, 324, 371, 373
Vasyluinas, Izidore 238
Vaughan, Henry 269, 272
Vaughan, Sarah 29

Vaughan Williams, Ralph 62, 265,
  444
Veen, Jan 194
Verdi, Giuseppe 121, 124, 126,
  219
Very, Jones 272
Vidal, Gore 249
Vietnam War 59, 379
Villa-Lobos, Heitor 141, 313, 338
Vincent, John (1902–1977) xiv–
  xv, 41–49, 419, 424–25,
  427, 431, 434, 436–37
  works:
    Consort 49
    Mary at Calvary 49
    The Phoenix, Fabulous Bird 49
    String Quartet No. 1 42, 44,
      45, 46
    String Quartet No. 2 49
    Symphonic Poem after Descartes
      42, 47
    Symphony in D 42, 47, **48**,
      431
    Symphony No. 2 49
    Three Grecian Songs 42, 44,
      46
    3 Jacks 42
  writings:
    The Diatonic Modes 42–44,
      425
Viscuglia, Felix 239
Vivaldi, Antonio 69, 133
Voisin, Roger 27, 239

Wagenaar, Bernard 70
Wagner, Richard 38, 42–43, 110,
  192, 237, 346, 349, 382,
  386, 407, 412, 421, 432,
  442
Wales 274
Wallenberg, Raoul 348
Waller, Marie 208
Waller, Thomas "Fats" 108
Walter, Bruno 11
Walther, Johann Gottfried
  260
Ward, John 361
Warren, B. (*see* Betsy Warren)

Warren, Betsy (b. 1921) xiv–xv,
    357, 364–66, 368–69,
    398, 426, 435–37
  works:
    Balloons and Frog Music 365
    Five Songs in 5 Minutes 365
    Gift of the Magi 365
    Mass in E 365
    Ride-A-Cock-Horse 364, 365
    Violin Sonata No. 1 365
Warren, Harry 398
Watts, Bob 376
Waxman, Franz 201
Weber, Max 153, 379
Webern, Anton 3, 80, 101, 113,
    147, 202, 237, 252, 286,
    302, 311, 316, 329, 343,
    349–50, 352, 354–55,
    361, 363, 402, 438, 442
Webster, Beveridge 209
Webster, Max 315
Weckmann, Matthias 260
Weigel, Eugene 257
Weill, Kurt 154
Weinberger, Jaromir 333
Weiner, Lazar 305, 310
Weisberg, Arthur 403
Weisgall, Hugo 432
Weiss, Neal 272
Welles, Orson 181, 186
Welty, Eudora 46
Werschinger, Carl 333
Westergaard, Peter (b. 1931) xv–
    xvi, 226, 323, 348–52,
    354–55, 428–30, 434–35,
    446–47
  works:
    Alonso's Grief 350
    Mr. and Mrs. Discobbolos 350,
      351, 352
    Symphonic Movement 348, 428
    The Tempest 352
    Variations for Six Players 350,
      435
  writings:
    *An Introduction to Tonal The-
      ory* 352
Wheelwright, Jack 9
Whiteman, Paul 18

Whiteside, Abby 315
Whitman, Walt 109, 128, 240,
    287
Whittier, John Greenleaf 190
Wilbur, Richard 128,
    272
Wilder, Thornton 15
Williams, John 48–49
Williams, William Carlos 110,
    272
Winston, George 392
Witten, David 242
Wodehouse, P.G. 31
Wolfe, Thomas 257
Wolff, Christian 371–72, 383–84,
    388, 431
Wolfskehl, Karl 288
Wolpe, Stefan 220
Wood, Grant 52
Woodworth, G. Wallace 135,
    160, 330
Woollen, Russell xv, 447
Wordsworth, William 157
World War I 420, 440
World War II (*see also* military
    service) xi, 25–26, 49–50,
    55–56, 58, 104, 108, 133,
    135, 140, 147, 182, 208,
    220, 231, 236, 422, 426–
    29
  Holocaust 288, 293–94, 333
  Office of War Information 55
Wright, James 199, 203, 413
Wyler, William 57
Wyner, Susan Davenny 307, 311,
    313
Wyner, Yehudi (b. 1929) xv, 64,
    295–96, 301, 304–15,
    320–22, 414–15, 428–29,
    431, 435–37, 446
  works:
    Cadenza! 312
    Composition (*see De Novo*)
    De Novo 312, 436
    Concert Duo 307, 308–9,
      310
    Fragments from Antiquity 312
    Friday Evening Service 312
    Intermedio (*see Romances*)

Intermezzo 313
Kodosh Ato 312
Memorial Music 312
The Mirror (incidental music)
    312
Old Glory (incidental music)
    312
Partita 306, 429
The Passover Offering 312
Piano Sonata 307
Romances 312–13, 314
R'tzey 312
Sections (see *3 Informal Pieces*)
Serenade 310–312, 431
3 Informal Pieces 312

3 Short Fantasies 312
Torah Service 312
*Two Preludes on Southern
    Hymns* 306

Yancey, Jimmy 266
Yeats, William Butler 50, 409,
    415
Yiddish music (see Jewish music)
Yugoslavia 63
Yun, I Sang 130

Zano, Anthony xv
Zaslaw, Neal 353
Zwilich, Ellen Taaffe 432

ABOUT THE AUTHOR

HOWARD POLLACK (B.M., University of Michigan; M.A., Ph.D., Cornell University) is assistant professor of music history at the University of Houston since 1987. He also has taught at the Rochester Institute of Technology and Cornell. His other books include *Walter Piston* (UMI, 1982) and a biography of John Alden Carpenter (Smithsonian, forthcoming). He is co-editor of *German Literature and Music: An Aesthetic Fusion (1890–1989)* (Fink, 1992) and a frequent contributor to professional journals in the areas of American music, 18th-century music, and piano literature. Most recently, he published an essay on Walter Piston in honor of the composer's upcoming centennial (G. Schirmer, 1992).